# THEORIZING THE SHARING ECONOMY

# RESEARCH IN THE SOCIOLOGY OF ORGANIZATIONS

| | |
|---|---|
| Volume 41: | Religion and Organization Theory |
| Volume 42: | Organizational Transformation and Scientific Change: The Impact of Institutional Restructuring on Universities and Intellectual Innovation |
| Volume 43: | Elites on Trial |
| Volume 44: | Institutions and Ideals: Philip Selznick's Legacy for Organizational Studies |
| Volume 45: | Towards a Comparative Institutionalism: Forms, Dynamics and Logics Across the Organizational Fields of Health and Higher Education |
| Volume 46: | The University Under Pressure |
| Volume 47: | The Structuring of Work in Organizations |
| Volume 48A: | How Institutions Matter! |
| Volume 48B: | How Institutions Matter! |
| Volume 49: | Multinational Corporations and Organization Theory: Post Millennium Perspectives |
| Volume 50: | Emergence |
| Volume 51: | Categories, Categorization and Categorizing: Category Studies in Sociology, Organizations and Strategy at the Crossroads |
| Volume 52: | Justification, evaluation and critique in the study of organizations: contributions from French pragmatist sociology |
| Volume 53: | Structure, content and meaning of organizational networks: extending network thinking |
| Volume 54A: | Multimodality, Meaning, and Institutions |
| Volume 54B: | Multimodality, Meaning, and Institutions |
| Volume 55: | Social Movements, Stakeholders and Non-Market Strategy |
| Volume 56: | Social Movements, Stakeholders and Non-Market Strategy |
| Volume 57: | Toward Permeable Boundaries of Organizations? |
| Volume 58: | Agents, Actors, Actorhood: Institutional Perspectives on the Nature of Agency, Action, and Authority |
| Volume 59: | The Production of Managerial Knowledge and Organizational Theory: New Approaches to Writing, Producing and Consuming Theory |
| Volume 60: | Race, Organizations, and the Organizing Process |
| Volume 61: | Routine Dynamics in Action |
| Volume 62: | Thinking Infrastructures |
| Volume 63: | The Contested Moralities of Markets |
| Volume 64: | Managing Inter-organizational Collaborations: Process Views |
| Volume 65A: | Microfoundations of Institutions |
| Volume 65B: | Microfoundations of Institutions |

RESEARCH IN THE SOCIOLOGY OF ORGANIZATIONS VOLUME 66

# THEORIZING THE SHARING ECONOMY: VARIETY AND TRAJECTORIES OF NEW FORMS OF ORGANIZING

EDITED BY

**INDRE MAURER**
*University of Göttingen, Germany*

**JOHANNA MAIR**
*Hertie School, Germany / Stanford University, USA*

**ACHIM OBERG**
*WU Vienna University, Austria / University of Mannheim, Germany*

emerald PUBLISHING

United Kingdom – North America – Japan
India – Malaysia – China

Emerald Publishing Limited
Howard House, Wagon Lane, Bingley BD16 1WA, UK

First edition 2020





**British Library Cataloguing in Publication Data**
A catalogue record for this book is available from the British Library

ISBN: 978-1-78756-180-9 (Print)
ISBN: 978-1-78756-179-3 (Online)
ISBN: 978-1-78756-181-6 (Epub)

ISSN: 0733-558X (Series)

Printed and bound by CPI Group (UK) Ltd, Croydon, CR0 4YY

# CONTENTS

*Contributor Biographies* *vii*

**Variety and Trajectories of New Forms of Organizing in the Sharing Economy: A Research Agenda**
*Indre Maurer, Johanna Mair and Achim Oberg* *1*

**Market, Hierarchy, or Clan? Types of Governance in the Sharing Economy**
*Philipp C. Mosmann and Jennifer Klutt* *25*

**Shaping Emotional Labor Practices in the Sharing Economy**
*Eliane Bucher, Christian Fieseler, Christoph Lutz and Gemma Newlands* *55*

**An Institutional Logics Perspective on the Gig Economy**
*Koen Frenken, Taneli Vaskelainen, Lea Fünfschilling and Laura Piscicelli* *83*

**The Sharing Economy as an Emerging and Contested Field – How Classic and Institutional Entrepreneurs Cope with Plural Theoretical Frames**
*Aurélien Acquier, Valentina Carbone and Laëtitia Vasseur* *107*

**Is the Sharing Economy a Field? How a Disruptive Field Nurtures Sharing Economy Organizations**
*Dominika Wruk, Tino Schöllhorn and Achim Oberg* *131*

**Category Kings and Commoners: Within and Cross-category Spill-overs in the Sharing Economy**
*Pinar Ozcan, Kerem Gurses and Mareike Möhlmann* *163*

**"Turning the Sharing Economy into a Fair Economy": Strategic Issue Work in the Vienna City Administration**
*Sebastian Vith and Markus A. Höllerer* 187

**Regulating the Sharing Economy: A Field Perspective**
*Stefan Kirchner and Elke Schüßler* 215

*Index* 237

# CONTRIBUTOR BIOGRAPHIES

**Aurélien Acquier** (Ph.D., HDR) is Professor of Management at the ESCP Europe Business School, Paris, France, and Co-director of the ESCP Europe – Deloitte Research Chair in Circular Economy. Combining institutional, organizational, and historical analysis, he explores how the sharing economy is framed both conceptually and empirically. Mapping out the heterogeneous and paradoxical roots of the notion, he explores how the sharing economy is giving birth to various societal promises and controversies, business models, and organizational forms. His research on the sharing economy has been published in *Technological Forecasting and Social Change, Revue Française de Gestion*, or the *Cambridge Handbook of the Law of the Sharing Economy.*

**Eliane Bucher** is an Assistant Professor with the Nordic Centre for Internet and Society, BI Norwegian Business School, Oslo, Norway. She received the Doctorate degree in Management from the University of St. Gallen, Switzerland, where she is currently a Lecturer for Digital Media and Communications Management. She was a visiting scholar at Scandinavian Consortium for Organizational Research, Stanford University as well as the Berkman Center for Internet and Society, Harvard University. Her research interests include digital platforms and algorithmic labor and virtual and hyper-connective work environments. In particular, she is interested in how workers make sense of and "reverse-engineer" algorithmic decision-making mechanisms in increasingly digital work environments. Her research has been published, among others, in the *Journal of Business Ethics, Academy of Management Discoveries, Computers in Human Behavior* and the *Journal of Managerial Psychology.*

**Valentina Carbone** (Ph.D., HDR) is Professor of Supply Chain Management and Sustainability at the ESCP Europe Business School, Paris, France, and Co-director of the ESCP Europe – Deloitte Research Chair in Circular Economy. Her current research covers the sustainable dimension of SCM, corporate social and environmental responsibility, and sharing and circular economy business models. She explores the theoretical and ideological roots of the sharing economy and the multiple organizational configurations observed in the field, and in particular in the transportation/logistics sector. Her research on the sharing economy has been published in the *Journal of Business Logistics*, the *International Journal of Physical Distribution and Logistics Management*, the *Revue Française de Gestion*, and the *Cambridge Handbook of the Law of the Sharing Economy.*

**Christian Fieseler** is Professor of Communication Management with the BI Norwegian Business School, Norway and Director of the Nordic Centre for Internet and Society, Norway. He received the Ph.D. degree in Management and

Economics from the University of St. Gallen, Switzerland, in 2008. Since then, his research is focused on the question how individuals and organizations adapt to the shift brought by new, social media, and how to design participative and inclusive spaces in this new media regime. In this field, he has over the last years, worked extensively on technology and new working modes in projects with the European Union and the Norwegian Research Council.

**Koen Frenken** is the Chair of Innovation Studies with the Copernicus Institute of Sustainable Development, Utrecht University, The Netherlands. He previously worked at the University of Amsterdam, the University of Grenoble, and Eindhoven University of Technology. His early works focused on technological change from an evolutionary economics perspective (Frenken, 2006, *Innovation, Evolution and Complexity Theory*, Edward Elgar). He then concentrated his research on developing an integral evolutionary approach to economic geography. Since 2015, he has been developing an interest in the study of the platform economy and published a policy report on platforms in 2017 with the Rathenau Institute ("A Fair Share") and a summary piece in 2017 on the sharing economy ("Putting the Sharing Economy into Perspective", in: *Environmental Innovation an Societal Transitions*, with Juliet Schor).

**Lea Fünfschilling** is Associate Senior Lecturer at the Department of Design Sciences and CIRCLE, Lund University, Sweden. She received the Ph.D. degree in Sociology from the University of Basel. Her research interests are centered around understanding and conceptualizing the dynamics of sustainability transitions. Special attention is devoted to the co-evolution of institutions, actors, and technology in different industries and regions, in particular during processes of institutionalization and destabilization. She is active in the board of the Sustainability Transitions Research Network and the Project Coordinator of the Swedish Transformative Innovation Policy Platform.

**Kerem Gurses** is Assistant Professor at La Salle Barcelona, Ramon Llull University, Spain. He holds a Ph.D. in Management from IESE Business School and an MBA from Illinois Institute of Technology. He specializes in industry change, particularly how industry practices and technologies change through firm corporate political strategies. He is the author of many academic articles and chapters on this topic at *Academy of Management Journal, European Management Journal*, and *The Oxford Handbook of Entrepreneurship and Collaboration* among others. Kerem has also done consulting and project work for food and aerospace industries.

**Markus A. Höllerer** is Professor in Organization Theory at UNSW Sydney, Australia. He is also affiliated with the Research Institute for Urban Management and Governance at WU Vienna University of Economics and Business, Austria. His scholarly work is focused on the study of institutions, meaning, and novel forms of organization and governance. His research interests include, among others, issues of collaborative governance at the interface of the private sector, public administration, and civil society. He has published in scholarly outlets such as the *Academy of Management Annals, Academy of Management Discoveries,*

*Academy of Management Journal, Academy of Management Review, Journal of Business Ethics, Journal of Management Studies, Organization Science, Organization Studies, Public Administration, Strategic Organization*, and *Urban Studies*. Currently, he is serving as the Chairman of the Executive Board of the *European Group for Organizational Studies*.

**Stefan Kirchner** is Professor of Sociology of Working Worlds' Digitalization at the Technical University Berlin, Germany. In his current research, he is especially interested in the transformative effects of digital technology for the organization of digital markets and the ensuing reorganization processes of work and value capture. He has published in journals such as *Industrial and Labor Relations Review, Socio-Economic Review, Kölner Zeitschrift für Soziologie und Sozialpsychologie* and *Zeitschrift für Soziologie*.

**Jennifer Klutt** is a Research and Teaching Assistant at the Chair of Organization and Corporate Development, University of Göttingen, Germany. Her research deals with the governance of business models of the sharing economy, especially within new forms of working contexts such as coworking spaces as shared workspaces. Recently, she has published her empirical work in the Journal of Business Ethics. She is currently working on her doctoral thesis.

**Christoph Lutz** is an Associate Professor with the Nordic Centre for Internet and Society, Norway, and with the Department of Communication and Culture, BI Norwegian Business School, Norway. He received the Ph.D. degree in Management from the University of St. Gallen, Switzerland. His research interests cover a broad spectrum of topics and lie in the field of social media and Internet-mediated communication. More specifically, he investigates digital inequalities, privacy, the sharing economy, new forms of work, and social robots. Over the last years, he has published in leading Internet, communication, information systems and business/management journals such as *New Media & Society; Information, Communication & Society*; *Social Media + Society*; *First Monday*; the *Journal of Management Information Systems*; *New Technology, Work and Employment*; *Academy of Management Discoveries*; *Big Data & Society*; and the *Journal of the Association for Information Science and Technology*.

**Johanna Mair** is Professor of Organization, Strategy and Leadership at the Hertie School in Berlin. She is a Distinguished Fellow and co-directs the Global Innovation for Impact Lab at the Stanford Center on Philanthropy and Civil Society. Her research examines how organizations tackle societal challenges and alter institutional contexts. She is particularly interested in specifying alternative forms of organizing and transformative mechanisms involved in this work. She has published articles in *Academy of Management Journal, Journal of Management Studies, Organization Studies, Journal of Management*, and other scholarly journals. She obtained her PhD in Management from INSEAD.

**Indre Maurer** is Professor of Organization Studies and Corporate Development at the University of Göttingen, Germany. Her research focuses on the governance of inter-organizational relationships and social capital. Her recent empirical work in these areas examines entrepreneurial, temporary and sharing economy organizations. She has published articles in *Administrative Science Quarterly, Journal of Management Studies, Organization Studies, Research Policy*, and other scholarly journals. She holds graduate degrees in business administration and in socio-economics from Augsburg University, where she also received her doctoral degree in business administration.

**Mareike Möhlmann** is Assistant Professor in Information Systems and Management at Warwick Business School, UK. Furthermore, she is a Teaching Fellow/Visiting Assistant Professor at the London School of Economics, UK. Previously, she worked as a Postdoc at New York University. She holds a Ph.D. from the University of Hamburg. Her current research focuses on digital innovation, digital platforms, the sharing economy, digital trust, and algorithmic management. Her work and comments have been featured in media outlets such as *The Times, the Financial Times*, the World Economic Forum, and the BBC.

**Philipp C. Mosmann** is a Research and Teaching Assistant at the Chair of Organization and Corporate Development, University of Göttingen, Germany. His research interests focus on the governance of communities in new organizational forms such as in the sharing economy. From a business history perspective, he is further interested in how both historical and modern forms of shared resource use are connected. He holds the doctoral degree from the University of Göttingen.

**Gemma Newlands** is a Ph.D. candidate with the University of Amsterdam, The Netherlands, and a Doctoral Stipendiary Fellow with the Nordic Centre for Internet and Society, BI Norwegian Business School, Norway. Her research explores the transformation of work in the digital economy, especially focusing on issues of platform-mediated workplace recognition and obfuscation in heterogeneous management settings. She is currently working on extending Axel Honneth's critical social theory of recognition to account for the spread of nonhuman agents in the workplace. Her research to date has been published in leading Internet, communication, and business journals such as *New Technology, Work and Employment, First Monday, Internet Research*, the *Journal of Business Research*, and the *Law and Ethics of Human Rights*.

**Achim Oberg** is Assistant Professor at the Institute for Organization Studies at the WU Vienna University of Economics and Business, Austria, and Senior Researcher at the Institute for SME Research at the University of Mannheim, Germany. His research focuses on digital social science and has been published in journals such as the *Journal of Business Ethics, Research in the Sociology of Organizations, Scandinavian Journal of Management, Policy & Politics*, and *Higher Education*. In his research, institutional theory and network analysis are combined to explore the structuration of new organizational fields. He holds a degree in Business Administration and Computer Science from the University of Mannheim, Germany, and completed his Ph.D. at the University of Jena, Germany.

**Pinar Ozcan** is Professor of Entrepreneurship and Innovation at Saïd Business School, Oxford University, UK. She specializes in strategy, entrepreneurship, and technology markets. She regularly publishes articles at academic journals such as *Academy of Management Journal* and *Strategic Management Journal* and chapters at prominent books such as *The Oxford Handbook of Entrepreneurship and Collaboration*. Pinar holds a Ph.D., a Master of Science, and dual Bachelor's degrees from Stanford University. She is the 2015 recipient of the British Academy Newton Grant for open innovation, the 2016 SWIFT award for disruption in the UK Banking sector. In 2017, Pinar was selected for the Top 40 Business School Professors under 40 by Poets and Quants. In 2018, she was selected for the Global Thinkers 50 list for emerging thinkers. Finally, in 2019, Pinar was chosen as a British Academy Mid-Career Fellow.

**Laura Piscicelli** is an Assistant Professor with the Innovation Studies Group, Copernicus Institute of Sustainable Development, Utrecht University, The Netherlands. Prior to this, she was a Research Fellow in Strategy, Innovation & Business Models with Cass Business School – City, University of London, UK, and a Postdoctoral Research Fellow with the University of Twente, The Netherlands. Her research interests are in the area of sustainable business and innovation, including the sharing economy, the circular economy, business models, digital platforms, and consumer behavior. She received her Ph.D. degree in sustainable consumption and design from Nottingham Trent University, UK. Her work on the sharing economy has been published in journals such as the *Journal of Cleaner Production, Transportation Research Part D*, and *Sustainability*.

**Tino Schöllhorn** is Researcher at the Institute for SME Research at the University of Mannheim, Germany. His research focuses on digital science and he has presented his work at international conferences and workshops such as the Academy of Management Annual Meeting, the European Group of Organizational Studies Colloquium, and the New Institutionalism Workshop. His research focuses on methods and techniques of collecting data about self-representations of organizations on the Internet and their interpretation from different theoretical perspectives. He holds a degree in Business Administration and Computer Science from the University of Mannheim.

**Elke Schüßler** is Professor of Business Administration and Head of the Institute of Organization Science at Johannes Kepler University in Linz. Her research interests include creativity and innovation, social and institutional change, and work and employment relations. She currently examines labor standards in global supply chains and new forms of digital organizing. She holds a doctorate in Business Administration from Freie Universität Berlin, an MSc in Industrial Relations from the London School of Economics and a BSc in Psychology from the University of Sussex.

**Taneli Vaskelainen** is an Assistant Professor with the Copernicus Institute of Sustainable Development, Utrecht University, The Netherlands. His research interests lie in the emergence dynamics of new industries and market categories. His studies mostly focus on empirical contexts with a promise of contributing to a more sustainable society (e.g., the sharing economy). His work has been published in academic journals in the fields of management, sustainability, and business ethics.

**Laëtitia Vasseur** is a Ph.D. candidate at the ESCP Europe Business School, France. She is working on planned obsolescence. She explores the institutional emergence of the public problem of extending products' lifespan and its impact on organizations as well as its links with the concept of circular economy. She has authored a master thesis on the emergence of the sharing economy by analyzing the OuiShare organization in 2015. She is also the Director and the Co-founder of the Association HOP.

**Sebastian Vith** is Research Associate at the Research Institute for Urban Management and Governance at WU Vienna University of Economics and Business, Austria. He holds degrees in Social and Political Theory as well as in Organization Studies from the University of Innsbruck. Between 2012 and 2016, he gained insights into various private and public sector organizations as a consultant, trainer for innovation management, and expert for new business development. He is currently writing his doctoral dissertation on the sharing economy from a public governance perspective.

**Dominika Wruk** is Senior Researcher at the Institute for SME Research at the University of Mannheim, Germany. She has published articles in journals such as the *Journal of Business Ethics, Journal of Business Economics*, and the *Zeitschrift für KMU und Entrepreneurship*. Her research focuses on the emergence and diffusion of new organizational forms and concepts and on how such processes shape and are shaped by institutional environments. She holds a doctoral degree from the University of Mannheim.

# VARIETY AND TRAJECTORIES OF NEW FORMS OF ORGANIZING IN THE SHARING ECONOMY: A RESEARCH AGENDA

Indre Maurer, Johanna Mair and Achim Oberg

The idea of "sharing instead of owning" – though it is not new – is currently experiencing a revival and becoming a major trend in modern (business) life (Belk, 2010; Botsman & Rogers, 2010; Frenken & Schor, 2017; Schor, 2014). It constitutes the defining principle of the so-called sharing economy, characterized by peer-to-peer-based sharing of access to goods and services, coordinated through information- and communication-technology platforms (Cohen & Kietzmann, 2014; Heinrichs, 2013). Starting as grassroots movements, initiatives associated with the sharing economy have gained increasing importance and diffused in different sectors and markets. A variety of new (and old) forms of organizing based on the basic idea of sharing, bartering, or lending have emerged and spread, changing or even disrupting existing ways of organizing in a number of markets, such as mobility, service delivery, and hospitality (Owyang, 2016; Stokes, Clarence, Anderson, & Rinne, 2014).

For scholars of organizations, such developments and implications provide a welcome opportunity for taking stock of and theorizing the sharing economy. Not surprisingly, the amount of sharing-economy research in organization and management studies has increased significantly in recent years – as it has in many other disciplines. This increase is reflected in the number of special issues in leading organization and management journals devoted to the topic (e.g., *Technological Forecasting and Social Change*, 2017; *Academy of Management Discoveries*, 2018; *Journal of Management Studies* (in preparation); *Entrepreneurship Theory and Practice* (in preparation); and *Journal of Business Ethics*, 2019) and in the abundance of literature on the sharing economy, with around 400 peer-reviewed articles published annually during the last years.

**Theorizing the Sharing Economy: Variety and Trajectories of New Forms of Organizing**
**Research in the Sociology of Organizations, Volume 66, 1–23**

**ISSN: 0733-558X/doi:10.1108/S0733-558X20200000066002**

The studies featured in these academic journals have contributed to our knowledge base on managing and organizing in the sharing economy in important ways. They have drawn attention to highly debated issues (Martin, 2016), strengthened our understanding of sharing-economy organizations' business models (Munoz & Cohen, 2017), and provided valuable insights on potential societal, economic, and ecologic consequences of this phenomenon (Hamari, Sjöklint, & Ukkonen, 2016; Parguel, Lunardo, & Benoit-Moreau, 2017; Plewnia & Guenther, 2018; Voytenko Palgan, Zvolska, & Mont, 2017). This body of literature has also placed exploration of the variety and trajectories of new forms of organizing in the sharing economy at the center of current research efforts (see Fig. 1). It has emphasized the unsettled nature of the sharing economy (Kornberger, Leixnering, Meyer, & Höllerer, 2018), described its complexity and paradoxical character (Acquier, Daudigeos, & Pinkse, 2017), and pointed to the different levels of analysis on which sharing-economy organizations can be studied (Mair & Reischauer, 2017).

While the multiple facets and inherent complexity of the sharing economy open up new ways for practice and theory to stimulate one another, at the moment these two perspectives seem out of sync (Belk, 2014; Cohen & Kietzmann, 2014). On the one hand, scholars complain that theoretical insights lag behind public discourse and practice (Acquier et al., 2017; Etter, Fieseler, & Whelan, 2019); on the other hand, much research remains rather descriptive and phenomenally driven instead of building on existing theoretical work (Vaskelainen & Münzel, 2017).

Therefore, the core of this special issue is empirical and conceptual work that explores the variety and trajectories of new forms of organizing in the sharing economy by harnessing, extending and recasting existing organization theories.

In the following, we first provide evidence that corroborates why understanding the variety and trajectories of new forms of organizing is at the top of the agenda for current organizational research on the sharing economy. Based on the most influential scholarly articles published in the last five years, we constructed a semantic network. This semantic network visualizes that terms such as "heterogeneous," "diverse," and "complex" are commonly linked to descriptions of the sharing economy. Patterns derived from this analysis illustrate that scholars have a shared understanding of the variety and dynamics of the sharing economy and that this understanding presents an important starting point for current research.

Second, we introduce a framework that helps to clarify different dimensions to advance theoretical work on the sharing economy in organization studies. This framework is informed by the studies in this volume and covers dimensions such as methodological approach, level of analysis, exploratory goal, explanatory mechanisms, and trajectory. Our hope is that it will facilitate and guide future theoretical inquiry into the variety and trajectories of sharing organizations. When introducing this framework, we describe how the contributions in this volume fit into it.

Third, we acknowledge the exploratory nature of this volume and summarize the individual contributions by grouping them according to theoretical themes that they touch upon. This concluding summary highlights how the chapters relate to the overall objective of this volume – theorizing the sharing economy – and provides a more granular thematic overview that connects the contributions to contemporary debates in organizational studies.

## DESCRIPTIONS OF THE SHARING ECONOMY AS A PHENOMENON OF VARIETY AND DYNAMICS

We found it helpful to first take stock of how scholars have described and started to theorize the sharing economy. To carry out this aim, we conducted a semantic-network analysis based on the most influential scholarly papers on the sharing economy[1] and the depictions the authors of these papers used to define and

*Fig. 1.* Semantic Network of Depictions of the Sharing Economy.

characterize the phenomenon.[2] From the co-occurrence of descriptions, we were able to construct a semantic network with clusters of high density (Blondel, Guillaume, Lambiotte, & Lefebvre, 2008) that shows those characteristics that are commonly mentioned together in depictions of the sharing economy. The analysis revealed that scholars perceive the sharing economy as a phenomenon of inherent variety and dynamics. This perception underscores the need for and potential fruitfulness of studying the variety and trajectories of new forms of organizing in the sharing economy. Fig. 1 illustrates these findings by visualizing the following four clusters of terms commonly used to describe the sharing economy and the organizations operating within it: "diverse and paradox," "new and contested," "growing and broad," and "ambiguous."

*Cluster 1 "diverse and paradox."* Many authors point to the diversity, heterogeneity, and paradoxical nature of the sharing economy (see Cluster 1 in Fig. 1). For instance, authors highlight the "great diversity" (Schor, 2014, p. 3) and "wide range of activities and business models" (Plewnia & Guenther, 2018, p. 3) of sharing-economy organizations. In addition, they emphasize that the sharing economy is "replete with paradoxes and tensions" (Acquier et al., 2017, p. 1) and point to its complex, disruptive, and paradoxical nature (Laamanen, Pfeffer, Rong, & Van de Ven, 2018; Martin, 2016; Schor, 2017), which imposes "paradoxes and dilemmas" (Munoz & Cohen, 2017, p. 2) on organizations operating within it.

*Cluster 2 "new and contested."* Other authors emphasize the newness and contested character of the sharing economy (see Cluster 2 in Fig. 1). They refer to its "new digitally-enabled sharing business models" (Junglas, Koch, Sundararajan, & Wang, 2017, p. iv), mention "new forms of organizations" (Etter et al., 2019, p. 3), or emphasize that the sharing economy as a whole represents a "new phenomenon" (Li, Tallmann, Qian, & Keil, 2018). While the democratization of the economy is mentioned as one of the expected contributions of these new forms of organizing, its realization is being increasingly questioned. This questioning results in heated debates that bolster the claim of the contested nature of the sharing economy (Etter et al., 2019).

*Cluster 3 "growing and broad."* A third group of authors points to the growth and breadth of the phenomenon (see Cluster 3 in Fig. 1). These authors view the sharing economy as an "umbrella term" (Codagnone, Biagi, & Abadie, 2016, p. 5) or "umbrella concept" (Heinrichs, 2013, p. 229) that subsumes current developments and models. At the same time, they commonly emphasize the rapid growth of the phenomenon (Cohen & Kietzmann, 2014; Fraiberger & Sundararajan, 2015), which is enabled by the spread of digital technologies as well as the increased digitalization of economy and society (Matzler, Veider, & Kathan, 2015; Schor, 2014).

*Cluster 4 "ambiguous."* A fourth group of authors highlights the ambiguous goals of sharing-economy organizations (see Cluster 4 in Fig. 1). The broad definition of the sharing economy as a "socio-economic phenomenon" (Plewnia & Guenther, 2018, p. 571) or "socioeconomic ecosystem" (Laamanen et al., 2018, p. 213) commonly applied by these authors indicates the lack of a shared definition and clear boundaries for the sharing economy and underscore its "ambiguous" nature (Erickson & Sørensen, 2016, p. 3; Plewnia & Guenther, 2018, p. 571).

Often, authors who emphasize the ambiguous character of the sharing economy also elaborate on whether and how sharing organizations contribute to social and ecologic goals. While non-economic goals were among the early promises of the sharing economy, researchers and practitioners increasingly question whether such promises can be kept and instead acknowledge that the sharing economy and the goals it represents are ambiguous (Etter et al., 2019; Hawlitschek, Teubner, & Gimpel, 2016; Martin, 2016).

Taken together, scholars seem to agree that the sharing economy and the organizations operating within it present a phenomenon that features diversity and paradoxes, newness and contestation, rapid growth and breadth as well as ambiguous goals. In combination, these features make theorizing the sharing economy a challenging and at the same time promising endeavor. These features also make clear that an important starting point for theorizing the sharing economy is understanding the variety and dynamics of organization forms within it. We argue that organization studies as a discipline is well suited for studying sharing-economy organizations because one of its strengths is dealing with a new and growing phenomenon of high levels of heterogenity and ambiguity.

## A FRAMEWORK FOR THEORIZING THE SHARING ECONOMY

The objective of this volume is to instigate and facilitate theoretical work on the sharing economy grounded in a deep understanding of the phenomenon. Inspired by the contributions in this volume, we lay out an organizing framework based on various dimensions: the methodological approach, level of analysis, exploratory goal, explanatory mechanism, and trajectory. These dimensions are particularly useful for future theorizing of the variety and trajectories of new forms of organizing in general, and they may also guide organization scholars in further theorizing the sharing economy specifically.

### *Methodological Approach*

To cope with the newness of the sharing phenomenon and a lack of understanding, one can rely on Weber's (1978) epistemological concept for the social sciences. In his view, one important aim of sociology is developing a meaningful understanding of social phenomena. Weber distinguishes between the complementary processes of "understanding" ("Verstehen") and "explaining" ("Erklären") to accomplish this aim. New phenomena typically have an ambiguous meaning and are therefore contested. A contested phenomenon demands an interpretative and theoretically driven description of actors, actions, and situations (Weber, 2013). In this view, "understanding" represents a systematic interpretative process in which researchers as outside observers relate to phenomena under study, make observations, and interpret them against a theoretical background – which is eventually further developed from insights gained about the new phenomena (Ringer, 1997).

Following Weber's ideas, "understanding" thus goes beyond purely descriptive approaches and rather relates to existing bodies of theory and knowledge. As methodological approaches, conceptual research and theoretically driven qualitative research can be particularly suitable for achieving this goal. Once a phenomenon is understood and explored, processes of "explaining" aim at testing alternative assumptions about the underlying mechanisms driving a phenomenon and the effects associated with it. Expectations derived from different theories can be operationalized and tested against each other using quantitative research as a methodological approach. Processes of "explaining" eventually lead to the creation of grounded or established knowledge of a phenomenon.

The history of science has shown that processes of "understanding" or "explaining," to some extent, take place in succession (Ruse, 2009). New phenomena are typically explored in conceptual and qualitative research to achieve a thorough "understanding" of the phenomenon against the background of existing theories, before hypotheses on relationships between drivers, new phenomena, and effects are developed; before concepts are operationalized; and before hypotheses are tested. In Weber's ideas of bureaucracy, for example, we observe such a sequence. Weber developed ideas on the relationships between elements of an idealized bureaucratic organization in the early twentieth century, but those ideas, in the sense of "explaining," were not tested until situational and contingency approaches emerged (Kieser, 1999) and large empirical research projects (Pugh, Hickson, Hinings, & Turner, 1968) were carried out in the 1960s.

Keeping these considerations of process in mind is helpful when reflecting on meaningful methodological pathways for studying organizations in the sharing economy. Conceptual and qualitative research approaches typically seek to gain a deeper understanding of a phenomenon as the basis for explanation, whereas quantitative research for the most part examines large-scale patterns in the search for explanations. Since, as already mentioned, the sharing economy is a new phenomenon, most of the current research on it is conceptual (e.g., Mair & Reischauer, 2017) as well as qualitative (e.g., Kornberger et al., 2018; Kyprianou, 2018; Reischauer & Mair, 2018a; Uzunca, Rigtering, & Ozcan, 2018). Similarly, the contributions in this volume predominantly cover conceptual research (Frenken, Vaskelainen, Fünfschilling, & Piscicelli, in this volume; Kirchner & Schüßler, in this volume) and qualitative research (Acquier, Carbone, & Vasseur, in this volume; Mosmann & Klutt, in this volume; Vith & Höllerer, in this volume; Wruk, Schöllhorn, & Oberg, in this volume) along with some contributions applying mixed methods (Bucher, Fieseler, Lutz, & Newlands, in this volume; Ozcan, Gurses, & Möhlmann, in this volume). These applied approaches help to further unpack and explore the variety of organization forms and provide an in-depth understanding of the trajectory of the sharing economy. In line with existing studies, the contributions in this volume rely on a range of empirical data sources: interviews or written surveys with founders and users, organizational documents or websites, media articles and other types of texts. They also employ a range of data-analysis methods – from inductive content analysis to (semantic) network approaches to statistical analysis (see Table 1 for an overview of the methodological approaches applied in the individual contributions in this volume). We believe that applying the diverse methodological repertoire we as organizational scholars have available – including ethnographic methods, topic modeling, or simulation – will be important for advancing our knowledge base on the sharing economy, and that this repertoire will allow us to mainstream the study of sharing-economy organizations in the larger field of organization research.

### *Levels of Analysis*

Research on new organizational forms in the sharing economy has started to explore the phenomenon at different levels of analysis. Fig. 2 provides an overview of possible levels that future research can consider. At the individual level, research has already begun to analyze why people participate in sharing models as providers or consumers and what drives their satisfaction (e.g., Hamari et al., 2016; Möhlmann, 2015). Another interest in current research at this level is in revealing the motivations and traits of sharing-organization founders (e.g., Cohen & Muñoz, 2016; Li et al., 2018). The diversity of models and application areas in the sharing economy has given rise to a number of studies at the organizational level, which to a large extent have focused on understanding the organizational and business models of sharing organizations (e.g., Cohen & Muñoz, 2016; Voytenko Palgan et al., 2017; Wruk, Oberg, Klutt, & Maurer, 2019) and their historical predecessors (e.g., Mosmann, 2019). Many of these new models rely on developing communities of suppliers and consumers who participate in value creation. The question of how to effectively establish and coordinate such communities is one of the research interests on the level of platforms and communities (e.g., Bucher et al., in this volume; Mosmann & Klutt, in this volume; Reischauer & Mair, 2018b). The rapid growth of the sharing economy in many industries has drawn attention to studies at the market level in specific subfields of the sharing economy – such as in the mobility, carsharing, and accommodation industries – focusing on how sharing organizations interact with each other and with industry incumbents (e.g., Shaheen & Cohen, 2007; Zervas, Proserpio, & Byers, 2017). A related set of studies has integrated industry associations, regulators, media organizations, and other social actors into its analyses, positioning

*Fig. 2.* Sharing Phenomena on Different Levels of Analysis.

these studies at the field level (Acquier et al., in this volume; Frenken et al., in this volume; Kirchner & Schüßler, in this volume; e.g., Laamanen et al., 2018; Wruk et al., in this volume).

As the contributions in this volume show, the variety within and trajectories of the sharing economy allow researchers to develop study designs that span multiple levels of analysis and also bridge literatures in adjacent fields such as political economy, legal studies, business history, or information systems (Mair & Rathert, 2019; Wruk, Oberg, & Maurer, 2019). (See Table 1 for an overview of the individual contributions in this volume and the level of analysis they present).

### *Understanding the Variety of New Forms of Organizing*

We now turn to developing a typology for systematizing different theoretical inquiries for understanding the variety of new forms of organizing. We discuss two common dimensions – exploratory goal and explanatory mechanism – that have proved particularly useful for mapping a heterogeneous yet connected body of research (Borgatti & Foster, 2003). From these dimensions, we construct a four-field matrix and use it to organize and briefly summarize both the general approaches for studying the variety of new organizational forms as well as the individual chapters in this volume.

#### *Exploratory Goal: Emergent Structuring of Variety Versus Governing Variety*

In line with the above-mentioned newness of our research object – the sharing economy – we introduce the "exploratory" goal (not explanatory goal) as one important dimension for organizing research on the variety of sharing organizations. This dimension captures the general approach a theory takes to understand the variety of new forms of organizing: Is its focus on the emergent structuring of variety or is it on the mechanisms for governing variety instead? The first approach aims at understanding the heterogeneity in the sharing economy as an emerging process. It is thus primarily interested in examining the process and implications of the emergent structuring of a field. The second approach emphasizes agency rather than structure: It focuses on governance and governing variety in the sharing economy and explores effective modes, strategies, or practices for coordinating actors to achieve desired outcomes. Neither approach is mutually exclusive, yet to demonstrate types of inquiry we differentiate between approaches that are primarily interested in either the emergent structuring of variety or in governing variety.

#### *Explanatory Mechanism: Cognition Versus Practice*

Independent of the exploratory goal, the explanatory mechanism presents another dimension, which helps to understand the variety of new forms of organizing in the sharing economy and explain the mechanisms at work. One fundamental difference within this dimension is between theories emphasizing cognition and logics and theories focusing on practices. Although cognition and practices are interrelated (as behavior and meaning, or talk and action) (e.g., Meyer &

Höllerer, 2010), most current research either focuses on cognition or practices when examining the phenomenon theoretically and empirically.

*Types of Theoretical Inquiry for Understanding Variety*

Together, exploratory goal and explanatory mechanism span a four-field matrix highlighting general approaches for exploring the variety of new organizational forms in the sharing economy, which for convenience – and to better illustrate these approaches – we term "logics and categories," "brokerage," "governance practices," and "governance approach." The contributions in this volume advance knowledge in these areas (see Fig. 3 and Table 1).

*Logics and Categories.* Research in this area of inquiry studies the emergent structuring of the sharing economy by considering its diverse, paradoxical, and contested nature; the multiple meanings, interpretations, and normative foundations it represents; the tensions arising between its various actors; and its resulting potential for changing or even disrupting existing institutional settings.

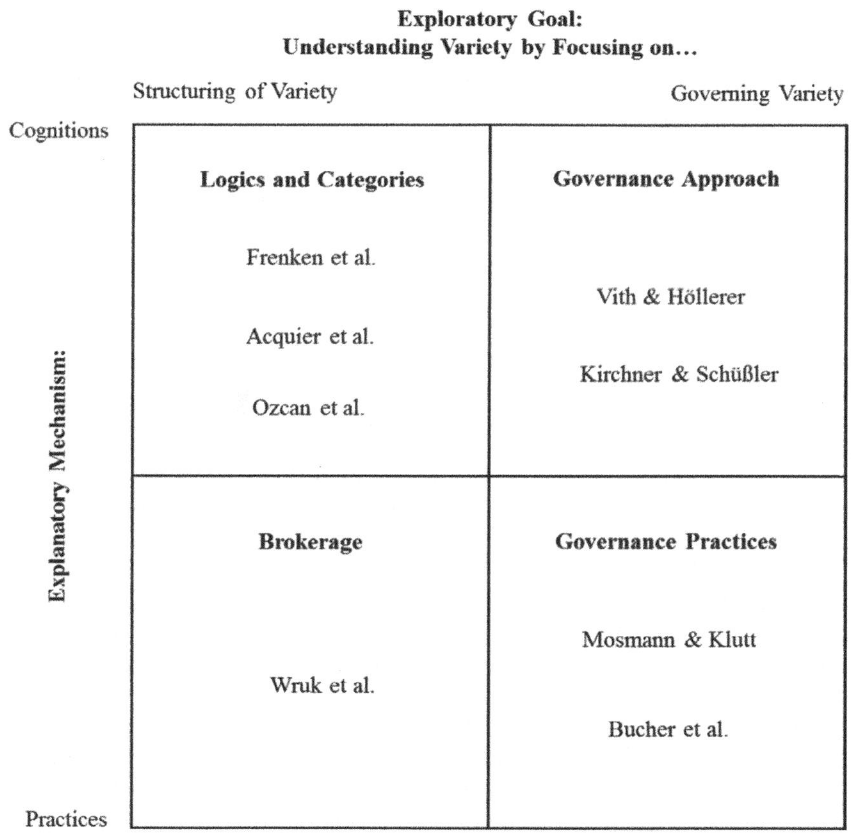


*Fig. 3.* Types of Theoretical Inquiry for Understanding Variety.

The theoretical approaches of "logics and categories" seem particularly suited for these types of investigations and are therefore strongly represented here.

Institutional logics are "socially constructed, historical patterns of material practices, assumptions, values, beliefs, and rules" that prescribe behavior and provide meaning in institutional settings and fields (Ocasio & Thornton, 1999, p. 804). To gain legitimacy and survive organizations follow the prescriptions of those logics that are characteristic for the institutional field they are embedded in (Thornton, Ocasio, & Lounsbury, 2012). Scholars studying the sharing economy with an institutional-logics lens commonly emphasize the tensions and paradoxes within this field and the resulting lack of a dominant logic or reference frame that can provide meaning, coherence, and predictability (Acquier et al., in this volume; Uzunca et al., 2018). To explore field emergence and structuring in a context of diverse and paradoxical logics, these scholars theorize around institutional plurality and complexity (e.g., O'Sullivan & O'Dwyer, 2015), a prominent research stream for organizations and fields (Greenwood, Raynard, Kodeih, Micelotta, & Lounsbury, 2011; Raynard, 2016; Reay & Hinings, 2009). Two chapters in this volume follow this approach and complement existing research in this line of inquiry: In their conceptual chapter, Frenken, Vaskelainen, Fünfschilling, and Piscicelli apply a conceptual framework of institutional logics (Thornton et al., 2012) to introduce a new platform-based rationale of economic exchange and show how this rationale breaks with established ones. Acquier, Carbone, and Vasseur use an institutional-logics lens to examine how plurality is produced and reproduced as the sharing economy as a field emerges and develops.

Categories are socially constructed labels that differentiate between those objects that have specific elements or features in common from those that do not, and thereby provide audiences with cognitive boundaries for category membership (Lamont, 2012). The idea of categories can be traced back to population ecology (Hannan, Pólos, Carroll, & Hsu, 2007; Hsu & Hannan, 2005) and institutional theory (DiMaggio, 1997; Zuckerman, 1999). Categories can be viewed as abstract cognitive schemes that help to structure fields and evaluate the organizations within a filed, such as the sharing economy (Durand & Paolella, 2013; Rao, Monin, & Durand, 2003; Wruk, Oberg, Klutt, et al., 2019). Categories, therefore, impact organizations and their survival (Durand & Paolella, 2013; Negro, Koçak, & Hsu, 2010). In this volume, the chapter by Ozcan, Gurses, and Möhlmann adopts this theoretical approach to help us understand category spill-overs in the sharing economy. More concretely, they examine how "category kings" (i.e., pioneering organizations like *Airbnb* and *Uber* that create and dominate new categories) affect "category commoners" (i.e., their less-prominent counterparts within the same category) and thereby provide insight into how the sharing economy as a whole and firms in its sub-categories co-evolve.

While the approaches of logics and categories are distinct, they both focus on the emergent structuring of the sharing economy as a field and the various actors operating within it, thus presenting ways of addressing one of the pressing issues in current research on the sharing economy (Mair & Reischauer, 2017).

*Brokerage*. The newness and variety characterizing the sharing economy provide opportunities to study processes of structuration by looking at practices of interaction and mutual recognition among various actors, which is why we term this area of inquiry "brokerage." The concept of the organizational field is a suitable one for studying these processes (DiMaggio & Powell, 1983). Fields emerge when previously disconnected organizations with individual organizational forms begin to have a shared purpose and start to recognize and interact with each other. From dyadic relationships, more complex relational patterns and roles (e.g., supplier, producer, and broker) develop over time (Powell & Oberg, 2017), and the structure of a field begins to take shape (Barley & Tolbert, 1997; Scott, 2013). As organizations within fields interact with each other more frequently and more purposefully than they do with organizations that are not members of the field (Scott, 2013), field boundaries emerge. Within a field, organizational forms that prove to be legitimate and successful proliferate, while others disappear (Lawrence, Hardy, & Phillips, 2002). In addition to the interactions that result from being jointly involved in value chains, organizations begin to observe and recognize the others as part of the same field. This development allows members and external observers to recognize the field as distinct (Greenwood et al., 2011). Besides the organizations providing services and products – in our case, sharing organizations – associations, regulators, researchers, dedicated media organizations, and other social actors can become part of the field and contribute to its structuration (Hinings, Logue, & Zietsma, 2017).

The breadth and variety of the sharing economy, which stems from both its diverse organization forms and from many industries and areas in which sharing organizations are active, challenge established assumptions about practices of interaction and mutual recognition and who is involved in these practices. This raises the question of what structure these practices have led to so far. The chapter by Wruk, Schöllhorn, and Oberg in this volume addresses this question by studying the structure and configuration of the field of the sharing economy. These authors are particularly interested in whether a stratified structure characterizes organizational fields (DiMaggio & Powell, 1983) or whether the focus of interactions among field members is on jointly contributing to debates and referencing each other. Both practices – stratifying and referencing – are helpful to understand issue fields (Wooten & Hoffman, 2008) and in combining the two, this chapter contributes to research on the field level and simultaneously demonstrates the fruitfulness of a field-level approach for understanding the emergent structuring of the sharing economy.

*Governance Practices*. Research that takes the variety and peculiarities of new forms of organizing as an opportunity for exploring effective "governance practices," meaning practices for organizing, controlling, and coordinating the behavior of actors to achieve a collective outcome (O'Mahony & Bechky, 2008; Williamson, 1999), can be located in this area of inquiry. When new forms of organizing, such as network organizations (Ebers & Oerlemans, 2013; Powell, 1990), temporary organizations (Bechky, 2006; Grabher, 2004), and online communities (O'Mahony & Ferraro, 2007; Sibai, De Valck, Farrell, & Rudd, 2015) initially emerged, they challenged the prevailing knowledge on effective governance and thereby presented an opportunity for scrutinizing and enlarging existing theories. Similarly, new forms of organizing in the sharing economy call for research on the governance of communities and their members. Within these organizations, communities are an integral part of value creation (Aaltonen & Lanzara, 2015; Davis, 2015; Reischauer & Mair, 2018a) and at the same time are characterized by fluid boundaries of membership, decentralized decision making, and a heterogeneous pool of individuals with multiple roles and responsibilities (Faraj & Johnson, 2011; Seidel & Stewart, 2011). The nature of these communities means that governance within sharing organizations is an important yet challenging task and calls for organization scholars to explore effective mechanisms that can help sharing organizations to coordinate the activities of their community members (Bucher et al., in this volume; Mosmann & Klutt, in this volume; Reischauer & Mair, 2018a).

In this volume, two chapters address this call: The chapter by Mosmann and Klutt leverages classical theories on market, hierarchy, and clan governance practices (Heide, 1994; Sibai et al., 2015) to understand how sharing organizations coordinate the activities of their community members. The chapter by Bucher, Fieseler, Lutz and Newlands, in contrast, draws on work on emotion regulation and emotional labor (e.g., Ashforth & Humphrey, 1993; Grandey, 2000; Morris & Feldman, 1996) and shows how sharing organizations can enforce emotional-labor practices among their members. Together, these chapters complement initial research on community governance in the sharing economy (e.g., Reischauer & Mair, 2018a) and put forward alternative theoretical approaches for advancing our knowledge on practices for governing variety in new forms of organizing.

*Governance Approach.* Finally, research in this area addresses questions about effective approaches for governing the sharing economy as a whole. The heightened relevance of the answers to these questions is prompted by the contested and ambiguous nature of the sharing economy and the resulting debates on the potential positive and negative effects of new forms of organizing in it (Codagnone et al., 2016; Etter et al., 2019). These debates concern issues such as distorted competition, precarious working conditions, tax evasion, and social inequality (Malhotra & Van Alstyne, 2014; Peticca-Harris, deGama, & Ravishankar, 2018; Scholz, 2017; Schor, 2017) and have prompted legal, regulatory, and administrative authorities at different levels to search for novel ways to shape, support, coordinate, or restrict the behavior of sharing-economy organizations (Vith, Oberg, Höllerer, & Meyer, 2019). Managing the tradeoff between supporting innovation and protecting the rights of users, workers, and incumbent organizations is viewed as one of the major challenges for developing appropriate governance approaches (Cohen & Sundararajan, 2015) and one that gives organization scholars an open invitation to theorize this phenomenon (Vith & Höllerer, in this volume). The last two chapters in this volume give researchers space to follow up on this invitation by looking closely at the underlying assumptions and ideas about the sharing economy and the actors in it.

Vith and Höllerer use framing theory (Meyer, 2004; Snow & Benford, 1988) to explore how (local) governments can respond to new social and economic phenomena (here, the sharing economy). By uncovering the "Viennese Way" of governing the sharing economy, they contribute to a deeper understanding of the strategic engagement and issue work that underlie policymaking in the context of a contested issue such as the sharing economy. From a different perspective, Kirchner and Schüßler build on literature on the sociology of markets (e.g., Fligstein, 2002) to show that governance approaches hinge on our understanding of the ways in which the sharing economy is organized; they also discuss the role market organizers play in regulating the sharing economy.

### *Understanding Trajectories of New Forms of Organizing*

One area of interest in organizational research is tracing the changes that follow from the emergence and spread of new forms of organizing. Such changes open up two general directions of trajectories that are fruitful for organizational analysis. One direction starts from a variety of new forms and studies the formation of structures and orders. Another direction is from order to variety, applied by organizational scholars interested in understanding how existing structures and orders are questioned and changed by the formation and proliferation of new forms. We provide an overview of different theoretical inquiries used to investigate trajectories from variety to order and from order to variety and elaborate on how these inquiries are particularly helpful for studying these trajectories. Fig. 4 summarizes the positioning of theoretical concepts on the trajectories between variety and order that are applied in the chapters of this volume.

#### *From Variety to Order*

In chapters relying on field theory (Wruk et al., in this volume), category research (Ozcan et al., in this volume), institutional work (Vith & Höllerer, in this volume), and standardization (Bucher et al., in this volume; Kirchner & Schüßler; Mosmann & Klutt, in this volume), the authors start from a point of highly unstructured variety and identify orders and ordering mechanisms. Chapters on standards and institutional work assume that actors try to influence governance of the sharing economy, while chapters on fields and categories describe the development of order as a process of emergence.

*Categories.* In new fields such as the sharing economy, organizational models are diverse and contested. Over time, however, as sharing organizations observe each other and become subject to similar environmental demands, successful and legitimate organizational forms should proliferate, potentially becoming taken-for-granted organizational categories (Durand & Paolella, 2013; Hsu & Hannan, 2005). Category research provides a set of theoretical concepts and ideas to capture this trajectory from variety to order. In this volume, Ozcan, Gurses, and Möhlmann take a category approach and study the development of order as a process of emergence and its underlying mechanisms.

*Fields.* Organizations that are active in the same field often have more frequent interaction with each other and observe others in this same field more closely than do organizations that are outside this field (DiMaggio & Powell, 1983). Because of this interaction and mutual recognition, the structural order of the field evolves as a relational network (DiMaggio & Powell, 1983; White, Owen-Smith, Moody, & Powell, 2004). In addition, other actors emerge or enter the field, and they contribute to structuration and ordering processes by shaping either the institutional infrastructure in the field or the discourse about it (DiMaggio & Powell, 1983; Hoffman, 1999). Taking a field-theory perspective is thus fruitful for studying trajectories from variety to order. Wruk, Schöllhorn, and Oberg take such a perspective in this volume, in their analysis of the relational network in the sharing economy on the World Wide Web, thereby exploring the structural order of the emerging field of the sharing economy.

*Standards*. The trajectory from variety to order can also be fruitfully studied from a standardization perspective. The development and diffusion of standardized practices is typically promoted by certain social actors, such as industry associations, social-movement actors, or other types of legitimate theorizers (Strang & Meyer, 1993; Strang & Soule, 1998). In this volume, how actors seek to influence and govern the sharing economy by advancing standards is the research interest of Kirchner and Schüßler. Similarly, the contributions by Mosmann and Klutt as well as Bucher, Fieseler, Lutz, and Newlands discuss mechanisms that help sharing organizations to set standards for and guide the behavior of their community members, given these members' various and divergent interests and motives.

*Institutional Work*. Analyzing the role social actors play in initiating and promoting changes to institutional environments is also of key interest for institutional-work research. Institutional work may thereby involve both the trajectory from order to variety and from variety to order (Hampel, Lawrence, & Tracey, 2017). New forms of organizing may be promoted in established fields, where an existing order is broken up and variety is created (Zietsma & Lawrence, 2010). Institutional work may also contribute to creating order in a field where diverse new forms of organizing exist. The contribution from Vith and Höllerer in this volume focuses on the second line of inquiry and studies how governmental actors participate in institutional work to create order in the sharing economy.

### *From Order to Variety*

Chapters applying a logics perspective (Acquier et al., in this volume; Frenken et al., in this volume), apply the hypothetical assumption that clearly ordered logics exist before these orders collide in everyday interaction and that this collision produces innovation and variety.

*Logics*. Institutional logics reflect the broader belief systems shaping the cognition and behavior of social actors (Friedland & Alford, 1991; Ocasio & Thornton, 1999). Each logic thereby represents its own order. Organizations are oftentimes confronted with expectations and influences from diverse institutional logics (Reay & Hinings, 2009). As a result, institutional logics as orders collide in everyday interactions and situations and produce innovation and a variety of organizational responses (Greenwood, Díaz, Li, & Lorente, 2010). In addition, new forms of organizing may introduce new logics in fields and thus bring newness and variety into an established order. In this volume, Acquier, Carbone, and Vasseur as well as Frenken, Vaskelainen, Fünfschilling, and Piscicelli take an institutional-logics perspective to trace trajectories from order to variety in the sharing economy.

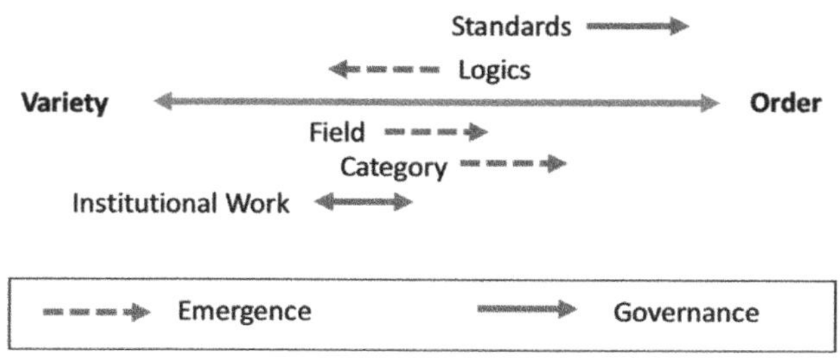


*Fig. 4.* Coping with Variety.

## OVERVIEW OF INDIVIDUAL CHAPTERS

To demonstrate how the dimensions of theoretical inquiry help to systematize current research on the sharing economy, we categorized the different chapters according to these dimensions (see Table 1): methodological approach, level of analysis, exploratory goal, explanatory mechanism, and trajectory.

## SITUATING THE VOLUME IN CONTEMPORARY RESEARCH ON ORGANIZATIONS

This volume set out to advance theorizing on the sharing economy. The contributions included here helped us to develop an organizing framework that can guide and facilitate such theorizing endeavors and underscore the potential of organization research to enhance understanding of the variety and the dynamics inherent in the sharing economy. These contributions also demonstrate the relevance of studying the sharing economy as a way to advance theoretical and empirical research on the variety and trajectories of new forms of organizing more generally (Mair & Rathert, 2019). And finally, these contributions help to connect research on the sharing economy with more generic themes and debates in research on organizations. In what follows, we briefly highlight how the chapters featured in this volume help advance contemporary debates and discussion.

First, research in this volume responds to debates on integrating community and concerns of legitimacy in theorizing organizations. The chapter by Mosmann and Klutt provides an insightful account of organizational governance types and practices in the sharing economy and thereby connects and enhances theoretical foundations on governance by taking seriously the importance of communities for sharing-economy organizations. Similarly, Bucher, Fieseler, Lutz, and Newlands focus on questions on coordination and control in the context of sharing-economy organizations and highlight the role of emotional labor in this process. Finally, Frenken, Vaskelainen, Fünfschilling, and Piscicelli use the sharing economy as a setting for laying out pathways for how legitimacy can be lost and regained.

Second, several contributions in this volume speak to the increasing amount of research studying the emergence and evolution of organizational fields and

***Table 1.*** Overview of Contributions of this Volume

| Authors | Methodological Approach | Level of Analysis | Understanding Variety | | Understanding Trajectories |
|---|---|---|---|---|---|
| | | | Exploratory Goals | Explanatory Mechanisms | |
| Mosmann & Klutt | Qualitative | Organization and community members | Governance of community members | Governance practices | From variety to order |
| Bucher et al. | Mixed method | Organization and community members | Governance of community members | Emotional practices | From variety to order |
| Frenken et al. | Conceptual | Field | Emergent structuring of field | Institutional logics | From order to variety |
| Acquier et al. | Qualitative | Field | Emergent structuring of field | Institutional logics | From order to variety |
| Wruk et al. | Qualitative | Field | Emergent structuring of field | Relational practices | From variety to order |
| Ozcan et al. | Mixed method | Field | Emergent structuring of field | Categories | From variety to order |
| Vith & Höllerer | Qualitative | Organization and field | Field governance | Governance approach | From variety to order |
| Kirchner & Schüßler | Conceptual | Field | Field governance | Governance approach | From variety to order |

how categories shape dynamics within these fields. Acquier, Carbone, and Vasseur examine the evolution of the sharing economy as a field in France between 2014 and 2017. Their analysis of entrepreneurs in the sharing economy shows how plurality in a field is produced and reproduced. Wruk, Schöllhorn, and Oberg apply a field-level analysis to the sharing economy and investigate the field at the social-relationship and discursive levels. A field-level analysis helps them to understand that the field is composed of organizations that are not necessarily sharing-specific ones, but also include organizations with greater experience leveraging new societal and technology developments aimed at disrupting other industries and fields. And finally, Ozcan, Gurses, and Möhlmann adopt a category lens to understand category spill-over and the resulting dynamics in the sharing economy.

And third, chapters in this volume bridge the micro and macro focus in organization research: they apply different theoretical perspectives yet all study organizations and organizing in the sharing economy as a means for integrating societal and regulatory aspects, arrangements, and dynamics. Vith and Höllerer, for example, use framing theory to explore the role of (local) governments and the repertoire they have for governing the sharing economy and its actors based on a case of policymaking in the Vienna City Administration. Complementing Vith and Höllerer, Kirchner and Schüßler build on literature on the sociology of markets to address pertinent questions on competition, labor conditions, and tax regimes in the sharing economy. They emphasize that regulatory solutions for the sharing economy hinge on our understanding of the ways in which the sharing economy is organized, and point to the role of standards; civil-society actors; and alternative, non-market forms of organizing as exerting a potential regulatory influence on the sharing economy.

Taken together, the contributions in this volume showcase the potential of organization research to enhance the understanding of the dynamics in the sharing economy. More importantly, they showcase the relevance of this discipline for advancing theoretical and empirical research on the variety and trajectories of new forms of organizing. In doing so, the contributions in this volume provide a first and important step toward proactively forging discussions across perspectives, levels of analysis, and even disciplinary divides, a step that further enhances the relevance of organization research for understanding evolving social and economic phenomena.

## NOTES

1. We used two sources to identify a collection of academic articles on the sharing economy. First, in August 2019, we searched Google Scholar for articles on the sharing economy, using a search term that captures what observers often proclaim is a diversity of labels used to describe the phenomenon under study (search term: "sharing economy" or "share economy" or "shareconomy" or "collaborative economy"). The resulting list of articles was arranged in descending order based on the number of citations the articles received according to Google Scholar. This list formed the basis of our analysis and included the most frequently cited articles (78 of them received between 38 and 1,624 citations). Second, we searched for special issues of academic journals dedicated to the sharing economy that were published within the last few years or that are currently in preparation. To deepen our

search for descriptions, we also added 13 introductory papers and calls for papers from these special issues to our collection of articles. To understand how the sharing economy is characterized in these papers, we analyzed the abstracts and introduction and definition sections in each for descriptions of the sharing economy.

2. We started with an inductive approach and collected labels that were used in definitions and descriptions of the sharing economy, such as adjectives and adverbs, and developed a list of all the labels that we found. For each article, we then coded which of the labels from our list it contained (binary coding). We grouped together labels (first-level codes) that were used more or less synonymously or that indicated the same ideas and used these labels to create depictions (second-level codes). We thus distinguish between depictions of the sharing economy and labels that make up these depictions.

From our coding of depictions (second-level codes), we created a co-occurrence matrix to see which depictions were used in combination. Based on this co-occurrence matrix, we developed a semantic network consisting of nodes that represent depictions of the sharing economy, and relationships capturing the number of co-occurring depictions that appeared in the sample of articles (Distel, 2010; Wasserman & Faust, 1994). To interpret the semantic network, we created a network visualization using Gephi, an open-source network analysis and visualization software package (Bastian, Heymann, & Jacomy, 2009) and applied the Fruchterman-Reingold algorithm (Fruchterman & Reingold, 1991). The algorithm positions nodes closely together if these nodes co-occur and are thus strongly connected. In addition, for each depiction in the co-occurrence matrix (second-level code) we added the labels that it subsumed (first-level codes). The resulting network visualization thus allows us to see which depictions of the sharing economy are used together in articles and which labels are used to make these depictions.

## REFERENCES


Aaltonen, A., & Lanzara, G. F. (2015). Building governance capability in online social production: Insights from Wikipedia. *Organization Studies*, *36*(12), 1649–1673.

Acquier, A., Carbone, C., & Vasseur, L. (2020). The sharing economy as an emerging and contested field – How classic and institutional entrepreneurs cope with plural theoretical frames. In I. Maurer, J. Mair, & A. Oberg (Eds.), *Theorizing the sharing economy. Research in the sociology of organizations* (pp. 107–129). Bingley: Emerald Publishing Limited.

Acquier, A., Daudigeos, T., & Pinkse, J. (2017). Promises and paradoxes of the sharing economy: An organizing framework. *Technological Forecasting and Social Change*, *125*, 1–10.

Ashforth, B. E., & Humphrey, R. H. (1993). Emotional labor in service roles: The influence of identity. *Academy of Management Review*, *18*(1), 88–115.

Barley, S. R., & Tolbert, P. S. (1997). Institutionalization and structuration: Studying the links between action and institution. *Organization Studies*, *18*(1), 93–117. doi:10.1177/017084069701800106

Bastian, M., Heymann, S., & Jacomy, M. (2009). Gephi: an open source software for exploring and manipulating networks. *ICWSM*, *8*, 361–362.

Bechky, B. A. (2006). Gaffers, Gofers, and Grips: Role-based coordination in temporary organizations. *Organization Science*, *17*(1), 3–21. doi:10.1287/orsc.1050.0149

Belk, R. (2010). Sharing. *Journal of Consumer Research*, *36*(5), 715–734.

Belk, R. (2014). Sharing versus pseudo-sharing in Web 2.0. *Anthropologist*, *18*(1), 7–23. doi:10.1080/09720073.2014.11891518

Blondel, V. D., Guillaume, J.-L., Lambiotte, R., & Lefebvre, E. (2008). Fast unfolding of communities in large networks. *Journal of Statistical Mechanics: Theory and Experiment*, *2008*(10), P10008. doi:10.1088/1742-5468/2008/10/P10008

Borgatti, S. P., & Foster, P. C. (2003). The network paradigm in organizational research: A review and typology. *Journal of Management*, *29*(6), 991–1013.

Botsman, R., & Rogers, R. (2010). What's mine is yours: The rise of collaborative consumption. Retrieved from https://books.google.de/books

Bucher, E., Fieseler, C., Lutz, C., & Newlands, G. (2020). Shaping emotional practices in the sharing economy. In I. Maurer, J. Mair, & A. Oberg (Eds.), *Theorizing the sharing economy. Research in the sociology of organizations* (Vol. 66, pp. 55–82). Bingley: Emerald Publishing Limited.

Codagnone, C., Biagi, F., & Abadie, F. (2016). *The passions and the interests: Unpacking the 'sharing economy'*. Institute for Prospective Technological Studies, JRC Science for Policy Report.

Cohen, B., & Kietzmann, J. (2014). Ride on! Mobility business models for the sharing economy. *Organization & Environment, 27*(3), 279–296. doi:10.1177/1086026614546199

Cohen, B., & Muñoz, P. (2016). Sharing cities and sustainable consumption and production: Towards an integrated framework. *Journal of Cleaner Production, 134*(Part A), 87–97.

Cohen, M., & Sundararajan, A. (2015). Self-regulation and innovation in the peer-to-peer sharing economy. *University of Chicago Law Review Online, 82*(1), 116.

Davis, G. F. (2015). What might replace the modern corporation: Uberization and the web page enterprise. *Seattle University Law Review, 39*, 501.

DiMaggio, P. (1997). Culture and cognition. *Annual Review of Sociology, 23*(1), 263–287.

DiMaggio, P., & Powell, W. (1983). The iron cage revisited: Institutional isomorphism and collective rationality in organizational fields. *American Sociological Review, 48*(2), 147–160. doi:10.2307/2095101

Distel, R. (2010). *Graph theory*. Berlin: Springer.

Durand, R., & Paolella, L. (2013). Category stretching: Reorienting research on categories in strategy, entrepreneurship, and organization theory. *Journal of Management Studies, 50*(6), 1100–1123. doi:10.1111/j.1467-6486.2011.01039.x

Ebers, M., & Oerlemans, L. (2013). The variety of governance structures beyond market and hierarchy. *Journal of Management, 42*(6), 1491–1529. doi:10.1177/0149206313506938

Erickson, K., & Sørensen, I. (2016). Regulating the sharing economy, 5(2). *Internet Policy Review*. doi:10.14763/2016.2.414

Etter, M., Fieseler, C., & Whelan, G. (2019). Sharing economy, sharing responsibility? Corporate social responsibility in the Digital Age. *Journal of Business Ethics, 159*, 935–942. 10.1007/s10551-019-04212-w

Faraj, S., & Johnson, S. L. (2011). Network exchange patterns in online communities. *Organization Science, 22*(6), 1464–1480.

Fligstein, N. (2002). *The architecture of markets: An economic sociology of twenty-first-century capitalist societies*. Princeton, NJ: Princeton University Press.

Fraiberger, S. P., & Sundararajan, A. (2015). Peer-to-peer rental markets in the sharing economy. *NYU Stern School of Business Research Paper, 6*.

Frenken, K., & Schor, J. (2017). Putting the sharing economy into perspective. *Environmental Innovation and Societal Transitions, 23*, 3–10.

Frenken, K., Vaskelainen, T., Fünfschilling, L., & Piscicelli, L. (2020). An institutional logics perspective on the gig economy. In I. Maurer, J. Mair, & A. Oberg (Eds.), *Theorizing the sharing economy. Research in the sociology of organizations* (pp. 83–105). Bingley: Emerald Publishing Limited.

Friedland, R., & Alford, R. R. (1991). Bringing society back in: Symbols, practices, and institutional contradictions. In W. W. Powell, & P. J. DiMaggio (Eds.), *The new institutionalism in organizational analysis* (pp. 232–263). Chicago, IL: University of Chicago Press.

Fruchterman, T. M., & Reingold, E. M. (1991). Graph drawing by force-directed placement. *Software: Practice and Experience, 21*(11), 1129–1164.

Grabher, G. (2004). Temporary architectures of learning: Knowledge governance in project ecologies. *Organization Studies, 25*(9), 1491–1514.

Grandey, A. A. (2000). Emotional regulation in the workplace: A new way to conceptualize emotional labor. *Journal of Occupational Health Psychology, 5*(1), 95.

Greenwood, R., Díaz, A. M., Li, S. X., & Lorente, J. C. (2010). The multiplicity of institutional logics and the heterogeneity of organizational responses. *Organization Science, 21*(2), 521–539.

Greenwood, R., Raynard, M., Kodeih, F., Micelotta, E. R., & Lounsbury, M. (2011). Institutional complexity and organizational responses. *Academy of Management Annals, 5*(1), 317–371. doi:10.1080/19416520.2011.590299

Hamari, J., Sjöklint, M., & Ukkonen, A. (2016). The sharing economy: Why people participate in collaborative consumption. *Journal of the Association for Information Science and Technology*, *67*(9), 2047–2059. doi:10.1002/asi.23552

Hampel, C., Lawrence, T. B., & Tracey, P. (2017). Institutional work: Taking stock and making it matter. In R. Greenwood, C. Oliver, T. B. Lawrence, & R. E. Meyer (Eds.), *The Sage handbook of organizational institutionalism* (pp. 558–590). London: Sage.

Hannan, M. T., Pólos, L., Carroll, G. R., & Hsu, G. (2007). Identity and audience. *Logics of Organization Theory: Audiences, Codes, and Ecologies* (pp. 100–120). Oxford: Princeton University Press.

Hawlitschek, F., Teubner, T., & Gimpel, H. (2016). Understanding the sharing economy – Drivers and impediments for participation in peer-to-peer rental. In *IEEE Hawaii International Conference on System Sciences*, At Kauai, USA (pp. 4782–4791).

Heide, J. B. (1994). Interorganizational governance in marketing channels. *Journal of Marketing*, *58*(1), 71–85.

Heinrichs, H. (2013). Sharing economy: A potential new pathway to sustainability. *GAIA-Ecological Perspectives for Science and Society*, *22*(4), 228–231.

Hinings, C. R., Logue, D. M., & Zietsma, C. (2017). Fields, institutional infrastructure and governance. In R. Greenwood, C. Oliver, T. B. Lawrence, & R. E. Meyers, *The Sage handbook of organizational institutionalism* (pp. 163–189). London: Sage.

Hoffman, A. J. (1999). Institutional evolution and change: Environmentalism and the U.S. Chemical Industry. *Academy of Management Journal*, *42*(4), 351–371. doi:10.2307/257008

Hsu, G., & Hannan, M. T. (2005). Identities, genres, and organizational forms. *Organization Science*, *16*(5), 474–490.

Junglas, I., Koch, H., Sundararajan, A., & Wang, P. (2017). Special Issue Editorial: Shared responsibility and blurring boundaries: Strategic implications of the sharing economy. *MIS Quarterly Executive*, *16*(4), iii–xiii.

Kieser, A., & Ebers, M. (2006). *Organisationstheorien*. Stuttgart: W. Kohlhammer Verlag.

Kieser, A. (1999). Der Situative Ansatz. In A. Kieser (Eds.), *Organisationstheorien* (pp. 169–198). Stuttgart: W. Kohlhammer Verlag.

Kirchner, S., & Schüßler, E. (2020). Regulating the sharing economy: A field perspective. In I. Maurer, J. Mair, & A. Oberg (Eds.), *Theorizing the sharing economy* (*Research in the sociology of organizations*) , Vol. 66, pp. 215–236). Bingley: Emerald Publishing.

Kornberger, M., Leixnering, S., Meyer, R. E., & Höllerer, M. A. (2018). Rethinking the sharing economy: The nature and organization of sharing in the 2015 refugee crisis. *Academy of Management Discoveries*, *4*(3), 314–335.

Kyprianou, C. (2018). Creating value from the outside in or the inside out: How nascent intermediaries build peer-to-peer marketplaces. *Academy of Management Discoveries*, *4*(3), 336–370.

Laamanen, T., Pfeffer, J., Rong, K., & Van de Ven, A. (2018). Editors' introduction: Business models, ecosystems, and society in the sharing economy. *Academy of Management Discoveries*, *4*(3), 213–219.

Lamont, M. (2012). Toward a comparative sociology of valuation and evaluation. *Annual Review of Sociology*, *38*(1), 201–221. doi:10.1146/annurev-soc-070308-120022

Lawrence, T. B., Hardy, C., & Phillips, N. (2002). Institutional effects of interorganizational collaboration: The emergence of proto-institutions. *Academy of Management Journal*, *45*(1), 281–290. doi:10.2307/3069297

Li, L., Tallmann, S., Qian, G., & Keil, T. (2018). Call for papers for special issue on the sharing economy: Entrepreneurial discovery and creative destruction across countries. Entrepreneurship Theory and Practice. Retrieved from https://journals.sagepub.com/pb-assets/cmscontent/ETP/ETP_CFP_EDCD.pdf. Accessed on August 16, 2019.

Mair, J., & Rathert, N. (2019). Alternative organizing with social purpose: Revisiting institutional analysis of market-based activity. *Socio-Economic Review*. doi:10.1093/ser/mwz031

Mair, J., & Reischauer, G. (2017). Capturing the dynamics of the sharing economy: Institutional research on the plural forms and practices of sharing economy organizations. *Technological Forecasting and Social Change*, *125*, 11–20. doi:10.1016/j.techfore.2017.05.023

Malhotra, A., & Van Alstyne, M. (2014). The dark side of the sharing economy… and how to lighten it. *Communications of the Association for Computing Machinery*, *57*(11), 24–27. doi:10.1145/2668893

Martin, C. J. (2016). The sharing economy: A pathway to sustainability or a nightmarish form of neoliberal capitalism? *Ecological Economics*, *121*, 149–159. doi:10.1016/j.ecolecon.2015.11.027

Matzler, K., Veider, V., & Kathan, W. (2015). Adapting to the sharing economy. *MIT Sloan Management Review*, *56*(2), 71.

Meyer, R. (2004). *Globale Managementkonzepte und lokaler Kontext: Organisationale Wertorientierung im österreichischen öffentlichen Diskurs*. facultas. wuv/maudrich.

Meyer, R. E., & Höllerer, M. A. (2010). Meaning structures in a contested issue field: A topographic map of shareholder value in Austria. *Academy of Management Journal*, *53*(6), 1241–1262. doi:10.5465/amj.2010.57317829

Möhlmann, M. (2015). Collaborative consumption: Determinants of satisfaction and the likelihood of using a sharing economy option again: Collaborative consumption-determinants of satisfaction and the likelihood of using a sharing economy option again. *Journal of Consumer Behaviour*, *14*(3), 193–207. doi:10.1002/cb.1512

Morris, J. A., & Feldman, D. C. (1996). The dimensions, antecedents, and consequences of emotional labor. *Academy of Management Review*, *21*(4), 986–1010.

Mosmann, P. (2019). Renaissance of shared resource use? The historical honeycomb of the sharing economy. In *Perspectives on the sharing economy*. Newcastle: Cambridge Scholars Publishing.

Mosmann, P., & Klutt, J. (2020). Market, hierarchy, or clan? Types of governance in the sharing economy. In I. Maurer, J. Mair, & A. Oberg (Eds.), *Theorizing the sharing economy. Research in the sociology of organizations* (Vol. 66, pp. 25–54). Bingley: Emerald Publishing Limited.

Munoz, P., & Cohen, B. (2017). Mapping out the sharing economy: A configurational approach to sharing business modeling. *Technological Forecasting and Social Change*, *125*, 21–37.

Negro, G., Koçak, Ö., & Hsu, G. (2010). Research on categories in the sociology of organizations. In *Categories in markets: Origins and evolution* (pp. 3–35). Bingley: Emerald Publishing.

O'Mahony, S., & Bechky, B. A. (2008). Boundary organizations: Enabling collaboration among unexpected allies. *Administrative Science Quarterly*, *53*(3), 422–459. doi:10.2189/asqu.53.3.422

O'Mahony, S., & Ferraro, F. (2007). The emergence of governance in an open source community. *Academy of Management Journal*, *50*(5), 1079–1106.

O'Sullivan, N., & O'Dwyer, B. (2015). The structuration of issue-based fields: Social accountability, social movements and the Equator Principles' issue-based field. *Accounting, Organizations and Society*, *43*, 33–55. doi:10.1016/j.aos.2015.03.008

Ocasio, W., & Thornton, P. H. (1999). Institutional logics and the historical contingency of power in organizations: Executive succession in the higher education publishing industry, 1958–1990. *American Journal of Sociology*, *105*(3), 801–843.

Owyang, J. (2016). Honeycomb 3.0: The collaborative economy market expansion. Retrieved from http://www.web-strategist.com/blog/2016/03/10/honeycomb-3-0-the-collaborative-economy-market-expansion-sxsw/. Accessed on November 13, 2018.

Ozcan, P., Gurses, K., & Möhlmann, M. (2020). Category kings and commoners: Within and cross- category spill-overs in the sharing economy. In I. Maurer, J. Mair, & A. Oberg (Eds.), *Theorizing the sharing economy. Research in the sociology of organizations* (Vol. 66, pp. 163–185). Bingley: Emerald Publishing Limited.

Parguel, B., Lunardo, R., & Benoit-Moreau, F. (2017). Sustainability of the sharing economy in question: When second-hand peer-to-peer platforms stimulate indulgent consumption. *Technological Forecasting and Social Change*, *125*, 48–57. doi:10.1016/j.techfore.2017.03.029

Peticca-Harris, A., deGama, N., & Ravishankar, M. (2018). Postcapitalist precarious work and those in the 'drivers' seat: Exploring the motivations and lived experiences of Uber drivers in Canada. *Organization*. doi:1350508418757332.

Plewnia, F., & Guenther, E. (2018). Mapping the sharing economy for sustainability research. *Management Decision*, *56*(3), 570–583.

Powell, W. W. (1990). Neither market nor hierarchy: Network forms of organization. *Research in Organizational Behavior*, *12*, 295–336.

Powell, W. W., & Oberg, A. (2017). Networks and institutions. In R. Greenwood, C. Oliver, T. B. Lawrence, & R. E. Meyer (Eds.), *Sage Handbook on organizational institutionalism* (pp. 446–476). Thousand Oaks, CA: Sage Publications.

Pugh, D. S., Hickson, D. J., Hinings, C. R., & Turner, C. (1968). Dimensions of organization structure. *Administrative Science Quarterly*, *13*(1), 65–105.

Rao, H., Monin, P., & Durand, R. (2003). Institutional change in Toque Ville: Nouvelle cuisine as an identity movement in French gastronomy. *American Journal of Sociology*, *108*(4), 795–843.

Raynard, M. (2016). Deconstructing complexity: Configurations of institutional complexity and structural hybridity. *Strategic Organization*, *14*(4), 310–335.

Reay, T., & Hinings, C. R. (2009). Managing the rivalry of competing institutional logics. *Organization Studies*, *30*(6), 629–652.

Reischauer, G., & Mair, J. (2018a). How organizations strategically govern online communities: Lessons from the sharing economy. *Academy of Management Discoveries*, *4*(3), 220–247.

Reischauer, G., & Mair, J. (2018b). Platform organizing in the new digital economy: Revisiting online communities and strategic responses. In L. Ringel, P. Hiller, & C. Zietsma (Eds.), *Research in the sociology of organizations: Vol. 57. Toward permeable boundaries of organizations?* (pp. 113–135). Bingley: Emerald Publishing.

Ringer, F. (1997). *Max Weber's methodology: The unification of the cultural and social sciences*. Cambridge, MA: Harvard University Press.

Ruse, M. (2009). *Philosophy after Darwin: Classic and contemporary readings*. Princeton, NJ: Princeton University Press

Scholz, T. (2017). *Uberworked and underpaid: How workers are disrupting the digital economy*. Hoboken, NJ: John Wiley & Sons.

Schor, J. (2014). Debating the sharing economy. *Journal of Self-Governance & Management Economics*, *4*(3), 7. doi:10.22381/JSME4320161

Schor, J. (2017). Does the sharing economy increase inequality within the eighty percent?: Findings from a qualitative study of platform providers. *Cambridge Journal of Regions, Economy and Society*, *10*(2), 263–279.

Scott, W. R. (2013). *Institutions and organizations: Ideas, interests, and identities*. London: Sage.

Seidel, M.-D. L., & Stewart, K. J. (2011). An initial description of the C-form. In C. Marquis, M. Lounsbury, & R. Greenwood (Eds.), *Research in the sociology of organizations: Vol. 33. Communities and organizations* (pp. 37–72). Bingley: Emerald Publishing.

Shaheen, S. A., & Cohen, A. P. (2007). Growth in worldwide carsharing: An international comparison. *Transportation Research Record*, *1992*(1), 81–89. doi:10.3141/1992-10

Sibai, O., De Valck, K., Farrell, A. M., & Rudd, J. M. (2015). Social control in online communities of consumption: A framework for community management. *Psychology & Marketing*, *32*(3), 250–264.

Snow, D. A., & Benford, R. D. (1988). Ideology, frame resonance, and participant mobilization. *International Social Movement Research*, *1*(1), 197–217.

Stokes, K., Clarence, E., Anderson, L., & Rinne, A. (2014). *Making sense of the UK collaborative economy*. London: Nesta.

Strang, D., & Meyer, J. W. (1993). Institutional conditions for diffusion. *Theory and Society*, *22*(4), 487–511.

Strang, D., & Soule, S. A. (1998). Diffusion in organizations and social movements: From hybrid corn to poison pills. *Annual Review of Sociology*, *24*(1), 265–290.

Thornton, P. H., Ocasio, W., & Lounsbury, M. (2012). *The institutional logics perspective: A new approach to culture, structure, and process*. Oxford: Oxford University Press on Demand.

Uzunca, B., Rigtering, J. P. C., & Ozcan, P. (2018). Sharing and shaping: A cross-country comparison of how sharing economy firms shape their institutional environment to gain legitimacy. *Academy of Management Discoveries*, *4*(3), 248–272.

Vaskelainen, T., & Münzel, K. (2017). The effect of institutional logics on business model development in the sharing economy: The case of German carsharing services. *Academy of Management Discoveries*, *4*(3), 273–293. doi:10.5465/amd.2016.0149

Vith, S., & Höllerer, M. A. (2020). "Turning the sharing economy into a fair economy…": Strategic issue work on the Vienna city administration. In I. Maurer, J. Mair, & A. Oberg (Eds.), *Theorizing the sharing economy. Research in the sociology of organizations* (Vol. 66, 187–213). Bingley: Emerald Publishing Limited.

Vith, S., Oberg, A., Höllerer, M. A., & Meyer, R. E. (2019). Envisioning the 'Sharing City': Governance strategies for the sharing economy. *Journal of Business Ethics*. doi:10.1007/s10551-019-04242-4

Voytenko Palgan, Y., Zvolska, L., & Mont, O. (2017). Sustainability framings of accommodation sharing. *Sustainability perspectives on the sharing economy*, *23*, 70–83.

Wasserman, S., & Faust, K. (1994). *Social network analysis: Methods and applications* (Vol. 8). New York, NY: Cambridge University Press.

Weber, M. (2013). *Gesammelte Aufsätze zur Wissenschaftslehre*. BoD–Books on Demand.

Weber, M. (1978). *Economy and society: An outline of interpretive sociology* (Vol. 1). Berkeley, CA: University of California Press.

White, D. R., Owen-Smith, J., Moody, J., & Powell, W. W. (2004). Networks, fields and organizations: Micro-dynamics, scale and cohesive embeddings. *Computational & Mathematical Organization Theory*, *10*(1), 95–117. doi:10.1023/B:CMOT.0000032581.34436.7b

Williamson, O. E. (1999). Strategy research: Governance and competence perspectives. *Strategic Management Journal*, *20*(12), 1087–1108.

Wooten, M., & Hoffman, A. J. (2008). Organizational fields: Past, present and future. In *The SAGE Handbook of organizational institutionalism* (pp. 131–147). London: Sage.

Wruk, D., Oberg, A., & Maurer, I. (2019). *Perspectives on the sharing economy*. Newcastle: Cambridge Scholars Publishing.

Wruk, D., Oberg, A., Klutt, J., & Maurer, I. (2019). The presentation of self as good and right: How value propositions and business model features are linked in the sharing economy. *Journal of Business Ethics*, *159*(4), 997–1021. doi:10.1007/s10551-019-04209-5

Wruk, D., Schöllhorn, T., & Oberg, A. (2020). Is the sharing economy a field? How a disruptive field nurtures sharing economy organizations. In I. Maurer, J. Mair, & A. Oberg (Eds.), *Theorizing the sharing economy. Research in the sociology of organizations* (Vol. 66, 131–162). Bingley: Emerald Publishing Limited.

Zervas, G., Proserpio, D., & Byers, J. W. (2017). The rise of the sharing economy: Estimating the impact of Airbnb on the hotel industry. *Journal of Marketing Research*, *54*(5), 687–705.

Zietsma, C., & Lawrence, T. B. (2010). Institutional work in the transformation of an organizational field: The interplay of boundary work and practice work. *Administrative Science Quarterly*, *55*(2), 189–221.

Zuckerman, E. W. (1999). The categorical imperative: Securities analysts and the illegitimacy discount. *American Journal of Sociology*, *104*(5), 1398–1438.

# MARKET, HIERARCHY, OR CLAN? TYPES OF GOVERNANCE IN THE SHARING ECONOMY

Philipp C. Mosmann and Jennifer Klutt


## ABSTRACT

*The rise of the sharing economy has brought with it a huge variety of new organizational forms and innovative business models. An integral part of these forms and models is the communities and members of sharing-economy organizations, since they significantly contribute to value creation for these organizations. Relying on community member contributions, though, is a challenge for these organizations because fluid community boundaries and voluntary membership makes it difficult to coordinate their activities. This chapter investigates the under-researched question of how sharing-economy organizations govern the actions of their community members. Following an abductive approach that included site visits, participant observations, and 67 interviews, we develop a framework that illustrates four different types of governance: pure market, pure clan, market-hierarchy hybrid, and clan-hierarchy hybrid. The framework explains differences among these types depending on the main activity (providing resources or producing jointly) and the primary aim of the community (business orientation or social orientation). This study thus contributes to research on both governance in general and to sharing-economy organizations in particular by capturing the variety and diversity of community forms, governance practices, and business-model configurations.*


**Keywords**: Community; governance types; control practices; sharing economy; business model; abductive approach

**Theorizing the Sharing Economy: Variety and Trajectories of New Forms of Organizing**
**Research in the Sociology of Organizations, Volume 66, 25–54**

**ISSN: 0733-558X/doi:10.1108/S0733-558X20200000066003**

## INTRODUCTION

The sharing economy – defined as a social and economic phenomenon of shared, swapped, or lent resource use (Acquier, Daudigeos, & Pinkse, 2017; Hamari, Sjöklint, & Ukkonen, 2016) – has opened up new, alternative ways for organizations to create and capture value and has disrupted traditional ways of doing business (Botsman & Rogers, 2011; Lamberton & Rose, 2012). These organizations – and the new and innovative forms of organizing they bring with them – are growing fast and are having an extensive impact on society. The heterogeneous practices and application areas of sharing-economy organizations are seen in for- and non-profit organizations and online and offline ones: in Business-to-Consumer (B2C), Business-to-Business (B2B), and Peer-to-Peer (P2P) models; in commercial and non-commercial platforms; in settings operating internationally (e.g., Couchsurfing), nationally (e.g., Stuffle), and locally (e.g., Food-sharing); and in both labor-intensive platforms (e.g., Uber) and capital-intensive ones (e.g., Airbnb).

Communities, and their importance to the respective organizations, are the common element of all these organizational forms and models that comprise the highly complex and multifaceted economic and social phenomenon of the sharing economy (Schor, 2014; Sundararajan, 2016). Communities are defined as all the individuals and members whose interactions are enabled and/or facilitated by the organization's business model (Reischauer & Mair, 2018). Within these communities, individuals and members take on multiple roles and responsibilities, and the communities themselves are characterized by fluid boundaries of membership, local or decentralized decision-making, and a fluid and heterogeneous pool of individuals whose mutually shared goals and voluntary commitment and engagement make it possible for them to communicate and interact (Faraj & Johnson, 2016; Seidel & Stewart, 2011). The informal structures, individual expertise, and self-efficacy beliefs of communities are central components of these organizations (O'Mahony & Lakhani, 2011; Puranam, Alexy, & Reitzig, 2014). Just as the business models in sharing-economy organization communities are diverse, so too are the specific communities themselves. The business models in the sharing economy are highly heterogeneous (Botsman & Rogers, 2011), and therefore the forms of sharing-economy communities vary widely as well, from communities of practice and innovation to epistemic ones (Gulati, Puranam, & Tushman, 2012; Lee & Cole, 2003; O'Mahony & Lakhani, 2011). For sharing-economy organizations, community governance – defined as the mode of control and coordination (Heide, 1994; Williamson, 1999) – is essential for building and consolidating an active community that will support exchange processes such as renting a flat (Airbnb), sharing a car (BlaBlaCar), or exchanging clothes (Kleiderkreisel). To sharing-economy organizations, the community is the "core of value creation" (Reischauer & Mair, 2018, p. 221) because it brings together suppliers and consumers to carry out the sharing, exchange, and lending processes that define these organizations. In sum, communities are a critical foundation of a sharing-economy organization's success and survival (Aaltonen & Lanzara, 2015).

The growing number of communities and community forms of organizing has been increasingly studied over the last decade (Porter & Donthu, 2008; Spaulding, 2010) and researchers have acknowledged that these communities and forms represent an alternative way of doing business (Demil & Lecocq, 2006; Galbreth, Ghosh, & Shor, 2012; Lee & Cole, 2003; Reischauer & Mair, 2018). Researchers stress that communities and community forms of organizing have peculiarities (Seidel & Stewart, 2011), offering conceptual, anecdotal, or single-case analyses (Kannan, Chang, & Whinston, 2000; O'Mahony & Ferraro, 2007). Despite the valuable insights of these studies, one limitation is their focus on single, specific community forms within one type of business model or organizational form, a focus that fails to provide a more holistic and comprehensive view (Faraj, Jarvenpaa, & Majchrzak, 2011; von Krogh, Spaeth, & Lakhani, 2003; O'Mahony & Ferraro, 2007). Therefore, we still know little about the governance of communities in sharing-economy organizations, which is highly diverse and distinct, since the sharing-economy phenomenon itself is so complex and encompasses such a wide range of different business models (Botsman & Rogers, 2011; Muñoz & Cohen, 2017). This study aims at overcoming this limitation and lack of knowledge by seeking to understand how sharing-economy organizations govern the actions and behavior of their communities and to uncover the underlying drivers of different types of governance. This investigation thus seeks to better understand the crucially important nature of community governance in sharing-economy organizations and responds to a recent call by Reischauer and Mair (2018), who recognize the highly strategic value of communities and how crucially important it is to understand their governance.

Since our empirical observations (site visits, participant observations, and 67 interviews) did not match existing theoretical frameworks, we used an abductive approach (Dubois & Gadde, 2002; Locke, Golden-Biddle, & Feldman, 2008) to develop a new framework, which allowed us to capture and reveal the diversity and complexity of governing the multiple community forms that comprise sharing-economy organizations. We identified four different types of governance: pure market, pure clan, market-hierarchy hybrid, and clan-hierarchy hybrid. These governance types reflect the different governance practices organizations use, and we discovered that the type of governance depends on the main activity the community carries out (providing resources or producing jointly) and the primary aim (business orientation or social orientation). Our research devotes more attention to new forms of organizing, since this focus fits to the objectives of our study: understanding practices of governance and how they help organizations achieve their organizational and community goals (Garrett, Spreitzer, & Bacevice, 2017).

## THEORY

### *Community and Governance in the Sharing Economy*

Communities play an integral role in sharing-economy organizations because community members' sharing, swapping, and lending transactions generate value (Faraj, van Krogh, Monteiro, & Lakhani, 2016; Lee & Cole, 2003; Seidel & Stewart, 2011). The role played by community members within these organizations depends on the organization's business model and can range from users, consumers, providers, and demanders to formal employees. For instance, while ride-sharing and crowdsourcing platforms consider their registered users as an (online) community, other P2P platforms such as neighborhood-sharing organizations work to create small (offline) village or neighborhood communities, while community gardens include in their definition of community employees, volunteers, and users of the community beds. We have identified the different forms that communities take within the sharing economy as communities of practice (e.g., Crowdwerk) (O'Mahony & Ferraro, 2007), online communities in general (e.g., Kleiderkreisel), communities of interest and transaction (e.g., Pumpipumpe and Stuffle) (Spaulding, 2010), as well as innovation communities (e.g., WeWork) (Franke & Shah, 2003). While we know much about the roles played within communities and the forms that these communities take, what is missing is an understanding of how varied communities are governed in sharing-economy organizations in order to achieve organizational goals and to exploit the communities' strategic potential. Research within this field is scarce. Reischauer and Mair (2018) have only just begun to acknowledge the importance of communities by examining organizational practices that govern online sharing-economy communities.

### *The Variety of Community Governance*

Research from the last decade has acknowledged that communities are an important component of new forms of organizing (Demil & Lecocq, 2006; Snow, Fjeldstad, Lettl, & Miles, 2011). Literature has focused on the different types and forms of communities in organizations' business models (Haefliger, Monteiro, Foray, & von Krogh, 2011; von Krogh et al., 2003; Spaulding, 2010). These types and forms range from online, innovation, and epistemic communities to communities of interest, transaction, and practice (von Hippel & von Krogh, 2003; O'Mahony & Ferraro, 2007). Researchers have emphasized the importance of these communities to organizations, such as their role in creating value (Spaulding, 2010), innovating (Faraj & Johnson, 2016; Schaarschmidt, Walsh, & von Kortzfleisch, 2015), and achieving transaction efficiencies (Adler, Kwon, & Heckscher, 2008). However, the idea that communities are a source of value creation adds a new logic, new activities, and distinct drivers to value creation (Stabell & Fjeldstad, 1998). A great body of literature has emphasized the importance of governance for ensuring that a community's activities actually *do* create value. Governance in this context comprises a mode of organizing, controlling, and coordinating interactions and transactions to infuse order in a setting where potential conflict threatens to undo or upset opportunities for realizing mutual gains (O'Mahony & Lakhani, 2011; Williamson, 1999) and is defined as "the way organizations control and coordinate the actions of individuals" (Sibai, de Valck, Farrell, & Rudd, 2015). In addition, the goal and function of governance changes as the needs of community interactions and relationships evolve. For instance, the aims of governance practices at different stages of community interaction are to initiate, maintain, and dissolve relationships. Governance practices that initiate interaction are designed to help organization members select a satisfactory interaction partner; practices of maintaining interaction seek to enhance parties' willingness to continue interacting; and in the final stage, termination practices are designed to complete, end, or dissolve a short- or long-term interaction (Kellog, Orlikowski, & Yates, 2006).

Types and practices of governing communities are multiple and evolving. In a multimethod study of one open-software community, O'Mahony and Ferraro (2007) found that members developed a shared basis of formal authority, bounded by democratic mechanisms that enable the community to experiment as conceptions of authority shifted over time. O'Mahony & Bechky (2008) also describe a form of governance that is open and allows members to participate in processes, ensuring independent and collective control without undoing firm influence. Aaltonen and Lanzara (2015) document how a collective governance capability was developed in a community and that steered the process of integrating distributed community knowledge into resources that produce value. Demil and Lecocq (2006) reveal another governance structure found in open-source communities based on specific legal contracts in open-source projects: bazaar governance. Bazaar governance, according to these authors, is characterized by low levels of control and weak incentives. Another form of governance is the C-Form, described by Seidel and Stewart (2011), is designed to capture the architecture of open-source software in organizations. Even though the focus of governance research in these studies is diverse, individually, none of them is entirely applicable to the variety of sharing-economy organizations, business models, and the communities that exist, nor do they help us understand what drives different types of governance in sharing-economy organizations.

### *The Concept of Governance Structure*

Similar to the approach of Demil and Lecocq (2006) and Seidel and Stewart (2011), we set out to identify governance types by building on established types of governance, including market, hierarchy, and clan governance (Powell, 1990). We chose these three because they are "discrete structural alternatives for any transaction" (Demil & Lecocq, 2006). Market governance follows the logic of economic exchange, and controls and coordinates transactions by relying on the price mechanism to coordinate competing suppliers, demanders, and outcomes (Adler, 2001). A typical example of market governance is one that involves a traditional transaction between a provider and a demander within a community. Each exchange in market types is governed by different contractual relations involving long-term relationships, clear role specifications, and organizational rule enforcement and monitoring (Ouchi, 1980). Hierarchy governance follows the logic of authority, using legitimate power as a source for creating and coordinating horizontal and vertical relationships and using the power of employment to get employees to submit to the legitimate right of the organization, both of which form the basis for an organization's implementing and enforcing rules. An example of this governance type is an interaction or transaction between community members and an administrator: in this governance type, the administrator unilaterally defines what is allowed and what is not. In contrast to market governance, hierarchy governance focuses on the input (e.g., processes or behavior) and not the output of economic exchange (Powell, 1990). In clan governance, sharing dominates as an exchange logic, and relies on community interaction, self-governance, and peer pressure to enforce rules, norms, and values (Heide, 1994). Within this governance type, community members are responsible for such things as regulating acceptable and appropriate behavior and actions among themselves (Sibai et al., 2015).

To grasp the different forms of governance within communities, Sibai et al. (2015) have introduced a set of distinct control and coordination practices executed during interactions within online communities through which specific goals and functions can be achieved. These practices are subsumed under market, hierarchy, or clan governance and underlie each form. Practices are designed to adjust individuals' behaviors to adhere to certain rules in a social group, to pre-empt social problems via socialization, and to resolve them via regulation. Such control practices are further sub-divided into separate phases and activities of interaction: (1) initiation seeks to select a satisfactory interaction partner; (2) maintenance aimed at enhancing a party's willingness to continue interacting; and (3) termination in which a short- or long-term interaction is completed (Sibai et al., 2015). The practices identified by Sibai et al. (2015), though, focus solely on command-and-control activities in *online* communities. They overlook how important communities are in creating value for organizations in both online and offline interactions (Harrison & Wellman, 2012). Despite these limitations, we suggest that this conceptual foundation can still be applied by adapting it to the different types of sharing-economy communities, since this practice framework clearly distinguishes interaction levels and whether practices are designed to control or coordinate.

Distinguishing governance types as market, hierarchy, clan, or bazaar makes clear the wide range of types, practices, and principles that are suitable for examining governance in the sharing economy, since these types of governance are employed in multiple business models and a great variety of community forms. Nevertheless, we chose to use only market, hierarchy, and clan governance, since these three provide a core foundation from which a (further) differentiation of governance types – such as bazaar or single governance – is possible (Ouchi, 1980; Powell, 1990). Table 1 illustrates our conceptual foundation, differentiating governance types into market, hierarchy, and clan. The advantage of these three forms is that they represent practices that are best able to capture the variety of communities, organizations, and business models in the sharing economy, in contrast to bazaar, and C-Form governance, which are either generically derived from market, hierarchy, or clan, or are limited to specific communities and contexts. To these three forms, we added bases from Heide (1994) and Sibai et al. (2015) to capture the variety and diversity of governance demands that sharing-economy organizations have.

**Table 1.** Market, Hierarchy, and Clan Governance.

| | | Market Governance | Hierarchy Governance | Clan Governance |
|---|---|---|---|---|
| Initiating interaction | Recruiting | No initiation process:<br>-Open Access<br>-Flexible Profile design | Selective entry<br>Skill training<br>Applying and inviting:<br>-Learning<br>-Occupational groups | Selective entry<br>Value training:<br>-Quiz<br>-Accompanied Tutorials |
| Maintaining interaction | Explicating roles | Narrowly defined in terms of minimum level of duties relevant to complete exchange:<br>-Seller/Provider<br>-Buyer/Demander | Defined career path<br>Roles imposed:<br>-Expert<br>-Advanced<br>-Beginner | Roles are closely intertwined and multidimensional:<br>-Roles depending on demand<br>-No fix role attribution |
| | Formalizing rules | Rights and responsibilities of exchange parties and contingency planning for inadequate transactions and transaction failures:<br>-General business conditions<br>-Compensation, liability | More broadly, proactively defined rules:<br>Freedom and rights and their boundaries, administrators powers and responsibilities, conflict resolution procedures:<br>-Procedure descriptions | Functional:<br>Guidelines ex-ante and narrowly defined:<br>-Golden rules<br>-User guidelines<br>-Codes of conduct |
| | Monitoring interactions | External/Internal and reactive action<br>Measurement of output:<br>-Administrators<br>-Moderation | External/Internal and reactive action<br>Measurement of input and behavior by administrator, moderator, community:<br>-Spontaneous control<br>-Security Check | Internal and proactive action<br>Based on self-control of community/group/team:<br>-Personal agreements<br>-Accompanied Groups |
| | Incentive system:<br>-Positive<br>-Negative | Tied to output<br>Short term:<br>-Digital currency<br>-Rewards | Tied to input and behavior<br>Short and long term:<br>-Experience levels<br>-Career path | Displayed commitment to the system and overt compliance (behavior)<br>Long term:<br>-Merit increase<br>-Awards |
| | | Tied to exchange and output:<br>-Banning<br>-Warning | Tied to input and behavior:<br>-Banning<br>-Warning | Tied to commitment and compliance:<br>-Interpersonal problem solving<br>-Discussion |
| Terminating interaction | Completion | Short-term relationship tied to individual exchange:<br>-Evaluation (Feedback)<br>-Payment | Fixed relationship length:<br>-Contractual agreements<br>-Member contracts<br>-Lease | Open-ending relationship:<br>-No termination<br>-Long-term commitment |

*Sources*: Heide (1994) and Sibai et al. (2015).

Enriching the *existing* foundations by structuring it along the logics of market, hierarchy, and clan governance also allows us to account for different measures and explanations: Market governance, for example, does not include an initiation process. This governance type can be considered as openly accessible to interested community members who can register and are presented with a flexible profile design that does not require them to participate more actively. Market governance contrasts with hierarchy and clan governance, both of which employ selective entry. Hierarchy governance might, for instance, use skill training as a means of initiation, by inviting prospective members to apply to learning and occupational groups before being accepted; in clan governance, organizations select members using an entry quiz or accompanied tutorials. Another difference between these two forms and market governance can be seen in community members' roles: within market governance, these roles are narrowly defined, primarily as provider or demander, and both are subjected to general business conditions and shared liabilities. Within this form, members' incentives are tied to the output and are in the form of short-term rewards. If output does not conform to expectations, community members are warned or even banned. By contrast, in some forms of hierarchy governance, members are provided with defined career paths and imposed roles and are identified by titles such as "expert," "advanced," or "beginner." Control is achieved by ex-ante defined rules and interactions, which are sporadically monitored and checked. Community-member incentives here are tied member input and can be long term, for instance, in the form of career paths. In clan governance, roles are closely intertwined and multidimensional; guidelines are narrowly defined and come in forms such as user guidelines or codes of conduct. In this governance type, interactions are monitored by such practices as personal agreements. Members who exhibit commitment to the system are rewarded with merit increases or awards, and problems are solved among members in personal discussions. Finally, there are other differences in terms of interactions and relationships: within market governance, individual exchange (such as payment) completes an interaction. Relationships in hierarchy governance have fixed lengths in the form of contractual agreements, while in clan governance, open-ended relationships are prevalent.

## RESEARCH APPROACH AND SAMPLE

When we looked to the sharing economy for examples of the fundamental governance types and practices (market, hierarchy, clan), we discovered that our given type and practice construct needed to expand to account for our observations. This discovery led us to follow an abductive approach, especially useful since our empirical observations do not match existing theoretical frameworks or foundations and prevent us from theorizing based on generic statements and explanations (Dubois & Gadde, 2002; Locke et al., 2008). More specifically, our approach is aimed at developing a new consensus framework by linking extant theory with new empirical observations, thus creating novel knowledge (Langley, Smallman, Tsoukas & Van de Ven, 2013). These aims are better achieved by examining the variety of different community forms and identifying the drivers of governing communities.

***Table 2.*** Overview of Sampled Case Organizations and Selecting Criteria.

| | Industry Area | Orientation | Year of Founding | Approx. No. of Employees | Approx. No. of Members |
|---|---|---|---|---|---|
| Redistribution markets | Food[a] | Non-profit | 2011 | 12 | 12.000 |
| | Goods_1[a] | For-profit | 2012 | 13 | 275.000 |
| | Goods_2[a] | For-profit | 2009 | 240 | 12 Mio. |
| | Goods_3[b] | Non-profit | 2014 | 65 | n/a |
| Product-service-systems | Transport[a] | For-profit | 2006 | 550 | 40 Mio. |
| | Service_1[b] | Non-profit | 2014 | 4 | n/a |
| | Service_2[a] | For-profit | 2011 | 6 | 1,278 |
| Collaborative lifestyle | Service_3[a] | For-profit | 2014 | 2 | 1,100 |
| | Space_1[b] | Non-profit | 2012 | 23 | 120 |
| | Space_2[b] | For-profit | 2011 | 10 | 210 |

[a]Organizations were pseudonymized according to their industry, function, and practice area.
[b]Online service-based business models.
[c]Offline service-based business models.

We chose the sharing economy in Germany as a research setting because it has given birth to a great variety of new business models and organizational forms (Lamberton & Rose, 2012) in which communities are an integral part of doing business (Botsman & Rogers, 2011). One of the main definitions of the sharing economy is an economy based on acts and processes of "distributing what is ours to others for their [temporary] use," "receiving or taking from others for our [temporary] use," or both (Belk, 2007, p. 126). These acts and processes are based on "the activity of sharing [...], and coordination through community-based [...] services" (Hamari et al., 2016).

We used theoretical sampling (Miles & Hubermann, 2004) to choose our sharing-economy study cases, all of which rely on communities but whose sharing-economy organization classifications differ. More concretely, the sharing-economy organizations in our case-study sample met the following criteria (see Table 2): they reflect the main types of collaborative consumption in the sharing economy, namely "redistribution markets," with pre-owned goods that are free, swapped, or sold for cash; include "product-service systems," in which privately owned goods are shared or rented via P2P marketplaces; and include "collaborative lifestyles," in which people with similar needs or interests share and exchange less-tangible assets such as business ideas (Botsman & Rogers, 2011). All of the organizations in our sample reflect the main industry, function, and practice areas that constitute the sharing economy (i.e., food, goods, transportation, space, and service) (Owyang, 2016); they include non-profit as well as for-profit organizations (Schor, 2014); and they offer their services both online and offline.

### *Data Collection*

This study is part of a larger research project,[1] and our intensive data-collection phase lasted over a year, from September 2015 to November 2016. We used multiple sources of evidence (Yin, 2012), including interviews, site visits, and participant observations.

We conducted 67 semi-structured *interviews* in 10 sharing-economy organizations that served as a primary source of data. Our interview partners were individuals (29 men, 38 women) who were founders, formal employees, or members of the organizations' communities, and were selected according to their functional role. Using snowball sampling, we asked our initial informants to give us the names of other organization employees so that our sample would be representative across hierarchies and levels, disciplines, and tenures. We recruited informants until we reached theoretical saturation. Two researchers were present at each interview, which were recorded and then transcribed verbatim in order to ensure reliability (Eisenhardt & Bourgeois, 1988).

During multiple *site visits*, we made both formal and informal *participant observations*, which gave us rich insights into the daily practices of organization members and users and the procedures they follow. By shadowing members of the organizations as they performed their daily work and by observing their interactions with each other and with users, we gained knowledge about both organizational and community governance. We also participated as registered users, which deepened our understanding of the role and function of community members (Table 3).

***Table 3.*** Data Sources.

| Organization | Interviewees[a] | Observation |
|---|---|---|
| Food | Executive director (1)<br>Ambassador (1)<br>User (2) | Active participation<br>Site visits |
| Goods_1 | Founder (1)<br>Employee (1)<br>User (2) | Active participation<br>Site visits |
| Goods_2 | Founder (1)<br>Employee (2)<br>User (12) | Active participation |
| Goods_3 | Executive director (1)<br>User (5) | Active participation |
| Transportation | Executive director (1)<br>Employee (2)<br>User (15) | Active participation |
| Service_1 | Founder (1)<br>User (2) | Active participation<br>Site visits |
| Service_2 | Founder (1)<br>User (2) | Active participation |
| Service_3 | Founder (1)<br>Executive director (1)<br>User (1) | Active participation |
| Space_1 | Executive Director (1)<br>Employee (2)<br>User (2) | Active participation<br>Site visits |
| Space_2 | Founder (1)<br>Employee (1)<br>User (4) | Active participation<br>Site visits |
| | 67 | |

[a]This column summarizes the number of informants () and their functions.

### *Data Analysis*

This study draws on and is guided by the conceptual literature on governance types and control practices in general (Heide, 1994), and more specifically, of communities (Shah, 2006; Sibai et al., 2015; Spaulding, 2010). As our empirical observations of governance practices and types do not match the existing theoretical foundations of network and bazaar governance in terms of how communities are controlled and coordinated in the sharing economy (Demil & Lecocq, 2006; O'Mahony & Ferraro, 2007; Powell, 1990; Reischauer & Mair, 2018), we followed an abductive approach (Dubois & Gadde, 2002; Locke et al., 2008). As hermeneutical circle, this approach guided our work, in which we constantly moved back and forth between empirical data and our initial understandings, since as interpreters we are informed by existing theory in governance types. While we interpreted our data in light of theory, we also remained open to critical questioning of our initial understandings of the sharing economy and the governance of communities (Mantere & Ketokivi, 2013). This approach helped us to develop a new framework that connects and matches extant theory to new empirical observations and allows us to generate "novel conceptual insight and distinctions" (Langley et al., 2013, p. 11).

For our qualitative data analysis, we used MAXQDA 12 software. By selecting data for single contol practices and moving away from raw data as we analyzed our cases, we were able to identify different types of governance within our cases. Our analysis consisted of four steps: (1) evaluating and systematically comparing existing literature and established categorizations of governance types; (2) iteratively identifying and building individual cases; (3) extending prevailing theoretical assumptions; and (4) conducting cross-case analyses (Miles & Hubermann, 2004). The extant conceptual foundation was constantly revised and adjusted throughout the data-collection and analysis process, as the data became more differentiated each time a new datum was added to it (Sibai et al., 2015). There was a constant overlap between data collection and data analysis. By following an abduction process, we acknowledge that "data analyses often alternate and iterate with data collection processes" (Edmondson & McManus, 2007, p. 1163).

The starting point for our data analysis was our interviews focusing on community and governance-related topics, from which we conceptualized and formed single cases of each organization in terms of how they control and coordinate their communities' interactions and behavior. We examined all relevant wordings from the interview transcripts to try and assess variance and similarities (i.e., common wording or phrasing) in our informants' statements, which we then used to examine different groups of control and coordination practices (recruiting, explicating roles, formalizing rules, monitoring, incentives, and completion). We applied techniques used by Van Maanen (1979) to categorize raw data and to code the statements. Triangulating the different sources of data (interviews, participant observation, and site visits) helped us to learn about the communities and relate this knowledge to the corresponding governance practices. We used the extant conceptual foundations of governance (Heide, 1994) and combined that with the characteristics of these organizations, as they related to the respective business models (Baden-Fuller & Mangematin, 2013; Lamberton & Rose, 2012; Yunus,

Moingeon, & Lehmann-Ortega, 2010). We coded governance practices and business-model characteristics for all cases and to categorize the governance practices as belonging to one of three forms (market, hierarchy, or clan). Reliability of the codes was assessed through independent second and third coders following standardized coding instructions. Any disagreements were resolved through consultation. We then analyzed each case to familiarize ourselves with the data. To increase our chances of capturing novel findings within the data, we used standard cross-case analysis techniques established by Miles and Hubermann (2004) and searched for similarities and differences across cases. This step allowed us to compare our initial impressions to our categorizations. To adjust and consolidate our framework, we looked for evidence across all cases. This step presented us with an emerging typology of governance. By applying replication logic, the insights derived from a set of multiple cases became the vehicle for generalizing to new cases. The multiple cases provide robust and compelling evidence, helping to confirm or refute the findings drawn from the other cases (Yin, 2012) by predicting similar or contrasting results. We chose theoretically relevant cases, collected case data, and conducted iterative analyses. These steps led us to expand our previously developed categorizations, which refined our understanding and allowed us to focus only on the most robust findings.

## FINDINGS

From our cases, we identified four governance types: pure market, pure clan, market-hierarchy hybrid, and clan-hierarchy hybrid. Our governance-type framework highlights differences in control practices (see Fig. 1). This new framework provides flexibility because it builds on existing governance types while also allowing us to extend and adjust these types to fit to the particularities of the different business models represented in our cases. Additionally, we identified that each

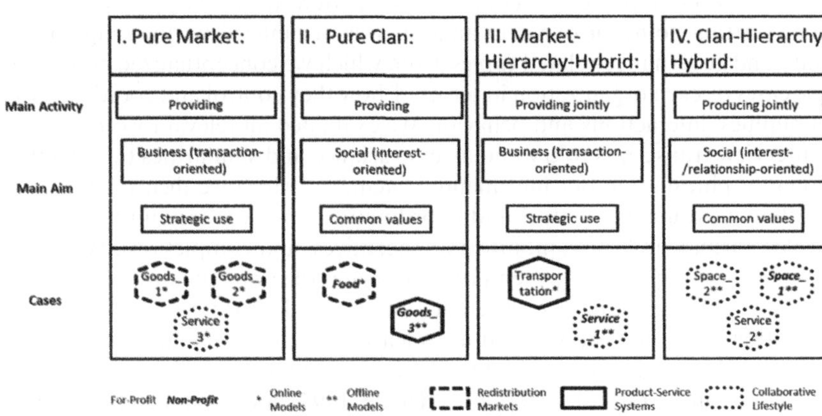


*Fig. 1.* Types of Governance.

governance type has one of two drivers – either the main activity of the community or the main aim.

The driver *main activity* indicates whether the community merely provides the resources for transactions or whether the community jointly produces them. In the latter case, organizations layer market or clan governance with hierarchical governance practices to form hybrid governance types. These hybrid types can be explained by transactional reasoning, which claims that organizations hierarchically integrate control and coordination activities (Makadok & Coff, 2009) to ensure value creation when faced with behavioral uncertainty and complex community structures. The *main aim* of the community captures whether it has a business or social orientation, and whether the community serves a strategic purpose for the organization or whether the organization focuses on promoting common values within the community (O'Mahony & Bechky, 2008). For some organizations, business-oriented communities serve a strategic purpose and are typically governed by market-like practices. In other organizations, the aim of communities is social, and the shared values of communities correspond to clan-like governance practices. Whether a community is governed by market or clan practices depends on institutional thoughts and which governance type seems legitimate given a specific aim in a specific context (DiMaggio & Powell, 1983). Fig. 1 depicts our case organizations and classifies them according to their dominant types of governance, illustrating how each type of governance is driven either by the main activity or the main aim of the organizations' communities.

### *Pure Market*

The way interaction is initiated in *pure-market* governance profoundly influences how relationships in this governance type are subsequently managed (Heide & John, 1990). Initiating interaction in pure-market governance involves neither specific *recruiting* nor initiation processes. Access to the community in this governance type is open, with no restrictions on members' becoming part of the organization nor requirements for social-profile transparency.

> You use your real name or just make something up [when registering]. It's up to you. You can create a profile picture of yourself or you don't [have to] if you want to keep it more anonymous. (Employee, Goods_2)

Even though pure-market organizations recommend or even impose minimum standards for new members when creating a profile, many organizations using pure-market governance are online sharing platforms that let community members decide how much personal information they want to disclose (pictures, bio, interests, etc.). The basic theoretical assumption behind this approach is that organizations with this type of governance (online sharing platforms and time banks) typically facilitate economic transactions for exchange parties whose identity is immaterial (Butler, 1983). Following initiation, maintaining interaction starts with practices of *explicating roles* to the different interaction partners (Loyd, Wang, Phillips, & Lount, 2013). In pure-market governance, roles are narrowly defined, with a minimum of duties that need to be carried out to complete interactions or transactions. Specific roles are inconsequential to members, and hence the organization makes no conscious effort to make the community or the organizational members aware of how these specific roles fit into the business model.

> There are the ones looking for something, and the ones selling their stuff, or both, since any seller can buy stuff here too. (Community member, Goods_2)

Roles in these communities are insignificant, primarily because the relationship between demander and provider is unidimensional, and except for engaging in transactions or creating platform traffic, community members do not typically do extra activities or take on additional responsibilities to create value.

The *formalization of rules* in pure-market governance specifies parties' responsibilities and rights as well as contingencies for incomplete or failed transactions (Sibai et al., 2015). Both the founder of Service_3 (a time-bank platform where users share knowledge in exchange for time credits) and the founder of Goods_1 (an online sharing platform for personal goods) confirm that except for agreeing to general business terms and following community guidelines when registering, members do not have to follow additional rules. Maintaining interaction in this governance-type results from *monitoring procedures*, which measure output via both internal and external reactive action. Monitoring here is limited to determining the extent to which contractual compliance has taken place. Across all cases, our informants report conflict and problem situations in which organization employees monitor community members' actions and behavior when they, for example, share their expertise on a specific topic or offer their used items for sale.

> Focusing on the final result, our customer support unit checks every new registration to detect people who have already registered and we [have] installed some alert systems. So, if someone has been suspended before, for example for selling broken or damaged goods, we recognize his or her phone number and he or she can't install the app again. (Customer support, Goods_1)

*Incentive systems* in pure-market types (Holmstrom & Tirole, 1989) are directly tied to the transactions, which are inherently short-term and focused on output. The founder of Service_3 says that these systems encourage members to become more active and to increase their commitment to establishing a community above and beyond sharing their skills and knowledge in transactions and engaging in frequent personal interactions. In addition to transactions, this commitment creates value, since social relationships that lead to additional future transactions are encouraged. The business models in pure-market governance organizations depend on the community frequently engaging; for example, as in Service_3, to reinvest their time credits.

> You can earn some [digital, non-monetary] assets, based on previous transactions you completed and depending on the quality of the output you provided, you can reinvest these assets in new transactions. [...] You have a certain account you can use for every new transaction you enter [into]. (Founder, Service_3)

In all cases of this governance type, banning or warning members are practices that serve as negative incentives or disincentives, are included in the general business terms community members agree to, and are intended to protect the organizations from the legal risks of bad member practices.

> Such members get banned from our platform, of course, if [...] it occurs several times that the transferred good does not match the description or [if it] is damaged. (Founder, Service_3)

The *completion* of discrete and repeated interactions is measured as individual short-term exchanges, with each completed transaction constituting a completed event (Heide, 1994) either in the form of sold personal goods, such as clothes, or completed transactions of individual expertise in exchange for time credit. The control practice of terminating interactions is tied exclusively to exchange and seeks to build the basis for new transactions by integrating positive and negative transaction evaluations as incentives with a strategic objective (Sibai et al., 2015).

Providing information and resources is the *main activity of the community* in pure-market governance: "The users are the ones providing the content on the platform" (Founder, Goods_2), creating value through an activity that supports organizations' goals of gaining new members, increasing turnover, and expanding organizational borders. These goals are achieved by keeping barriers to entry low and maintaining easy or open access. The cases that fit within this governance type indicate that the *main aim of the community* is almost exclusively business oriented, as indicated by community members themselves when describing their role:

> Everyone's got something to sell or finds it interesting to constantly check out the supply of goods [geographically] nearby. (Community member, Goods_2)

As, for instance, sharing-platform organizations offer for sale such things as clothes, skills, or pre-owned items and are generally business oriented, the communities in this governance-type stress the importance of having rules that stipulate the "liability for the exchange parties" as well as "usage rights" and "general duties and responsibilities" (General Business Terms, Goods_2). Since these organizations typically foster discrete exchanges, the rules are limited to individual transactions or to reactive problem solving (Heide, 1994). Hence, monitoring practices are also tied to the output of exchange relationships. In addition, as the *main aim of the community* in this governance type is business oriented, providing positive incentives is necessary to foster positive member behavior (Heide, 1994). Organizations with pure-market governance use these incentives to increase the willingness of community members to engage in future transactions. Across all cases, strategically using the community to grow the business and achieve a critical mass is a necessary and fundamental aim, since organizations' communities represent a unique selling point:

> The community is what makes us different. It starts by approaching them on a personal level and binding them on our platform. (Founder, Service_3)

### *Pure Clan*

Initiation of potential members in *pure-clan* governance is considered more stringently than in the other types of governance, and members are evaluated based on a combination of their skills, qualifications, and specific attitudes and values (Heide, 1994; Benkler & Nissenbaum, 2006). Organizations that have adopted this type of governance, such as food-sharing and neighborhood-help platforms, pre-test and cultivate relationship-specific attitudes with potential members using cultural and socialization processes prior to new members' joining, and these evaluations have two aims: eliminating as much as possible the divergence between members' and the organization's goals, and better aligning the members' incentives with the organization's goals (Ouchi, 1979; Sibai et al., 2015). One form of *recruiting* in clan-governance organizations within our sample is mostly carried out via a comprehensive quiz, requiring potential members to study the information the organization provides in the form of a wiki and prove their knowledge and commitment before becoming a member:

> Possible new users have to pass a quiz first to become [a member] of the organization. [...] And they have to go through accompanied tutorials, after which they get the official go. Only then do we consider them ready to be responsible and reliable members. We need to make sure that they are aware of the rules. (Founder, Food)

Organizational members who have already attained a certain amount of experience introduce potential new members to the norms and values of the organization in these tutorials in order to ensure that they understand the routines and practices of the interactions required to, for example, pick up food (leftovers) from stores. It is this understanding that supports a smooth-functioning organization (O'Mahony & Bechky, 2008). *Explication of roles* in these organizations is designed to enhance members' willingness to continue interacting by defining the closely intertwined and multidimensional roles among interaction parties. Community members can assume different roles after climbing up an internal ladder and advancing through promotion stages. At Food, new members are given the title of "Foodsavers" and then eventually become "Ambassadors" or even part of the central organizing committee, depending on the degree of their commitment and engagement.

> Basically, everyone's a Foodsaver – part of the organization and also part of the system [...]; that is, everyone working in the organization team is either employed as Ambassador or Saver. (Community Member, Food)

*Formalization of rules* in pure-clan-governance organizations specifies the rights and responsibilities of transaction parties both during transactions and with future contingencies in mind. In these organizations, the rules are broadly defined by function and designed ex-ante. These rules are very important because pure-clan organizations and its community members deal with sensitive goods, and to ensure an organization's smooth operations, members must follow organizational procedures. If pick-ups are disorganized and poorly executed, the result might be legal consequences.

> We offer a wiki, let me call it the policy of our organization, where users have access to all relevant information which guides them through every process and explains [expected] behavioural patterns. [Also], we have a code of practice of how to approach other organizations and suppliers so that our members know how to behave and what to do in worst-case scenarios. (Employee, Food)

Additionally, procedures of *monitoring* delineate internal and ex-ante actions and are designed to establish community self-control across all different functions and community levels, and these procedures are carried out by members themselves (Ouchi, 1979):

> The Ambassador is responsible for [ensuring] every pickup [is] punctual and smooth. (Ambassador, Food)

> There is always that self-control mechanism [among] the community members […]. It is left to the community members. (Founder, Goods_3)

Recording interaction-parties' behaviors also allows clan-governance organizations to identify social problems (Sibai et al., 2015). These self-control practices can be seen in community-monitoring procedures, which are aimed at inculcating patterns of reciprocity, personal pride, and respect (Faraj & Johnson, 2016) and help to foster online and offline interpersonal relations. These patterns are extremely important for organizations whose business models rely on their community members to interact both virtually and/or physically. Self-control is ex-ante imposed through ongoing and intense interactions among community members, and these interactions promote trust, mutual concern, and sometimes effective multilateral enforcement of group norms (Bowles & Gintis, 2002).

Positive *incentive systems* within clan governance are directly linked to the level of commitment community members' display toward the system and their overt interest in a long-term engagement (Heide, 1994; Ouchi, 1979). By distributing rewards based on behavior, clan-governance organizations can strengthen members' identification with the organization and the system. The clan-governance organizations represented in our cases apply measures that include rewarding members with possible "promotion … and the chance to assume more responsibilities after a certain amount of time and effort" (Community Member, Food) after successfully completing transactions, rewards that are bestowed on members based on how other community members and the responsible ambassadors of the organization evaluate them. Clan governance typically fosters and utilizes incentives that have been traditionally deployed to regulate joint activity (Bowles & Gintis, 2002). Negative incentive systems are frequently built-in to measure member commitment and overt compliance, but in clan governance these activities are often carried out on a member-to-member level:

> Problems that arise on-site will be solved on-site and directly by other community members so that you don't [have] any administrative burden. Possibilities to do so are group discussions […] warnings, and as last option, a forced break with the organization. (Employee, Food)

Complementing these control practices are individual members' altruistic motivations and interests in such goals as actively reinforcing the idea of saving food and reducing waste or creating a neighborhood, and these goals encourage positive and mutually beneficial interactions among members who have shared interests. The organizations' visions, which are primarily centered around social, ecological, or sustainability goals, such as in Food or Goods_3, unite the community members and their motivations are made manifest in their actions and behavior (respecting the belongings of others, treating each other fairly). Cases in this form of governance are entirely founded on open-ended relationships with no finite or foreseeable *completion* (Heide, 1994).

Pure-clan governance organizations are constituted by and contingent on various factors that determine which control practices are used. The function and *main activity of the community* of this governance type is to provide resources and information to community members or interaction partners. As the transaction object is fundamental for configuring business models in this governance type, and as the shared personal information about supporters and partner organizations requires members to treat this information responsibly, reliably, and in legally permitted ways, it is important that these organizations build in and promote common values among their community (Code of Conduct, Food).

The business models of organizations represented in our cases reveal overarching value-driven goals. To ensure that the community is displaying commitment to and working toward that common goal, the organization needs to ensure that members share certain values. One case interview in this organization form describes the primary *aim of the community*:

> With this project called Snowflake, currently we are working on the democratization of our organization. We want – even [at] the lowest level in the respective teams on-site – to communicate that everyone is involved and has to participate, for instance, in decision-making and therefore feel a part of the whole. We need to build a common ground, [...] involving everyone and bringing them on the same side. (Founder, Food)

Whereas in pure-market-governance organizations transactions and a business orientation predominate, in pure-clan-governance organizations, a clear social orientation is present (Spaulding, 2010) because community members find in these forms an opportunity and a necessity to physically work together, meet each other, and get to know other personally:

> You get to know each other on a very friendly basis. Being part of this [organization] is not mandatory [...] you're here on a voluntary basis trying to do something good. It's like you're doing something with friends and family together. (Founder, Food)

Compared to other governance types with a more purely business orientation, incentive systems in pure clan-governance appear to be of secondary importance. Instead, formalized rules and monitoring procedures are designed with a social orientation in mind, serve as an incentive in themselves, and support a degree of self-control and voluntary commitment that motivates the community (Seidel & Stewart, 2011; Shah, 2006). We attribute this secondary importance of incentives to the voluntary nature of community involvement, despite pure-clan governance having the highest entry barriers and the most stringent recruiting processes of all types of governance. Because of these stringent recruiting practices, community members are expected to display high levels of commitment and involvement and to share the organization's values and goals.

### *Market-Hierarchy Hybrid*

The *market-hierarchy hybrid* governance type entails no concrete *recruiting* process, but instead is open to all, with community-member profiles that can be easily created and eventually changed, as one community member of a ride-sharing platform explained:

> After I'm sure about the exact date and route, I run my advertisement online [...] basically whenever I want. [...] You register online and create a profile [...] but they [the organization] just recommend to you how to do so, for example, without any obligation to mention something. Basically, you say what you've got and wait till it's your turn. That's all, plain and simple. (Community member, Transportation)

*Explication of roles* in market-hierarchy hybrid types combines market and hybrid practices of governance, including narrowly defined roles, with a minimal number of duties members are required to complete during an exchange or are needed to advance along defined career paths. This type of governance clearly distinguishes between users as providers and users as demanders, but members in market-hierarchy hybrid organizations have the opportunity to switch roles and to participate in jointly producing a resource (Gläser, 2001), a common practice in many repair cafés or on ride-sharing platforms, for example. Additionally, in one ride-sharing organization, providing community members with a defined career path gives them opportunities to advance stepwise, moving from such titles as Rookie to Ascender to Advanced to Expert, all the way up to Ambassador (Observation, Transportation). Furthermore, in market-hierarchy hybrid organizations *rules are formalized*, a practice similar to pure-market governance. Also, in market-hierarchy hybrid governance, there is no difference between for-profit and non-profit business models, as both strictly adhere to general business terms that address liability and compensation issues, and in both models formal rules and procedures are detailed to ensure community members' behavior and social order conforms to expectations (Aaltonen & Lanzara, 2015). Legal terms function as enforceable contractual guarantees for providers and demanders. Exchange-party rights and responsibilities are in place as a contingency if transactions are inadequately executed or fail (Sibai et al., 2015):

> We heavily depend on our users to come back and engage in interactions frequently in order to help us maintain our work here. We cannot afford to get sued or something; that's why we need to protect ourselves against any kind of financial or legal risks, of course. People coming here always have to sign our legal disclaimer and right before every repair our volunteers remind them of the fact that it's possible, well, that the repair can go wrong. (Founder, Service_1)

Legal protection is important for organizations and is incorporated into their general business terms, since they deal with personal goods, such as in repair cafés where volunteers are not professionals, or with passenger services. *Monitoring of interactions* within this hybrid governance type consists of both output and input measurements conducted by the organization and undertaken reactively:

> Practices of input measurements mean, for example, that all profiles, photos, offers and descriptions are moderated by our organization. [...] We have colleagues reading every description and message in our system. (Community member, Transportation)

Another practice in this governance type, applicable above all in offline business models, is spontaneous "physical control" or sometimes just the "physical presence" of organizational members who monitor the interactions of the community

(Founder, Service_1). To guarantee smooth processes and stable operations, *incentive systems* for members are also linked to the organizations' output and input measurement because member behavior that conforms to expectations and members with a high degree of engagement is crucial. "Career paths and experience levels" serve as positive incentives for members "to behave properly and according to the legal terms" (Community member, Transportation). In the case of Service_1, providing community members with the chance to do something good by helping a local non-profit organization also supports organizations in steering both member and community output and proper behavior, as does the fact that many organizational members work voluntarily to support the organization and its philosophy, mission, or values, such as conserving resources (sustainability) or helping people in need.

In addition to these positive incentives, market-hierarchy hybrids also use practices of warning and banning, as described by an employee of Transportation:

> In many cases [what users are doing] doesn't work out or fit in our corporate philosophy or it's just against our legal conditions, so we have to first block and sometimes even ban single users from our platform. Sometimes it is almost a criminal act happening there and regarding their offer […] it's just against the law in some cases. [These] cases [confirm and justify] the monitoring and disincentives we set. (Employee, Transportation)

Hierarchical control practices of warning or banning single members of the community are also used in cases of "inappropriate behaviour" (Founder, Service_1). Such behavior includes being late (Observation, Transportation) or cutting the line at repair cafés (Observation, Service_1). Disincentives are seen less often in Service_1 than they are in Transportation because the physical presence of organizational members lowers the likelihood of misbehavior (Shah, 2006). Finally, *completed* interactions are measured primarily by market-based practices of filling out a feedback questionnaire (Observation, Service_1), also called the evaluation of the output (punctuality, driving style, and communication frequency) (Observation, Transportation), after each completed transaction.

The *main activity of the community* in market-hierarchy hybrids is in jointly providing resources and providing information about the resource and the interaction partner. "As soon as I'm sure about the day, time, and route, I put my offer online," explains a community member of Transportation. Besides information about the transaction object, community members also provide information about their age, their vehicle, the individual rider, the route, the driving time, and ride preferences (Observation, Transportation). Within this governance type, however, the *main aim of the community* is business or transaction oriented, as community members of Service_1 and Transportation explained:

> Once a month I can try to get my personal stuff fixed for free, learn something, well at least how to do it. (Community member, Service_1)

> If you look carefully, for the user it's just about getting from A to B and saving money both for the provider and the demander. (Community member, Transportation)

Organizations with this type of governance use market and hierarchy practices of role explication, rule formalization, and monitoring because they need to ensure every exchange and interaction and to signal to each member trustworthiness via the general business terms, including liability and compensation clauses (Sibai et al., 2015). The *main aim of the community* – jointly providing resources or information – is a strategic one: an employee of Transportation stated that

> in the end, every provider needs a demander and vice versa. We're the ones profiting from increasing demand and increasing supply. We're the ones profiting from a growing community, clearly.

Both case organizations within this governance type try to bind the community to the organization and to guarantee as many securities and benefits for members as possible so that the organization can use the community for marketing purposes or to achieve a critical mass. Thus, practices follow a clear business orientation (Spaulding, 2010): "We need them to publicize us" (Employee, Transportation) and to "help us spread the idea" (Founder, Service_1).

### *Clan-Hierarchy Hybrid*

*Recruiting* practices in *clan-hierarchy hybrids* entail selectively choosing community members: individuals can apply to work on certain tasks or are invited by other community members (Observation Service_2). Organizations with the clan-hierarchy hybrid governance type include crowdsourcing platforms, whose recruiting practices are described by one organization's founder:

> I selectively pick the right people fitting to my tasks and my questioning is aimed at getting the people I want in there. Otherwise, I wouldn't get to know those people of value [because they can help the person to complete a task] for me and my task. (Founder, Service_2)

The *roles* within clan-hierarchy hybrids operate according to clan governance, which can be seen in the names given to multidimensional roles, such

> "as volunteers, experts, users. Whatever your function and role is in here, they overlap and you just try to have a look at each other and make this a better place. (Founder, Space_1)

The *formalization of rules* within this hybrid governance type encompasses functional practices of narrowly and ex-ante defined guidelines of clan governance, such as golden rules (Observation, Space_2), user guidelines, and codes of conduct (Observation, Space_1). Golden rules in one organization, for instance, are in a computer file that all users must download, read, and study. Although it has the name "rules," this document is more about how members are expected to behave and explains that members should treat each other with respect while working or sharing the space (Observation, Space_2). Although these rules are formalized, they are flexible and can be adapted to changing needs and dynamics when relying on community engagement or commitment (Heide, 1994). Thus, *monitoring* procedures in clan-hierarchy hybrids come in the form of internal and ex-ante community practices based on measuring input:

> The feeling prevails that our community has a strong self-regulating mechanism; combined with a leap of faith from us as [an] organization when it comes to how they behave and what they do here. (Founder, Space_2)

Members of the community monitor the behavior of other members, holding them accountable for their actions (Observation, Space_1) and as a result, patterns of interaction are characterized by direct reciprocity (Faraj & Johnson, 2016), such as in community gardens and coworking spaces. We also see evidence of monitoring practices undertaken by the organization, which supports reciprocity within the community, as one employee explained:

> There is always one of our team [members] on-site and available [...] in any case of questions or concerns from our community or any interested person [...] right at the entrance at our information point. We also [initiated] a community service [requirement] every member has to deliver. By doing so we make sure that our community members participate here. (Employee, Space_1)

The founder of the crowdsourcing organization Service_2 additionally states that "there is always the self-control of the community. Among community members, you can distinguish very active members and members with a rather low level of commitment." These examples show how monitoring, interaction, and explicated roles in clan-hierarchy hybrids relate to one another. The explicated roles in the business model of Service_2 involve different commitment levels, which serve as a positive *incentive system*. Community members with high levels of commitment are rewarded, as their activities form the basis of the business model in community gardens, coworking spaces, and crowdsourcing platforms, all of which are included in this governance type:

> Once every quarter [the organization] awards users for special achievements on the platform. In addition, every community member also has the chance to offer a reward for every user who participated in the task and produced high-quality output. (Community member, Service_2)

Disincentive practices, by comparison, are those that warn and ban community members for poor-quality input and bad behavior and for not following the rules, such as using genetically modified seeds (Observation, Space_1) or making a phone call in the workplace (Observation, Space_2). Clan-hierarchy hybrids typically involve open-ended relationships with no concrete *completion* of interaction. The community garden Space_1, for example, offers the opportunity for everyone passing the area "to just participate or join the activities of our organizations on-site, which is completely free." However, there are also lease or "member contracts" (Community member, Space_2) that provide for a temporary right of use with a fixed relationship length, combining both hierarchy and clan-governance practices. This model is designed to be open and allows members to decide whether to engage with the organization based on the (mainly) social (e.g., inclusion and participation) or ecological (e.g., sustainable use of resources) values it represents.

In the clan-hierarchy hybrid governance type, our cases reveal that the *main activity of the community* is jointly producing something, which can be a tangible product, such as a fixed asset, or intangible, such as a working atmosphere or specific knowledge (Marquis, Lounsbury, & Greenwood, 2011). Interestingly, the jointly produced resources can be used both by individuals and the organizational by, for example, incorporating voluntary labor into the business model (Seidel & Stewart, 2011). Space_1 incorporates voluntary labor employed for the common good by "offering space for non-profit purposes and other organizations within a local area." "Interns" mainly do these activities, which are supervised and coordinated by organizational members (employee, Space_1). A Service_2 community member further explains: "You can develop and produce something on a platform jointly with the other members you engage in such a process." The underlying assumption of such business models is articulated by the founder of Space_1: "The idea basically is to do something jointly. Our space is there for the community and of course to use this as a community space." The *main aim of the community* is therefore a social one oriented toward both interests and relationships, as described by one employee:

> Some are seeking social exchange; some are looking for support with their work and getting new perspectives and input from people of maybe different professional backgrounds. They are looking for the opportunity to work with others on their stuff and to get feedback; not on a formal level paying a lot of money for it. And here it's that both parties benefit from each other. (Employee, Space_2)

The organization encourages community members "to make use of the organization and the resulting possibilities to interact with others" (Community member, Space_2). Accordingly, another main aim of this organization is to instill common values within the community. To this end, fostering reciprocity and trust among the community supports monitoring procedures. "Community duties" (Founder, Space_1) are one example of practices designed to instill these common values by building a foundation for collaboration and joint production of goods through mandatory services in the community garden or coworking space, such as maintenance work. If these organizations do not create and impose these duties, they run the risk of interaction problems (Heide, 1994). In fact, fostering community members' embeddedness has a strong positive effect on values, beliefs, and the image of the organization (Porter & Donthu, 2008), aligning organizational goals and visions with community members' goals (Participant observation, Space_1).

## CONCLUSION AND DISCUSSION

In this study, we set out to identify types of governance in sharing-economy organizations. We draw on prior literature on governance and community management (Makadok & Coff, 2009; O'Mahony & Ferraro, 2007; Preece, 2000) and focus on organizations that rely on their communities to do business and create value (Bardhi & Eckhardt, 2012; Botsman & Rogers, 2011; Lamberton & Rose, 2012; O'Mahony & Lakhani, 2011). Using an abductive approach, we developed a new framework that captures the variety and diversity of community forms, governance practices, and business-model configurations in the sharing economy and introduce the idea that each governance type is driven either by the main activity of an organization's community or the main aim. In developing this framework and identifying these drivers, we show that prevailing value configurations (Stabell & Fjeldstad, 1998) as well as governance types (Heide, 1994) need to be expanded to include community configurations of value creation and hybrids and to assess sharing-economy organizations and their communities as a whole. In addition, we show that instead of traditional categorizations of sharing-economy organizations, such as sectors or industry areas, these drivers and configurations serve as factor explaining which governance types an organization uses. Our theorizing broadens and combines existing approaches to accurately reflect the state and the potential of the sharing economy (Aaltonen & Lanzara, 2015; Puranam et al., 2014).

Our results contribute to the literature on governance of communities in new forms of organizing (Gulati et al., 2012; Puranam et al., 2014) and to the current debate on how organizations in the sharing economy control and coordinate their communities (Acquier et al., 2017; Reischauer & Mair, 2018). We build on studies that focus on online communities (Faraj et al., 2016), communities of practice (O'Mahony & Ferraro, 2007), collaborative communities (Fjeldstad, Snow, Miles, & Lettl, 2012), and communities of interest and transaction (Spaulding, 2010). Thus, our study is more comprehensive than, and expands on, the findings of prior studies since we provide a framework that captures the great variety of governance types that operate within the sharing economy. A new framework is essential for representing and understanding a new phenomenon and new forms of organizing such as the sharing economy, which encompasses various cores and principles of organizing, grants community members access to resources, enables resource exchange, and promotes interaction among them (Ozanne & Ballantine, 2010).

Another contribution of both theoretical and practical relevance is our identification of what drives the choice of each different governance type. One finding, for example, is that faced with the choice between market or clan governance, a sharing-economy organization's decision is rooted in the aims of the community. These results are in line with institutional theory (DiMaggio & Powell, 1983), which claims that organizations have to meet certain expectations of their environments in order to gain legitimacy. We find this claim to be true for both our pure governance types – market and clan – which are adapted to fit the main aims of their organizations' communities. While organizations with business-oriented communities (e.g., Uber and Car2go) claim to achieve legitimacy by market governance, organizations with social-oriented communities (e.g., community gardens and Couchsurfing) utilize clan governance to ensure legitimate structural design and member action patterns. Organizations with business-oriented communities, such as the sharing-platform Goods_2, have incorporated a "praise-function" for community members to evaluate each other after successfully completing transactions, a practice inspired by and adopted from other online as well as social-media platforms, which conforms to established practices and through which this organization gains legitimacy (Sanders & Tuschke, 2007). In contrast, organizations with social-oriented communities, such as the organization, such as the community garden Space_2, have implemented mandatory "community duties" for community members. This sharing-economy organization draws on historically evolved and established practices to gain legitimacy. Such practices for ensuring smooth operations and encouraging social interactions have historical roots: in commons and machinery rings, for example, these practices built the foundation for desired operational and social outcomes (Becker & Mosmann, 2017; Bradley & Pargman, 2017).

In this sense, our findings confirm that an organization's governance practices have to accord with community members' expectations, meet these members' aims, and by doing both, are considered legitimate. Meeting the expectations of their communities and aligning themselves to the aims of their communities are the result of adjustment processes that seek to give organizations either a business or social orientation that can help them retain existing community members and attract potential new ones. In business-oriented communities, these expectations and aims translate to an emphasis on sales opportunities or cost-efficient and flexible access to resources such as clothes or cars, whereas in social-oriented communities, organizations promote integration, neighborhood help, or social change (Martin, 2016). Market governance thus supports short-term transactions without restricting entry and focuses on price mechanisms to ensure frequent, smooth, and safe transactions. This support and focus are a direct response to the business orientation of the community. Clan governance, by contrast, fosters self-control while relying on commitment – in the form of long-term relationships – to ensure meaningful interactions and engagement, which also conforms to the expectations of these organizations' socially oriented communities (Sibai et al., 2015).

Similarly, hybrid governance types are distinct from pure markets or pure clans. Our findings emphasize that market and clan governance should neither be understood as two ends of a continuum nor are there just pure forms, but must also allow for hybrid types of both (Ebers & Oerlemans, 2016). We find hybrid types of governance in which hierarchical practices are layered onto pure market and clan forms. Whenever joint production or provision of resources – a key component of value creation for hybrid-governance organizations – is the main activity of the community, organizations implement a high degree of hierarchy and combine this governance type with either market or clan governance. While our results are in line with transaction-cost theory (Butler, 1983; Williamson, 2002), which argues that governance is designed to minimize costs and ensure successful transactions, we also add to the literature by identifying the core variables that can explain when hybrid types of governance are chosen (Ebers & Oerlemans, 2016). In pure types of governance, the individual provision of resources and information by community members predominates; we find, however, that joint production or provision – characterized by high asset specificity, frequency, and uncertainty (Williamson, 1991) – calls for a strict set of rules to control and coordinate while also ensuring value creation, all in a governance type that blends elements of market or clan governance. In terms of asset specificity, when joint production or provision is the main activity of a community, specific human capital (knowledge and capabilities) as well as investments in reputation is essential, since the outcome of the main activity is directly linked to the image of the organization. In addition, community members frequently carry out transactions and exchange information, engage in interactions, and spend a lot of time and effort in such activities as joint community gardening or crowdsourcing, all of which requires close coordination. These tasks are especially challenging for organizations to coordinate and control since communities are a heterogeneous group of individuals with diverse interests, roles, and functions (Reischauer & Mair, 2018; Seidel & Stewart, 2011). These activities represent complex structures and are highly uncertain, since they often result in opportunistic behavior, such as withholding information or disregarding rules. To restrict such behavior, organizations apply hierarchical governance, which relies on defined functions, strict procedural rules, and input and behavior measurement, actions that adds up to market governance and secure mutually dependent interaction or transaction partners (Makadok & Coff, 2009; Ménard, 1996). Combining hierarchy with market and clan governance as a hybrid type is done to align the governance type with the social or business orientation of the communities while simultaneously ensuring that the main community activity can be quickly adapted to changing demands. These findings are significant and contribute both theoretically and practically, as many researchers and organizations themselves claim – on the one hand – that the sharing economy seeks to promote a post-market society and is based on political, legal, and ideological dimensions rather than on economic ones (Acquier et al., 2017; Muñoz & Cohen, 2017); and on the other hand, that organizations themselves struggle with the community's need for autonomy and the organization's need for control (Möhlmann & Zalmanson, 2017). Thus, organizations have to ensure smooth operations and a functioning business model, especially when they uphold social or ecological ideals and visions in organizations such as community gardens, repair cafés, or food-sharing platforms. These organizations also deal with sensitive goods such as food or personal belongings, and to guarantee the proper handling of such goods, organizations add hierarchical governance practices and rely on strict procedural rules or define clear responsibilities that their community members have to follow.

We acknowledge that our study has limitations, yet also acknowledge how these limitations present possible fruitful avenues for future research. First, using in-depth, qualitative data offer an opportunity to better understand a new research field and build theory in areas that we currently know little about. However, a limitation of this method is that the resulting theory runs the risk of being idiosyncratic and not generalizable (Eisenhardt, 1989). That said, we believe that the characteristics of the communities and community management in our cases have wider applicability, since organizations outside the sharing economy may also have different objectives and business-model configurations, yet rely on their communities to carry out and achieve these different objectives. We would therefore expect our findings to apply to other organizations outside the sharing economy in which communities play an integral role, such as in society, other (grassroots) initiatives, or new forms of cooperatives (Pazaitis, Kostakis, & Bauwens, 2017). We cannot confirm this assumption from our study, though, and therefore encourage researchers to empirically test our findings to discover the extent to which they can be generalized. Second, studies focusing on motivations and perceptions of community members would complement our findings, as would business-model research to derive the implications of the design of architecture and archetypes (Hamari et al., 2015; Hawlitschek, Teubner, & Gimpel, 2018). Although we recognize that our observations are based on different organizing cores and principles across organizations in the sharing economy, our observations link to and account for this diversity. Therefore, we suggest that future research focus more on comparing organizing cores and principles and identifying the sources of convergence and divergence between governance types and business models. Researchers who approach the sharing economy from an organization-studies perspective could add to our research by drawing distinct conceptual and definitional boundaries to determine the factors and aspects that constitute the sharing-economy phenomenon. Likewise, we encourage scholars to reassess boundaries of communities in organizations, as our study shows that organizations in the sharing economy take on various forms and definitions, with different roles and functions within them that are distinct from prevailing conceptualizations. Furthermore, we encourage future research to focus on hierarchical governance, since our findings suggest that this form of governance is combined with market and clan forms and – critically – reflects a possible interface that hybrid governance types can offer in the context of algorithmic management (Möhlmann & Zalmanson, 2017). Since the sharing economy is a very young field, the question of whether these types will consolidate and become even clearer and more distinct will be answered over time. We suggest further investigation of how organizations both in and outside the sharing economy might still be applying and using strict procedural rules to govern their communities' behavior and activities, especially since many of them specifically promote (or at least claim to support) a transformation of the economy and society in the direction of post-bureaucratic organizing (Acquier et al., 2017). Taken together, we hope this study provides some inspiration for further research on governance of communities in a broad range of organizational types with differing boundaries, in different forms of communities and business configurations.

## NOTE

1. The overall aim of the research project *i-share* is to capture the economic, ecological, and social impact of the sharing economy in Germany. For further information, see https://www.i-share-economy.org/en.

## REFERENCES

Aaltonen, A., & Lanzara, G. F. (2015). Building governance capability in online social production: Insights from Wikipedia. *Organization Studies*, *36*(12), 1649–1673.

Acquier, A., Daudigeos, T., & Pinkse, J. (2017). Promises and paradoxes of the sharing economy: An organizing framework. *Technological Forecasting and Social Change*, *125*, 1–10.

Adler, P. S. (2001). Market, hierarchy, and trust: The knowledge economy and the future of capitalism. *Organization Science*, *12*(2), 215–234.

Adler, P. S., Kwon, S. W., & Heckscher, C. (2008). Professional work: The emergence of collaborative community. *Organization Science*, *19*(2), 359–376.

Baden-Fuller, C., & Mangematin, V. (2013). Business models: A challenging agenda. *Strategic Organization*, *11*(4), 418–427.

Bardhi, F., & Eckhardt, G. M. (2012). Access-based consumption: The case of car sharing. *Journal of Consumer Research*, *39*(4), 881–898.

Becker, P. K., & Mosmann, P. C. (2017). Von der ruralen Notwendigkeit zum urbanen Lifestyle. Historische Formen und aktuelle Entwicklungen einer Sharing Economy am Beispiel der Gartennutzung. *ScriptaMercaturae*, *46*, 183–215.

Belk, R. (2007). Why not share rather than own? *Annals of the Academy of Political and Social Science*, *611*(1), 126–140.

Benkler, Y., & Nissenbaum, H. (2006). Commons-based peer production and virtue. *Journal of Political Philosophy*, *14*(4), 394–419.

Botsman, R., & Rogers, R. (2011). *What's mine is yours*. London: Collins.

Bowles, S., & Gintis, H. (2002). Social capital and community governance. *The Economic Journal*, *112*(483), F419–F436.

Bradley, K., & Pargman, D. (2017). The sharing economy as the commons of the 21st century. *Cambridge Journal of Regions, Economy and Society*, *10*, 231–247.

Butler, R. J. (1983). Control through markets, hierarchies and communes: A transactional approach to organizational analysis. In A. Francis, J. Turk, & P. Willman (Eds.), *Power, efficiency and institutions* (pp. 137–158). London: Heinemann Educational Books.

Demil, B., & Lecocq, X. (2006). Neither market nor hierarchy nor network: The emergence of Bazaar Governance. *Organization Studies*, *27*(10), 1447–1466.

DiMaggio, P. J., & Powell, W. W. (1983). The iron cage revisited: Institutional isomorphism and collective rationality in organizational fields. *American Sociological Review*, *48*(2), 147–160.

Dubois, A., & Gadde, L.-E. (2002). Systematic combining: An abductive approach to case research. *Journal of Business Research*, *55*(7), 553–560.

Ebers, M., & Oerlemans, L. (2016). The variety of governance structures beyond market and hierarchy. *Journal of Management*, *42*(6), 1491–1529.

Edmondson, A., & McManus, S. (2007). Methodological fit in management field research. *Academy of Management Review*, *32*(4), 1155–1179.

Eisenhardt, K. M. (1989). Building theory from case study research. *Academy of Management Review*, *14*(4), 532–550.

Eisenhardt, K. M., & Bourgeois, L. J. (1988). Politics of strategic decision making in high-velocity environments: Toward a midrange theory. *Academy of Management Journal*, *31*(4), 737–770.

Faraj, S., Jarvenpaa, S. L., & Majchrzak, A. (2011). Knowledge collaboration in online communities. *Organization Science*, *22*(5), 1224–1239.

Faraj, S., & Johnson, S. L. (2016). Network exchange patterns in online communities. *Organization Science*, *22*(6), 1464–1480.

Faraj, S., van Krogh, G., Monteiro, E., & Lakhani, K. (2016). Special section introduction – Online community as space for knowledge flows. *Information Systems Research*, *27*(4), 668–684.

Fjeldstad, Ø. D., Snow, C. C., Miles, R. R., & Lettl, C. (2012). The architecture of collaboration. *Strategic Management Journal*, *33*(6), 734–750.

Franke, N., & Shah, S. (2003). How communities support innovative activities: An exploration of assistance and sharing among end-users. *Research Policy*, *32*(1), 157–158.

Galbreth, M. R., Ghosh, B., & Shor, M. (2012). Social sharing of information goods: Implications for pricing and profits. *Marketing Science*, *31*(4), 603–620.

Garrett, L. E., Spreitzer, G. M., & Bacevice, P. A. (2017). Co-constructing a sense of community at work: The emergence of community in coworking spaces. *Organization Studies*, *38*(6), 821–842.

Gläser, J. (2001). "Producing Communities" as a theoretical challenge. Paper presented at the TASA 2001 Conference, Sydney.

Gulati, R., Puranam, P., & Tushman, M. (2012). Meta-organization design: Rethinking design in interorganizational and community contexts. *Strategic Management Journal*, *33*(6), 571–586.

Haefliger, S., Monteiro, E., Foray, D., & von Krogh, G. (2011). Social software and strategy. *Long Range Planning*, *44*(5–6), 297–316.

Hamari, J., Sjöklint, M., & Ukkonen, A. (2016). The sharing economy: Why people participate in collaborative consumption. *Journal of the Association for Information Science and Technology*, *67*(9), 2047–2059.

Harrison, R., & Wellman, B. (2012). *Networked: The new social operating system*. Cambridge, MA: MIT Press.

Hawlitschek, F., Teubner, T., & Gimpel, H. (2018). Consumer motives for peer-to-peer sharing. *Journal of Cleaner Production*, *204*, 144–157.

Heide, J. B. (1994). Interorganizational governance in marketing channels. *Journal of Marketing*, *58*(1), 71–85.

Heide, J. B., & John, G. (1990). Alliances in industrial purchasing: The determinants of joint action in buyer-supplier relationships. *Journal of Marketing Research*, *27*(1), 24–36.

Holmstrom, B., & Tirole, J. (1989). The theory of the firm. In R. Schmalensee & R. Willig (Eds.), *Handbook of industrial organization* (pp. 61–133). New York, NY: Elsevier.

Kannan, P. K., Chang, A.-M., & Whinston, A. B. (2000). Electronic communities in e-business: Their role and issues. *Information Systems Frontiers*, *1*(4), 415–426.

Kellog, K. C., Orlikowski, W. J., & Yates, J. (2006). Life in the trading zone: Structuring coordination across boundaries in postbureaucratic organizations. *Organization Science*, *17*(1), 22–44.

Lamberton, C. P., & Rose, R. L. (2012). When is ours better than mine? A framework for understanding and altering participation in commercial sharing systems. *Journal of Marketing*, *76*(4), 109–125.

Langley, A., Smallman, C., Tsoukas, H., & Van de Ven, A. H. (2013). Process studies of change in organization and management: Unveiling temporality. *Activity and Flow. Academy of Management Studies*, *56*(1), 1–13.

Lee, G. K., & Cole, R. E. (2003). From a firm-based to a community-based model of knowledge creation: The case of Linux Kernel development. *Organization Science*, *14*(6), 633–649.

Locke, K., Golden-Biddle, K., & Feldman, M. S. (2008). Making doubt generative: Rethinking the role of doubt in the research process. *Organization Science*, *19*(6), 907–918.

Loyd, D. L., Wang, C. S., Phillips, K. W., & Lount, R. B., Jr. (2013). Social category diversity promotes premeeting elaboration: The role of relationship focus. *Organization Science*, *24*(3), 757–772.

Makadok, R., & Coff, R. (2009). Both market and hierarchy: An incentive-system theory of hybrid governance forms. *Academy of Management Review*, *34*(2), 297–319.

Mantere, S., & Ketokivi, M. (2013). Reasoning in organization science. *Academy of Management Review*, *38*(1), 70–89.

Marquis, C., Lounsbury, M., & Greenwood, R. (2011). Introduction: Community as an institutional order and a type of organizing. In C. Marquis, M. Lounsbury, & R. Greenwood (Eds.), *Communities and Organizations* (pp. xi–xxix). Bingley: Emerald Publishing.

Martin, J. (2016). The sharing economy: A pathway to sustainability or a nightmarish form of neoliberal capitalism? *Ecological Economics*, *121*, 149–159.

Ménard, C. (1996). On clusters, hybrids, and other strange forms: The case of the French poultry industry. *Journal of Institutional and Theoretical Economics*, *152*, 154–183.

Miles, M. B., & Hubermann, A. M. (2004). *Qualitative data analysis: An expanded sourcebook* (2nd ed.). Thousand Oaks, CA: Sage.

Möhlmann, M., & Zalmanson, L. (2017). Hands on the wheel: Navigating algorithmic management and Uber Drivers' Autonomy. In Proceedings of the 2017 *international conference on information systems* (ICIS), Seoul, South Korea, (pp. 1–17).

Muñoz, P., & Cohen, B. (2017). Mapping out the sharing economy: A configurational approach to sharing business modeling. *Technological Forecasting and Social Change*, *125*, 21–37.

O'Mahony, S., & Bechky, B. A. (2008). Boundary organizations: Enabling collaboration among unexpected allies. *Administrative Science Quarterly*, *53*(3), 422–459.

O'Mahony, S., & Ferraro, F. (2007). The emergence of governance in an open source community. *Academy of Management Journal*, *50*(5), 1079–1106.

O'Mahony, S., & Lakhani, K. R. (2011). Organizations in the shadow of communities. In C. Marquis, M. Lounsbury, & R. Greenwood (Eds.), *Communities and organizations* (pp. 3–36). Bingley: Emerald Publishing.

Ouchi, W. G. (1979). A conceptual framework for the design of organizational control mechanisms. *Management Science*, *25*(9), 833–848.

Ouchi, W. G. (1980). Markets, bureaucracies, and clans. *Academic Science Quarterly*, *25*(1), 129–141.

Owyang, J. (2016). Honeycomb 3.0: The collaborative economy market expansion. Retrieved from http://www.web-strategist.com/blog/2016/03/10/honeycomb-3-0-the-collaborative-economy-market-expansion-sxsw/. Accessed on February 8, 2017.

Ozanne, L. K., & Ballantine, P. W. (2010). Sharing as a form of anti-consumption? An examination of toy library users. *Journal of Consumer Behaviour*, *9*(6), 485–498.

Pazaitis, A., Kostakis, V., & Bauwens, M. (2017). Digital economy and the rise of open cooperativism: The case of the enspiral network. *European Review of Labour and Research*, *23*(2), 177–192.

Porter, C. E., & Donthu, N. (2008). Cultivating trust and harvesting value in virtual communities. *Management Science*, *54*(1), 113–128.

Powell, W. W. (1990). Neither market nor hierarchy: Network forms of organization. *Research in Organizational Behavior*, *12*, 295–336.

Preece, J. (2000). *Online communities: Designing, usability, supporting sociability*. Chichester: John Wiley & Sons.

Puranam, P., Alexy, O., & Reitzig, M. (2014). What's 'new' about new forms of organizing? *Academy of Management Review*, *39*(2), 162–180.

Reischauer, G., & Mair, J. (2018). How organizations strategically govern online communities: Lessons from the sharing economy. *Academy of Management Discoveries*, *4*(3), 220–247.

Sanders, W. M., & Tuschke, G. (2007). The adoption of institutionally contested organizational practices: The emergence of stock option pay in Germany. *Academy of Management Journal*, *50*(1), 33–56.

Schaarschmidt, M., Walsh, G., & von Kortzfleisch, H. F. (2015). How do firms influence open source software communities? A framework and empirical analysis of different governance modes. *Information and Organization*, *25*(2), 99–114.

Schor, J. (2014). Debating the sharing economy. Great Transiotion Initiative. Retrieved from http://www.greattransition.org/publication/debating-the-sharing-economy. Accessed on January 6, 2016.

Seidel, M.-D. L., & Stewart, K. (2011). An initial description of the c-form. In C. Marquis, M. Lounsbury, & R. Greenwood (Eds.), *Communities and organizations* (pp. 37–73). Bingley: Emerald Publishing.

Shah, S. K. (2006). Motivation, governance, and the viability of hybrid forms in open source software development. *Management Science*, *52*(7), 1000–1014.

Sibai, O., de Valck, K., Farrell, A. M., & Rudd, J. M. (2015). Social control in online communities of consumption: A framework for community management. *Psychology and Marketing*, *32*(3), 250–264.

Snow, C. C., Fjeldstad, Ø. D., Lettl, C., & Miles, R. E. (2011). Organizing continuous product development and commercialization: The collaborative community of firms model. *Journal of Product Innovation Management*, *28*(1), 3–16.

Spaulding, T. J. (2010). How can virtual communities create value for business. *Electronic Commerce Research and Applications*, *9*(1), 38–49.

Stabell, C. B., & Fjeldstad, Ø. D. (1998). Configuring value for competitive advantage: On chains, shops, and networks. *Strategic Management Journal*, *19*(5), 413–437.

Sundararajan, A. (2016). *The sharing economy. The end of employment and the rise of crowd-based capitalism*. Cambridge, MA: MIT Press.

Van Maanen, J. (1979). The fact of friction in organizational ethnography. *Administrative Science Quarterly*, *24*(4), 539–550.

von Hippel, E. V., & von Krogh, G. V. (2003). Open source software and the "private-collective" innovation model: Issues for organization science. *Organization Science*, *14*(2), 209–223.

von Krogh, G., Spaeth, S., & Lakhani, K. R. (2003). Community, joining, and specialization in open source software innovation: A case study. *Research Policy*, *32*(7), 1217–1241.

Williamson, O. E. (1991). Comparative economic organization: The analysis of discrete structural alternatives. *Administrative Science Quarterly*, *36*(2), 269–296.

Williamson, O. E. (1999). Strategy research: Governance and competence perspectives. *Strategic Management Journal*, *20*(12), 1087–1108.

Williamson, O. E. (2002). The theory of the firm as governance structure: From choice to contract. *Journal of Economic Perspectives*, *16*(3), 171–195.

Yin, R. K. (2012). *Case study research: Design and methods* (4th ed.). Thousand Oaks, CA: Sage.

Yunus, M., Moingeon, B., & Lehmann-Ortega, L. (2010). Building social business models: Lessons from the Grameen experience. *Long Range Planning*, *43*(2–3), 308–325.

# SHAPING EMOTIONAL LABOR PRACTICES IN THE SHARING ECONOMY*

Eliane Bucher, Christian Fieseler, Christoph Lutz and Gemma Newlands

## ABSTRACT

*Independent actors operating through peer-to-peer sharing economy platforms co-create service experiences, such as shared car-rides or home-stays. Emotional labor among both parties, manifested in the mutual enactment of socially desirable behavior, is essential in ensuring that these experiences are successful. However, little is known about emotional labor practices and about how sharing economy platforms enforce emotional labor practices among independent actors, such as guests, hosts, drivers, or passengers. To address this research gap, we follow a mixed methods approach. We combine survey research among Airbnb and Uber users with content analysis of seven leading sharing economy platforms. The findings show that (1) users perform emotional labor despite not seeing is as necessarily desirable and (2) platforms actively encourage the performance of emotional labor practices even in the absence of direct formal control. Emotional labor practices are encouraged through (hard) design features such as mutual ratings, reward systems, and gamification, as well as through more subtle (soft) normative framing of desirable practices via platform and app guidelines, tips, community sites, or blogs. Taken together, these*

*All authors contributed equally to this chapter.

**Theorizing the Sharing Economy: Variety and Trajectories of New Forms of Organizing**
**Research in the Sociology of Organizations, Volume 66, 55–82**

**ISSN: 0733-558X/doi:10.1108/S0733-558X20200000066004**

*findings expand our understanding of the limitations of peer-to-peer sharing platforms, where control over the service experience and quality can only be enforced indirectly.*

**Keywords:** Emotional labor; sharing economy; service co-creation; online platforms; control; peer-to-peer sharing

## INTRODUCTION

Organizations have a vested interest in encouraging positive behaviors among their workforce, such as engagement, commitment, and citizenship behaviors (Katz, 1964; LePine, Erez, & Johnson, 2002; Mowday, Steers, & Porter, 1979; Organ, 1988; Smith, Organ, & Near, 1983). These behaviors, in turn, positively impact outcome variables, such as service quality (Bienstock, DeMoranville, & Smith, 2003) and customer satisfaction (Koys, 2001). In contexts where workers interact directly with customers, organizations may also encourage individuals to display specific emotional expressions toward relevant audiences and even alter their feelings. Here, frontline staff such as receptionists, waitresses, or customer service representatives may be expected to display positive emotions such as happiness, interest, or kindness (Hochschild, 1983; Leidner, 1999). Other professions, such as bailiffs or undertakers, may be expected to display neutral or negative emotions such as aggression or sadness (Brook, 2009; Hochschild, 1983). The collective practices of emotion and expression management for organizational purposes have been discussed in the academic literature under the umbrella term emotional labor (Ashforth & Humphrey, 1993; Grandey, 2000; Hochschild, 1983; Morris & Feldman, 1996, 1997).

In the peer-to-peer sharing economy, platform-mediated service experiences are provided by private individuals offering their own assets (Bardhi & Eckhardt, 2012; Botsman & Rogers, 2010; Guttentag, 2015). An Airbnb host, for instance, offers their own home to a guest, while an Uber driver ferries passengers around in their private vehicle. Rather than being framed as a purely economic transaction, such service experiences are imbued with the norms of social hospitality and accordingly expectations of positive interpersonal interaction on both sides (Bucher, Fieseler, Fleck, & Lutz, 2018). A successful sharing experience, therefore, depends on the readiness of providers (hosts, drivers) and consumers (guests, passengers) to manage their feelings and emotional displays. This is because misalignment between provider and consumer expectations regarding the level and modality of social interaction can reduce perceived service quality, user satisfaction, and future use-intention (Kim, Park, & Lee, 2019).

As a new paradigm of commercial peer-to-peer social interaction emerges, academic research has started to investigate emotional labor practices in the sharing economy. While initial work focused on the specific context of Uber drivers (Raval & Dourish, 2016; Rosenblat & Stark, 2016; Stark, 2016), more recent research has expanded to also consider emotional labor across a variety of sharing economy platforms, as well as among both providers and consumers (Lutz, Newlands, & Fieseler, 2018; Marquis, Kim, Alahmad, Pierce, & Robert, 2018; Newlands, Lutz, &

Fieseler, 2019). However, there is limited academic research into how organizations instill such emotional labor practices in contexts where organizations act as mediators between independent actors. Unlike traditional organizations, which can communicate objectives to employees, monitor performance, and punish problematic behavior (Lindsay, Lindsay, & Irvine, 1996; Otley & Berry, 1980), service experiences in the sharing economy are delivered not by employees, but by independent actors outside of formal organizational boundaries. Accordingly, there is a significant tension between, on the one hand, desired platform control over the quality of social interaction and, on the other hand, the expected autonomy of providers who participate with their own assets and of consumers who are unaccustomed with being the subject of such expectations (Lutz et al., 2018).

In this chapter, we follow a mixed methods approach which combines survey research and correspondence analysis with content analysis to better understand how emotional labor practices are instilled among providers and consumers of the sharing economy. In particular, we show (1) how pronounced emotional labor is in home-sharing and ride-hailing and how the propensity to engage in emotional labor is influenced by a variety of antecedents (user side) and (2) how sharing platforms with limited direct power over their participants encourage and enforce emotional labor practices (platform side). Here, we put a special emphasis on the role of (a) platform design choices, such as rating and review systems and (b) narrative frames of desirable practices, as conveyed through guidelines, communities, or blogs. This contribution will inform future work on instilling behavioral practices, such as emotional labor, outside the traditional spheres of organizational influence. The results may further enrich the current debate on inequality, power, and exploitation in the sharing economy, placing particular emphasis on the potential individual costs and externalities associated with emotional labor. We also expect our results to add to the ongoing debate on provider classification (Newlands, Lutz, & Fieseler, 2018), which may inform current debates in regulation and policymaking.

## LITERATURE REVIEW

### *Emotional Labor*

The ability to regulate internal emotional responses, as well as the corresponding outward affective display, may be a prerequisite for successful participation in both society and organizations. When our emotions stand in contrast to a given situation or norm, we try to regulate our emotional responses so that they better serve our goals (Gross, 2002). For instance, instead of displaying a state of boredom during a monotonous meeting, we may either attempt to take a genuine interest in the content (cf. Hochschild, 1983: "deep acting"; Gross, 1998: "antecedent focused emotion regulation") or otherwise adopt an outward display of interest (cf. Hochschild, 1983: "surface acting"; Gross, 1998: "response focused emotion regulation"). Gross (2002, p. 282) defines emotional regulation as "processes by which we influence which emotions we have, when we have them, and how we experience and express them." Emotion regulation strategies may entail efforts to influence (increase, maintain, or decrease) negative emotions, such as anger, jealousy, or boredom, as well as positive emotions, such as joy, contentment, or love (Parrott & Schulkin, 1993). However, not all emotion regulation is consciously performed. Emotion regulation practices range from "explicit, conscious, effortful, and controlled regulation to implicit, unconscious, effortless, and automatic regulation" (Gross, 1998, p. 275). These can be referred to as "explicit" and "implicit" display rules, highlighting the contrast between external performance and internal moderation.

In the context of organizational psychology and work sociology, emotion regulation is often referred to as emotional labor (Ashforth & Humphrey, 1993; Brook, 2009; Grandey, 2000, 2003; Grandey & Melloy, 2017; Harris, 2002; Hochschild, 1983). Workers perform emotional labor when they have to follow certain display rules in order to fulfill the organizational requirements of their role (e.g., a waiter smiling to a customer). Emotional labor is also performed when workers are rated on the quality of their affective delivery, by either customers or superiors (e.g., through tips or promotions). Building on earlier theoretical work on emotional labor (Ashforth & Humphrey, 1993; Hochschild, 1983), Grandey (2000, p. 97) proposes an integrated definition of emotional labor as "the process of regulating both feelings and expressions for organizational goals." In this contribution, we are interested in emotional labor practices outside the direct influence-sphere of the mediating organization. Therefore, we propose to frame Grandey's (2000) integrated definition more generally so that it can be applied to various social actors and contexts. Accordingly, we understand emotional labor as the "process of regulating both feelings and expressions for a specific goal."

While emotion regulation in general (Gross, 2002) and emotional labor in particular (Grandey, 2017) are neither good nor bad per se, the conditions in which the emotional work occurs may create situations of conflict when the emotions felt do not match the emotions expected by relevant audiences, such as co-workers, supervisors, or customers. Here, workers may experience "emotional dissonance" (Grandey, 2015; Morris & Feldman, 1996, 1997) which may in turn lead to detrimental outcomes such as burnout, dissatisfaction, cynicism, service misbehavior, or turnover intention (Brotheridge & Grandey, 2002; Grandey, 2000; Hülsheger & Schewe, 2011; Jin & Guy, 2009; Karatepe & Aleshinloye, 2009; Lee & Ok, 2012; Wharton, 1993). In general, detrimental effects of emotional labor may be alleviated by strong role identification. If a particular role reflects a "valued identity", individuals are more willing to engage in emotional labor to fulfill the expectations associated with it (Humphrey, Ashforth, & Diefendorff, 2015). In general, the more consistent the display rules of a specific role (e.g., cheerful waiter, caring nurse, and welcoming hotelier) are with elements of one's own personal identity, the more authentic role-conforming behavior is bound to be. In this case, "being true to the role, […] is tantamount to being true to oneself" (Humphrey et al., 2015, p. 754).

Research into emotional labor throughout various service industries such as retail, aviation, or medical services has burgeoned in the last three decades (Fisher & Ashkanasy, 2000; Götz, 2013; Zapf, 2002). Studies have looked at emotional labor as performed by office assistants (Grandey, 2000), customer service workers

(Dahling & Perez, 2010), barristers and paralegals (Harris, 2002; Pierce, 1999), service personnel (Ashforth & Humphrey, 1993; Ogbonna & Wilkinson, 1990), care workers and nurses (Brotheridge & Grandey, 2002; Henderson, 2001; Lopez, 2006) as well as flight attendants (Williams, 2003), fast-food frontline workers (Leidner, 1999), and university professors and lecturers (Bellas, 1999). While research has mainly focused on face-to-face contexts, some work has also examined emotional labor in e-commerce transactions (Ishii & Markman, 2016).

In the emotional labor literature of the past three decades, the customer is often perceived as a passive audience member whose emotions are there to be managed and influenced (Gountas, Ewing, & Gountas, 2006; Groth, Hennig-Thurau, & Walsh, 2009; Pugh, 2001; Tang, Seal, Naumann, & Miguel, 2013; Tsai & Huang, 2002). In the case of the sharing economy, sharing experiences are inherently co-created by both providers and consumers and thus predicate emotional engagement on both sides.

### *Emotional Labor in the Sharing Economy*

Widespread technological advancements as well as shifts in consumer attitudes toward access enabled the growth of the "sharing economy" (Bardhi & Eckhardt, 2012; Belk, 2013; Botsman & Rogers, 2010; Cohen & Kietzmann, 2014). Although a variety of different exchange relationships have been included within the umbrella of the sharing economy (Arnould & Thompson, 2016; Codagnone, Biagi, & Abadie, 2016), in this chapter, we focus on peer-to-peer sharing of tangible assets, mediated through digital platforms. Key areas of academic investigation into the sharing economy have included conceptual clarifications (Howcroft & Bergvall-Kåreborn, 2019; Sutherland & Jarrahi, 2018), labor issues (Carboni, 2016; Glöss, McGregor, & Brown, 2016; Peticca-Harris, deGama, & Ravishankar, 2018), trust (Wentrup, Nakamura, & Ström, 2019), "algorithmic" management (Möhlmann & Zalmanson, 2017), motivations for sharing (Bucher, Fieseler, & Lutz, 2016; Cheng, 2016; Hamari, Sjöklint, & Ukkonen, 2016; Jabagi, Croteau, Audebrand, & Marsan, 2019), as well as marketing and consumer research (Guttentag, 2015).

Although a handful of studies have considered emotional labor in the sharing economy (Gandini, 2018; Glöss et al., 2016; Lutz et al., 2019; Marquis et al., 2018), most studies have focused on the context of ride-hailing or home-sharing. Raval and Dourish's (2016) survey among Uber drivers, for instance, points toward several instances where providers might be engaging in emotional labor. The authors conclude that being a worker in the sharing economy might require "a combination and alternation of positive and negative emotional display, empathy generation, building one's social capital" (p. 6). Similarly, Rosenblat and Stark's (2016) work on algorithmic labor finds that the metrics and rating systems encourage Uber drivers to employ emotional labor practices as they use "a combination of friendly conversational attempts with eye contact and general demeanor" to gauge whether or not customers want to be entertained or left alone (p. 3775). In his discussion of the social costs of Uber, Rogers (2016) argues that Uber's rating system may require both drivers and passengers to engage in emotional labor, which makes him the first to point toward emotional labor being present on both sides of the peer-to-peer sharing transaction. This thread of research was expanded by Newlands et al. (2019), who outlined that sharing-economy consumers across both home-sharing and ride-hailing platforms perform emotional labor during sharing experiences, but find the necessity to act in socially desirable ways frustrating and coercive.

Sharing platforms, reliant as they are on service experiences co-created by independent actors, face a challenge in that they only have limited direct power when it comes to enforcing specific emotional, cognitive, or behavioral practices among participants. A growing body of research has investigated mechanisms of control available to platforms over the conditions of participation, controlling duration, intensity, and even selectivity (Wentrup et al., 2019). However, direct control is limited as a result of regulatory restrictions. Providers are explicitly classed as either independent contractors or as "consumers" of platform's matching services (Aloisi, 2016; Carboni, 2016; Newlands et al., 2018). As such, implementation of formal managerial requirements over how the sharing experience is executed increases the liability for providers to be re-classified as employees of the platform.

Platforms can approach this problem in two ways. First, to preclude moral hazard and to set a baseline for quality assurance, platforms can establish (hard) reputation-based feedback mechanisms. In Hochschild's (1983) discussion of emotional labor among airline personnel, the presence of passenger feedback, in the form of letters or opinion polls, translated into rewards or punishments. In the sharing economy, emotional labor can be similarly encouraged by the presence of mutual feedback mechanisms, taking the form of reviews, ratings, and rewards. While reputation-based feedback systems provide information about past transactions, increasing mutual trust (Mayzlin, 2016), they also act as a factor in determining the overall success of a transaction. Participants with bad feedback can face negative consequences such as discrimination in future encounters or ejection from the platform (Rosenblat & Stark, 2016). Ratings are thus not only associated with establishing a service mentality among providers (Lee, Kusbit, Metsky, & Dabbish, 2015; Newlands et al., 2019), but also with establishing control in general (Cockayne, 2016; Horton & Golden, 2015; Van Doorn, 2017). While reputation and reward systems are expected to be effective on both the provider and consumer side, the increasing proliferation of services results in a scenario where providers compete in a crowded market and consistently high ratings have become crucial for success (Rosenblat & Stark, 2016; Stark, 2016). Reputation systems combine control mechanisms (Haman and Putnam, 2008), namely managerial control (e.g., rewards for compliant behavior and punishment for non-compliant behavior) and peer-based control, where individual members reinforce organizational culture and enforce behavioral norms among each other (e.g., Barker, 1993; Tracy, 2000).

As a softer way to influence behavior outside their direct sphere of influence, organizations can also use normative messaging such as signs, guidelines, or stories which convey the desired attitudes, beliefs, and perceptions (Cialdini, 2003; Schultz, Khazian, & Zaleski, 2008). The goal of this normative social influence is to alter perceived implicit rules and standards within a group "without the force of laws" (Cialdini & Trost, 1998, p. 152). Cialdini (2003) has demonstrated the effectiveness of such normative messaging by using the example of energy conservation behavior among hotel customers. Influencing behavior through normative frames is in line with what Haman and Putnam (2008) describe as attempts of cultural control, where organizations try to cultivate a sense of identification with organizational symbols, values, and missions (Kunda & Van Maanen, 1999).

## RESEARCH DESIGN

This chapter follows a mixed or integrative method approach, where quantitative survey measures (regression analysis, correspondence analysis) are combined with qualitative content analysis (platform content). Mixed methods research is a systematic integration of quantitative and qualitative methods in a single study for purposes of obtaining a full picture and deeper understanding of a phenomenon. Mixed methods combine "more than one kind of technique for gathering, analyzing, and representing human phenomena, all for the purpose of better understanding" (Greene, 2006). In the present contribution, a mixed methods' approach was deemed fitting to allow for the exploration and combination of multiple viewpoints, perspectives, and positions. Given limited previous research on the topic, the research design is exploratory rather than confirmatory. At the same time, we attempt to cover the topic holistically and thus opted for a mixed methods' approach that captures different aspects of the topic. Table 1 shows the overall research design and methodological approach. Data collection took place in three subsequent and complementary phases between June and November 2017. The first phase was a large-scale multi-country survey on the sharing economy more generally (Newlands, Lutz, & Fieseler, 2017b; survey 1 in the remainder of this chapter). Emotional labor was included as one aspect in this survey due to

***Table 1.*** Research Methodology Overview.

| Phase | Method | Sample and Data | Purpose |
|---|---|---|---|
| 1 (June 2017) | Online survey (1st wave) | Representative survey in 12 European Countries $N = 6{,}111$ Sub-sample of 985 Airbnb and Uber users | Establish the emotional labor construct and its antecedents among sharing-economy providers and consumers in Europe |
| 2 (October 2017) | Qualitative platform analysis | Analysis of 7 sharing platforms yielded 231 instances where emotional labor practices were suggested | Show how sharing platforms suggest and enforce emotional labor practices among participants |
| 3 (November 2017) | Online survey (2nd wave) | Online survey among four major online communities $N = 726$ Airbnb and Uber users | Confirm emotional labor construct and its antecedents in a different setting and among dedicated communities |
| | Correspondence analysis | Collection of ideal host/guest, driver/passenger traits in four major online communities ($N = 726$ Airbnb and Uber users) | Provide an overview of perceived ideal character traits of consumers and providers in the sharing economy |

an extensive literature review on power-related aspects of the sharing economy (Newlands, Lutz, & Fieseler, 2017a). Survey 1 in general served descriptive purposes and was intended to map under-covered issues in the sharing economy in Europe from a user-centric perspective. In this chapter, the first step of the analysis, including quantitative results from surveys 1 and 2 (phases 1 and 3) through a linear regression analysis, also serves to set the scene and provide an overview of the prevalence and antecedents of emotional labor in a relatively generalizable manner. The second phase was an in-depth qualitative platform analysis. This phase complements the first and third phase, focusing on the role of the platforms rather than user practices and expectations. For more clarity in the argument, the results of the platform analysis are reported after the results of both surveys are presented, even though data collection occurred before the second survey. The third phase was a user-centered and tailored survey that specifically focused on emotional labor (survey 2 in the remainder of this chapter). It accompanied and built on survey 1 by including the same emotional labor questions and antecedents, thus enabling comparability. However, it substantially expanded on survey 1 by including a set of open-ended questions that assessed not only emotional labor practices and antecedents but also expectations and contextual prompts. Survey 2 resulted in a validation of the European findings through a regression analysis and in a correspondence analysis.

## QUANTITATIVE SURVEYS

In terms of the quantitative data, we performed (1) a linear regression (How prevalent is emotional labor among consumers and providers?) and (2) a correspondence analysis (Which are ideal traits of consumers and providers?). This two-step approach allows to compare emotional labor practices on the one hand and perceptions, ideals, and expectations on the other hand, revealing a holistic perspective of the phenomenon on the user side.

### *Linear Regression*

#### *Sample and Data*

The first wave of data collection took the form of a representative survey conducted in Denmark, France, Germany, Ireland, Italy, the Netherlands, Norway, Poland, Portugal, Spain, Switzerland, and the UK. The survey was in the field in June and July 2017. For the recruitment of participants, we collaborated with an ESOMAR-certified, globally leading survey provider with experience in recruiting respondents for surveys on the sharing and gig economy. A total of 6,111 respondents was collected, with a nationally representative profile of the age group 18–65 in terms of age, gender, and area of residence. The respondents received a small financial reward. The median response time was 760 seconds and quality assurance on the side of the survey provider guaranteed that low-quality respondents (e.g., those speeding or through-lining) were replaced.

Respondents were grouped into one of four response streams, depending on their answer to a filter question: providers, consumers, aware non-users, and non-aware non-users. For providers and consumers, we subsequently asked which sharing-economy platform they used most frequently via an open text field. In all, 556 (9%) respondents in our sample were classified as providers, 1,143 (19%) as consumers, 3,818 (62%) as aware non-users, and 593 (10%) as non-aware non-users. In the following, we focus on the provider and consumer groups ($N = 1{,}699$), where Airbnb (645 respondents), Uber (340 respondents), and BlaBlaCar (268 respondents) clearly emerged as the most frequently used platforms. However, on aggregate, a relatively large proportion of users (446 in total) used smaller platforms such as the German Kleiderkreisel or Italian Gnammo most frequently. To be able to compare survey 1 and survey 2 (see below), we only included Airbnb and Uber users in the analysis of survey 1, leaving us with a sub-sample of 985 respondents. Among these 985 respondents, the average age is 36.7 (SD = 12.5). In all, 51.7% are male and 48.3% female.

Data collection for survey 2 took place in November 2017. We limited our attention to Airbnb and Uber and used four data sources to survey users of these two platforms: Amazon Mechanical Turk (AMT), Prolific, UberPeople, and Airhostsforum. UberPeople (https://uberpeople.net/) is an online forum for Uber drivers. Airhostforum (https://airhostsforum.com/) is an online community for Airbnb hosts. Online communities are an important space for providers to interact (Reischauer & Mair, 2018) and both of these communities are off-platform and moderated by volunteers rather than Uber or Airbnb community managers. On AMT and Prolific, we posted four separate surveys, targeted at Uber drivers, Uber passengers, Airbnb hosts, and Airbnb guests. Overall, 748 participants were recruited in survey 2. Also, 22 respondents were removed for quality reasons (speeding), leaving a total number of 726 participants. Among those, 283 primarily defined themselves as Uber drivers, 104 as Uber passengers, 144 as Airbnb hosts, and 194 as Airbnb guests. In the survey 2, the average age is 33.3 years (SD = 9.4). In all, 53.7% of respondents identified as male, 45.0 as female and 1.3% either prefer not to say or identify as neither male nor female. Also, 62.7% of respondents reside in the USA (455 in total) and 29.9% in the UK, with the remaining 7.4% residing in a variety of countries.[1]

*Measures*

We measured emotional labor with four items, adapted from Best, Downey, and Jones (1997). The question prompt for each item was *When you interact with passengers/drivers/guests/hosts, how often do you the following?* The items were, in the respective order: *express feelings of sympathy (e.g., saying you are sorry to hear about something, saying you understand)*; *express friendly emotions (e.g., smiling, giving compliments, making small talk)*; *hide your disapproval about something someone has done*; *and hide your annoyance about something someone has done*. Respondents could answer on a five-point scale ranging from "Not at all" (1) to "Very much" (5). Initial principal component analysis (in SPSS, Kaiser criterion) showed that all items load on one factor (Cronbach's $\alpha$ of 0.75).

For the independent constructs, we included respondents' sharing frequency with the question "How frequently do you provide on the sharing platform?" for providers and "How frequently do you use the sharing platform?" for consumers. Respondents could answer on a 9nine-point scale. To assess users' motivations for using sharing platforms, we used four items oriented on motive typologies from previous studies (Bucher et al., 2016; Hamari et al., 2016; Hawlitschek et al., 2016). One item captured financial benefit, one the social aspects of sharing (e.g., meeting new people), one hedonic aspects (e.g., having fun), and one social responsibility (e.g., sharing is the right thing to do). For rating system assessment (positive and negative) and rating experience, we did not find suitable established scales. Therefore, these measures were newly developed. Positive rating system assessment was measured with two items: *The rating/review system is fair* and *The rating/review system works well.* In both surveys, the scale had sufficient reliability, with a Cronbach's $\alpha$ of 0.73 in survey 1 and 0.80 in survey 2. Negative rating system assessment was measured with two items: *The rating/review system takes into account elements beyond my control* and *The rating/review system should be removed.* The scale had a Cronbach's $\alpha$ of 0.35 in survey 1 and of 0.28 in survey 2, showing insufficient reliability.[2] Despite the low Cronbach's $\alpha$, the factor loadings for negative rating system assessment in both surveys were satisfactory (0.78 for both items in survey 1 and 0.76 for both items in survey 2). Finally, we measured critical ratings with three items: *Consumers/providers rate me too harshly*; *The rating/review systems gives consumers/providers power over me*; and *Consumers/Providers have unrealistic expectations.* The Cronbach's $\alpha$ for both surveys was 0.67, close to the threshold of 0.70. However, the composite reliability is substantially higher in both surveys (0.82), showing sufficient convergent validity. Appendix A displays descriptive statistics for the variables included in the regression that are not directly interpreted in the text, and Appendix B displays the correlations between these variables. For all variables consisting of more than one item, we used principal component analysis (SPSS, Kaiser criterion, save "Regression" command) to aggregate the variable across items for the ensuing regression analysis.

*Method*

We used linear regression to test the influence of the independent variables on the dependent variable of emotional labor. The analysis was conducted with Stata (v.14) and robust standard errors to account for possible heteroscedasticity in the data. We also checked for multicollinearity but none of the VIFs exceeded 2.59, indicating the absence of serious multicollinearity.

*Results*

Table 2 displays the results of the regression analysis. Consumers in survey 1 perform more emotional labor than providers. Gender is the only statistically significant demographic variable, with women scoring higher on emotional labor than men. Frequency of use has a weak but positive effect. More frequent sharing-economy users report more emotional labor. One of the four motives assessed affects emotional labor significantly: financial motives. The positive sign shows that users who

***Table 2.*** Results of the Regression Analysis.

| Independent Variable | Survey 1: EU-12 | | Survey 2: Users | |
|---|---|---|---|---|
| | Unstandardized Coefficient (Robust Standard Error) | Beta | Unstandardized Coefficient (Robust Standard Error) | Beta |
| Group: Consumer (Reference = Provider) | 0.177* (0.085) | 0.070* | −0.534*** (0.111) | −0.263*** |
| Platform (Reference = Airbnb) | −0.026 (0.063) | −0.013 | −0.027 (0.086) | −0.013 |
| Age | −0.002 (0.002) | −0.003 | 0.004 (0.004) | 0.033 |
| Gender (Reference = Female) | −0.288*** (0.056) | −0.150*** | −0.234** (0.069) | −0.117** |
| Education | −0.009 (0.029) | −0.010 | 0.019 (0.039) | 0.019 |
| Country (Reference = Denmark/US) | | | 0.014 (0.082) | 0.006 |
| France | −0.078 (0.139) | −0.026 | | |
| Germany | 0.222 (0.198) | 0.046 | | |
| Ireland | 0.072 (0.122) | 0.025 | | |
| Italy | −0.041 (0.138) | −0.012 | | |
| Netherlands | 0.291 (0.170) | 0.061 | | |
| Norway | −0.026 (0.135) | −0.007 | | |
| Poland | 0.047 (0.157) | 0.010 | | |
| Portugal | 0.383** (0.126) | 0.117** | | |
| Spain | 0.002 (0.134) | 0.001 | | |
| Switzerland | 0.184 (0.136) | 0.056 | | |
| UK | 0.023 (0.127) | 0.008 | | |
| Volunteering | 0.046 (0.034) | 0.046 | 0.094* (0.041) | 0.094* |
| Materialism | 0.048 (0.032) | 0.050 | 0.092* (0.042) | 0.092* |
| Frequency of Use | 0.052** (0.017) | 0.103** | 0.064** (0.023) | 0.147** |
| Motives: Financial | 0.062* (0.029) | 0.068* | 0.096** (0.034) | 0.101** |
| Motives: Social | 0.038 (0.037) | 0.046 | −0.051 (0.041) | −0.068 |
| Motives: Fun | 0.044 (0.035) | 0.053 | 0.019 (0.037) | 0.025 |
| Motives: Social Responsibility | 0.040 (0.037) | 0.047 | −0.004 (0.038) | −0.006 |
| Positive Rating System Assessment | 0.206*** (0.035) | 0.204*** | 0.087* (0.041) | 0.087* |
| Negative Rating System Assessment | 0.078* (0.037) | 0.078* | 0.104** (0.038) | 0.104** |
| Critical Ratings | 0.178*** (0.037) | 0.178*** | 0.105* (0.046) | 0.105* |
| Constant | −0.681** (0.250) | | 0.253 (0.309) | |
| $R^2$ | 0.217 | | 0.191 | |
| $N$ | 985 | | 726 | |

*Note*: Dependent variable: emotional labor factor; independent variables $F$ for survey 1 = 11.30, Prob. > $F$ = 0.000; $F$ for survey 2 = 11.73, Prob > $F$ = 0.000.

are more motivated financially will perform more emotional labor. The fact that financial motives are the only significant motivational predictor could point to the increasingly service-oriented and commercial nature of the sharing economy (Martin, Upham & Budd, 2015; Murillo, Buckland & Val, 2017), our focus is on commercial platforms rather than grassroots initiatives, and the high competition and oversupply among providers (Smorto, 2018). Finally, all rating factors assessed influence emotional labor positively and strongly. Positive rating system assessment has the strongest effect, followed by critical ratings, and negative rating system assessment. This indicates that emotional labor and ratings are, in fact, connected. While the qualitative platform analysis will elaborate on this association, the findings are in line with earlier research where we found evidence for the conditioning effect of ratings mechanisms in terms of emotional labor (Newlands et al., 2019).

The group effect is significant in survey 2 but in a different direction compared with survey 1: In survey 2, providers score substantially higher on emotional labor than consumers. This could be due to the different composition of the sample. However, running the regression only on non-US respondents did not change the directionality or significance of the group effect. In fact, the effect was still significant at the 1% level and the beta was even higher. As in survey 1, women report significantly higher values of emotional labor than men. Unlike before, volunteering and materialism have a weak and positive effect on emotional labor. Those who report to be more materialistic and those who report to volunteer more perform more emotional labor. However, these effects become insignificant when removing the US-based respondents. Like in survey 1, financial motivations are a significant driver of emotional labor and the frequency of engaging in the sharing economy is positively related to emotional labor, so that frequent users perform more emotional labor than infrequent users. This effect becomes insignificant when removing the US-based respondents. Finally, all three rating-related factors have a significant effect on emotional labor. In this case, the effect of critical ratings is strongest, followed by negative and then positive rating system assessment.

Taken together, the results of the quantitative analyses show how the rating system of sharing platforms might nudge users to perform emotional labor. Moreover, across a range of contexts, the results suggest a gender effect, with women performing more emotional labor than men. Finally, we found evidence across both studies of the predictive power of financial motives. Thus, respondents who use sharing platforms for financial reasons will perform more emotional labor than those who do not.

### *Correspondence Analysis*

To conduct a correspondence analysis, we asked the participants of survey 2 to describe their ideal sharing-economy provider and consumer with three characteristics, adjectives, or traits. Uber users were asked to describe both the ideal Uber passenger and Uber driver with three words each in an open text box. Similarly, Airbnb users were asked to describe their ideal Airbnb guest and Airbnb host with three words each in an open text box. Participants were thus completely free in their description of an ideal user. The open text field responses were subsequently processed and brought into table form to analyze them with correspondence analysis (in SPSS, v.23). For each of the four user categories (Uber driver and passenger; Airbnb host and guest), we created separate frequency tables that ranked the traits based on how many times they were mentioned. From this set, we selected the top ten most mentioned traits per user category. Twenty two traits in total were in the top ten at least once and only four of them were mentioned in all four user categories: friendly, clean, polite, and kind. A further 6 traits were in the top 10 in two user categories (respectful, quiet, punctual, honest, professional, and courteous). The remaining 12 traits were only in the top 10 list for one user category (e.g., responsible, helpful, and welcoming). Across all four user categories, the most mentioned traits were: friendly (435 mentions), clean (270), respectful (210), polite (191), quiet (160), and kind (134).

The numerous mentions of placid functional attributes, such as clean, and introspective adjectives, such as quiet, shows that for many sharing-economy participants, the ideal user is not overly talkative or intrusive. In fact, traits that indicate a strong social and communicative element, such as outgoing, warm, and talkative, were mentioned only infrequently. If traits were mentioned that relate to emotional labor, they were generic (friendly, polite, respectful) and tied to general social conventions rather than specific sharing norms.

To synthesize the results, we used the 22 traits that had shown up in at least one of the top 10 lists for a correspondence analysis, with two dimensions. Fig. 1 shows a graphical representation. The *x*-axis, or first dimension, shows variation in both the traits and user categories. Positive values on the *x*-axis denote providers (Uber driver, Airbnb host), whereas negative values denote consumers (Airbnb guest, Uber passenger). Airbnb guests have the lowest values on the *x*-axis, while Airbnb hosts and Uber drivers have vastly similar positive values. The fact that Uber passengers are in the middle between Airbnb guests and providers (both Airbnb hosts and Uber drivers) on the *x*-axis indicates that this category might share more traits with providers than Airbnb guests share.

In terms of the adjectives, the *x-axis* differentiates between professionalism- and service-related characteristics on the right side and personal characteristics on the left side. The traits with high and positive values on the *x*-axis describe actively helping or engaged. These are more strongly connected to providers than consumers. Traits with negative values on the *x*-axis refer to being non-intrusive. In the middle, with values close to 0 on the *x*-axis, we find generic traits that include elements of both professional and personal type such as kind, friendly, nice, and polite. Thus, the first dimension refers to the dichotomy between professional and personal.

The *y*-axis, or second dimension, differentiates between the two major platforms. Positive values describe Airbnb users and negative values describe Uber users. While Uber passengers and drivers have similar values on the *y*-axis, Airbnb hosts score higher than Airbnb guests. It seems that there is more difference and platform distinction between Airbnb guests and hosts than between Uber passengers and drivers. For the traits, the *y*-axis seems to differentiate more expressive characteristics from more self-contained and transactional characteristics. Traits with negative values on the *y*-axis, such as safe, efficient, and punctual, all refer to a transactional understanding of sharing (i.e., sharing as a professional, frictionless service that uses established parameters in judging the success of the transaction). On the other side, we find traits which are associated with a more intrinsic understanding of sharing, stressing the social, expressive, and emotional elements (welcoming, accommodating, honest, and understanding). Thus, the second dimension refers to the dichotomy between intrinsic and expressive on the one hand and extrinsic and transactional on the other hand.

The combined visualization of traits and user types shows that the ideal Uber passenger, according to other users, is polite, quiet, nice, and courteous.

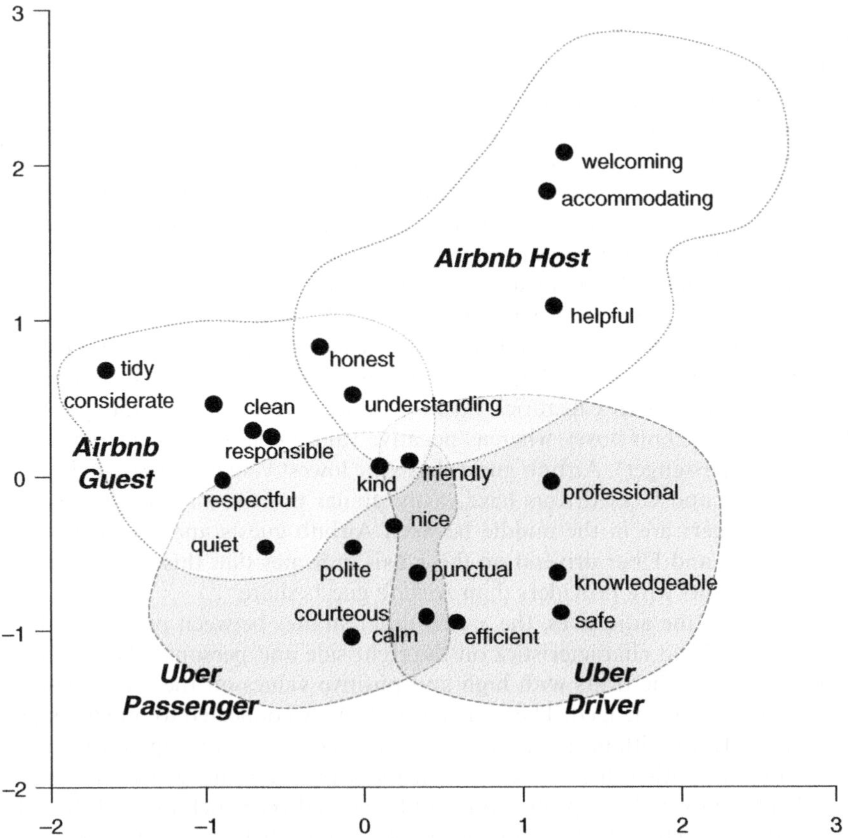


*Fig. 1.* Graphical Representation of Correspondence Analysis.
*Note*: The graph displays desired and ideal user characteristics in a two-dimensional space. *x*-axis: Personal (negative values) versus professional (positive values). *y*-axis: Extrinsic and transactional (negative values) versus intrinsic and expressive (positive values).

This reflects a passive and emotionally uninvolved transaction. The ideal Uber driver is punctual, knowledgeable, safe, efficient, calm, and nice. Again, we do not find strong emotional traits. The ideal Airbnb guest is respectful, responsible, considerate, clean, and tidy. This describes an almost aseptic guest, with little emotional engagement and a primary intention of not disturbing anyone. Finally, the ideal Airbnb host is welcoming, accommodating, helpful, honest, and understanding. Of all the user categories, Airbnb host is by far the most pronounced in terms of emotional expectations. Several ideal traits of Airbnb hosts, with frequent mentions but not making it in the top 10, have even more emotional undertones. For example, warm (20 mentions), caring (14), fun (11), and communicative (10) all describe a more active role of this category compared with the other categories. Thus, in contrast to the actual practices, where we did not find significant differences between

Airbnb and Uber and inconclusive differences between providers and consumers in the two surveys, the correspondence analysis suggests a clearer picture when it comes to expectations and ideals. Emotional labor seems more expected among providers than consumers and more so in the context of home-sharing (Airbnb) than ride-hailing (Uber). Of the four categories, only Airbnb hosts face clear emotional labor expectations. These differences between practices and expectations lead to an interesting tension and question: Why do users engage in emotional labor when it is not clearly desired by the transaction partner? In light of the research on emotional labor in traditional organizations and the identified risks (e.g., cynicism, service misbehavior, or turnover intention), the behavior seems not only superfluous but also potentially straining and harmful. However, to answer this question holistically we need to consider the role of the platform and ask a second question: How and why do platforms instill emotional labor practices? The next section sets out to answer this question.

## QUALITATIVE PLATFORM ANALYSIS

### *Data and Sample*

The platform analysis was carried out with the goal of identifying the narrative frames employed by platforms to suggest emotional labor practices to both consumers and providers. Within the scope of our analysis were five multi-national home-sharing platforms (Airbnb, Couchsurfing, Guest-to-Guest, Wimdu, and Papvacances), as well as three ride-sharing/ride-hailing platforms (Uber, BlaBlaCar, and Lyft). The platforms were derived from the first survey where participants were asked to name sharing platforms they had used before. Some platforms from the survey were omitted because they either no longer existed as separate organizations (e.g., mitfahrgelegenheit.de) or because they did not fit our sharing definition (e.g., professional home rentals).

### *Method*

The qualitative content analysis of policies, guidelines, and community content was carried out according to the walk-through method originally proposed for the analysis of (web) apps by Light, Burgess, and Duguay (2018). Here, two researchers assumed a user's position and systematically and forensically stepped through the various stages of the platform, mimicking a prototypical user flow which includes (1) registration, profile setup and login, (2) transactions pertaining to everyday use, and finally (3) discontinuation of use or logoff (Table 3).

During the walk-throughs, behavioral practices were collected which were either directly or indirectly suggested by the platform. Direct suggestions include content sections like "tips", "help," or "guidelines" where providers and consumers are given specific and straightforward advice on how to address or behave in certain situations. Indirect suggestions include content sections such as "blogs," "stories," or "community" where providers and consumers learn about prototypical practices through storytelling and third person anecdotes.

*Table 3.* Step-by-step Walk-through of Sharing Platforms.

| | Focus | Examples for Platform Sections | Purpose |
|---|---|---|---|
| Step 0 | Vision<br>Operating model<br>Governance | Frontpage, About us, Our Story, Our Values, and Vision | Confirmation of sharing model<br>-peer-to-peer nature<br>-joint usage of resources<br>-reputation system |
| Step 1 | Entry and profile setup | Getting Started, How it works | Collection of suggested transactional and emotional labor practices |
| Step 2 | Everyday use and tips | Help, Help-Center, Resource Center, FAQ, Tips, Guidelines, Rules | |
| Step 3 | Blog and community | Community Center, Stories, and Blog | |

*Source*: Light et al. (2016).

During the collection of practices, we employed a very broad definition of emotional labor. Practices were collected if they either directly pertained to regulating feelings and expressions (e.g., smiling to the other party) or if they demanded prior emotional involvement (e.g., preparing a handwritten note). In line with Light et al. (2016) we also contextualized the findings from the walk-through within a review of the sharing platform's vision, operating model, and governance in order to confirm the sharing model of the platform. Coding was carried out according to what Hsieh and Shannon (2005) termed "conventional content analysis" where codes are derived directly from the data during data analysis. Coding was in a first step carried out through a descriptive coding approach. As a second step, we used interpretive coding to summarize the descriptive codes and pattern coding to categorize behavioral practices identified in the data (Yin, 2002). It is important to note that the qualitative content analysis applied here goes beyond counting words and is instead about creating categories that represent similar meanings as well as identifying themes or patterns within these categories (Hsieh & Shannon, 2005; Weber, 1990).

### *Results*

In the course of the analysis, a total of 231 suggested emotional labor practices were identified, 144 (62%) of which address providers, 44 (19%) address consumers, and 43 (19%) address both providers and consumers. In the course of the analysis, seven practices had to be excluded, because they did not fit into our definition of emotional labor. For example, general rules of safety, such as "driving safely" or "not bringing a firearm to the car," did not qualify as emotional labor. The remaining practices were grouped into four overarching themes. Each theme encompasses both low-involvement practices (e.g., "welcome your guests with a smile" [Airbnb]) as well as high involvement practices (e.g., "exchange stories, songs and food" [Couchsurfing]).

The first theme encompasses practices which contribute to a *comfortable sharing environment*. These practices pertain predominantly (but not exclusively) to the home-sharing context and include adding personal touches like flowers, extra amenities, or small gifts. Airbnb, for instance, tells their hosts that guests "love special touches, like wine [...] or a handwritten note." Furthermore, they portray numerous hosts who go even further and create highly personalized greeting rituals such as baking fresh cookies to create an inviting smell or – in one particularly elaborate example – gifting flower leis in the guest's favorite color with a handwritten welcome message in the guest's language. Consumers on the other hand are often given more low-involvement advice like taking good care of the environment, tidying up after themselves when exiting a car, or leaving the environment cleaner than they found it.

The second theme *empathy* also addresses consumers and providers alike and can be seen as a "cornerstone of the guest-host relationship." Sharing platforms ask participants to listen closely to others, to read their behavioral cues, or to put themselves in their shoes. Uber tells their passengers that they should "take cues" from their drivers when deciding whether or not to engage in conversation. Empathy is further put forth as a way of approaching different viewpoints. Couchsurfing, for example, suggests that users "try to listen to and understand others with whom [they] may disagree."

*Respect* emerged as a third theme, encompassing practices such as granting personal space and refraining from asking overly personal questions. Particular emphasis is placed on respecting personal boundaries. Several platforms ask participants not to initiate romantic or sexual advances of any kind. Uber explicitly tells users to not "touch or flirt with other people in the car." Instead, participants are asked to be "personable, polite, respectful, and friendly," to smile and "dress professionally." While the respect theme pertains to both the home- and ride-sharing context equally, practices surrounding personal boundaries are more relevant in the physically confined exchanges of ride-sharing.

The fourth theme pertains to practices of *social interaction* and is the largest cluster. Here, we find many practices which are discussed in the traditional emotional labor literature, such as showing interest or building a positive and friendly rapport with the other party. The social interaction theme spans low-involvement practices, such as initiating conversation and small talk, as well as high-involvement practices, such as sharing personal information and even making friends or inviting others into the family. Practices are conveyed mostly through third person anecdotes in the format of blogs or community sites. Typical anecdotes may include instances where "strangers" met through the platform and felt "like a close circle of friends" or "like family." Social interaction is particularly pronounced in the home-sharing context, where the sharing parties are physically close to each other for an extended period of time – a proximity normally only occurring among friends and family. Emotional labor practices in this theme also encompass sharing one's interests or passions as well as "stories, songs or food."

## DISCUSSION AND CONCLUSION

In the course of this study, we have shown that emotional labor plays an important role in the sharing economy – both on the provider and on the consumer side. Our study thus contributes to the growing number of studies of work practices in the gig and economy (Aloisi, 2016; Keegan & Meijerink, 2019; Kuhn, 2016; Stanford, 2017), and specifically to an emerging research strand on emotional labor

(Raval & Dourish, 2016; Rosenblat & Stark, 2016). While the former primarily raise the issue of the nature and design of platform work necessitate emotional labor, we were primarily interesting in providing a deeper account of such practices, and an initial exploration how they are encouraged via platform providers (that themselves straddle a balancing act of guiding contributors with whom they formally they do not share an employment relationship that would justify such demands).

Our research has shown that for a sharing transaction to be considered successful, both for the provider as well as the requester side argued, participants are expected to alter their behavior in a way that emphasizes positive traits such as being friendly, kind, calm, welcoming, or polite (see Fig. 1). However, organizations in the sharing economy have only limited direct control over participants who remain independent actors within the value network. Sharing platforms approach this challenge in two steps: First, they use platform content (guidelines, community content, storytelling, etc.) to provide narratives frames of ideal sharing experiences centered around the themes of empathy, respect, socialization, and comfort (see Table 4). Second, they use platform design features such as peer-based reputation systems, notifications or rewards to encourage and enforce the desired values and practices.

***Table 4.*** Qualitative Platform Analysis and Illustrative Vignettes.

| Illustrative Vignettes (Practices Collected During Walk-Through of Homesharing and Ride-sharing Platforms) | EL-Practices (2nd Order Themes) | EL-Themes (1st Order Themes) |
|---|---|---|
| • Hosts, tidy up your space before Couchsurfers arrive. Surfers, leave it better than you found it. Keep your things in order and **always clean up after yourself** *(Couchsurfing)*<br>• And by tidying up after yourself – whether it's taking your trash home or cleaning up a spilled drink – you'll **keep the car in good condition** and ensure the next person has a pleasant ride, too *(Uber)* | Be tidy and clean | Comfortable Environment |
| • Guests enjoy touches like **flowers or extra pillows** *(Airbnb)*<br>• Check out your guest's profile before they arrive, and ask them why they're traveling. **Consider tailoring your amenities**. For example, you could offer sunscreen and earplugs for people going to a music festival *(Airbnb)* | Add personal touches | |
| • A thoughtful, **personal greeting ritual** can help you connect with guests, build trust, and make them feel excited to have arrived in your space. Guests say they love special touches, like wine, a welcome basket, or a **handwritten note** *(Airbnb)*<br>• **I always find out my guests fav color** and get a Hawaiian Lei for the female in that color … with a note written along with it in their language expressing Welcome *(Airbnb)* | Provide personal greeting | |
| • Similarly, the guest at the end of his stay will leave the house in the same conditions he found it, and will **offer a small gift** to thank the host for his hospitality *(Guest-to-Guest)*<br>• provide **bottled water, snacks, gum, mints**, and cell phone chargers *(Uber)*<br>• **A small gift of wine or flowers** makes guests happy *(Wimdu)*<br>• It is always nice to leave **a small welcoming present** for your guest. It could be a local culinary specialty or a small souvenir. They will love the surprise! *(Guest-to-Guest)* | Offer small gifts | |

*Table 4.* Qualitative Platform Analysis and Illustrative Vignettes.

| Illustrative Vignettes (Practices Collected During Walk-Through of Homesharing and Ride-sharing Platforms) | EL-Practices (2nd Order Themes) | EL-Themes (1st Order Themes) |
|---|---|---|
| • Try to **listen to and understand others** with whom you may disagree *(Couchsurfing)*<br>• "**People become more vulnerable**, and are more open to tell you things that they might be embarrassed or ashamed to tell people back home" [...] *(Airbnb)*<br>• "And **when you hear these personal tales**, you feel like you carry a piece of it in your heart" *(Airbnb)* | Listen closely | Empathy |
| • **Reading guests' behavior** is a skill it takes time to develop, but it can go a long way toward making your guest feel more comfortable and cared for *(Airbnb)* | Read behaviour | |
| • Approaching your environment with a **sense of empathy** for your guests can help you imagine how to make their experience more positive and comfortable *(Airbnb)*<br>• Empathy is the cornerstone of the host–guest relationship. When you **put yourself in your guest's shoes**, you can learn a lot about making them feel at home *(Airbnb)* | Put yourself in their shoes | |
| • **Don't touch or flirt** with other people in the car. As a reminder, Uber has a no sex rule *(Uber)*<br>• **Don't contact other members for dating**, or use the site to find sexual partners *(Couchsurfing)*<br>• [Don't be abusive...] For example, **asking overly personal questions**, using verbal threats, and making comments or gestures that are aggressive, sexual, discriminatory, or disrespectful *(Uber)* | Respect boundaries | Respect |
| • **Help with luggage and bags** when it's safe to do so *(Uber)*<br>• **Keep the conversation polite**, professional, and respectful *(Uber)*<br>• It's **common courtesy** not to shout, swear or slam the car door *(Uber)*<br>• **Welcome your guests with a smile** and half your job is done *(Airbnb)* | Be courteous | |
| • Try **asking your host about their favorite neighborhood spots**! *(Airbnb)*<br>• Opening with broad questions like, **"What brings you to the area?"** can help you identify whether the guest would be happy in your space. [...] Looking at their profile, reviews, and online presence can assist you in figuring out what to ask *(Airbnb)*<br>• If the rider is willing, engage them in a conversation. But **take your cues from them, and if they'd rather keep to themselves, respect that** *(Uber)* | Initiate conversation | Social Interaction |
| • Be it **stories, songs, food or your favorite coffee shop**, Couchsurfing is about sharing and connection *(Couchsurfing)*<br>• **Share your story** in the bio section of your profile, and get a Verified ID. Hosts prefer to know who's asking to stay with them *(Airbnb)*<br>• **Share your passions** in your profile and you're more likely to draw guests with similar tastes and interests. Providing details about your home can help guests connect with the unique accommodations and experiences that interest them *(Airbnb)* | Share personal information | |
| • Spend time with your host or surfer. **Make new friends** and help each other discover new things about the world *(Couchsurfing)*<br>• "We were hanging out in the yard with a group of guests, and **they started to feel like a circle of friends** – and it's always a great experience to have those human connections" *(Airbnb)*<br>• I actually kept in contact with one of the guys I met from the Krakow to Budapest journey and it turned out he was travelling in the UK so he came and stayed with me for a few nights and **now we're good friends**! *(BlaBlaCar)* | Make friends | |

That platforms provide such type of guidance is interesting in itself. Although it is acknowledged that platforms need to control and coordinate the efforts of their participants (Adner, 2017), the emotional practices described in our research are more in search of excellence (the equivalent of delivering five-star service), and have hitherto not been addressed as such. Research at present is more concerned with platforms (fairly or unfairly) trying to ensure a bottom-line performance. Rosenblat and Stark (2016), for instance, have discussed how Uber drivers are offered instructions on how to improve their passenger ratings and earnings, and McKeown (2016) has looked into pre-employment training for free-lancers. In their desire to avoid establishing an employment relationship, platform firms would normally not offer any further training possibilities to gig workers, withhold selected secondary benefits, and provide limited instructions for work performance (Keegan & Meijerink, 2019). The practices encouraged by platforms in our research nudge closer to a "leadership role" that platforms enact on their users (Breidbach & Brodie, 2017).

Being a more general description of user practices, there are limitations to the degree of granularity that our study may offer. For future research, it would be interesting to go into deeper depth on how platform straddle this balance between being a marketplace and encouraging their users to strive for excellence, which in our opinion quickly resembles more traditional managerial impulses. Reischauer and Mair (2018) have for instance shown in their research on community governance that platforms at least implicitly tend to nudge social relations among their users and steer users into certain directions. Likewise, research on platform governance suggests different manners of promoting and enforcing specific types of behavior among users through design incentives, network access, transaction costs, and reputation management (Choudary, 2018; Rosenblat, Levy, Barocas, & Hwang, 2017; Schreieck, Wiesche, & Krcmar, 2016; Sibai, de Valck, Farrell, & Rudd, 2015). Connecting this with research on software design and boundary objects (Ghazawneh & Henfridsson, 2013) could be an interesting way forward.

The results suggest that participants' general readiness to alter their behavior is at least in part dependent on such design mechanisms, such as the peer-based rating systems provided as hard design features by sharing platforms. This is in line with general notions of managerial control and peer-based control (Haman & Putnam, 2008). While reputation systems serve as an incentive for users to engage in emotional labor, they do not shape the actual emotional labor practices. Thus, while users may know that their behavior is being rated, and even care about achieving a good rating themselves (as was shown in the quantitative survey), they do not automatically know which behavioral practices will ultimately be regarded as excellent or "five-star-worthy" in a given context and community.

Here, users may gauge their own behavior in relation to the (assumed) attitudes, beliefs, and perceptions of prototypical users (Turner 1991; Turner, Oakes, Haslan, & McGarty, 1994). Knowledge about typical actors (e.g., excellent Airbnb hosts, excellent Uber drivers) is derived not just by often limited individual experiences (e.g., actual interactions with users), but also by narrative frames provided by platforms in the form of guidelines, help sections, or community sites. As the results of our qualitative analysis suggest, users across platforms are advised to alter their behavior, expressions and feelings in a way that they are perceived to be *emphatic, respectful, social* and creating a *welcoming* environment. Yet, the specific practices pertaining to these themes may be varying across platforms and we therefore encourage future research to take a closer look into these differences. It would be interesting to look into the development of suggested behavioral practices over time. A first impression suggests that younger and more regional platforms demand less emotional labor from their users than their more mature counterparts. Lastly, while the behaviors suggested by the sharing platform themselves may be an important factor in shaping expectations, other relevant sources should be considered as well. Namely, users may adopt behavioral practices from third parties (e.g., online forums, social media, and newspapers) or from experiences in neighboring industries (e.g., hotel or taxi industry) – either by approximation or by distinction. The sources for such knowledge go well beyond what platforms provide, such as community forums, and social media (such as specifically WhatsApp groups and YouTube), resembling a form of learning from others, variably termed friendsourcing (Bernstein, Tan, Smith, Czerwinski, & Horvitz, 2016).

Our results suggest that in the sharing economy, narrative frames (*defining good practices*) and peer-based rating systems (*rewarding good practices*) may be complementary mechanisms which incentivize users to engage in emotional labor and to actively contribute to highly personalized experiences. While this may be a good way to ensure quality among sharing offerings, it is also possible that platforms which portray increasingly elaborate practices raise entry barriers for new users. In order to get a good rating and to be considered an attractive sharing partner, it may not be sufficient anymore to "just" provide a spare bedroom or to behave like an anonymous hotel guest. Recently, Airbnb has introduced a "host-mentor program" (Airbnb, 2017) where tenured members support new hosts in reaching "their goals as a host," which suggests that becoming successful as a host has to be learned and developed over time. Future research may put a particular emphasis on perceived entry barriers and thresholds for new participants in particular sharing contexts. Costs to meet high expectations also lie with the participants: It is the hosts who provide welcome presents and homemade cookies. It is the guests who take time to engage with others and make an effort to build a connection. While traditional organizations often have coping resources in place for overwhelmed employees, participants in the sharing economy often lack such structures. It remains to be seen whether the sharing economy might continue its rise if platforms do take adequate measures to make the emotional demands reasonable and bearable.

## NOTES

1. The following five countries had more than one respondent: Armenia (2 respondents), Germany (2 respondents), Italy (3 respondents), Portugal (18 respondents), and Spain (12 respondents).
2. Based on the review by Eisinga, Te Grotenhuis, and Pelzer (2013), Cronbach's α seems not particularly suitable for two-item scales because it underestimates the true reliability. It should only be used "under rather restrictive assumptions" (p. 641).

## ACKNOWLEDGMENTS

This work was generously supported by the *Research Council of Norway* under the grants "Future Ways of Working in the Digital Economy" (Grant Number 275347) and "Fair Labor in the Digitized Economy" (Grant Number 247725) and the *EU Horizon 2020* project "Ps2Share: Participation, Privacy and Power in the Sharing Economy" (Grant Number 732117)

## REFERENCES

Adner, R. (2017). Ecosystem as structure: An actionable construct for strategy. *Journal of Management, 43*(1), 39–58.

Airbnb. (2017). What is the host mentor program? Airbnb help center. Retrieved from https://www.airbnb.ch/help/article/1149/what-is-the-host-mentor-program? Accessed on July 31, 2018.

Aloisi, A. (2016). Commoditized workers: Case study research on labor law issues arising from a set of on-demand/gig economy platforms. *Comparative Labor Law & Policy Journal, 37*(3), 653–690.

Arnould, E. J., & Thompson, C. J. (2005). Consumer culture theory (CCT): Twenty years of research. *Journal of Consumer Research, 31*(4), 868–882.

Ashforth, B. E., & Humphrey, R. H. (1993). Emotional labor in service roles: The influence of identity. *Academy of Management Review, 18*(1), 88–115.

Bardhi, F., & Eckhardt, G. M. (2012). Access-based consumption: The case of car sharing. *Journal of Consumer Research, 39*(4), 881–898.

Barker, J. R. (1993). Tightening the iron cage: Concertive control in self-managing teams. *Administrative Science Quarterly, 38*(3), 408–437.

Belk, R. W. (2013). Extended self in a digital world. *Journal of Consumer Research, 40*(3), 477–500.

Bellas, M. L. (1999). Emotional labor in academia: The case of professors. *The Annals of the American Academy of Political and Social Science, 561*(1), 96–110.

Bernstein, M. S., Tan, D., Smith, G., Czerwinski, M., & Horvitz, E. (2010). Personalization via friendsourcing. *ACM Transactions on Computer-Human Interaction, 17*(2), 1–28.

Best, R. G., Downey, R. G., & Jones, R. G. (1997, April). Incumbent perceptions of emotional work requirements. Paper presented at the12th annual conference of the Society for Industrial and Organizational Psychology, St. Louis, MO.

Bienstock, C. C., DeMoranville, C. W., & Smith, R. K. (2003). Organizational citizenship behavior and service quality. *Journal of Services Marketing, 17*(4), 357–378.

Botsman, R., & Rogers, R. (2011). *What's mine is yours: How collaborative consumption is changing the way we live*. New York, NY: Harper Business.

Breidbach, C. F., & Brodie, R. J. (2017). Engagement platforms in the sharing economy: Conceptual foundations and research directions. *Journal of Service Theory and Practice, 27*(4), 761–777.

Brook, P. (2009). In critical defence of 'emotional labour' refuting Bolton's critique of Hochschild's concept. *Work, Employment and Society, 23*(3), 531–548.

Brotheridge, C. M., & Grandey, A. A. (2002). Emotional labor and burnout: Comparing two perspectives of "people work". *Journal of Vocational Behavior, 60*(1), 17–39.

Bucher, E., Fieseler, C., Fleck, M., & Lutz, C. (2018). Authenticity and the sharing economy. *Academy of Management Discoveries, 4*(3), 294–313.

Bucher, E., Fieseler, C., & Lutz, C. (2016). What's mine is yours (for a nominal fee): Exploring the spectrum of utilitarian to altruistic motives for Internet-mediated sharing. *Computers in Human Behavior, 62*, 316–326.

Carboni, M. (2016). A new class of worker for the sharing economy. *Richmond Journal of Law & Technology, 22*(4), 11–56.

Cheng, M. (2016). Sharing economy: A review and agenda for future research. *International Journal of Hospitality Management, 57*, 60–70.

Choudary, S. P. (2018). The architecture of digital labour platforms: Policy recommendations on platform design for worker well-being. ILO Future of Work Research Paper. International Labour Organization.

Cialdini, R. B. (2003). Crafting normative messages to protect the environment. *Current Directions in Psychological Science*, *12*(4), 105–109.

Cialdini, R. B., & Trost, M. R. (1998). Social influence: Social norms, conformity, and compliance. In D. T. Gilbert, S. T. Fiske, & G. Lindzey (Eds.), *The Handbook of Social Psychology* (4th ed., Vol. 2, pp. 151–192). Boston, MA: McGraw-Hill.

Cockayne, D. G. (2016). Sharing and neoliberal discourse: The economic function of sharing in the digital on-demand economy. *Geoforum*, *77*, 73–82.

Codagnone, C., Biagi, F., & Abadie, F. (2016). The passions and the interests: Unpacking the 'sharing economy'. Digital Economy Working Paper 2016/01, Institute for Prospective Technological Studies.

Cohen, B., & Kietzmann, J. (2014). Ride on! Mobility business models for the sharing economy. *Organization & Environment*, *27*(3), 279–296.

Dahling, J. J., & Perez, L. A. (2010). Older worker, different actor? Linking age and emotional labor strategies. *Personality and Individual Differences*, *48*(5), 574–578.

Eisinga, R., Te Grotenhuis, M., & Pelzer, B. (2013). The reliability of a two-item scale: Pearson, Cronbach, or Spearman-Brown? *International Journal of Public Health*, *58*(4), 637–642.

Fisher, C. D., & Ashkanasy, N. M. (2000). The emerging role of emotions in work life: An introduction. *Journal of Organizational Behavior*, *21*(1), 123–129.

Fjeldstad, Ø. D., & Snow, C. C. (2017). Business models and organization design. *Long Range Planning*, *0*(0), 1–8.

Gandini, A. (2019). Labour process theory and the gig economy. *Human Relations*, *72*(6), 1039–1056.

Ghazawneh, A., & Henfridsson, O. (2013). Balancing platform control and external contribution in third-party development: The boundary resources model. *Information Systems Journal*, *23*(2), 173–192.

Glöss, M., McGregor, M., & Brown, B. (2016, May). Designing for labour: Uber and the on-demand mobile workforce. In *Proceedings of the 2016 CHI conference on human factors in computing systems* (pp. 1632–1643).

Goffman, E. (1959). *The presentation of self in everyday life*. New York, NY: Doubleday Anchor.

Goffman, E. (1969). *Strategic interaction*. Philadelphia, PA: University of Pennsylvania Press.

Götz, I. (2013). Encountering Arlie Hochschild's concept of "Emotional Labor" in gendered work cultures: Ethnographic approaches in the sociology of emotions and in European ethnology. In G. Koch, & S. Everke (Eds.), *Pathways to empathy: New studies on commodification, emotional labor and time binds* (pp. 183–200). Frankfurt, Germany: Campus.

Gountas, S., Ewing, M. T., & Gountas, J. I. (2007). Testing airline passengers' responses to flight attendants' expressive displays: The effects of positive affect. *Journal of Business Research*, *60*(1), 81–83.

Grandey, A. A. (2000). Emotional regulation in the workplace: A new way to conceptualize emotional labor. *Journal of Occupational Health Psychology*, *5*(1), 95.

Grandey, A. A. (2003). When "the show must go on": Surface acting and deep acting as determinants of emotional exhaustion and peer-rated service delivery. *Academy of Management Journal*, *46*(1), 86–96.

Grandey, A. A., & Melloy, R. C. (2017). The state of the heart: Emotional labor as emotion regulation reviewed and revised. *Journal of Occupational Health Psychology*, *22*(3), 407.

Greene, J. C. (2006). Toward a methodology of mixed methods social inquiry. *Research in the Schools*, *13*(1), 93–98.

Gross, J. J. (1998). The emerging field of emotion regulation: An integrative review. *Review of General Psychology*, *2*(3), 271.

Gross, J. J. (2002). Emotion regulation: Affective, cognitive, and social consequences. *Psychophysiology*, *39*(3), 281–291.

Groth, M., Hennig-Thurau, T., & Walsh, G. (2009). Customer reactions to emotional labor: The roles of employee acting strategies and customer detection accuracy. *Academy of Management Journal*, *52*(5), 958–974.

Guttentag, D. (2015). Airbnb: Disruptive innovation and the rise of an informal tourism accommodation sector. *Current Issues in Tourism*, *18*(12), 1192–1217.

Haman, M., & Putnam, L. L. (2008). In the gym: Pressure and emotional management among co-workers. In S. Fineman (Ed.), *The emotional organization: Passions and power* (pp. 61–73). Malden, MA: Blackwell.

Hamari, J., Sjöklint, M., & Ukkonen, A. (2016). The sharing economy: Why people participate in collaborative consumption. *Journal of the Association for Information Science and Technology*, *67*(9), 2047–2059.

Harris, L. C. (2002). The emotional labour of barristers: An exploration of emotional labour by status professionals. *Journal of Management Studies*, *39*(4), 553–584.

Henderson, A. (2001). Emotional labor and nursing: An under-appreciated aspect of caring work. *Nursing Inquiry*, *8*(2), 130–138.

Hochschild, A. R. (1983). *The managed heart: Commercialization of human feeling*. Berkeley, CA: University of California Press.

Horton, J., & Golden, J. (2015). *Reputation inflation: Evidence from an online labor market*. Working Paper, NYU.

Howcroft, D., & Bergvall-Kåreborn, B. (2019). A typology of crowdwork platforms. *Work, Employment and Society*, *33*(1), 21–38.

Hsieh, H-F., & Shannon, S. E. (2005). Three approaches to qualitative content analysis. *Qualitative Health Research*, *15*(9), 1277–1288.

Hülsheger, U. R., & Schewe, A. F. (2011). On the costs and benefits of emotional labor: A meta-analysis of three decades of research. *Journal of Occupational Health Psychology*, *16*, 361–389.

Humphrey, R. H., Ashforth, B. E., & Diefendorff, J. M. (2015). The bright side of emotional labor. *Journal of Organizational Behavior*, *36*(6), 749–769.

Ishii, K., & Markman, K. M. (2016). Online customer service and emotional labor: An exploratory study. *Computers in Human Behavior*, *62*, 658–665.

Jabagi, N., Croteau, A. M., Audebrand, L. K., & Marsan, J. (2019). 'Gig-workers' motivation: Thinking beyond carrots and sticks. *Journal of Managerial Psychology*, *34*(4), 192–213. doi:10.1108/JMP-06-2018-0255

Jin, M. H., & Guy, M. E. (2009). How emotional labor influences worker pride, job satisfaction, and burnout: An examination of consumer complaint workers. *Public Performance & Management Review*, *33*(1), 88–105.

Karatepe, O. M., & Aleshinloye, K. D. (2009). Emotional dissonance and emotional exhaustion among hotel employees in Nigeria. *International Journal of Hospitality Management*, *28*(3), 349–358.

Katz, D. (1964). The motivational basis of organizational behavior. *Systems Research and Behavioral Science*, *9*(2), 131–146.

Kim, N., Park, Y., & Lee, D. (2019). Differences in consumer intention to use on-demand automobile-related services in accordance with the degree of face-to-face interactions. *Technological Forecasting and Social Change*, *139*, 277–286.

Kuhn, K. M. (2016). The rise of the "Gig Economy" and implications for understanding work and workers. *Industrial and Organizational Psychology*, *9*(1), 157–162.

Kunda, G., & Van Maanen, J. (1999). Changing scripts at work: Managers and professionals. *The Annals of the American Academy of Political and Social Science*, *561*(1), 64–80.

Lee, M. K., Kusbit, D., Metsky, E., & Dabbish, L. (2015). Working with machines: The impact of algorithmic and data-driven management on human workers. In *Proceedings of the 33rd annual ACM conference on human factors in computing systems* (pp. 1603–1612).

Lee, J. J., & Ok, C. (2012). Reducing burnout and enhancing job satisfaction: Critical role of hotel employees' emotional intelligence and emotional labor. *International Journal of Hospitality Management*, *31*(4), 1101–1112.

Leidner, R. (1999). Emotional labor in service work. *The Annals of the American Academy of Political and Social Science*, *561*(1), 81–95.

LePine, J. A., Erez, A., & Johnson, D. E. (2002). The nature and dimensionality of organizational citizenship behavior: A critical review and meta-analysis. *Journal of Applied Psychology*, *87*(1), 52–65.

Light, B., Burgess, J., & Duguay, S. (2018). The walkthrough method: An approach to the study of apps. *New Media & Society*, *20*(3), 881–900.

Lindsay, R. M., Lindsay, L. M., & Irvine, V. B. (1996). Instilling ethical behaviour in organizations: a survey of Canadian companies. *Journal of Business Ethics*, *15*(4), 292–407.

Lopez, S. H. (2006). Emotional labor and organized emotional care: Conceptualizing nursing home care work. *Work and Occupations*, *33*(2), 133–160.

Lutz, C., Newlands, G., & Fieseler, C. (2018). Emotional labor in the sharing economy. In *Proceedings of the 51st Hawaii international conference on system sciences* (pp. 636–645).

Marquis, E. B., Kim, S., Alahmad, R., Pierce, C. S., & Robert, L. P. Jr. (2018, October). Impacts of perceived behavior control and emotional labor on gig Workers. In Companion of the 2018 ACM *conference on computer supported cooperative work and social computing* (pp. 241–244).

Martin, C. J., Upham, P., & Budd, L. (2015). Commercial orientation in grassroots social innovation: Insights from the sharing economy. *Ecological Economics*, *118*, 240–251.

Mayzlin, D. (2016). Managing social interactions. In Y. Bramoull´e, B. W. Rogers, & A. Galeotti (Eds.), *The Oxford handbook of the economics of networks* (pp. 792–809). Oxford: Oxford University Press.

McKeown, T. (2016). A consilience framework: Revealing hidden features of the independent contractor. *Journal of Management & Organization*, *22*(6), 779–796.

Meijerink, J., & Keegan, A. (2019). Conceptualizing human resource management in the gig economy. *Journal of Managerial Psychology*, *34*(4), 214–232.

Möhlmann, M., & Zalmanson, L. (2017, 10–13 December). Hands on the wheel: Navigating algorithmic management and Uber drivers' autonomy. In *Proceedings of the international conference on information systems*, Seoul, South Korea (pp. 1–17). Atlanta, GA: Association for Information Systems - AIS.

Morris, J. A., & Feldman, D. C. (1996). The dimensions, antecedents, and consequences of emotional labor. *Academy of Management Review*, *21*(4), 986–1010.

Morris, J. A., & Feldman, D. C. (1997). Managing emotions in the workplace. *Journal of Managerial Issues*, *9*(3), 257–274.

Mowday, R. T., Steers, R. M., & Porter, L. W. (1979). The measurement of organizational commitment. *Journal of Vocational Behavior*, *14*(2), 224–247.

Murillo, D., Buckland, H., & Val, E. (2017). When the sharing economy becomes neoliberalism on steroids: Unravelling the controversies. *Technological Forecasting and Social Change*, *125*, 66–76.

Newlands, G., Lutz, C., & Fieseler, C. (2017a). Power in the sharing economy. SSRN Electronic Journal. Retrieved from https://papers.ssrn.com/sol3/papers.cfm?abstract_id=2960938

Newlands, G., Lutz, C., & Fieseler, C. (2017b). European perspectives on power in the sharing economy. SSRN Electronic Journal. Retrieved from https://papers.ssrn.com/sol3/papers.cfm?abstract_id=3046473

Newlands, G., Lutz, C., & Fieseler, C. (2018). Collective action and provider classification in the sharing economy. *New Technology, Work and Employment*, *33*(3), 250–267.

Newlands, G., Lutz, C., & Fieseler, C. (2019). The conditioning function of rating mechanisms for consumers in the sharing economy. *Internet Research*. *29*(5), 1090–1108. doi:10.1108/INTR-03-2018-0134

Ogbonna, E., & Wilkinson, B. (1990). Corporate strategy and corporate culture: The view from the checkout. *Personnel Review*, *19*(4), 9–15.

Organ, D. W. (1988). *Organizational citizenship behavior: The good soldier syndrome*. Lexington, KY: Books/DC Heath and Com.

Otley, D. T., & Berry, A. J. (1980). Control, organization, and accounting. *Accounting Organizations, and Society*, *5*, 231–246.

Parrott, W. G., & Schulkin, J. (1993). Neuropsychology and the cognitive nature of the emotions. *Cognition & Emotion*, *7*(1), 43–59.

Peticca-Harris, A., deGama, N., & Ravishankar, M. N. (2018). Postcapitalist precarious work and those in the 'drivers' seat: Exploring the motivations and lived experiences of Uber drivers in Canada. *Organization*. doi:10.1177/1350508418757332

Pierce, J. L. (1999). Emotional labor among paralegals. *The Annals of the American Academy of Political and Social Science*, *561*(1), 127–142.

Pugh, S. D. (2001). Service with a smile: Emotional contagion in the service encounter. *Academy of Management Journal*, *44*(5), 1018–1027.

Raval, N., & Dourish, P. (2016, 27 February – 2 March). Standing out from the crowd: Emotional labor, body labor, and temporal labor in ridesharing. In *Proceedings of the 19th ACM conference on computer-supported cooperative work & social computing*, San Francisco, California (pp. 97–107). New York, NY: ACM.

Reischauer, G., & Mair, J. (2018). How organizations strategically govern online communities: Lessons from the sharing economy. *Academy of Management Discoveries*, *4*(3), 220–247.

Rogers, B. (2016). Employment rights in the platform economy: Getting back to basics. *Harvard Law & Policy Review*, *10*, 479.

Rosenblat, A., Levy, K. E., Barocas, S., & Hwang, T. (2017). Discriminating tastes: Uber's customer ratings as vehicles for workplace discrimination. *Policy & Internet*, *9*(3), 256–279.

Rosenblat, A., & Stark, L. (2016). Algorithmic labor and information asymmetries: A case study of Uber's drivers. *International Journal of Communication*, *10*(1), 3758–3784.

Schreieck, M., Wiesche, M., & Krcmar, H. (2016, June 12–15). Design and governance of platform ecosystems – Key concepts and issues for future research. In 2016 Twenty-fourth European conference on information systems, İstanbul, Turkey (pp. 1–20).

Schultz, W. P., Khazian, A. M., & Zaleski, A. C. (2008). Using normative social influence to promote conservation among hotel guests. *Social Influence*, *3*(1), 4–23.

Sibai, O., de Valck, K., Farrell, A. M., & Rudd, J. M. (2015). Social control in online communities of consumption: A framework for community management. *Psychology & Marketing*, *32*(3), 250–264.

Smith, C. A., Organ, D. W., & Near, J. P. (1983). Organizational citizenship behavior: Its nature and antecedents. *Journal of Applied Psychology*, *68*(4), 653.

Smorto, G. (2018). Regulating (and self-regulating) the sharing economy in Europe: An overview. In M. Bruglieri (Ed.), *Multidisciplinary design of sharing services* (pp. 111–126). Cham, Switzerland: Springer.

Stanford, J. (2017). The resurgence of gig work: Historical and theoretical perspectives. *The Economic and Labour Relations Review*, *28*(3), 382–401.

Stark, L. (2016). Recognizing the role of emotional labor in the on-demand economy. *Harvard Business Review*. Retrieved from https://hbr.org/2016/08/recognizing-the-role-of-emotional-labor-in-the-on-demand-economy. Accessed on November 17, 2017.

Sutherland, W., & Jarrahi, M. H. (2018). The sharing economy and digital platforms: A review and research agenda. *International Journal of Information Management*, *43*, 328–341.

Tang, C., Seal, C. R., Naumann, S. E., & Miguel, K. (2013). Emotional labor: The role of employee acting strategies on customer emotional experience and subsequent buying decisions. *International Review of Management and Marketing*, *3*(2), 50.

Tracy, S. J. (2000). Becoming a character for commerce: Emotion labor, self-subordination, and discursive construction of identity in a total institution. *Management Communication Quarterly*, *14*(1), 90–128.

Tsai, W. C., & Huang, Y. M. (2002). Mechanisms linking employee affective delivery and customer behavioral intentions. *Journal of Applied Psychology*, *87*(5), 1001.

Turner, J. C. (1991). *Social influence*. Milton Keynes: Open University Press.

Turner, J. C., Oakes, P. J., Haslam, S. A., & McGarty, C. (1994). Self and collective: Cognition and social context. *Personality and Social Psychology Bulletin*, *20*(5), 454–463.

Turner, J. C., & Reynolds, K. J. (2011). Self-categorization theory. In *Handbook of theories in social psychology* (Vol. 2, pp. 399–417).

Van Doorn, N. (2017). Platform labor: On the gendered and racialized exploitation of low-income service work in the 'on-demand' economy. *Information, Communication & Society*, *20*(6), 898–914.

Weber, R. P. (1990). *Basic content analysis*. Newbury Park, CA: Sage Publications.

Wentrup, R., Nakamura, H. R., & Ström, P. (2019). Uberization in Paris: The issue of trust between a digital platform and digital workers. *Critical Perspectives on International Business*, *15*(1), 20–41.

Wharton, A. S. (1993). The affective consequences of service work: Managing emotions on the job. *Work and Occupations*, *20*(2), 205–232.

Williams, C. (2003). Sky service: The demands of emotional labour in the airline industry. *Gender, Work & Organization*, *10*(5), 513–550.

Yin, R. K. (2002). *Case study research: Design and methods*. Thousand Oaks, CA: SAGE Publications.

Zapf, D. (2002). Emotion work and psychological well-being: A review of the literature and some conceptual considerations. *Human Resource Management Review*, *12*(2), 237–268.

# APPENDIX A: DESCRIPTIVE STATISTICS

| Construct<br>*Items* | Survey 1 | Survey 2 |
|---|---|---|
| *Emotional Labour* | **3.06 (0.72)** | **3.27 (0.91)** |
| Express feelings of sympathy | 3.17 (1.00) | 3.18 (1.28) |
| Express friendly emotions | 3.50 (0.97) | 4.05 (1.08) |
| Hide your disapproval | 2.76 (0.95) | 2.88 (1.30) |
| Hide your annoyance | 2.80 (0.97) | 2.96 (1.28) |
| *Volunteering* | **2.78 (1.03)** | **3.18 (1.09)** |
| I do volunteer work to help people in need | 2.79 (1.29) | 3.24 (1.32) |
| I get involved in issues such as health or safety, that affect my community | 2.94 (1.15) | 3.17 (1.21) |
| I work with a group to solve a problem in the community where I live | 2.61 (1.20) | 3.12 (1.28) |
| *Materialism* | **3.01 (0.95)** | **3.23 (1.04)** |
| I'd be happier if I could afford to buy more things | 3.43 (1.13) | 3.56 (1.19) |
| I like a lot of luxury in my life | 2.91 (1.19) | 3.12 (1.27) |
| I admire people who own expensive homes, cars and clothes | 2.68 (1.18) | 3.01 (1.34) |
| *Frequency of Use* (1–9 ascending frequency scale) | **3.33 (1.90)** | **5.08 (2.30)** |
| *Motives* | **2.85 (0.79)** | **2.99 (0.95)** |
| Financial | 3.70 (1.05) | 3.89 (1.06) |
| Social | 2.40 (1.14) | 2.50 (1.34) |
| Fun | 2.79 (1.15) | 3.00 (1.34) |
| Social responsibility | 2.48 (1.13) | 2.55 (1.40) |
| *Positive Rating System Assessment* | **3.54 (0.73)** | **3.69 (0.94)** |
| The rating/review system is fair | 3.47 (0.82) | 3.63 (1.02) |
| The rating/review system works well | 3.62 (0.82) | 3.74 (1.04) |
| *Negative Rating System Assessment* | **2.70 (0.74)** | **2.70 (0.88)** |
| The rating/review system takes into account elements beyond my control | 3.19 (0.85) | 3.24 (1.10) |
| The rating/review system should be removed | 2.20 (1.04) | 2.16 (1.21) |
| *Critical Ratings* | **2.86 (0.72)** | **3.49 (0.91)** |
| Consumers/providers rate me too harshly | 2.56 (0.97) | 3.14 (1.20) |
| The rating/review systems gives consumers/providers power over me | 3.09 (0.94) | 3.68 (1.12) |
| Consumers/providers have unrealistic expectations | 2.93 (0.89) | 3.64 (1.21) |
| *N* | **985** | **726** |

Arithmetic means are displayed (standard deviations in brackets); Arithmetic mean for the overall factor (in bold) is the arithmetic mean of the factor variable. The factor variable is calculated as the sum of all values of the respective items divided by the number of items; Unless otherwise specified, all items were assessed on 1–5 Likert scales.

# APPENDIX B: CORRELATIONS

*Table B1. Correlations in Survey 1*

| Construct | EL | VO | MA | FoU | MO | PR | NR |
|---|---|---|---|---|---|---|---|
| VO | 0.16*** | | | | | | |
| MA | 0.17*** | 0.10** | | | | | |
| FoU | 0.20*** | 0.24*** | 0.24*** | | | | |
| MO | 0.13*** | 0.27*** | 0.24*** | 0.31*** | | | |
| PR | 0.23*** | 0.07 | 0.09** | 0.05 | 0.17*** | | |
| NR | 0.16*** | 0.17*** | 0.18** | 0.25*** | 0.19*** | −0.14*** | |
| CR | 0.21*** | 0.18*** | 0.22*** | 0.22*** | 0.19*** | −0.14*** | 0.50*** |

* $p<0.05$, ** $p<0.01$, *** $p<0.001$.
EL: Emotional labor; VO: Volunteering; MA: Materialism; FoU: Frequency of use; MO: Motives; PR: Positive rating system assessment; NR: Negative rating system assessment; CR: Critical ratings; Pairwise correlations between the factor vari ables (as per the table note in Appendix A) are displayed; $N=726$.

*Table B2. Correlations in Survey 2*

| Construct | EL | VO | MA | FoU | MO | PR | NR |
|---|---|---|---|---|---|---|---|
| VO | 0.16*** | | | | | | |
| MA | 0.17*** | 0.07 | | | | | |
| FoU | 0.27*** | 0.12*** | 0.21*** | | | | |
| MO | 0.19*** | 0.31*** | 0.32*** | 0.35*** | | | |
| PR | 0.04 | 0.04 | 0.08* | −0.18*** | 0.13*** | | |
| NR | 0.18*** | 0.12** | 0.12** | 0.24*** | 0.20*** | −0.24*** | |
| CR | 0.00 | 0.02 | 0.07 | −0.21*** | −0.02 | 0.09* | −0.00 |

* $p<0.05$, ** $p<0.01$, *** $p<0.001$
EL: Emotional labor; VO: Volunteering; FoU: Frequency of use; MO: Motives; PR: Positive rating system assessment; NR: Negative rating system assessment; CR: Critical ratings; Pairwise correlations between the factor variables (as per the table note in Appendix A) are displayed; $N=985$.

# AN INSTITUTIONAL LOGICS PERSPECTIVE ON THE GIG ECONOMY

Koen Frenken, Taneli Vaskelainen, Lea Fünfschilling and Laura Piscicelli

## ABSTRACT

*We witness rising tensions between online gig-economy platforms, incumbent firms, regulators, and labor unions. In this chapter, we use the framework of institutional logics as an analytical lens and scheme to understand the fundamental institutional challenges prompted by the advent of the online gig economy. We view gig-economy platforms as corporations that organize and self-regulate markets. In doing so, they span two parallel markets: the market for platforms competing to provide intermediation services and the market for the self-employed competing on platforms to provide peer-to-peer services. Self-regulation by platforms also weakens the traditional roles of the state. While the corporation and market logics empower the platform, they weaken self-employed suppliers as platforms' design constrain suppliers to grow into a full-fledged business by limiting their entrepreneurial freedom. At the same time, current labor law generally does not classify suppliers as employees of the platform company, which limits the possibility to unionize. The current resolutions to this institutional misalignment are sought in "band aid solutions" at the level of sectors. Instead, as we argue, macro-institutional reform may be needed to re-institutionalize gig work into established institutional logics.*

**Keywords:** Platform; gig economy; sharing economy; institution; regulation; labor union

**Theorizing the Sharing Economy: Variety and Trajectories of New Forms of Organizing**
**Research in the Sociology of Organizations, Volume 66, 83–105**

**ISSN: 0733-558X/doi:10.1108/S0733-558X20200000066005**

## INTRODUCTION

Digital platforms are rapidly changing the economy, and their expected impact has been compared to the industrial revolution (Kenney & Zysman, 2016). In a generic sense, platforms have been defined as infrastructures mediating social and economic interactions online (Kenney & Zysman, 2016). Strikingly, platforms have enabled individuals to connect and exchange directly, by-passing large corporations and traditional intermediaries. Such platforms are sometimes called "peer-to-peer" platforms and have caused disruption in the music (e.g., Napster), retail (e.g., eBay), and media sectors (e.g., Facebook). More recently, we witnessed the rise of "sharing economy" platforms enabling individuals to rent out homes, cars, and other consumer items (e.g., Airbnb, Drivy, and Peerby) and "gig economy" platforms where individuals provide personal services like deliveries, cleaning jobs, and taxi rides (e.g., Deliveroo, Helpling, and Uber). With the advent of these platforms, a significant share of work done by traditional businesses and their employees is substituted by self-employed offering their services directly to clients, supported by a platform.

While digital platforms have raised controversy in virtually all sectors they entered (Kenney & Zysman, 2016; Schor, 2016), the gig economy is currently mostly debated as tensions rise between gig-economy platforms, incumbent firms, regulators, and labor unions. These tensions emerged as platforms have been able to partly neutralize the role of unions and state regulations due to unclear legal jurisdictions regarding labor rights and platform responsibilities. At the same time, transactions remain hidden for tax agencies as platforms are unwilling to share personal data for privacy reasons. While governments try to respond with new regulations to the rise of platforms and their intended consequences, their solutions remain ad hoc and sector-specific. Given the strong position of gig economy platforms in broad sectors like transportation and domestic services, and their growing presence in other sectors including education, journalism, care, and legal sectors (van Dijck, Poell, & de Waal, 2018), a more comprehensive approach to platforms seems desirable without denying sectoral and national specificities.

However, considering the growth and impact of gig-economy platforms, the phenomenon remains surprisingly undertheorized. Some institutional scholars have called for new frameworks as to uncover the platforms' institutional underpinnings and how these affect the behavior of platforms and their users (Grinevich, Huber, Karataş-Özkan, & Yavuz, 2019; Hinings, Gegenhuber, & Greenwood, 2018; Mair & Reischauer, 2017; Vaskelainen & Münzel, 2018). There is also indicative evidence that the way the platform gets regulated is highly contingent on local institutions (Thelen, 2018; Uzunca, Rigtering, & Ozcan, 2018). A focus on the institutional changes that platforms bring about thus seems an apt one.

In order to make sense of the changes prompted by gig-economy platforms, we will draw on the framework of institutional logics as laid out by Thornton, Ocasio, and Lounsbury (2012). We will particularly focus on the changing nature of the market logic and the corporation logic in the era of the platform economy.

As gig-economy platforms are themselves corporations that organize markets, they reconfigure the institutional logics of both the market and the corporation in a new way. At the same time, they deal with gig workers as self-employed business, yet constrain them in their entrepreneurial freedoms. An institutional logics perspective thus allows us to conceptualize an eventual new platform-based rationale of economic exchange and enables us to trace how it breaks with many of the established ways built up in the past and why the state logic gets weakened in the process.

We start by outlining the essence of the institutional logics approach, focusing in particular on the traditionally dominant rationale of economic exchange centered on institutions, such as the market, the corporation, and the state. We then go on to show how gig-economy platforms disrupt these institutional settings and, as a consequence, are perceived as illegitimate. Where relevant, we will also discuss differences and similarities between gig-economy and sharing-economy platforms (mainly referring to the case of Airbnb). Finally, we lay out four scenarios of how the platforms could gain legitimacy, either as a result of the platforms aligning with existing institutional configurations or by societal institutional arrangements changing in such a way as to accommodate the platforms.

## INSTITUTIONAL LOGICS

Institutional logics are defined as

> the socially constructed, historical patterns of material practices, assumptions, values, beliefs, and rules by which individuals produce and reproduce their material subsistence, organize time and space, and provide meaning to their social reality. (Thornton & Ocasio, 1999, p. 804)

It is one of the many concepts found in organizational institutionalism to describe and make sense of an organization's environment. It depicts the institutional setting that shapes actors' behavior and the diffusion of practices. One of the seminal arguments in organizational institutionalism is that organizations need to adhere to the expectations of their immediate surroundings and of modern society as a whole if they are to survive (DiMaggio & Powell, 1983; Meyer & Rowan, 1977). Legitimacy, and not merely efficiency, becomes the explanatory variable for organizational survival. Organizations must be legitimate to key stakeholders both socio-politically and cognitively (Aldrich & Fiol, 1994). Socio-political legitimacy refers to an organization being perceived as appropriate and proper with regard to laws and norms in its environment. Cognitive legitimacy refers to the outputs or the form of the organization being understood and well known. If the key stakeholders do not understand the organization, the latter might fail even though its operations would be socio-politically proper and efficient.

In order to determine the relevant content of this socially constructed system, institutional scholars have brought forward the concept of "organizational field." Over the years, fields have been defined in various ways, but in general they represent "a recognized area of institutional life" (DiMaggio & Powell, 1983, p. 148) for a certain set of actors that interact on a regular basis with each other and, in doing so, contribute to a common meaning system. Fields could, for instance, form around specific industries (e.g., automotive industry or the energy sector), professions (e.g., engineers or doctors), social movements (e.g., labor rights), or thematic areas (e.g., sustainability or equality) (Wooten & Hoffman, 2008; Zietsma, Groenewegen, Logue, & Hinings, 2017). Fields represent the relevant, socially constructed institutional environment that guides actors' behavior and sense-making in those areas.

Earlier scholarly contributions mainly focused on studying the effects of organizational fields on actors, pointing toward isomorphism among actors caused by various coercive, normative, and mimetic institutional pressures (DiMaggio & Powell, 1983; Meyer & Rowan, 1977). However, the institutional content per se and its origins were often left aside. The question of why fields are dominated by some institutions and not others was largely ignored or, how Friedland and Alford (1991, p. 244) put it: "… they do not have the theoretical tools by which to understand the institutional content whose diffusion they do analyze …." The idea of institutional logics was thus developed with the purpose of specifying the institutional content of an organization's environment – not by referring to some form of technical functionality or organizational interests and power struggles as previously done, but rather by acknowledging overarching, societal institutions that affect all fields to different degrees.

Friedland and Alford (1991) argued that also interests, power structures, or notions of uncertainty and functionality are institutionally embedded: individual and organizational perception, sense-making and agency is always shaped by macro-level, societal institutions. The authors argued that the most important institutions of contemporary Western societies come with a distinct "central logic – a set of material practices and symbolic constructions – which constitutes its organizing principles and which is available to organizations and individuals to elaborate" (Friedland & Alford, 1991, p. 248). These overarching institutional orders included the capitalist market, bureaucratic state, democracy, nuclear family, and Christian religion.[1] This list was later complemented and modified by Thornton (2004) and Thornton et al. (2012) by adding the professions, the corporation, and the community as institutions with a distinct logic, resulting in seven institutional logics: family, religion, state, market, profession, corporation, and community. A similar, yet distinct framework was developed by Boltanski and Thévenot (2006 [1991]) who instead speak of six orders of worth (inspired, domestic, fame, civic, market, and industrial), which actors invoke in settlements of dispute or controversy (Boltanski & Thévenot, 1999; Patriotta, Gond, & Schultz, 2011).[2]

All of the institutional logics brought forward by Thornton et al. (2012) are ideal types (Doty & Glick, 1994). They are simplified theoretical constructions with clear boundaries and categories that sharpen the interpretation of cultural content. This also means that the ideal types do not represent a single unified logic present in the society, nor should a logic be understood as static

(Boltanski & Thévenot, 1999). For example, nouvelle cuisine arose to challenge classical cuisine as the dominant professional institutional logic in the French gastronomy market (Rao, Monin, & Durand, 2003), and new public management has affected classical bureaucratic principles but without substituting the dominant state logic as such (Meyer & Hammerschmid, 2006).

Each of the main institutions come with a distinct logic, that is, a specific institutional order containing different sources of legitimacy and identity, different basis of norms and strategy, and unique control mechanisms (Table 1). For example, the basis of strategy in family logic is increasing family honor, in state logic it is increasing community good, and in market logic it is increasing profits (Thornton et al., 2012). The assumption then is that actors can draw from these societal-level institutional orders, which get reconfigured and materialized in different organizational fields.

In order to achieve legitimacy, organizations are thus expected to conform to their institutional setting, that is, the institutional logics present in the fields they are embedded in. For example, the CEO of a company replacing jobs by robots in the workplace would probably get very different reactions depending on whether he or she worked in a private company (market logic), state-owned company (state logic), or family owned company (family logic). A CEO of a private company would most likely be applauded by the shareholders because downsizing is usually linked to increased profits (Greenwood, Díaz, Li, & Lorente, 2010). However, the CEO of a family owned company that believes in traditions and long-term employment might have difficulties with the same move because it might stain the family honor (Greenwood et al., 2010). In a state-owned company, a mere profit motive might not be an adequate reason for layoffs because the company would be expected to contribute to community good by employing people within its home country (Greenwood et al., 2010; Greve & Zhang, 2017).

Fields thus differ regarding the dominance of different institutional logics and the degree to which different logics co-exist and intertwine (Greenwood, Raynard, Kodeih, Micelotta, & Lounsbury, 2011), but the institutional repertoire they have to make sense of reality and adjust their behavior is principally the same. Much of recent research on organizational fields has thus been centered on understanding the composition of different institutional logics within fields and their degree

***Table 1.*** Institutional Logic Ideal Types.

| Logic | Family | Community | Religion | State | Market | Profession | Corporation |
|---|---|---|---|---|---|---|---|
| Source of legitimacy | Loyalty | Reciprocity | Faith | Democracy | Share price | Expertise | Market power |
| Source of authority | Parent | Ideology | Charisma | Bureaucracy | Shareholder | Professional association | Board of directors |
| Basis of strategy | Honor | Status | Symbolism | Community good | Profit | Reputation | Size |

*Source*: Adapted from Thornton et al. (2012).

of elaboration and coherence (Zietsma et al., 2017). Institutional complexity and institutional pluralism have become central themes in institutional theory to explain organizational behavior and field-level institutional change (Greenwood et al., 2011; Raynard, 2016; Vermeulen, Zietsma, Greenwood, & Langley, 2016). The main aim of this research is to analyze organizational behavior when confronted with heterogeneous institutional demands, mostly stemming from different institutional logics. The assumption is that being exposed to institutional complexity might open up windows of opportunity for agency, innovation, and change because actors can draw from and refer to different institutional logics (Greenwood et al., 2011; Raynard, 2016). Field-level change is thus ultimately seen as a consequence of which and how many different institutional logics are institutionalized to what degree (Zietsma et al., 2017).

The effect of complexity in institutional logics and their reconfiguration process are thus well-studied phenomena (Lounsbury, 2002, 2007; Reay & Hinings, 2005). Most often, however, these studies focus on field-level changes of institutional logics, that is, in specific markets or industries, and do not investigate the reconfiguration of the actual societal-level institutional orders. In the coming sections, we argue that the advent of platforms holds the potential to cause a *macro*-level change by reconfiguring the essence of the institutions of the market, the corporation and the state, and their interrelation.

## THE HISTORICAL CONFIGURATION OF CORPORATION, MARKET, AND STATE LOGICS

The capitalist market is one of the five seminal institutions brought forth by Friedland and Alford (1991) in their first essay presenting the institutional logics. Companies are embedded in market logics through their outputs. The products and services are given a monetary price and the customers do their purchasing decisions based on whether they perceive that they get enough value for the price. A well-working market will then pick the winning companies, who produce most value for money. These companies consequently grow in size as the customer spending accrues to them.

Besides market logic, all growth aspiring companies are also embedded in the corporation logic. Indeed, an important addendum by Thornton (2004) and Thornton et al. (2012) to the original institutional logics framework of Friedland and Alford (1991) has been to separate the corporation logic from the market logic. This addendum is consonant with a similar distinction made by Boltanski and Thévenot (2006 [1991]) between the industrial order and the market order. The top management embedded in the corporation logic usually bases its strategy on the pursuit of growth due to the fact that the legitimacy is based on the market position of the firm: the legitimacy of the players is measured by revenue and market share (Thornton, 2004). Even though the word corporation refers to a type of organization, Thornton et al. (2012) argue that it is an institutional innovation as well: limited liability, assimilation of capital and ability to engage in contracts make it a separate institutional order that is governed by its own rules and norms. Employees of a modern corporation, then, do not only derive their identity from the professional logics that they represent, but also from their role and status in the corporate bureaucracy (Thornton et al., 2012). Also note that the routines and practices of the corporations do not stem only from the employees' professions, but are saved in the collective memory of the corporation, both in tacit and in codified (and increasingly algorithmic) forms (Nelson & Winter, 1982).

Because of the significance of publicly traded companies in organizing the society, the institutions of the corporation and the market, even if analytically separate, are tightly intertwined. Yet, the corporation and market logics are not inherently aligned. In this context, it is helpful to distinguish between the product market logic and the capital market logic. Many companies are embedded both in product markets where they sell their goods and services and in capital markets where they raise capital for investment. Investors do not value companies primarily by the goods or service they produce, but perceive them as profit-maximizing entities that produce cash flows for their shareholders. As extensively theorized in various disciplines, the key contradiction between the capital market logic and the corporation logic can be conceived as a principal-agent problem that is managed through corporate governance (Greve & Zhang, 2017). In the context of corporations, this refers to shareholders (principals) hiring the managers (agents) to manage the companies they own. The principal-agent problems stem from information asymmetry between the shareholders and the managers: the shareholders have large stakes in how the company is operated, but not the knowledge of the day-to-day operations. The management, on the other hand, possesses this knowledge, but without governance mechanisms (e.g., stock options) it does not necessarily have as high stakes in the success of the company. This may lead to managers following primarily the corporation logic of growing the company, for example, by new business development, geographical market expansion, and mergers & acquisitions. This growth orientation, however, may well conflict with the maximization of profit *casu quo* shareholder value characterizing the market logic. For example, a well-researched finding holds that most mergers seem to have detrimental effect on the performance of the two companies (Dickerson, Gibson, & Tsakalotos, 1997; Tuch & O'Sullivan, 2007).

Over time, the capital market logic has been gaining dominance over the corporation logic. The locus of power within corporations has slowly moved from outputs to customers to cash flows to shareholders: the first power shift moved from engineering to sales and later from sales to the finance departments (Fligstein, 1993). For most of the twentieth century, the shareholders worked mainly as passive observers of the corporations: if they were dissatisfied with the management of a corporation they reacted by selling its shares from the portfolio (Green, Babb, & Alpaslan, 2008; Ocasio & Radoynovska, 2016). However, this changed during the 1970s and 1980s. The shareholders took a more active role and changed boards with hostile takeovers when they were dissatisfied with the management of the company (Green et al., 2008). In addition, by rewarding managers not only by wages but also by shares, interests of managers and shareholders could be further aligned.

The strong alignment between the market and the corporation logic should also be understood with reference to the institution of the state. States stabilize markets to enhance market exchange by enforcing property rights and establishing governance structures and rules for exchange (Fligstein, 1996). In a similar vein, also the institution of the corporation is strongly aligned with the state. As a nexus of the interest of various stakeholders (consumers, shareholders, labor, and environmentalists), the modern corporation is institutionalized by laws to protect the rights of consumers, shareholders, labor, and nature, respectively. Such laws pertaining to markets and corporations are mostly defined at the national level, and differences among countries can aptly be described as "varieties of capitalism" (Hall & Soskice, 2001). At the same time, national governments have harmonized national legislations in multi-lateral arrangement as well, especially regarding trade and, to a lesser extent, labor and environmental policies.

Generally, the institutional logics approach assumes that states are interested in the well-being of their citizens (Thornton et al., 2012). The states enforce this through command-and-control frameworks that are based on the implemented laws (Lee & Lounsbury, 2015). In terms of the relationship between the state, the corporation and the market, two legal frameworks are especially important when it comes to platforms: labor laws and anti-trust laws. Labor laws are there to protect workers from exploitation from the corporations, who are usually more powerful in the negotiations than individual employees. For example, laws regarding minimum wages and statutory pauses ensure that corporations do not exploit the workers, and laws regarding health insurances guarantee that the employees do not fall outside the safety nets of the society. The latter also make sure that corporations foster the well-being of citizens, a cornerstone of the state logic. Anti-trust laws are needed to guarantee that competition in the product and service markets is based on independent price-setting without collusion. Crucially, a historical exemption was granted to labor, which is allowed to unionize for collective bargaining of wages, labor conditions, and social security benefits.

## INSTITUTIONAL MISALIGNMENTS IN THE PLATFORM ECONOMY

Using the framework of institutional logics as outlined above and focusing on the institutional alignment between market, corporate, and state logics as they have become dominant over the past 50 years in the West, we can now assess the rise of online platforms through an institutional lens. It can first be noted that, in an important sense, online platforms epitomize the marketization trend. Few exceptions aside (e.g., Wikipedia and PLoS), platforms are generally run as corporations that compete on intermediation markets as well as on markets for (venture) capital and maximize shareholder value. Compared to most corporations, one may also argue that platforms suffer relatively little from the tension between the profit interest of shareholders and the growth interest of managers. For one, managers often have a significant share in the company. Second, in the platform economy, the growth objective pursued by managers is fully compatible with the profit objective of shareholders, because the value of platforms in terms of expected future profits is primarily driven by the size of the network of users. The more users are active on a particular platform, the more they profit from network externalities stemming from the size of the user group, the higher the commission that users are willing to pay (Rysman, 2009).

While being a corporation, platforms organize markets. That is, platforms do not produce any particular good or service, but rather provide a digital infrastructure that allows peers to trade goods and services. It should be emphasized that such online, peer-to-peer marketplaces are not "free markets." Platforms to a great extent moderate transactions by categorizing items, matching supply and demand, and recommending or setting prices. What is more, a platform can police who is allowed to transact on the platform in the first place (Kirchner & Schüßler, 2018; McKee, 2017). Thus, the intermediation service provided by the platform can be understood as what economists call a "club good" as their service is non-rival (as a public good) but nevertheless excludable (as a private good). The platform acts as a self-regulatory body excluding participants who do not qualify according to the platform's (implicit) criteria. Often, a quality assessment is made based on negative reviews or ratings. Thus, platforms do not necessarily apply ex ante state or professional regulations regarding licenses, quality standards, or diplomas, but rely primarily on participants' mutual assessments in the form of reviews and ratings ex post. From an institutional logics perspective, then, a platform unites functions previously distributed among the institutional logics of the corporation, the market, the profession, and the state in a single organizational form.

### *Parallel Market Logics*

Having said this, we put forward the thesis that online platforms have created new and fundamental contradictions between the corporation logic and the market logic. The root of this contradiction lays in the nature of services that platforms offer. Instead of employing capital and labor to produce goods and services, platform organize digital marketplaces to enable two or more sides to exchange goods and services among themselves ("peer-to-peer"). This implies that the platform economy is characterized by two *parallel market logics*. First, there exists competition by platforms on the market for intermediation services (e.g., eBay vs Amazon, Uber vs Lyft, Airbnb vs Booking.com). Here, platforms compete for dominance by aggressive growth strategies funded by venture capital. Hence, this market is primarily driven by the capital market logic even if their growth in turn depends on the satisfaction of both suppliers and consumers making use of a platform. Second, platforms organize a digital marketplace where providers (sellers on eBay, home owners on Airbnb, drivers on Uber) compete on platforms to reach out to end consumers. Clearly, this market operates according to the product market logic, with providers being paid and reviewed by consumers according to their perceived quality.

Although the two parallel markets are different and distinct, they are intrinsically tied to one another by governance. The market for intermediation services can be considered as "a market for producing a market." Platforms produce a market primarily by algorithmic matching, (dynamic) price-setting and actively monitoring of providers by tracking technology and customer reviews. In this way, platforms lower transaction costs in peer-to-peer markets between strangers (Frenken & Schor, 2017). We can characterize peer-to-peer platforms by using the five governance principles that apply to markets as proposed by Ahrne, Aspers, and Brunsson (2015): deciding on membership, governing rules, monitoring rule compliance, sanctioning non-compliance, and establishing hierarchy. Whereas historically the control of these governance principles was delegated to different organizations, digital platforms may control all of them (Kirchner & Schüßler, 2018). For example, with ride-hailing platforms such as Uber or Lyft, all of these roles are performed by the platform: they decide who can join, they decide the rules that should be followed, and they can dismiss drivers that do not follow the rules. It is also important to note here that as platforms assume such a strong self-regulatory role, they diminish the need for state regulations or professional organizations.

Arguably, even if self-employed individuals are subject to more competition among themselves than platforms are among themselves, the market *logic* applies more to platforms in their race to dominate the market in order to create shareholder value than to the self-employed who operate in a highly surveilled, regulated, and constrained online environment. This is why some legal scholars have argued that, by exercising control over paid self-employed, a platform should be classified as an employer under current labor law (De Stefano, 2016; Sachs, 2015). Despite platforms indeed exercise control by algorithmically allocating assignments, monitoring quality and banning malfunctioning gig workers from the platform, gig work can still be considered a freelance job with gig workers deciding when to work, what assignment to accept and how to carry out the gig "on the ground." This ambiguity is also reflected in the reluctance of judges to take a clear stance on the issue. Instead, judges call for governments to adapt the labor law as to provide them with clearer guidance in specific cases.

### *Parallel Corporation Logics*

At the same time, the platform economy also involves two parallel corporation logics. Legally, both the platform and the peer providers are classified as corporations. The nature of the two types of corporations, however, could not be more different with platforms' value being mainly based on intangible assets (know-how, Intellectual Property Rights (IPR), brand value, and software), while self-employed suppliers being fully dependent on their own labor alone. The platform's business is fully compatible with the corporation logic as being oriented toward growth. Online platforms are easily scalable as the marginal costs of serving an additional supplier (or consumer) are close to zero. In effect, the growth of a platform can even be self-reinforcing. The value of a platform increases with the number of participants on the two sides of the market since more participants implies higher chances of a good match (Rysman, 2009), a phenomenon known as network externalities (Arthur, 1989).

The self-employed supplier operating on the platform, however, is dependent on its labor and thus physically constrained in the number of hours (s)he can be active. Despite self-employed suppliers being allowed to re-sell any assignment outside the platform as a means to grow their business, their membership on the platform is technologically tied to a single account and profile, limiting the opportunities to grow their business beyond their own labor efforts. In this regard, though both being corporations in a legal sense, the corporation logic applies much more to platforms than to the self-employed workers on the platform.

As self-employed individuals are suppliers to the platform, the resulting market structure is one of monopsony: the self-employed have little choice than to offer their service through one or two platforms. As a result, the surplus can be almost fully appropriated by the platform, as evidenced by their commission fees that range between 15% and 30%. Different from employees in corporations, the anti-trust regulations prohibit self-employed individuals to collectively bargain a minimum price (as well as labor conditions, right to privacy, social security, etc.). Here, it is the role of the state to enforce competition law (using anti-trust agency) and, accordingly, to consider the self-employed as running a business. That is, from a state's perspective, both the platform and the self-employed are categorized as a corporation.

The "precarity" of self-employed individuals working via platforms, then, does not only lie in traditional roots of precarity including low pay, informality, and discrimination, but also in their asymmetric dependency relations with the online platforms. While the latter operates under full support of the institutional logics of the corporation and the market, the self-employed cannot rely on such support in the same way employees do in the corporation logic and entrepreneurs do in the market logic. Regarding the corporation logic, self-employed individuals do not fit in even if they are legally classified as a corporation, as the nature of work and their digital identity provide little opportunities to grow their business in size beyond their individual efforts due to physical limits on one's working hours. Regarding the market logic, self-employed individuals nevertheless compete for income on markets, but they do so with little entrepreneurial freedom as platforms largely pre-design technologically how to offer and price one's labor services and how supply and demand are matched algorithmically.

The questions of surplus and control are intertwined when viewed from the pre-existing configuration of institutional logics. Following the corporation logic, the corporation employs labor, which collectively negotiates the surplus (wages, bonus, allowances, promotion criteria, benefits, etc.). In return, the corporation is allowed to exercise control by means of work instructions. Refusal to follow such instructions is a valid ground to fire an employee. By contrast, a self-employed individual is autonomous in deciding what work to accept and how to carry out the task at hand. This renders such freelancers self-employed and, hence, subject to competition law. Surplus can no longer be collectively negotiated, but it is established by market prices resulting from competition. To ensure the freelance status of their providers, platforms thus navigate the fine line of exercising control of freelancers without explicitly instructing them. This is feasible as long as the end-consumer is the one that specifies the assignment (e.g., by sending an order through the app) and reviews the work ex post (e.g., by rating and writing reviews in the app). At the same time, by not acting as an employer, the platform also avoids responsibility for how the self-employed carry out their job (e.g., regarding permits, health and safety regulations, and sexual harassment) and also can remain agnostic about their tax duties.

### *Weakening State Logics*

While the platform is empowered by the corporation and market logics it is subject to, the regulatory role of governments has become more limited. Where governments traditionally controlled entry to markets by permits and diplomas, platform companies decide themselves who enters their platform. Just as a home-sharing platform like Airbnb does not check if home owners have a permit to rent, gig-economy platforms may not check work licenses or diplomas (the recent exception being Uber in Europe, as explained below). Platform companies – be it in second-hand markets, social media, sharing economy, or gig economy – also control exit: they retain the right to ban users from their platform. Platforms do so in case a user does not adhere to the (otherwise implicit) norms that a platform expects users to adhere to, and they may base their decision on low ratings and reviews that a user received in the past (van Dijck et al., 2018; Frenken, Van Waes, Pelzer, Smink, & Van Est, 2019). The platform's policing capacity, which allows it to control the entry and exit of users, is de facto substituting government-controlled institutions such as licenses, diplomas, and worker rights that were put in place to ensure quality, safety, and anti-discrimination. Platforms indeed frame ratings and reviews as effective quality-control mechanisms that, in their view, render license-based or diploma-based regulations redundant and outdated (Frenken et al., 2019; Pelzer, Frenken, Boon, 2019).

Apart from seeing its regulations increasingly being ignored, governments also seek to weigh the economic and social effects that platform generate. On the one hand, the economic benefits for consumers seem obvious as, with the advent of platforms, consumers now enjoy a host of services at lower prices and at higher flexibility. Platforms also lower the entry barriers for freelance work thus providing many with the possibility to generate extra income. These economic benefits stemming from innovation and competition were particularly highlighted by the European Commission (2016) in its agenda on the sharing and gig economy. However, as explained, national governments struggle with how to apply their labor laws, which are meant to protect dependent workers (De Stefano, 2016; Sachs, 2015). Arguably, with platforms exercising so much control over self-employed individuals, they can, indeed, be regarded as dependent rather than independent contractors. As platforms do not take up the responsibility for the protection and well-being of the self-employed, the state logic has become misaligned. While government delegated principles including decent work conditions, anti-discrimination, employment protection, and income security to a large extent to modern corporation and the unions, such principles need not be adhered to by a platform vis-à-vis the self-employed workers.

For now, gig-economy platforms continue to operate with self-employed and show little willingness to make sure that these self-employed adhere to government regulations regarding work permits, licenses, diplomas, and anti-discrimination. As a notable exception, in Europe, Uber changed its UberPop model with unlicensed chauffeurs into a "license-based only" model. This change followed from court cases in European member states and later cumulated in a judgement by the European Court of Justice in December 2017 (Case C-434/15). The latter court speaks of Uber's "decisive influence" in each transaction between a driver and a passenger, because the algorithm decides the matching between drivers and passengers as well as the transaction's price. The court thus views Uber as a transportation company rather than as an "information society service" provider under the E-Commerce directive (which would have exempted them from national regulations in the transport sector). As a consequence, transportation regulations in each European member state apply equally to Uber, notably, the license requirement. Note, however, that the classification of Uber as a transportation company does not alter the freelance status of its drivers, which has been the main concern of unions. Hence, while Uber in Europe aligned with taxi regulations by accepting only licensed chauffeurs on their platforms, its business model based on self-employed, algorithmic control, and client ratings remains unaffected.

While the UberPop case in Europe may be understood as a sign that the state reaffirms its power and legitimacy, it seem unlikely that the same legal reasoning will apply to platforms whose influence on the transaction is arguably less "decisive" than in the case of Uber. Indeed, Uber can be thought of as an extreme case in which the platforms is in charge of matching and pricing, while on most other platforms gig workers enjoy somewhat more freedom in terms of matching, pricing, and offerings. Such subtle differences precisely mark the legal distinction between a classification as an E-Commerce platform (which exempt a platform from sectoral regulations) and a classification as a sector participant. As an illustrative example, a preliminary ruling by the Advocate General of the European Court of Justice in April 2019 (Case C-390/18) was of the opinion that Airbnb should be regarded as providing "information society services" as an E-Commerce platform, because Airbnb "does not exercise control over the essential procedures for the provision of those services." As a consequence, according to the Advocate General, Airbnb falls under the E-Commerce directive, and as such, cannot be regulated by national real-estate regulations. Following this reasoning, current EU law is likely to regard gig-economy platforms for domestic services, legal services, education, and care all as E-Commerce platforms, as long as their suppliers have similar freedoms as Airbnb hosts in terms of who to choose as a client and what price to charge.

### *Where Gig and Sharing Platforms Differ*

While the institutional tensions between platforms and users have been most visible in gig-economy platforms where people sell their labor to make an income, our analysis also extends to sharing economy platforms. In the case of Airbnb, for example, the main service consists of facilitating home owners to rent out their home. That is, sharing economy entails renting out an (under-utilized) asset, while gig economy entails renting out one's own labor (Frenken & Schor, 2017). Yet, even in the case of renting out a home, some form of labor is implied, for example, answering questions by prospective guests and cleaning the house (irrespective of whether these tasks are, in turn, outsourced by the home owner to others). Thus, as on gig-economy platforms, individuals carry out work on sharing economy platforms to generate an income and, just like gig-economy platforms, sharing economy platforms actively surveil such activities and sanction misconduct.[3]

Nevertheless, the institutional nature of the tensions caused by gig-economy platforms is quite different from the tensions caused by sharing economy platforms. In both cases, individuals are constrained in growing their business. However, while the constraint in gig-economy platforms stems from the physical limitations in terms of the number of hours a single individual can offer his/her services, the business constraints on sharing economy platforms are purposefully imposed (Frenken et al., 2019). First, government regulations prohibit excessive trade among peers. For example, many cities worldwide limit the number of days that a house can be rented out through Airbnb. Also, the Dutch government started taxing revenues from car sharing above a certain threshold, as individuals exceeding this threshold are regarded as a professional business. In other cases, a platform itself may actively police excessive trade by suppliers to avoid allegations of facilitating unfair competition with professional rental agencies (Frenken et al., 2019). For example, some peer-to-peer car sharing platforms actively monitor if a particular car is rented out on a permanent basis and, if so, remove the offering from the platform. In terms of institutional logics, then, the constraints on individuals to expand their sharing economy business are due to a particular configuration between the state and corporation logics, where the boundary between peer-to-peer sharing and professional businesses is maintained by imposing caps on the activities that individuals can undertake before they will be classified as a regular professional business. By contrast, gig-economy activities are considered a (freelance) business activity by default, and the opposition between amateur and professional business does not apply.

## RESOLVING INSTITUTIONAL MISALIGNMENTS

Platforms are well embedded in traditional market and corporation logics. They are very capable of attracting a large amount of capital to grow their company in size and, since the shareholder value of a platform primarily stems from its size in terms of user numbers, the objectives of managers and shareholders are well aligned. Moreover, platforms profit from extant state logics welcoming them as "disruptors" bringing innovations, empowering consumers and lowering prices. At the same time, the advent of online platforms has rendered self-employed suppliers an institutional anomaly. They are caught in the middle between corporation, market, and state logics. Despite being legally classified as a corporation, they cannot grow their business as other corporations do. Despite being active on markets, they cannot operate in an independent entrepreneurial manner as platforms strongly mediate market exchanges. In addition, they are ill-protected by territorial social laws and state regulations.

The misalignment of market, corporate, and state logics has become evident from the growing tensions and controversies surrounding online platforms. Platforms, in their current form, are perceived as illegitimate especially in the eyes of unions trying to protect precarious gig workers, that is, the self-employed who work via platforms. Governments also struggle with platforms that facilitate peer-to-peer transactions without enforcing government regulations and tax obligations (Frenken et al., 2019). Yet, while governments and unions are critical, the public at large seems to consider platforms as legitimate, as witnessed by their growing popularity among consumers. This also explains why government agencies may differ considerably in their assessment of platforms. For example, while inspection agencies and employment ministries raise questions, innovation agencies and competition authorities seem to emphasize the apparent consumer welfare benefits.

The resulting institutional complexity is often dealt with differently in different sectors and different countries. We discuss two trends taking place alongside each other, consistent with "compromise" and "criticism" (Boltanski & Thévenot, 1999, pp. 373–375) as two ways of dealing with disputes stemming from misalignments between logics (or, in the terminology of Boltanski and Thévenot: orders of worth). On the one hand, we observe a number of more pragmatic "band aid" solutions that go into the direction of containing the institutional tensions through ad hoc compromises. Here, actors seek to contribute to the common good without clarifying the contradictory nature of the logics that lie at the root of the dispute (Boltanski & Thévenot, 1999). On the other hand, we see more fundamental attempts to take platforms out of the problematic market/corporation nexus. Here, actors denounce the contradictions between the market and corporation logic that platforms generate, and call for a consistent application of one or the other logic. Such attempts can be considered examples of what Boltanski and Thévenot (1999) called criticism as the second way of dealing with dispute. Interestingly, while criticisms logically call for platforms to be institutionalized into either the corporation or the market logic, some criticisms propose a radical, alternative route to institutionalization following a community logic.

### *Band Aid Solutions*

With some platforms growing fast and raising controversies, governments understandably turn to pragmatic solutions. More fundamental resolutions would, from a government point of view, require a lengthy and (politically) uncertain process, for example, regarding a re-design of the fundamental laws regarding competition and labor (and, possibly, regarding privacy and anti-discrimination as well). Instead, the most pressing problems are addressed by ad hoc regulations targeted at specific platforms in specific organizational fields.

Three examples may help to exemplify this trend. First, in the taxi field, new regulations legalized the ride-hailing practices started by Lyft and Uber where ordinary people with permits would provide taxi services through the platform's app. In the USA, this was made possible by the introduction of a new category of "Network Transportation Companies" as distinct from traditional taxi companies (Tzur, 2019). By doing so, a "third" regulatory category was created between taxi companies and E-Commerce companies. Interestingly, while this solution has been accepted in most US states, European countries resisted the platforms' proposal to copy this US solution and institutionalized ride-hailing apps within traditional taxi law instead accepting licensed drivers only (Thelen, 2018).

Second, Uber and Deliveroo launched a health insurance scheme for self-employed individuals similar to services provided by employers to employees (Musaddique, 2018; Rosemail, Barzic, Pitas, & Smith, 2018). This may indeed be possible without platforms being automatically classified platforms as employers, because such classification issues depend much more on the issue of control than on the services and benefits that a platform would provide. Though this institutional pathway does not take away the (legal) issue of control of a platform over the self-employed, it nevertheless provides self-employed individuals with health insurance benefits that employees currently enjoy, meeting some of the concerns of unions regarding the precarious position of platform labor.

Third, in the hotel sector, home sharing has become legalized in many cities around the world by adopting specific regulations. In most cases, home sharing is allowed but only for a limited number of days and to a limited number of people. Again, this can be understood as a third-way solution striking a balance between state logic of zoning where residential houses would be meant for permanent residents only and home sharing should be forbidden, and the market logic of hotels and bed-and-breakfasts which are allowed to rent out rooms the whole year long (Frenken & Schor, 2017).[4]

The mentioned examples can be understood as typical organizational field-level responses. Regulatory responses concern single organizational fields in single geographical environments (e.g., the taxi sector in California). By and large, these solutions are quite favorable to the existing platforms. Even though they might create some boundaries for how the platforms conduct business, they leave the overall business model of platforms intact. The compromises are understood as field-level responses to platforms, which result into highly sector- and country-specific institutional changes (Thelen, 2018; Uzunca et al., 2018; Frenken et al., 2019). In this way, governments are able to regulate platforms in different organizational fields as a response to conflicting interests, while maintaining the institutional logics of market and corporation as built up in the past and that continue to govern the rest of the economy. Therefore, these solutions do not address let alone solve the fundamental contradiction between the market and the corporation logic that leaves gig workers misaligned with both corporation and market logics.

### *Corporation Logic*

Regarding the most pressing issue of the legal status of self-employed individuals, many advocate a simple way out by classifying platforms an employer and the self-employed as employees. In that case, platforms are being re-institutionalized in the old regime and tensions are resolved: wages can be negotiated collectively and platform can exercise control over labor. It would also solve the problem of regulatory compliance as regulatory responsibilities are then re-allocated from the self-employed to the platform. This scenario means that the corporation logic fully applies to platform work, thereby undoing the tensions caused by the parallel realities of competition by platforms and competition on platforms. The Danish domestic cleaning platform Hilfr serves as an example. It signed a union agreement in April 2018 changing the self-employed status of its workers into employees, who are thereby protected by EU and national labor law (Munkholm & Schjøler, 2018). The agreement covers pension contributions, holiday pay, and sickness benefits. It is further noteworthy that the agreement assigns new cleaners a default status as freelancer for the first 100 hours of services, which is automatically converted into that of employee afterward. It remains to be seen if such collective agreements will take place more often in the future. From a market logic point of view, one may expect that most platforms would oppose such an institutionalization pathway because their profit margins would deteriorate as labor would get a larger share of the surplus, while at the same time the total surplus is likely to decline as well as the total costs go up.

### *Market Logic*

A second pathway would go into the opposite direction and institutionalize platforms more fully as markets, that is, as technologies that facilitate exchange and transactions but otherwise do not exercise control over labor. This would entail a change in some of the business model characteristics of many platforms that now often set prices and match supply and demand algorithmically and may even preferentially select workers with good ratings. If platforms were to comply more faithfully to the market logic, they would have to decentralize decision-making to workers who are free to decide with whom to work and for what price. Indeed, this is visible in, for example, the domestic cleaning platform Helpling, which abandoned setting prices and now leaves it up to the cleaners to do so. Similarly, in response to imminent legal action, Uber decided to change its system for the allocation of rides, no longer disincentivizing drivers to reject a ride request in accordance to their freedom as a self-employed. Though such business model adaptations would make platforms less vulnerable against the threat of being classified as an employer, for now a key governance mechanism remains: platforms retain the right to close off access to workers who, in their eyes, underperform.

### *Community Logic*

A third pathway, which has been much more debated than empirically observed (Scholz & Schneider, 2016), is to overcome the corporation logic altogether by founding platforms as cooperatives with workers owning and controlling the platform. These kind of "platform co-ops" would likely be embedded in a community logic. The rule setting, then, would probably be community-based as the members of the community would decide on the rules, how they are monitored and how the offenders are sanctioned. Cooperatives then, would most likely emerge from local communities that use a platform to serve local consumers, as in most gig economy and sharing economy markets. In such context, an online community of providers can easily interact offline as well (Reischauer & Mair, 2018; Vaskelainen & Piscicelli, 2018), thus leveraging the physical proximity of providers operating in local markets. In particular cases, the membership of a platform co-op may be tight formally to a membership of a (national) professional organization as well, or otherwise informally to professional values and identities. It should be noted that the government would probably not deem these platforms as illegitimate as some of the privately owned platforms because the members would themselves be able to influence the platform and, thus, they would not need state protection. The unions would also be likely to accept these kinds of platforms at least in a scenario where they would be active in creating them. However, regarding platform co-ops, it remains unclear in what ways such initiatives are allowed under current competition law and whether any constraints will be lifted by governments as to facilitate such initiatives.

## RESEARCH AGENDA

The framework of institutional logics provides a useful analytical lens and scheme to understand the fundamental institutional challenges prompted by the advent of online platforms. Platforms are corporations that organize markets. In doing so, they span two parallel markets: the market for platforms competing to provide intermediation services and the market for the self-employed (and unpaid labor) competing on platforms to provide peer-to-peer services. While the corporation and market logics empower the platform, they weaken self-employed suppliers as platforms constrain them to grow into a full-fledged business and limit their entrepreneurial freedom by their platform design.

Our institutional logics' analysis made it clear that, apart from ad hoc field-level responses, many proposed institutional changes are calls to privilege one logic over another. There are calls to re-classify self-employed individuals as employees of the platform, which would resolve the conflicts of surplus and control in the traditional way and bring gig workers into the corporation logic. At the same time, there are also signs that platforms adapt their business model to avoid such future re-classification, for example, by reducing the level of control they exercise over the self-employed, thus adhering closer to the market logic. Finally, we witness some attempts to found platforms as cooperatives to enable self-employed individuals to take control over the platform and its algorithm and business model, which can be subsumed under the community logic.

From this analysis, a number of research questions can be derived for future institutional research on the platform economy:

- How can we explain the varying field-level institutional responses in different sectors and countries?
- What institutional logic can be expected to prevail depending on the business model characteristics of a platform (cf. Vaskelainen & Münzel, 2018)? A useful distinction here is between advertisement-based, subscription-based, and commission-based business models.
- What logic can be expected to prevail depending on sectoral characteristics? A first distinction here is between social media (viz. unpaid labor), gig work, and sharing assets. Furthermore, whether or not people rely on a platform for their main income can be a further important distinction.
- What logic can be expected to prevail depending on the variety of capitalism (cf. Thelen, 2018)? Operating in a (global) institutional void, platforms have entered many countries with, initially, very similar business model. Over time, one may expect such business models to adapt to local and national institutional demands, which themselves are co-evolving with platform technologies as well.

In addition to questions regarding the variance of institutional logics in different business model, sectoral and national contexts, a challenging question holds how the macro-level institutional logics themselves are subjected to change with the rise of the platform economy. Indeed, Friedland and Alford (1991) presented the institutional logics perspective to raise the analysis from the organizational level to societal level, as did Boltanski and Thévenot (2006) in their orders of worth framework. Yet, most of the work on institutional logics has focused on how organizations maintain legitimacy by conforming to or decoupling from institutional logics in particular institutional fields (Dunn & Jones, 2010; Lounsbury, 2007; Pache & Santos, 2013; Reay & Hinings, 2009; Thornton, 2004). In this view, organizations are seen as constrained by abstract macro-institutional logics, which downplay actors' deliberate attempts to reconfigure institutional logics through competent institutional work (Patriotta et al., 2011). While research on the institutional work of the platforms has been called for, research hitherto largely focused on the level of single organization or organizational field (Mair & Reischauer, 2017; Pelzer et al., 2019).

In the light of our essay, we argue that platforms hold the potential of creating a new institutional logic of their own based on algorithmic control (Zuboff, 2019) similar to how the corporation initially emerged as an organizational innovation, but later became established as a new institutional logic (Thornton et al., 2012). Further research could focus on examining how disruptive organizational innovations, such as platforms, mold the macro-level institutional orders. For example, is there a tipping point when many organizational field-level changes lead to change in the institutional order or is the change gradual, resulting from the alignment efforts of the new kinds of actors with the existing logics? Investigating how the platforms shape and change existing societal institutions and their logics will contribute to a better understanding of how innovations, technological and social, affect institutional change. Also, even if a new logic will not emerge, platforms are nevertheless likely to continue to affect the institutional logics of state, corporation and market, and their interrelations. Either way, we encourage scholars to engage in research that goes beyond the level of single fields as to understand the evolution of institutional logics as a societal process in the era of the platform economy.

## NOTES

1. The fact that only Christian religion is mentioned probably stems from the fact that the authors concentrated on the major institutional logics of the Western world.

2. For a useful discussion on the similarities and differences between the framework of institutional logics and orders of words, see Patriotta et al. (2011).

3. Whether or not the same analysis may extend to social media platforms is less clear. Social media apply a different business model than sharing and gig platforms, in that they connect advertisers to consumers through micro-targeted marketing algorithms. Hence, the market logic in social media pertains primarily to the two sides of advertisers and consumers. At the same time, social media platforms are also peer-to-peer media platforms where users upload the content for others to read and watch, but without remuneration. This has been considered a form of free labor (Terranova, 2000), where platforms enable people to express themselves and share knowledge, while at the same time appropriate such cultural expressions as data for commercial purposes. The surplus is taken by the platform altogether, recently prompting proposals for data property rights and data unions. Whereas the control over the content to produce is obviously much less in social media compared to paid work, there is nevertheless a form of control as platform retains the right to remove content and user accounts.

4. Social media platforms serve as a fourth example. Here, the dichotomy between host and editor has dominated; platforms self-identify as mere host of content that is produced "peer-to-peer," thereby escaping the status of an editor and the roles and expectations attached to it. Though, legally, it would be hard to classify social media platforms as editors, they assume editorial roles by removing content themselves. More recently, however, we see true attempts by governments to institutionalize this role of platforms in the face of fake news. In particular, European governments are exploring new regulations that could compel such platforms to rapidly remove misinformation (Helberger, Pierson, & Poell, 2017). Again, we can consider this attempt as a band aid solution by introducing regulation that would assign the role of editors to platforms that remain, legally, classified as hosts.

## ACKNOWLEDGMENTS

We thank Wouter Boon, Andrea Herrmann, and the participants of the workshop "The Rise of the Platform Economy" (Utrecht, April 2018), the 5th International Workshop on the Sharing Economy (Mannheim, June 2018), the 6th International Workshop on the Sharing Economy (Utrecht, June 2019), and the 35th EGOS colloquium (Edinburgh, July 2019) for useful comments. The usual caveat applies.

## REFERENCES

Ahrne, G., Aspers, P., & Brunsson, N. (2015). The organization of markets. *Organization Studies*, *36*(1), 7–27.

Aldrich, H. E., & Fiol, C. M. (1994). Fools rush in? The institutional context of industry creation. *Academy of Management Review*, *19*(4), 645–670.

Arthur, W. B. (1989). Competing technologies, increasing returns, and lock-in by historical events. *The Economic Journal, 99*(394), 116–131.

Boltanski, L., & Thévenot, L. (1999). The sociology of critical capacity. *European Journal Social Theory, 2*(3), 359–377.

Boltanski, L., & Thévenot, L. (2006). *On justification: Economies of worth*. Princeton, NJ: Princeton University Press (translated from French, first published in 1991).

De Stefano, V. (2016). *The rise of the "just-in-time workforce": On-demand work, crowdwork and labour protection in the "gig economy"*. Geneva, Switzerland: ILO.

Dickerson, A. P., Gibson, H. D., & Tsakalotos, E. (1997). The impact of acquisitions on company performance: Evidence from a large panel of UK firms. *Oxford Economic Papers, 49*(3), 344–361.

van Dijck, J., Poell, T., & de Waal, M. (2018). *The platform society. Public values in a connective world*. Oxford: Oxford University Press.

DiMaggio, P., & Powell, W. W. (1983). The iron cage revisited: Collective rationality and institutional isomorphism in organizational fields. *American Sociological Review, 48*(2), 147–160.

Doty, D. H., & Glick, W. H. (1994). Typologies as a unique form of theory building: Toward improved understanding and modeling. *Academy of Management Review, 19*(2), 230–251.

Dunn, M. B., & Jones, C. (2010). Institutional logics and institutional pluralism: The contestation of care and science logics in medical education, 1967–2005. *Administrative Science Quarterly, 55*(1), 114–149.

European Commission. (2016, June 3). *A European agenda for the collaborative economy*. Brussels, Belgium: European Commission.

Fligstein, N. (1993). *The transformation of corporate control*. Cambridge, MA: Harvard University Press.

Fligstein, N. (1996). Markets as politics: A political cultural approach to market institutions. *American Sociological Review, 61*(4), 656–673.

Frenken, K., & Schor, J. (2017). Putting the sharing economy into perspective. *Environmental Innovation and Societal Transitions, 23*, 3–10.

Frenken, K., Van Waes, A., Pelzer, P., Smink, M., & Van Est, R. (2019). Safeguarding public interests in the platform economy. *Policy & Internet*. doi:10.1002/poi3.217

Friedland, R., & Alford, R. R. (1991). Bringing society back in: Symbols, practices and institutional contradictions. In W. W. Powell & P. J. DiMaggio (Eds.), *The new institutionalism in organizational analysis* (pp. 232–263). Chicago, IL: University of Chicago Press.

Green, S. E., Babb, M., & Alpaslan, C. M. (2008). Institutional field dynamics and the competition between institutional logics. *Management Communication Quarterly, 22*(1), 40–73.

Greenwood, R., Díaz, A. M., Li, S. X., & Lorente, J. C. (2010). The multiplicity of institutional logics and the heterogeneity of organizational responses. *Organization Science, 21*(2), 521–539.

Greenwood, R., Raynard, M., Kodeih, F., Micelotta, E. R., & Lounsbury, M. (2011). Institutional complexity and organizational responses. *The Academy of Management Annals, 5*(1), 317–371.

Greve, H. R., & Zhang, C. M. (2017). Institutional logics and power sources: Merger and acquisition decisions. *Academy of Management Journal, 60*(2), 671–694.

Grinevich, V., Huber, F., Karataş-Özkan, M., & Yavuz, Ç. (2019). Green entrepreneurship in the sharing economy: Utilising multiplicity of institutional logics. *Small Business Economics, 52*(4), 859–876.

Hall, P.A., & Soskice, D. (2001). *Varieties of capitalism. The institutional foundations of comparative advantage*. Oxford: Oxford University Press.

Helberger, N., Pierson, J., & Poell, T. (2018). Governing online platforms: From contested to cooperative responsibility. *The Information Society, 34*(1), 1–14.

Hinings, B., Gegenhuber, T., & Greenwood, R. (2018). Digital innovation and transformation: An institutional perspective. *Information and Organization, 28*(1), 52–61.

Kenney, M., & Zysman, J. (2016). The rise of the platform economy. *Issues in Science and Technology, 32*(3). (online journal).

Kirchner, S., & Schüßler, E. (2018). The organization of digital marketplaces: Unmasking the role of Internet platforms in the sharing economy. In G. Ahrne, & N. Brunsson (Eds.), *Organization outside organizations. The abundance of partial organization in social life* (pp. 131–153). Cambridge: Cambridge University Press.

Lee, M.-D. P., & Lounsbury, M. (2015). Filtering institutional logics: Community logic variation and differential responses to the institutional complexity of toxic waste. *Organization Science*, *26*(3), 847–866.

Lounsbury, M. (2002). Institutional transformation and status mobility: The professionalization of the field of finance. *Academy of Management Journal*, *45*(1), 255–266.

Lounsbury, M. (2007). A tale of two cities: Competing logics and practice variation in the professionalizing of mutual funds. *Academy of Management Journal*, *50*(2), 289–307.

Mair, J., & Reischauer, G. (2017). Capturing the dynamics of the sharing economy: Institutional research on the plural forms and practices of sharing economy organizations. *Technological Forecasting and Social Change*, *125*, 11–20.

McKee, D. (2017). Neoliberalism and the legality of peer platform markets. *Environmental Innovation and Societal Transitions*, *23*, 105–113.

Meyer, R. E., & Hammerschmid, G. (2006). Changing institutional logics and executive identities: A managerial challenge to public administration in Austria. *American Behavioral Scientist*, *49*(7), 1000–1014.

Meyer, J. W., & Rowan, B. (1977). Institutionalized organizations: Formal structure as myth and ceremony. *American Journal of Sociology*, *83*(2), 340–363.

Munkholm, N. V., & Schjøler, C. H. (2018). Platform work and the Danish model: Legal perspectives. *Nordic Journal of Commercial Law*, *1*, 117–145.

Musaddique, S. (2018, May 8). Food start-up Deliveroo to spend $13 million on driver medical insurance but stops short of other benefits. Retrieved from https://www.cnbc.com/2018/05/08/deliveroo-offers-drivers-medical-insurance-but-stops-short-of-other-benefits.html. Accessed on July 24, 2019.

Nelson, R. R., & Winter, S. G. (1982). *An evolutionary theory of economic change*. Cambridge, MA: Belknap Press.

Ocasio, W., & Radoynovska, N. (2016). Strategy and commitments to institutional logics: Organizational heterogeneity in business models and governance. *Strategic Organization*, *14*(4), 287–309.

Pache, A.-C., & Santos, F. (2013). Inside the hybrid organization: Selective coupling as a response to competing institutional logics. *Academy of Management Journal*, *56*(4), 972–1001.

Patriotta, G., Gond, J.-P., & Schultz, F. (2011). Maintaining legitimacy: Controversies, orders of worth and public justifications. *Journal of Management Studies*, *48*(8), 1804–1836.

Pelzer, P., Frenken, K., & Boon, W. (2019) Institutional entrepreneurship in the platform economy: How Uber tried (and failed) to change the Dutch taxi law. *Environmental Innovation and Societal Transitions*, *33*, 1–12. doi:10.1016/j.eist.2019.02.003

Rao, H., Monin, P., & Durand, R. (2003). Institutional change in Toque Ville: Nouvelle cuisine as an identity movement in French gastronomy. *American Journal of Sociology*, *108*(4), 795–843.

Raynard, M. (2016). Deconstructing complexity: Configurations of institutional complexity and structural hybridity. *Strategic Organization*, *14*(4), 310–335.

Reay, T., & Hinings, C. R. (2005). The recomposition of an organizational field: Health care in Alberta. *Organization Studies*, *26*(3), 351–384.

Reay, T., & Hinings, C. R. (2009). Managing the rivalry of competing institutional logics. *Organization Studies*, *30*(6), 629–652.

Reischauer, G., & Mair, J. (2018). Platform organizing in the new digital economy: revisiting online communities and strategic responses. In L. Ringel, P. Hiller, & C. Zietsma (Eds.), *Toward permeable boundaries of organizations? Research in the sociology of organizations* (Vol. 57, pp. 113–135). Bingley: Emerald Publishing Limited.

Rosemail, M., Barzic, G., Pitas, C., & Smith, A. (2018, August 6). Uber expands health insurance benefit to drivers in 21 European countries. Retrieved from https://www.insurancejournal.com/news/international/2018/05/24/490210.htm. Accessed on July 24, 2019.

Rysman, M. (2009). The economics of two-sided markets. *Journal of Economic Perspectives*, *23*(3), 125–143.

Sachs, B. (2015, September 25). Uber: Employee Status and "Flexibility". Retrieved from https://onlabor.org/uber-employee-status-and-flexibility/. Accessed on 24 July 2019.

Scholz, T., & Schneider, N. (2016). *Ours to hack and to own. The rise of platform cooperativism. A new vision for the future of work and a fairer Internet*. New York, NY: OR Books.

Schor, J. (2016). Debating the sharing economy. *Journal of Self-Governance and Management Economics*, *4*(3): 7–22.

Terranova, T. (2000). Free labor: Producing culture for the digital economy. *Social Text*, *18*(2), 33–58.

Thelen, K. (2018). Regulating Uber: The politics of the platform economy in Europe and the United States. *Perspectives on Politics*, *16*(4), 938–953.

Thornton, P. H. (2004). *Markets from culture: Institutional logics and organizational decisions in higher education publishing*. Stanford, CA: Stanford University Press.

Thornton, P. H., & Ocasio, W. (1999). Institutional logics and the historical contingency of power in organizations: Executive succession in the higher education publishing industry, 1958–1990. *American Journal of Sociology*, *105*(3), 801–843.

Thornton, P. H., Ocasio, W., & Lounsbury, M. (2012). *The institutional logics perspective: A new approach to culture, structure, and process*. Oxford: Oxford University Press.

Tuch, C., & O'Sullivan, N. (2007). The impact of acquisitions on firm performance: A review of the evidence. *International Journal of Management Reviews*, *9*(2), 141–170.

Tzur, A. (2019). Uber Über regulation? Regulatory change following the emergence of new technologies in the taxi market. *Regulation & Governance*, *13*(3), 340–361.

Uzunca, B., Rigtering, J. C., & Ozcan, P. (2018). Sharing and shaping: A cross-country comparison of how sharing economy firms shape their institutional environment to gain legitimacy. *Academy of Management Discoveries*, *4*(3), 248–272.

Vaskelainen, T., & Münzel, K. (2018). The effect of institutional logics on business model development in the sharing economy. *Academy of Management Discoveries*, *4*(3), 273–293.

Vaskelainen, T., & Piscicelli, L. (2018). Online and offline communities in the sharing economy. *Sustainability*, *10*(8), 2927 (online journal).

Vermeulen, P., Zietsma, C., Greenwood, R., & Langley, A. (2016). Strategic responses to institutional complexity. *Strategic Organization*, *14*(4), 277–286.

Wooten, M., & Hoffman, A. J. (2008). Organizational fields: Past, present and future. *The Sage Handbook of Organizational Institutionalism*, *1*, 131–147.

Zietsma, C., Groenewegen, P., Logue, D. M., & Hinings, C. R. (2017). Field or fields? Building the scaffolding for cumulation of research on institutional fields. *Academy of Management Annals*, *11*(1), 391–450.

Zuboff, S. (2019). *The age of surveillance capitalism: The fight for a human future at the new frontier of power*. New York, NY: PublicAffairs

# THE SHARING ECONOMY AS AN EMERGING AND CONTESTED FIELD – HOW CLASSIC AND INSTITUTIONAL ENTREPRENEURS COPE WITH PLURAL THEORETICAL FRAMES

Aurélien Acquier, Valentina Carbone and Laëtitia Vasseur

## ABSTRACT

*This chapter explores how classic and institutional entrepreneurs in the sharing economy (SE) frame and make sense of the emergent, plural, and contested SE concept. The authors address this question through an investigation of an attempt to institutionalize the SE as a separate field in France, through data collected among SE entrepreneurs gravitating around OuiShare, a leading institutional entrepreneur for the SE. To analyze the plurality of discursive framings within the SE field, we explored how classic entrepreneurs affiliated with the SE and institutional entrepreneurs made sense of the concept and its related practices by referring to different theories and narratives. The results reveal that classic entrepreneurs used and combined four distinct theoretical currents (access economy, commons, gift, and libertarianism) to frame their projects. This framing diversity was further reinforced at the meso level by specific forms of institutional entrepreneurship which reflected and actively built*

**Theorizing the Sharing Economy: Variety and Trajectories of New Forms of Organizing**
**Research in the Sociology of Organizations, Volume 66, 107–129**

**ISSN: 0733-558X/doi:10.1108/S0733-558X20200000066006**

*on such framing diversity. However, over time, such heterogeneity negatively affects the internal coherence of the field. Based on these results, the authors discuss the impact of enduring framing diversity on the SE organizational field emergence and development.*

**Keywords:** Sharing economy; field emergence; discursive framing; theorization; organizational fields; diversity

## INTRODUCTION

By making use of technologies that allow individuals to share resources and skills on a large scale and decentralize the production and consumption of good and services (Botsman & Rogers, 2010; Schor, 2014), the sharing economy (SE) has experienced rapid growth, causing profound changes in a number of business sectors such as the hotel industry, transport, food, product design, and the repair or reuse of objects (Sundararajan, 2016). As an economic and social innovation, the SE raises complex questions in terms of institutional change (Mair & Reischauer, 2017) and has different impacts on organizational fields, that is, "sets of organizations that, in the aggregate, constitute a recognized area of institutional life" (DiMaggio & Powell, 1983; Wooten & Hoffman, 2017). First, the SE transforms established fields, as SE organizations disrupt or re-shape existing markets (such as the accommodation, transportation, or food industries) through the development of new organizational forms and business models based on digital platforms governing peer-to-peer transactions (Acquier, 2018; Acquier, Carbone, & Massé, 2019; Mair & Reischauer, 2017). In this perspective, the SE is mostly viewed as an economic phenomenon (see, e.g., Habibi, Davidson, & Laroche, 2017) which is closely related – not to say conflated with – the emergence of a new type of platform capitalism (Srnicek, 2017).

Beyond transforming established fields, the SE also involves processes of field creation and may be analyzed as an emergent field on its own. In this view, the SE is not only a new type of economic transactions: it is a socially and culturally complex phenomenon re-grouping diverse organizations which deserves understanding and regulation in its own right. For example, Martin (2016) analyzed the SE as a separate "niche of innovation" likely to drive a wider process of socio-technical transition toward sustainability (Geels, 2005). In this perspective, several organizations were set up over the last decade to promote the SE concept (Shareable – a global internet site – was founded in 2009, OuiShare – a global network and think-tank organizing professional conferences – was founded in France in 2012, and ShareNL – a similar type of organization in the Netherlands – has been active at least since 2013). Beyond the diffusion of ideas and the promotion of the SE concept, these organizations played a role to frame policy orientations and shape the field practices and meanings. Various reports were issued [such as a report committed by the French Prime Minister to the Deputy Pascal Terrasse (2016)] to assess the economic importance of the field and design a relevant regulatory framework for SE platforms. Also, while an increasing number of entrepreneurs started to affiliate with the SE, the development of the SE led to legal reflexions and propositions on how to regulate this emerging and growing field (Davidson, Finck, & Infranca, 2018). Accordingly, this chapter explores the efforts toward establishing the SE as a separate organizational field, which remains to date an under investigated research question (Mair & Reischauer, 2017).

Considering the ambivalent, controversial, and paradoxical nature of the SE, its multiple meanings, interpretations and normative foundations and the considerable difficulty to draw clear boundaries around the notion, we explore the processes of field emergence in a context of multiple and heterogeneous discursive framings. More specifically, we address two questions: at the micro level of analysis, which theoretical currents irrigate classic entrepreneurs' discourse to make sense of the SE and legitimize their projects? And at the meso level of analysis, which forms of institutional entrepreneurship are at work during the stage of field creation in a context of frame plurality? We tackle these questions through an investigation of an attempt to institutionalize the SE, relying on data collected between 2014 and 2017, among SE entrepreneurs gravitating around *OuiShare*, a leading institutional entrepreneur for the SE in France.

To analyze the plurality of discursive framings within the SE field, we explored how classic entrepreneurs, as well as institutional entrepreneurs made sense of the SE concept by relating their initiative to different theoretical currents. Our results reveal that two processes contributed to maintain frame diversity during the stage of field emergence: at the micro level, classic entrepreneurs combined four distinct theoretical currents (access economy, commons, gift, and libertarianism) to legitimize and assign meaning to their projects. This framing diversity was further reinforced and sustained at the meso level by specific forms of institutional entrepreneurship from OuiShare which reflected and actively built on such framing diversity. However, we argue that over time, such heterogeneity negatively affects the internal coherence of the field and may limit its institutionalization.

## FRAMINGS PLURALITY AND ENTREPRENEURSHIP IN EMERGING AND CONTESTED FIELDS

### *The SE: An Essentially Contested Concept*

Despite its development, the SE remains a controversial notion, given its heterogeneous nature and the difficulty in defining its boundaries. As a complex socio-economic phenomenon (Munoz & Cohen, 2017), the SE is characterized by a multitude of approaches, normative foundations, and gives way to contradictory interpretations (Acquier & Carbone, 2018; Acquier, Daudigeos, & Pinkse, 2017; Mair & Reischauer, 2017; Martin, 2016). Some authors view the SE as a reformist and activist movement that creates fertile ground for innovation in political and organizational governance (Laloux, 2014; Sundararajan, 2016) and new forms of solidarity or collective commons (Bauwens, 2006). They present the concept as an opportunity for individual liberation and environmental progress in the face of hierarchical and traditional corporations inherited from the Second Industrial Revolution (Filippova & OuiShare, 2015). Others view the SE as a potential lever to promote ecological stewardship, thereby making it possible to reduce the ecological footprint of consumption (Heinrichs, 2013; Parguel, Lunardo, & Benoit-Moreau, 2017). Others dismiss those visions as idealistic, and see the SE as a "low-cost" access economy (Bardhi & Eckhardt, 2012) founded on "business models" that jeopardize employment relationships and call into question the very concepts of the corporation and salaried employees (Murillo, Buckland, & Val, 2017; Slee, 2016). As a reflection of this heterogeneity, there are many semantic and conceptual debates within the field regarding its definition and appropriate terminology (Frenken & Schor, 2017).

As Acquier, Carbone, & Massé (2017) propose it, the SE appears both as an umbrella concept (Hirsch & Levin, 1999) covering a set of diverse phenomena, and an essentially contested concept (Gallie, 1956), that is, a concept imbued with normative values (here the notion of "sharing") which "inevitably involve endless disputes about their proper uses on the part of [their] users" (1956, p. 169). In this perspective, the SE should be considered as a concept in tension, built around three organizing cores: access economy, the platform economy, and community-based economy (see Acquier et al., 2017, p. 4). As each core corresponds to specific ideals of the SE and refers to different types of ideology and values, their co-existence creates a multiplicity of promises, but also tensions and paradoxes because of the potential incompatibility among such framings.

### *Plural Framings and Entrepreneurial Action*

Cognitive and discursive framing plays a central role in the elaboration of social movements (Snow & Benford, 1988) as well as in institutionalization processes (Maguire & Hardy, 2009). Agreement over a dominant discursive framing makes a field coherent, understandable and predictable, which plays a key role to secure stakeholder support (Phillips, Lawrence, & Hardy 2004; Zilber, 2008). However, a dominant discursive frame is absent in the SE (Acquier et al., 2017). In his analysis of online discourse on the SE, Martin (2016) spotted six different discursive framings within the field. He showed how "regime actors" (i.e., classic corporate interests from established fields) tended to reframe the SE as a purely economic – rather than a social and organizational – opportunity or pointed to its internal incoherence, thus either "coopting" the SE or weakening its potential to drive a transition toward sustainability. As discursive framing has a strategic dimension in shaping an emergent field (Lawrence & Phillips, 2004), how framing diversity is "invested" and reflected by entrepreneurs in an emerging field deserves to be analyzed.

Analyzing how entrepreneurs frame SE initiatives to give meaning and legitimize their projects may be done by exploring how they relate their initiatives to specific theoretical currents of the SE. By doing so, we join Thornton, Ocasio, and Lounsbury (2012, pp. 150–155) who show how narratives and rhetorical framing strategies are shaped by theories, which are key to legitimize change since they provide "general guiding principles that explain why and how institutional structures and practices should work." Theories tend to frame the problems, discourses, and narratives of actors in a field. They serve as different ideologies of value creation that project leaders use to theorize their initiatives (Greenwood, Suddaby, & Hinings, 2002) and frame the normative registers through which they wish to be evaluated.

Accordingly, we explore how entrepreneurs in the SE field link their actions and projects to various theoretical currents of the SE, which they use to legitimize and give meaning to their activities. Our first research question is the following: *Which theoretical currents do classic entrepreneurs use to frame and legitimize their projects?*

### *Institutional Entrepreneurship and Theorization in a Pluralistic Field*

Within entrepreneurial processes, institutional entrepreneurship refers to the "activities of actors who have an interest in particular institutional arrangements and who leverage resources to create new institutions or to transform existing ones" (Maguire, Hardy, & Lawrence, 2004, p. 657). Institutional entrepreneurs play a pivotal role in the creation or change of institutional fields (DiMaggio, 1988; Hardy & Maguire, 2008).

Theorization constitutes a central dimension of institutional entrepreneurship and refers to the way institutional entrepreneurs frame the practices they wish to promote, systematize their discourse, and explain and convince others of the merits of their innovation or the institutional field itself (Greenwood et al., 2002; Maguire & Hardy, 2009). Theorization is critical to the process of institutional change, since it provides a discursive regime that frames its roles and practices and defines its boundaries (Mena & Suddaby, 2016). Thus, Rao, Monin, and Durand (2003) showed how theorization of new practices around "nouvelle cuisine" was key to building a movement, creating a new school of thought and practices, and orchestrating institutional change in a very well-structured and well-established organizational field.

Established fields provide a well-defined scope for action, in which actors share a set of coercive, normative, and mimetic institutions (Scott, 1995). In contrast, things are very different for emerging organizational fields (Fligstein & McAdam, 2012; Maguire et al., 2004). Marcus and Anderson (2013, p. 4) indicate that an emerging organizational field "is typically enveloped in a sea of controversy and skepticism about what it does, about the quality, reliability, and performance of its products." In emerging fields, institutional entrepreneurs are supposed to engage into theorization and framing efforts to reduce such complexity and promote a single logic of action that would fit their interest (Barth & Ihl, 2018), to obtain the support of public and private stakeholders (regulators, entrepreneurs, traditional companies, the general public, etc.) and to render the field desirable, intelligible, understandable, and consistent (Phillips et al., 2004; Zilber, 2008).

However, harmonizing the field may not be easily done when fields are built on essentially contested concepts such as the SE. As a result, an important research avenue concerns how institutional entrepreneurs cope with such complexity in their efforts to frame an emerging field marked by framing pluralism.

Accordingly, our second research question is: What forms of institutional entrepreneurship are at work during a stage of field creation in a context of frame plurality?

## METHODOLOGY

To explore the parallel dynamics of classic and institutional entrepreneurial framing processes of the SE, we build on data collected in France between 2014 and 2017, in the context of a research project[1] sponsored by the French Ministry of Sustainable Development and aiming at analyzing the social and environmental impacts of the SE in the physical good sector (design, production, renting, or exchange of goods). *OuiShare* was studied as the main "institutional entrepreneur" in the field (Sundararajan, 2016), engaged in mainstreaming the concept of SE in France, framing its boundaries and theorizing the emerging field. *OuiShare* is a non-profit organization, which creates events and coordinates networks, produces studies and publications and organizes debates and public discussions on the SE. As an active supporting member of the research consortium, *OuiShare* contributed to identifying "classic entrepreneurs" active in the SE emerging field. Accordingly, interviewees, that is, project leaders, founders, or leading members of SE organizations, were identified within the OuiShare ecosystem: via lists of speakers and participants in conferences, public events and meetings organized by the organization. The sampling was designed to represent the diversity of organizational forms and governance models, including profit-oriented, non-profit, and hybrid initiatives.

We had 32 face-to-face interviews with classic entrepreneurs who had launched projects to produce, rent, or exchange material goods. Semi-structured interviews were organized along three themes: the project leader's individual background and motivations, the organizational configuration and value creation model of the initiative, and its potential social and environmental impacts.

We engaged into inductive coding (Thomas, 2006) of our primary data to draw out representative categories of discourse. Following the model of Thornton et al. (2012), we differentiated between narratives, rhetorical framing strategies, and theories (see Table 1). We first clustered the accounts of entrepreneurs presenting and explaining their approach in order to grasp the "narratives" promoted by entrepreneurs; we then related these narratives to intermediate theories [i.e., the rhetorical framing strategies of Thornton et al. (2012)]. These intermediate theories provide broader and more systematic discursive repertoires which serve as frames of reference for actors in the field, combined with currents of thought and value creation ideologies. They come from the theorization of gurus, academics, essayists, and organizations seeking to promote a particular vision of the SE. Connecting entrepreneurs' accounts to intermediate theories was either explicit when interviewees overtly referred to a specific source representing a school of thought, or more implicit if they expressed adherence to a "worldview" and ideas typical of a particular theory.

***Table 1.*** Organization of Data.

| Type of Data | Collection Method and Data Collected |
|---|---|
| *1. Entrepreneur narratives*<br>- Accounts of entrepreneurs seeking to present/dramatize and explain their approach | 32 face-to-face interviews with entrepreneurs (founders, co-founders, or leading managers) from 29 collaborative initiatives (name of the initiative, duration of the interview): Comment Réparer, 128 minutes; Recup.net, 79 minutes; Co-recyclage, 134 minutes; Vestaire Collective, 79 minutes; Share Voisin, 57 minutes; Mutum, 100 minutes; Repair Café Cœur d'Alsace, 61 minutes; Leroy Merlin, 97 minutes; Brocante Lab, 63 minutes; Peerby, 71 minutes; Peuplade, 41 minutes; Open Source Ecologie, 20 minutes; L'Etablisienne, 37 minutes; Ici Montreuil, 62 minutes; Place de la Loc, 82 minutes; La Nouvelle Fabrique, 46 minutes; C'est Bon Esprit, 83 minutes; Mon Atelier en Ville, 62 minutes; Kikawa, 62 minutes; Fablab de Rennes, 109 minutes; Volumes, 51 minutes; ElectroLab, 114 minutes; A Little Market, 53 minutes; Hall Couture, 54 minutes; Woma, 47 minutes; FacLab, 66 minutes; DressWing, 60 minutes; Maforladies, 58 minutes; La Ruche Qui Dit Oui, 88 minutes |
| *2. Intermediate theories (institutional entrepreneurs)*<br>- Interviews with the founders of *OuiShare*<br>- Field configuring events<br>- Outreach materials with a specific framing of the collaborative economy | 11 interviews with OuiShare members (60–92 minutes each): Connectors, Co-founders, Editors *OuiShare* Magazine, Co-founders Lab OuiShare, Members<br>Non-participatory observation in the "*OuiShare Fest*" in 2015 and 2016, and analysis of the topics in the 2014, 2015, and 2016 "*OuiShare Fest*" programs<br>4 publications studied:<br>• Botsman and Rogers (2010)<br>• Gansky (2012)<br>• Filippova and OuiShare (2015)<br>• Bauwens (2015) |

In order to characterize the types of institutional entrepreneurship in the field of the SE in France, we focused on the role of *OuiShare*, interviewing its main members and scrutinizing the content and the messages of the *OuiShare Fest*, the major event organized by the Community, a three-day annual SE event held in Paris, between 2013 and 2017. It is billed as "an interdisciplinary festival that brings together creative leaders, entrepreneurs, movement builders, purpose-driven organizations, and communities from across sectors and countries that want to drive systemic and meaningful change." The *OuiShare Fest* plays an important role in synthesizing, framing, and theorizing the SE field and can be seen as a field configuring event (Hardy & Maguire, 2010; Lampel & Meyer, 2008).

We conducted, transcribed, and coded a series of interviews with five co-founders and six active members of the *OuiShare* collective. To better analyze the different theorizations and rhetorical frames, we participated in two editions of *OuiShare Fest* in Paris (2015 and 2016) and analyzed the programs and session summaries from 2014 to 2017. We also scrutinized four publications showcased in a SE bookstore present at each Fest, through in-depth reading and note-taking.

## RESULTS

We present our results in our two research questions successively. We first develop the four theoretical currents mobilized by SE entrepreneurs to legitimize and give meaning to their own initiatives, and then turn to the forms of institutional entrepreneurship observed in a field characterized by plural framings and heterogeneous values.

### *Access Economy, Gift, Commons, and Libertarianism*

Concerning our first research question, we identified four theoretical currents providing the main cultural and cognitive frames of reference to the entrepreneurs of the SE: access economy, gift, commons, and libertarianism. SE entrepreneurs infuse their own initiative with value creation logics inspired from these theories, which echo the framing strategies developed by *OuiShare*, through the choice of the topics of debates and conferences occurring at the different editions of the *OuiShare Fest*, and through the publications showcased in the *OuiShare Fest* bookstore (see Tables 2 and 3).

#### *The Access Economy: Shifting from Property to Usage*

The first theoretical current emerging from the narratives of the SE entrepreneurs is that of the access economy – also called functional economy – (Stahel, 1986, 2008). This approach aims at re-designing business models in order to promote use and access over ownership and a shift toward service-driven business models (Bardhi & Eckhardt, 2012). Product-service systems solutions, defined by Botsman and Rogers (2010) as one of the three main areas of SE, are considered as a potential vehicle to enhance new consumption modes while fostering environmental sustainability. Such rationales where highlighted by several entrepreneurs, in particular in the fields of P2P renting, exchange of goods or services, repair or gift systems. Two examples are: Peerby, a platform for sharing goods (for free or for a fee) among individuals, founded in the Netherlands, and its French homolog Mutum:

> [Through our platform, people] use products more intensively. What we are trying to create is basically a platform that will ultimately incentivize manufacturers to start supplying goods that are no longer designed for a single consumer, but products that are designed for a community. What we want to offer to manufacturers is a way to sell products by the hour or per use so that the more durable the product that they create, the more money they can make. (Peerby)

> Basically what we do by having people share products in the long run is reducing the amount of products needed. Let's say if a street now requires one lawn mower per house with the proper infrastructure you could do one for all. (Mutum)

Entrepreneurs embracing this approach often blame the environmental impacts of planned obsolescence strategies from manufacturers, and tend to embrace principles, which seek to minimize the environmental impact of a good or service throughout its life cycle (Braungart & McDonough, 2009), without renouncing to economic sustainability.

***Table 2.*** Illustration of the Links Between the Data Collected and Theoretical Currents in the Collaborative Economy Field.

| | Theoretical Currents | | | |
|---|---|---|---|---|
| | The Access Economy | The Gift Economy | The Commons | Libertarianism |
| Entrepreneur narratives | "We consume on a massive scale, it piles up in our closets and we don't have any more space left [...] DressWing is a site that allows individuals to rent out high-end and luxury clothing and accessories to each other." (DressWing)<br>"People say that thanks to us, you can access goods and services that you couldn't have bought, or don't want to buy, by renting them. [...] before we would buy compact disc (CDs). Now we don't want to buy CDs, we want to listen to music." (Place de la Loc) | "I wanted to donate my refrigerator and I couldn't find a single organisation that was interested. [...] so I felt like creating something that would allow me to sell this refrigerator, and simply give the money to a charity." (C'est Bon Esprit)<br>"Our key message is sharing objects for free among neighbours. There is always a potential source of goods and services near us, since we all have neighbours. Our philosophy is based on free mutual aid between neighbors (...)." (ShareVoisin) | 'We believe in the "hacker" spirit, exemplified by open-source software and Do-It-Yourself. At its core: sharing knowledge, emulation, freedom to do things, and the desire to understand. Whether its by creating new objects and tools, or by continuously improving those that already exist, hacker culture's spirit of finding new uses for things beyond their intended purpose goes well with this desire for independence and experimentation that drives all our members.' (Electrolab) | "[...] In 2010, we weren't yet talking about the collaborative economy, but we were already talking about platforms. [...] We were already starting to see traditional economic players being destroyed by digital technology. I came to La Ruche Qui Dit Oui a very pragmatically, by telling myself that this project would allow us to give power back to consumers and producers. Thanks to the power of the Internet and platforms." (La Ruche Qui Dit Oui) |

***Table 2.*** *(Continued)*

| | Theoretical Currents | | | |
|---|---|---|---|---|
| | The Access Economy | The Gift Economy | The Commons | Libertarianism |
| Intermediate theories | "Transitioning Toward a Functional and Cooperation Economy" (Bernasconi and Sempels, *OuiShare Fest* 2015)<br>"The Functional and Cooperation Economy as Innovative Business Models" (Sempels, *OuiShare Fest* 2015)<br>"An increasing number of people from different backgrounds and all ages are shifting to a 'usage mind-set' whereby they pay for the benefit of a product – what it does for them – without needing to own the product outright." (Botsman & Rogers, 2010, p. 71) | "From Gift Culture to Gift Cosmology." (Eisenstein, *OuiShare Fest* 2013)<br>"Education Powered By Gift: The Story of Maya Universe Academy." (Manjil, *OuiShare Fest* 2014)<br>"A culture of 'indirect reciprocity' is often referred to as the "gift economy," one where people give goods and services without any explicit agreement for immediate or future reward. This model is at work in Freecycle." (Botsman & Rogers, 2010, p. 132) | "In order to address the scarcity of natural resources, we have to put an end to the scarcity of information, knowledge, and know-how. […] This is the goal of 'open-source' innovator communities that are producing contributive and intangible common goods. Reproducibility is at the core of their sustainable organizational principles." (Filippova & OuiShare, 2015, p. 95)<br>"Mozilla, Creative Commons, Wikipedia, and Architecture for Humanity remain strong embodiments of that ethos. The result is continuously organic improvement of the Web experience for all. These open communities and platforms are a terrific demonstration of the culture of gifting and generosity that fuelled the 'Web economy' in the mid-1990s. I believe it remains central to nurturing the next generation of healthy social innovations." (Gansky, 2012, p. 77) | "An Anatomy of Misfit Philosophies: How to Hack Systems." (Clay, *OuiShare Fest* 2014)<br>"How to finance your platform? Getting real about private, public and peer opportunities with Robin Chase, the successful founder and former CEO of ZipCar." (*OuiShare Fest* 2015)<br>"[…] these collaborative logics […] were obviously made possible by the Internet. When I say the Internet I'm referring to the technical network and practices as well as the visions and ideologies that gravitate around it. And this requires going back to the origins of the Internet, which were a little alternative, a little counter-cultural, and the way in which this counter-cultural heritage influenced the development of the Internet has meaning for the collaborative economy." (Co-founder, *OuiShare*) |

***Table 3.*** OuiShare Fest Evolution 2013–2017.

| | 2013 | 2014 | 2015 | 2016 | 2017 |
|---|---|---|---|---|---|
| Title | OuiShare Fest | The age of communities | Lost in Transition? | After the gold rush | Cities of the world, Unite! |
| Scope | 700 participants from 25 countries | 1,100 participants | 1,350 participants | 1,500 participants from 51 countries | NA |
| Main themes | Platforms, collaborative consumption, communities, collaborative practices | SE and start-up, virtual and local community management, new consumer behaviors, gift economy | Post-capitalism, crowdfunding, bitcoin, e-reputation, open source, democracy and digitalization, societal impact | Block-chain, scaling, makers movement, decentralization, horizontal governance | Communities, cities, citizens, civic-tech, open governance, democracy |
| Main features *(words and phrases from interviews)* | Enthusiasm, novelties, candor, bubbling | Professionalization, consolidation, wider gathering, public contributions | Beginning to question, taking distance, SE is only 1 theme out of 13 | Posture of defiance, disenchantment, openness | New horizons, beyond private initiatives, new energy, wider scope |
| Role of OuiShare *(words in inverted commas extracted from the interviews)* | "Pioneer," "disseminator of ideas," "ambassador," search for legitimacy | Assuming the role of institutional entrepreneur through awards ceremony and the erection of the festival as a flagship event | Increasing its own legitimacy, opening a space to criticisms and questions, and exploring new issues | "Critical thinker," defying the contested field of the SE, inviting the community to dig deeper into main societal issues | "Thinker of the future," Shifting the focus of the festival on a broader, territorialized field, the governance of and by the cities |

> For me, the starting point was in 2011, when I watched video report on planned obsolescence called "ready to dump." Like many other people, I was utterly shocked and started to think about something I could do about it … For a month, I was thinking of a solution … to save the world, basically! […] The subject of planned obsolescence has been an important topic of visibility for my site, on social networks. I started to make the site known also to make humorous posters where there was a message I was spreading via Facebook, which was basically "The industry makes products that are not sustainable. Conclusion: they think we are pigeons. We must act." (commentréparer.fr)

> And it seemed interesting to me to think about different actions on the product life cycle and different actions on consumer action. Where can behavior be changed to make products last as long as possible? There's this constant question nurturing our project. I am still convinced that making products last is the best possible action for the environment. […] By renting devices rather than buying them, etc., by working on maintenance systems. I believe there is a way not to kill the economy or growth while making the devices last longer. (commentreparer.fr)

*The Gift Economy: The Importance of "Social Relationships"*

Actors in the SE refer to the gift economy by promising a sense of meaning, a purpose for their own initiative, which goes beyond a simple market exchange, and is supposed to strengthen and renew social connections (Belk, 2010). They acknowledge that the practice of gifting is at the same time one of society's most ancient forms of exchange (Mauss, 1954), but still quite common in the business world (Cheal, 2015). Following Botsman and Rogers (2010), they believe that several SE practices (such as Recup.net, an online platform which organizes the gift of physical objects from peers to peers) could make it possible to regain a sense of community and connection that has been lost.

> For me, the great success of Recup.net is that it has allowed us to rediscover values that we had forgotten: social exchange, relationships between people, the social bond. We're not making this up, people were already doing it. Recup.net helped us find this, look up and think about our neighbor who might be interested in something we have at home and are about to throw away. As a result, we become interested in each other, make new contacts or renew old ones, or maintain them. (Recup.net)

A gift is usually understood as a transfer with no expectation of direct return or reward (Komter, 2007), as the immediate reciprocity that is required in a financial exchange or barter would actually destroy the social relationship (Boyle, 2012).

> I read a book that clearly shows the opposition between monetizable and commercial behavior on one side and the gift, "giving," on the other side, with examples of situations where, for example, lawyers and experts are asked to help people in need for a small fee. And lawyers refuse because it devalues their work. It devalues their expertise. And they don't want to get paid. On the other hand, they agree to do so free of charge. That is, the gift, you choose to bring something to a cause you care about. And we're off the commercial register. As soon as we enter the commercial register and evaluate things and bill them and pay them, we get into how much I am worth. We're in the same situation. (Commentréparer.fr)

As the act of gifting encompasses both the pursuit of individual advantage and openness to others through generous actions (Cheal, 2015), one of the leading platforms for borrowing/lending objects tried to estimate the positive social outcome generated by the exchanges occurring through their intermediation.

> Research shows that people that have at least some weak connections in their neighborhoods even if they are weak live longer and are healthier. There is a health impact in being connected to your neighbor. [...] What this research on our impact showed is that ... (I think it was in 2014) we generated roughly I think 2 million euros in social capital and I think what's important to realize is that we are growing by 500 to 600% per year. This year that could be 10 million and next year that could be 50 million. [...] A research team looked at the increase in happiness caused by lending or borrowing through our platform, and they compared that to an increase in salary. They tried to see how well being is influenced by salary and what is the impact of this platform. (Peerby)

These examples illustrate how SE entrepreneurs hold the SE's promise of fostering new forms of relationships between people that are not just friends, neighbors, or members of the same community, but are ready to "share with strangers" (Belk, 2014).

> Luckily there are guys who are out there to make gifts and who allow other people, people they do not know, to furnish themselves for zero euros. Because if we can get a table or a keyboard for free, it's because someone is willing to give an object, who is willing to make this gesture, but all the more is willing to give his time to take the photos, prepare the announcement. It is so much easier to throw it away! (Co-recyclage)

*The Commons: Toward Decentralized and Shared Governance*

Ideals of self-organized and distributed forms of governance, taking inspiration from the seminal work of Elinor Ostrom (1990) on the governance of the "commons," are recurrent in the discourse of the entrepreneurs of the SE, and in particular of those involved in the creation and management of knowledge, software, or skills (Benkler & Nissenbaum, 2006; Jemielniak, 2014).

> [I believe that, as a society,] the only reason we ever needed hierarchical organizations is because we didn't have the technology to connect people on an individual basis like peers in a network that has at the same time authority and power. I think peer-to-peer is really the logical next step of governance, in the same way that the centralized model was kind of an invention to be able to do things that were bigger than us. (Peerby)

This ideology is closely linked with Internet-related developments, such as the GNU project leading to Linux, a free and open-source operating system (Stallman, Lessig, & Gay, 2006) or the hacker movement (Lallement, 2015), which all rely on a decentralized technology to undermine established hierarchies and promote free, open, and universal access for users.

> We identify with the "hacker" spirit, which is expressed in free software and DIY. At the core of this is knowledge sharing, emulation, freedom to do things and the desire to understand. (Electrolab Hackerspace)

> Here, like in many other FabLabs, you have the freedom of choosing any economic model from non-profit to for profit, but you are obliged to share knowledge and you are obliged to train people. So, there is a vocation displayed which is a vocation of evangelization, sharing of information and engagement to train the totality of the people who use the tools and methods. Basically, the open world is to make sure that what I invent can be improved by others. (Fablab Rennes)

Michel Bauwens, one of the architects of the P2P foundation platform, calls for an alternative to closed business models, and encourages the emergence of a "mode of production and value creation that is free, fair, and sustainable," and encourages the sharing and co-creation of value with "commoners" (Bauwens, 2006, 2015).

> We do not want to be an engineering club, we want to be a citizen community, a network for sharing productive techniques, reappropriating technology and productive tools. So for that, we need an engaged citizen base, not just engineers. [...] We try to move from competition to collaboration and decentralization. And the idea is to try to go beyond competition since, in any case, knowledge must be published. To properly respect the terms of open source, it is necessary that the information is really available. We are not allowed to publish something a little and keep little secrets to in fact corner the market behind it. To be open source, you must be fair. (Open Source Ecology)

*Libertarianism: Start-ups and the Disruption of Large Bureaucratic Institutions*

Libertarianism stands as the fourth theoretical current emerging from the narratives of the SE entrepreneurs. Libertarianism is a collection of political philosophies (from the right as well as from the left wing) that uphold liberty as a core principle (Boaz, 1997). Actors that subscribe to this logic put forward the virtues of autonomy and entrepreneurship, praise the start-up culture, advocate for disruption and the end of bureaucratic and centralized organizations.

> Us, what we do, if we want to be factual, we do peer-to-peer, that is, we allow individuals who create to sell to individuals who want to buy a small, unique product. It's not necessarily "sharing" in the pure sense of the term, rather it is an amplification of the market by technologies. It is the freedom to make a profit by valuing what we know and love to do. If we are free to do what we want our creativity will go very far. [...] Our values are freedom and initiative taking. (A little Market)

American libertarian philosophers (Read, 1975; Rothbard, 1978) gave prominence to individual entrepreneurs and emphasized a drive for profits that irrigated an ideology built on individualism and the cult of inventiveness. Entrepreneurs in the SE have also taken from the ideology of American libertarianism, the aspiration to change the world and disrupt the economic rent of large established institutions (States and big companies).

This perspective is typical of explicitly disruptive initiatives such as Uber [whose founder Travis Kalanick has publicly declared his passion for Ayn Rand's masterpiece *Atlas Shrugged* (1957)] or Airbnb, which promotes an entrepreneurial and liberal vision challenging national regulations and attacking positions that it views as monopoly rents.

> Roughly speaking, I think that the sharing economy is a rather enormous opportunity, it is the rebirth of the market, moreover, it works very well in France. France is a country that is very well positioned. So my recommendation is to avoid the pitfalls that we have everywhere in France, always trying to regulate in all directions, and to see that more as an opportunity than a threat. The entrepreneurial freedom amplified by the power of Internet can do a lot of good to our country. (A little Market)

According to Turner (2008), who sees the development of Internet as rooted in 1960s American hippie counter culture, whose ideologies – first socialist libertarian and communitarian, then libertarian – are expressed in the development of new web technologies, the Silicon Valley is the icon of the emergence of a world that rejects regulations and the rent-seeking behavior of large bureaucratic companies (e.g., IBM in the 1970s). Such model heavily relies upon start-ups and venture capitalists.

> In companies that come from the Web, like ours, there is this start-up culture that means that you have to raise funds and capital, invest in technology, and it costs a lot. Obviously, after a while, we find ourselves faced with a tension between investors who are used to this culture, and quite different stakeholders, consumers, citizens, politicians, etc., who look for a different model for us. (The Food Assembly)

*Joint Mobilization of Plural Framings in the SE Field*

Despite the differences among each of the four theoretical currents, they are obviously not impervious, incompatible, or exclusive. A number of collaborative projects simultaneously draw on and "tweak" several theories by combining them: for example, an initiative such as CommentReparer.com (a platform developing a common pool of knowledge to repair broken objects), borrows simultaneously from the access economy (promoting reparability and combatting product obsolescence), the gift and the "commons" (free sharing and spreading knowledge to repair objects). Similarly, a project such as *La Ruche Qui Dit Oui*, The Food Assembly (a platform that organizes micro-markets for food distribution in order to re-localize food and promote more direct exchanges between consumers and producers), borrows from aspects of libertarianism while also promoting a community-based vision of value creation. Lastly, a project such as POC 21 (a prototyping space for solutions to major planetary issues) builds on the commons (open-source solutions) and the access economy. Each collaborative project can thus be developed by combining and hybridizing several theoretical currents and their underpinning value creation logics, providing opportunities for creativity and organizational innovation.

### *Institutional Entrepreneurship in the SE Field*

Concerning our second research question, aiming at characterizing the specific forms of institutional entrepreneurship at work in the emerging field of the SE, we identified three main distinctive features incarnated by *OuiShare*: first, it constitutes a strong collective of founders, which relies upon a coordinated network of members (connectors) promoting individual initiatives; second, it values the diversity of values and postures of each member; third, it seeks less to structure the field than to showcase/stage its tensions and dynamics.

*A Coordinated Network Led by Strong Leaders*

*OuiShare*, established in Paris in 2012, has been an institutional entrepreneur for the SE for several years: the primary goal of its co-founders was to offer a platform to bring together and connect actors, initiatives, supporters and all those interested in the movement. Most co-founders are under 30 years old, live in Paris, and had no children when they founded the organization. They have completed higher education up to Master level (Bac + 5), in prestigious academic institutions in Management, Engineering, or Political Science. They all had previous professional experience, mainly in the economic and entrepreneurial world, providing them with specific know-how and a varied professional network.

The network has been expanding and at the end of 2017, it was relying on several thousand sympathizers and contributors, in 20 countries in Europe, Latin America, North America and North Africa (OuiShare, 2017). Sympathizers and contributors represent all those who identify themselves in the mission of *OuiShare*, its values, its culture, and who participate in the activities of the community. They are supervised by "Connectors" (in the number of 80, at the end of 2017), that is, the most active members, thinkers, and entrepreneurs who participate in strategic decisions and voluntarily take in charge one or more projects, such as the organization of events (the *OuiShare Fest* and other local events), conducting studies, consulting and training to associations or companies, or writing articles for *OuiShare* Magazine, the association's main online media. Finally, the "Core Connectors" represent the group of executives of the movement, including the "Parisian core team" (mainly the co-founders) and some other local active connectors.

> I like to think of OuiShare as an incubator of people: a shared platform for experimentation that gives Connectors and members access to a common pool of knowledge, tools and an international network of people they can learn and draw inspiration from. (Connector & Co-founder OuiShare Fest)

Despite such formalization, *OuiShare* celebrates initiative, autonomy, and participation. Do-ocracy, meant as the principle according to which decision-making is led by action and experimentation, is one of core values put forward by the network.

> A large part is left to experimentation. Within OuiShare, if you are in a minority position, nothing prevents you from launching a project or testing an idea. Either it works and we follow it, or it doesn't work and it doesn't matter, there has been learning around the mistakes made. [...] The more you do the more visible, the more legitimate you become. (OuiShare Connector)

Proposals for new initiatives and experiments are discussed during the "*OuiShare* Summits," where decisions are mainly taken by consensus (overall agreement without strong objection). This reflects the willingness to adopt a horizontal, collaborative governance model, aligned with the societal vision promoted by the Association, although power struggles are not absent.

> And we realize that finally the tension between autocracy, that is to say making decisions either alone or in small groups (our founders), versus democracy where you make decisions to a large number of people, is constantly present in OuiShare, and in fact you are obliged to have both. [...] I wouldn't say that OuiShare is a completely horizontal organization because such organization doesn't really exist, but I think we have succeeded in putting in place several measures, such as our OuiShare summits or a rotating leadership system, that is, on certain areas or projects, for example, you could be responsible for one project and the next day work for or with me who will be project manager on another project. These postures and mechanisms prevent the same person from always imposing his ideas. (OuiShare Member)

*A Network of Individuals, a Plurality of Values and Postures*
*OuiShare* describes itself as

> a collective, a community, an accelerator of ideas and projects working towards the emergence of the collaborative society: a society based on principles of openness, collaboration, trust, and sharing of value. (OuiShare.net/fr)

Such broad definition allows members with different values and adopting alternative postures to co-exist within the network, as diversity is established as an indispensable value for *OuiShare* members.

> What I like about OuiShare's identity is that it is multiple, you can ask 80 people what OuiShare is and you will get 80 different answers. That's what makes OuiShare OuiShare. It's not a company. We're all in our own interpretation. Within OuiShare what makes the common denominator is this aspiration to try to build a model of society, very humbly, where people are not constantly in competition, self-destruction but in benevolence and collaboration. Otherwise we have a diversity that is our DNA, a diversity of ideas, which does not prevent us from having stronger ideas than others on how to build our future. (OuiShare Connector)

Throughout its activities, *OuiShare* also reflects the plurality of values and meanings revealed by classic entrepreneurs (cf. Table 2, which shows how the program of the Fest tends to reflect the same theoretical frames). In the same vein, *OuiShare* members convey different visions of the SE: for some, it is enabled by distributed digital technologies, vector of political innovation, catalyst of positive social change (the commons), and the main tool to enact entrepreneurial initiative (libertarianism); for some others it is linked to the need to move beyond internal crises raised by capitalism, or to more sustainable forms of production and consumption (functional economy, gift):

> We all embrace the digital technologies, we think that's what is going to bring us things to change. There are many anti-technological socialists …. Our idea is to include this technology in the commons, to combine them and not having to have the market do the regulation but another mechanism that would be digital technologies. (Connector and Co-founder OuiShare Fest)

> I do not think that everyone in OuiShare would formulate the idea that the objective is to move to a post-capitalist society, but for me, yes, capitalism is in direct contradiction with a distributed and equitable economic model. (Editor *OuiShare* Magazine)

> Our society, its institutions and the economic world are struggling to respond to the environmental issues and social challenges of our century: preservation of natural resources and protection of biodiversity, fight against pollution and climate change (*OuiShare* book, edited by an *OuiShare* Co-founder).

Such plurality of espoused values suggests the reluctance of *OuiShare* to adopt a too normative position, centered on one single specific framing, potentially marginalizing their discourse on the SE. Against such plurality of values and meanings, the common ambition of all members of the organization seems to be their ambition to change the whole society from inside.

> We try to have one foot in each world, we have our asses between two chairs, but what characterizes us is not the ambition to form a counter-culture but to infuse a discourse that would be applicable to the entire society, we are still far from it, but we have more this sensitivity. We are critical of the mainstream, but we have a vocation to be mainstream while being aware of the dangers associated with the mainstream. (Editor *OuiShare* Magazine)

*Showcasing Dynamics, Contradictions, and Controversies*

The third feature of *OuiShare* institutional entrepreneurship is linked to its ability to anticipate trends, nurture debates, and favor criticism.

> What distinguishes OuiShare is that we have always tried to remain critical of ourselves and critical of our subject. And that is why we have also evolved: we have evolved because we have always kept a critical eye on the main theme. (OuiShare Connector)

> In a defined field, fixed and framed, there are no borders to explore, we don't need a lighthouse in the daylight …. I've worked in consulting, I make big shortcuts but one of my main bosses told me "when there is blur, we have work." For me, OuiShare is the lighthouse of the Sharing Economy field. (OuiShare Member)

Building on the critical and reflexive perspective advocated by *OuiShare*, and through an analysis of the evolution of the *OuiShare* fest, we show that the main objective of the Network was not to structure and give coherence to the SE heterogeneous field, but to showcase the different values and meanings and the controversial dynamics riddling the field, to increase their own legitimacy as institutional entrepreneurs in the field and beyond it, in the wider context of societal innovation. Between 2013 and 2017, the focus of the *OuiShare Fest* has shifted from a celebration of the SE to a profound re-examination of such emerging practices, and its role have evolved from "ambassador" to "critical thinker," and even "thinker of the future" (see Table 3).

In 2013, the festival was presented as "the first major European event on the SE" (YouTube channel *OuiShare*). In 2014, the Fest was associated with the *OuiShare* Village at the *Foire de Paris*, an event gathering thousands of people, to celebrate "the SE week" (*OuiShare*, 2014). A turning point was the 2015 edition of the festival, which had to face a major challenge: to renew itself to always attract media and participants, and anticipate growing criticisms to the SE. Thus, *OuiShare* made the strategic choice to stage the controversies in the collaborative economy.

> We wanted to show reality in a more raw light. Criticism is part of our DNA, we are convinced that the ability to highlight defects is a step in the search for solutions. (Connector and Co-founder OuiShare Fest)

In 2016, this critical positioning was accentuated: the definition of the Fest evolves to become "four days of intense discussion, experimentation and collaboration to work on solutions" (YouTube channel, OuiShare).

> The Gold rush is over. What's left? The seeds we have planted: the projects, the processes and the things we have documented. (Official Program of OuiShare Fest 2016)

> It was then a question of recognizing the conceptual failure of the term Sharing Economy, and turning to the study of other deeper transformations, of which the sharing economy was only the tip of the iceberg: the future of work, the redistribution of value, the problems of governance and decentralization. (Editor *OuiShare* Magazine)

We observe a shift from an event centered on the SE from 2013 to 2015 to a space for reflection with strong critical connotations in 2016, to a more territorialized definition in 2017, calling for the participation of cities to enact the envisioned societal transformation toward collaboration, horizontality, and a more sustainable world. The promise behind this redefinition is to offer each year a space for critical and stimulating reflection, playful and original, due to the Festival format, on main contemporary societal subjects.

## DISCUSSION AND CONCLUSION

Through this chapter, we make several contributions. First, we contribute to the SE literature by conceptualizing the SE as a separate and emergent field, and showing how the plural framings of the field are mobilized by classic entrepreneurs to make sense of and legitimize their own initiatives. Second, we complement existing approaches to institutional entrepreneurship by showing how maintaining a plurality of frames during the institutionalization process of emerging fields involves specific forms of institutional entrepreneurship, that actively maintain and encourage – instead of discouraging – such plurality. Finally, we discuss the ambivalent effects of such framing plurality on the institutionalization of the field. In particular, we show that while plurality of framings provides entrepreneurs with opportunities for action and hybridization, this also creates problems related to identity, coherence, and external comprehension, and runs the risk of causing controversy or even fragmenting the field.

### *Contributions to the SE*

By identifying four distinct repertories in SE entrepreneurs' discourse, we reveal how heterogeneous frames are mobilized and invested by classical and institutional entrepreneurs to legitimize and give meaning to their initiatives. By exploring actors' promises, discursive strategies, and theoretical roots, we show how the SE involves various – and sometimes conflicting – visions of value creation and distribution.

By drawing on the discourse of entrepreneurs who affiliate with the field, our work offers an empirical contribution to current conceptual debates concerning the definition and boundaries of the field (Frenken & Schor, 2017; Schor, 2014). While some voices call for clarifying and restricting the conceptual and empirical scope of the field (Belk, 2014; Frenken & Schor, 2017), our empirical results suggest that entrepreneurs tend to adopt a broad understanding of the SE reflecting a wide array of theoretical frames, value creation logics, and organizational forms (Mair & Reischauer, 2017). Our empirical results based on entrepreneurial discourses tend to fit existing conceptual definitions of the SE as a multi-dimensional construct combining access-based economy, platform-based economy, and community-based economy (Acquier et al., 2017). We also refine this tri-dimensional model by showing how community-based economy may be reflected into two different field-specific framings, the "gift" and the "commons." Our discursive approach to the plural framings of the SE complements previous work based on configurational approaches to business model design in the SE field (Acquier et al., 2019) which had pointed to the co-existence of varied and conflicting value creation and distribution logics in the field.

Our insights on the framing strategies at work in the field shed light on the struggle over meanings involved in the institutionalization process (Zilber, 2008). Future research may connect discursive to configurational approaches to articulate their joint implications for our understanding of the social construction of the SE field.

*Contribution to the Theorization of Institutional Entrepreneurship in a Context of Framing Plurality*

A second contribution concerns the theorization of institutional entrepreneurship in a context of framing plurality. We have shown how such framing diversity within the SE creates a specific context for action for entrepreneurs, creating both opportunities and constraints. The entrepreneurial appeal of the SE is related to the field's framing plurality, creating diverse opportunities for legitimacy, creativity, and social innovation. However, such framing plurality also appears as a double-edge sword, as it may reveal internal contradictions between field-level values and meanings, raising problems of consistency and complexity for external stakeholders such as regulators, consumers, or citizens. As a result, a key question concerns the forms of institutional entrepreneurship likely to cope with such diversity. We contributed to this question by showing how emerging fields shaped by plural framings may involve specific forms of institutional entrepreneurship (DiMaggio, 1988; Greenwood et al., 2002; Maguire et al., 2004). The action of *OuiShare* offers a good example of how an institutional entrepreneur, in the form of a collective organization, can sustain plural diversity over time (instead of infusing a single dominant frame), through division of labor and a variety of espoused values reflecting such diversity, and process formalization to develop strong organizational capabilities. Similarly, rather than regulate, homogenize, and define the boundaries of the field and its normative foundations, they tend to create arenas (such as *OuiShare Fest*) to promote and organize its internal diversity and instability.

At the same time, the thematic evolution of the OuiShare Fest also reflects the difficulty to maintain equilibrium among different framings over time. The increasing critical perspective and distance of *OuiShare* from the concept of the SE is a sign that the concept (and field) is hard to sustain, which may eventually lead to fragmentation or, ultimately, construct collapse (Hirsch & Levin, 1999). In this case, the SE would constitute a plural and temporary field, creating entrepreneurial opportunities by offering legitimacy resources to entrepreneurs before the field gets fragmented and contested. In this case, entrepreneurs (both institutional and classic) would first affiliate to the field to grasp legitimacy opportunities, before diversifying with emergent concepts or re-affiliating with other fields when the notion becomes contested.

To further explore such perspectives, future research should draw on comparative studies among different countries, and extend the analysis to future trends to explore the institutionalization of the field, account for the tensions between empirical and conceptual developments of the SE, and show how such tensions are reflected in field configuring events (Lampel & Meyer, 2008).

## NOTE

1. PICO: Pioneers of Collaborative Economy, https://www.iddri.org/en/project/sharing-economy-and-sustainable-development.

## REFERENCES

Acquier, A. (2018). Uberization meets organizational theory: Platform capitalism and the rebirth of the putting-out system. In F. Davison, & Infranca (Eds.), *The Cambridge handbook of the law of the sharing economy* (pp. 11–25). Cambridge: Cambridge University Press.

Acquier, A., & Carbone, V. (2018). Sharing economy and social innovation. In F. Davidson, & Infranca (Eds.), *The Cambridge handbook of the law of the sharing economy* (pp. 51–64). Cambridge University Press.

Acquier, A., Carbone, V., & Massé, D. (2017). À quoi pensent les institutions? Théorisation et institutionalisation du champ de l'économie collaborative [What do institutions think about? Theorizing and institutionalizing the field of the sharing economy]. *Revue Française de Gestion [French Management Journal]*. *4*(265), 25–50.

Acquier, A., Carbone, V., & Massé, D. (2019). How to create value (s) in the sharing economy: Business models, scalability, and sustainability. *Technology Innovation Management Review*, *9*(2), 5–24.

Acquier, A., Daudigeos, T., & Pinkse, J. (2017). Promises and paradoxes of the sharing economy: An organizing framework. *Technological Forecasting and Social Change*, *125*, 1–10.

Bardhi, F., & Eckhardt, G. M. (2012). Access-based consumption: The case of car sharing. *Journal of Consumer Research*, *39*(4), 881–898.

Barth, G., & Ihl, C. (2018). How institutional entrepreneurs diffuse institutional logics to shape an emerging field. In *Academy of management proceedings* (Vol. 2018, p. 11066). Briarcliff Manor, NY: Academy of Management.

Bauwens, M. (2006). The political economy of peer production. *Post-autistic Economics Review*, *37*, 33–44. http://www.paecon.net/PAEReview/issue37/Bauwens37.htm.

Bauwens, M. (2015). *Sauver le Monde: Vers une Société Post-Capitaliste avec le Peer-to-Peer [Saving the World: Towards a Post-Capitalist Society with Peer-to-Peer]*. Paris, France: Les Liens qui libèrent.

Belk, R. (2010). Sharing. *Journal of Consumer Research*, *36*(5), 715–734.

Belk, R. (2014). You are what you can access: Sharing and collaborative consumption online. *Journal of Business Research*, *67*(8), 1595–1600.

Benkler, Y., & Nissenbaum, H. (2006). Commons-based peer production and virtue. *Journal of Political Philosophy*, *14*(4), 394–419.

Boaz, D. (1997). *Libertarianism: A primer*. New York, NY: Simon & Schuster.

Botsman, R., & Rogers, R. (2010). *What's mine is yours how collaborative consumption is changing the way we live*. London: Collins.

Boyle, M. (2012). *The moneyless manifesto: Live well. Live rich. Live free*. East Meon: Permanent Publications.

Braungart, M., & McDonough, W. (2009). *Cradle to cradle*. London: Penguin.

Cheal, D. (2015). *The gift economy*. Oxford: Routledge.

Davidson, N. M., Finck, M., & Infranca, J. J. (2018). *The Cambridge handbook of the law of the sharing economy*. Cambridge: Cambridge University Press.

DiMaggio, P. J. (1988). *Interest and agency in institutional theory, institutional patterns and organizations*. Cambridge: Ballinger.

DiMaggio, P. J., & Powell, W. W. (1983). The iron cage revisited: Institutional isomorphism and collective rationality in organizational fields. *American Sociological Review*, 147–160.

Filippova, D, & OuiShare. (2015). *Société Collaborative: La Fin des Hiérarchies [Collaborative Society: The End of Hierarchies]*. Paris, France: Rue de l'échiquier.

Fligstein, N., & McAdam, D. (2012). *A theory of fields*. New York, NY: Oxford University Press.

Frenken, K., & Schor, J. (2017). Putting the sharing economy into perspective. *Environmental Innovation and Societal Transitions*, *23*, 3–10.

Gallie, W. B. (1956). Essentially contested concepts. *Proceedings of the Aristotelian Society*, *56*(1955–1956), 167–198.

Gansky, L. (2012). *The mesh: Why the future of business is sharing*. New York, NY: Portfolio.

Geels, F. W. (2005). *Technological transitions and system innovations: A co-evolutionary and socio-technical analysis*. Cheltenham: Edward Elgar Publishing.

Greenwood, R., Suddaby, R., & Hinings, C. R. (2002). Theorizing change: The role of professional associations in the transformation of institutionalized fields. *Academy of Management Journal*, *45*(1), 58–80.

Habibi, M. R., Davidson, A., & Laroche, M. (2017). What managers should know about the sharing economy. *Business Horizons*, *60*(1), 113–121.

Hardy, C., & Maguire, S. (2008). Institutional entrepreneurship. In R. Greenwood, C. Oliver, R. Suddaby, & K. Sahlin (Eds.), *The SAGE handbook of organizational institutionalism* (pp. 198–217). London: SAGE Publications Ltd.

Hardy, C., & Maguire, S. (2010). Discourse, field-configuring events, and change in organizations and institutional fields: Narratives of DDT and the Stockholm convention. *Academy of Management Journal*, *53*(6), 1365–1392.

Heinrichs, H. (2013). Sharing economy: A potential new pathway to sustainability. *GAIA – Ecological Perspectives for Science and Society*, *22*(4), 228–231.

Hirsch, P. M., & Levin, D. Z. (1999). Umbrella advocates versus validity police: A life-cycle model. *Organization Science*, *10*(2), 199–212.

Jemielniak, D. (2014). *Common knowledge?: An ethnography of Wikipedia*. Palo Alto, CA: Stanford University Press.

Komter, A. (2007). Gifts and social relations the mechanisms of reciprocity. *International Sociology*, *22*(1), 93–107.

Lallement, M. (2015). *L'âge du faire : Hacking, travail, anarchie [The age of doing it: Hacking, work, anarchy]*. Paris, France: Seuil.

Laloux, F. (2014). *Reinventing organizations*. Toronto: Nelson Parker.

Lampel, J., & Meyer, A. D. (2008). Guest Editors' Introduction : Field-configuring events as structuring mechanisms: How conferences, ceremonies, and trade shows constitute new technologies, industries, and markets. *Journal of Management Studies*, *45*(6), 1025–1035.

Lawrence, T. B., & Phillips, N. (2004). From Moby Dick to Free Willy: Macro-cultural discourse and institutional entrepreneurship in emerging institutional fields. *Organization*, *11*(5), 689–711.

Maguire, S., & Hardy, C. (2009). Discourse and de-institutionalization: The case of DDT. *Academy of Management Journal*, *52*(4), 148–178.

Maguire, S., Hardy, C., & Lawrence, T. B. (2004). Institutional entrepreneurship in emerging fields: HIV/AIDS treatment advocacy in Canada. *The Academy of Management Journal*, *47*(5), 657–679.

Mair, J., & Reischauer, G. (2017): Capturing the dynamics of the sharing economy: Institutional research on the plural forms and practices of sharing economy organizations. *Technological Forecasting & Social Change*, *125*, 11–20.

Marcus, A. A., & Anderson, M. H. (2013). Commitment to an emerging organizational field: An enactment theory. *Business et Society*, *52*(2), 181–212.

Martin, C. J. (2016). The sharing economy: A pathway to sustainability or a nightmarish form of neoliberal capitalism? *Ecological Economics*, *121*, 149–159.

Mauss, M. (1954). *The gift: Forms and functions of exchange in archaic societies*. London: Cohen & West.

Mena, S., & Suddaby, R. (2016). Theorization as institutional work: The dynamics of roles and practices. *Human Relations*, *69*(8), 1669–1708.

Munoz, P., & Cohen, B. (2017). Mapping out the sharing economy: A configurational approach to sharing business modeling. *Technological Forecasting and Social Change*, *125*, 21–37.

Murillo, D., Buckland, H., & Val, E. (2017). When the sharing economy becomes neoliberalism on steroids: Unravelling the controversies. *Technological Forecasting and Social Change*, *125*, 66–76.

Ostrom, E. (1990). *Governing the commons: The evolution of institutions for collective action*. Cambridge: Cambridge University Press.

Parguel, B., Lunardo, R., & Benoit-Moreau, F. (2017). Sustainability of the sharing economy in question: When second-hand peer-to-peer platforms stimulate indulgent consumption. *Technological Forecasting and Social Change*, *125*, 48–57.

Phillips, N., Lawrence, T. B., & Hardy, C. (2004). Discourse and institutions. *Academy of Management Review*, *29*(4), 635–652.

Rand, A. (1957). *Atlas shrugged* (p. 1088). London: Penguin.

Rao, H., Monin, P., & Durand, R. (2003). Institutional change in Toque Ville: Nouvelle Cuisine as an identity movement in French gastronomy. *American Journal of Sociology*, *108*(4), 795–843.

Read, L. E. (1975). *The love of liberty*. Atlanta, GA: Foundation for Economic Education.

Rothbard, M. N. (1978). *For a new liberty: The libertarian manifesto*. Auburn, AL: Ludwig von Mises Institute.

Schor, J. (2014). Debating the sharing economy. *Great Transition Initiative* (online article; greattransition.org). New York.

Scott, W. R. (1995). *Institutions and organizations*. London: SAGE.

Slee, T. (2016). *What's yours is mine*. New York, NY: OR Books.

Snow, D. A., & Benford, R. D. (1988). Ideology, frame resonance, and participant mobilization. *International Social Movement Research*, *1*(1), 197–217.

Srnicek, N. (2017). The challenges of platform capitalism: Understanding the logic of a new business model. *Juncture*, *23*(4), 254–257.

Stahel, W. R. (1986). The functional economy: Cultural and organizational change. *Science & Public Policy*, *13*(4), 91–100.

Stahel, W. R. (2008). In K. B. Misra (Ed.), *The performance economy: business models for the functional service economy in handbook of performability engineering* (pp. 127–138). London: Springer.

Stallman, R. M., Lessig, L., & Gay, J. (2006). *Free software, free society: Selected essays of Richard M. Stallman*. Boston, MA: Free Software Foundation, Inc.

Sundararajan, A. (2016). *The sharing economy: The end of employment and the rise of crowd-based capitalism*. Cambridge, MA: The MIT Press.

Terrasse, P. (2016). Rapport du Député Pascal Terrasse sur le développement de l'économie collaborative en France. Retrieved from https://www.gouvernement.fr/partage/6421-rapport-de-pascal-terrasse-sur-le-developpement-de-l-economie-collaborative

Thomas, D. R. (2006). A general inductive approach for analyzing qualitative evaluation data. *American Journal of Evaluation*, *27*(2), 237–246.

Thornton, P. H., Ocasio, W., & Lounsbury, M. (2012). *The institutional logics perspective: A new approach to culture, structure, and process*. Oxford: Oxford University Press.

Turner, F. (2008). *From counterculture to cyberculture: Stewart brand, the whole earth network, and the rise of digital utopianism*. Chicago, IL: University of Chicago Press.

Wooten, M., & Hoffman, A. J. (2017). Organizational fields: Past, present and future. In R. Greenwood, C. Oliver, T. Lawrence, & R. E. Meyer (Eds.), *The SAGE handbook of organizational institutionalism* (pp. 55–74). London: Sage.

Zilber, T. B. (2008). The work of meanings in institutional processes. In R. Greenwood, C. Oliver, R. Suddaby, & K. Sahlin (Eds.), *The SAGE handbook of organizational institutionalism* (pp. 151–170). London: Sage.

# IS THE SHARING ECONOMY A FIELD? HOW A DISRUPTIVE FIELD NURTURES SHARING ECONOMY ORGANIZATIONS

Dominika Wruk, Tino Schöllhorn, and Achim Oberg

## ABSTRACT

*Is the sharing economy a field? Answering this question is crucial to understanding how sharing organizations look and behave, as well as how the sharing economy might develop. In this chapter, the authors applied two different field conceptions – organizational field and issue field – as a starting point for an explorative empirical analysis. To capture both field concepts, the authors collected relational data and data on organizations' self-representations to see how organizations engaged in the debate on the sharing economy relate to each other. The observed network of organizations suggests that the sharing economy is an issue field. In addition, the core of this network shows the relational structure of an organizational field. Surprisingly, it is not an organizational field of the sharing economy. Instead, it is a field of organizations heavily engaged in proselytizing new organizational forms that will change other fields. What the authors observed is a new field configuration – the authors call it a* disruptive field *– that is, less inward-oriented than other fields but much more engaged in changing other fields' structures and dynamics. With these insights, the authors contribute to institutional research on field configuration and shed light on the phenomenon of the sharing economy and its potential development.*

**Keywords:** Organizational field; issue field; disruptive field; relational perspective; discursive perspective; sharing economy; field configuration

**Theorizing the Sharing Economy: Variety and Trajectories of New Forms of Organizing**
**Research in the Sociology of Organizations, Volume 66, 131–162**

**ISSN: 0733-558X/doi:10.1108/S0733-558X20200000066007**

## INTRODUCTION

In recent years, entrepreneurs have founded an increasing number of organizations that apply modes of sharing, lending, renting, or commonly using products, services, and spaces in various industries and business domains (Botsman & Rogers, 2010). These organizations range from local nonprofit initiatives and citizens' initiatives to corporations running large international platforms (Wruk, Oberg, Klutt, & Maurer, 2019). Besides newly founded organizations, established firms (e.g., in the mobility sector) have entered the sharing economy with their own offers and models. In addition to these sharing organizations, collective actors such as activist groups, informal networks, and organizations have evolved (e.g., Ouishare, Shareable, and P2P Foundation). They have started to take over the role of industry associations by convening events and meetings of sharing economy organizations, publishing reports, engaging in lobbying work, and providing support and guidance to (potential) founders of sharing organizations (Mair & Reischauer, 2017; Martin, 2016).

Local, national, and international authorities engage in furthering the development of legal and regulatory frameworks to shape and govern the sharing economy or to provide favorable conditions for sharing economy start-ups (Cohen & Sundararajan, 2015; European Commission, 2016; Katz, 2015; Vith, Oberg, Höllerer, & Meyer, 2019). The sharing economy is also subject to academic and public debates. Researchers and journalists discuss best (and worst) practices (e.g., Belk, 2014; Malhotra & Van Alstyne, 2014; Scholz, 2016; Schor, 2016) and theorize on the meaning of the label sharing economy (Martin, 2016), thereby contributing to the definition of legitimate members and boundaries of the sharing economy (Navis & Glynn, 2010; Strang & Meyer, 1993).

In sum, the discussion of a shared issue, the emergence of new forms around this issue, the voice of first associations, and the ongoing theorization of the sharing economy could be interpreted as the first signs of an emerging field of the sharing economy (Grodal, 2007; Negro, Koçak, & Hsu, 2010; Powell, Oberg, Korff, Oelberger, & Kloos, 2017). Until now, we have known little about the structure and configuration of this field: is it an organizational field with dense interactions and internal cohesion (DiMaggio & Powell, 1983)? Or is the field still in a state where actors of various fields discuss the issue without a stratified structure (Wooten & Hoffman, 2008)? On a theoretical level, is the sharing economy field an organizational field or an issue field?

Understanding the configuration of the sharing economy from a field perspective is crucial to accessing further development perspectives. If the sharing economy starts to form an organizational field, then it will develop field-internal expectations about proper forms and activities in the field. Such mutually agreed expectations will then shape the everyday behavior of organizations (DiMaggio & Powell, 1983; W. R. Scott, 2013). Additionally, organizational fields have the tendency to perpetuate the internal structuration of the field, which creates relatively stable environments for organizations in the field. If the sharing economy remains an issue field without developing organizational field characteristics, then the debates about sharing might influence the adoption and adaptation of single sharing practices by organizations and the reception of the sharing economy in the broader society (Wooten & Hoffman, 2008) without creating a stabilizing environment for sharing organizations. Sharing organizations will then represent specific forms in other fields.

To answer the question of whether the sharing economy in its current stage is still an issue field or if it is already an organizational field, we apply a conceptual lens that reconstructs fields from a network perspective (Powell & Oberg, 2017). We reconstructed the network of organizations involved in the shared issue of sharing on the World Wide Web on a global level. By analyzing the configuration within this network, we observed that a densely linked community of organizations shows characteristics of an organizational field. However, this community is not primarily populated by sharing organizations. Instead, it is a field heavily engaged in discussing, theorizing, and legitimizing sharing organizations. We discuss these observations in light of field theories and argue that we observed an interesting configuration – the *disruptive field* – that is oriented toward changing other fields' debates and structures.

## THEORY

To conceptualize configurations of fields, we distinguish a relational and a discursive perspective and describe two major forms of fields – organizational fields and issue fields – from these perspectives.

### *Relational Perspective on Organizational Fields*

DiMaggio and Powell (1983) define an organizational field as follows:

> By organizational field, we mean those organizations that, in the aggregate, constitute a recognized area of institutional life: key suppliers, resource and product consumers, regulatory agencies, and other organizations that produce similar services or products (p. 148).

As the production of societally relevant services and products needs various kinds of knowledge and abilities, organizations specialize in particular domains and form production chains through interacting with each other. During these repeated interactions, reciprocal expectations about responsibilities and results of interaction partners are formed and confirmed by successful interactions (Berger & Luckmann, 1991; Schütz, 1967). Over time, relationships created for single transactions become stable interaction relationships among organizations. Repeated successful interactions increase the likelihood that such established relationships are used more frequently and fatefully than other relationships (Scott, 2013). Consequently, such relationships among organizations with similar sets of expectations become dense and form the center of an emerging organizational field, leading to high internal cohesion and low connectivity with field-external organizations.

Within the center of a field, organizations are aware of each other, even when they have not established direct collaboration partnerships. Furthermore, organizations in the periphery recognize actors in the center. In the early stages of a field, when new organizational forms strive for societal legitimacy, such mutual awareness in the field is publicly highlighted by mutual references. Such endorsements increase public awareness of new forms and help to increase legitimacy for the field and its members (Baum & Oliver, 1991; Walker, McCarthy, & Baumgartner, 2011).

Publicly visible references and endorsements contribute to two field-internal structuration processes: on a vertical dimension, the differences between central and peripheral organizations are visible and are recognized by field members (DiMaggio & Powell, 1983; Greenwood, Raynard, Kodeih, Micelotta, & Lounsbury, 2011). Over time, these differences become more nuanced, and in many cases the field-internal hierarchy is documented for a broader society in rankings, which enforce stratification processes even further (Espeland & Sauder, 2007). On a horizontal dimension, organizations that have connections to other similar organizations in the field become structurally equivalent. The higher the structural equivalence between two organizations, the easier it is for their existing partners to switch to the equivalent other organization. Consequently, structurally equivalent organizations observe each other carefully to make sure that potential competitive advantages of respective others are copied as fast as possible (DiMaggio & Powell, 1983). Both structuration processes – hierarchical stratification and structural equivalence – can be assessed from a social network perspective on organizational fields and "may provide a route for the a priori identification of … fields" (White, Owen-Smith, Moody, & Powell, 2004, p. 96).

### *Discursive Perspective on Organizational Fields*

The discursive perspective captures the organizations' expression of identity and their participation in public debates. The identity expressed in self-representations of organizations in organizational fields is influenced by the purpose of the field and by the relational positions of organizations within the field.

Organizational fields develop around societally relevant products and services (DiMaggio & Powell, 1983). The health care field with clinics, doctors, and pharmacies is an example. In such fields, the societal relevance becomes part of the shared purpose of the fields' organizations. The members of the field may have divergent goals regarding profit making, but they share the goal of fulfilling the purpose of the field together with other field members. In established organizational fields, the shared purpose is reflected in organizational self-representations (Glynn & Abzug, 2002). For instance, universities in the field of higher education developed a vocabulary of symbols for enlightenment in their logos to reflect their role in society (Drori, Delmestri, & Oberg, 2013). Such shared textual and visual vocabularies evolve and diffuse among field members over time and reflect a collective identity (Glynn & Navis, 2013; Strang & Meyer, 1993). This ensures that field membership of individual organizations can be identified by members and external observers (Greenwood et al., 2011).

Besides the shared purpose with its vocabulary, field-internal structuration processes influence individual organizations' identities and self-representations. The vertical and horizontal structuration described previously leads to different positions and roles in the field. For instance, in the field of car manufacturing, a distinction between manufacturers and suppliers on multiple tiers emerged over time. This hierarchical internal differentiation is often reflected in the organizations' activities in public debates: typically, suppliers on lower tiers follow the lead of manufacturers. Furthermore, field-specific meta-organizations, which represent field members and their concerns, emerge in fields. For instance, industry associations try to influence governmental regulations of specific fields and field-specific media outlets inform about field-internal developments (DiMaggio, 1991; Hinings, Logue, & Zietsma, 2017; Maguire, Hardy, & Lawrence, 2004; O'Sullivan & O'Dwyer, 2015). Successful meta-organizations become part of the center of an organizational field and are highly recognized inside and outside of the field, although they are not directly involved in producing services or products.

### *Relational Perspective on Issue Fields*

Another field concept understands fields as "centers of debates in which competing interests negotiate over issue interpretation" (Hoffman, 1999, p. 351). In contrast to the idea that fields emerge around services and products, this conception focuses on contested societal issues that are debated (Furnari, 2018; Meyer & Höllerer, 2010; O'Sullivan & O'Dwyer, 2015; Zietsma & Lawrence, 2010).

An issue can emerge among organizations that are already strongly connected because they are jointly involved in production chains or have a shared purpose as in organizational fields (Furnari, 2018). For instance, the question of how to design sustainable cars is a heavily debated issue in the organizational field of the automotive industry. Various car manufacturers position themselves with alternative technologies, industry associations organize meetings and conferences to discuss solutions, and governments introduce incentives or regulations to steer the field into a specific direction. This is an example of an issue field within an organizational field with the potential to change practices dramatically. Furthermore, such a change of practices can affect the relational positions of organizations in the field. For example, the newly founded car manufacturer Tesla challenges established incumbents like Mercedes and BMW by introducing electronic cars in a high prestige customer segment. With this strategy, Tesla addressed the issue of sustainable cars more radically than incumbents and gained a prominent position in a previously stable organizational field. Tesla thus changed the relational structure of an established organizational field by taking a radical position in an issue field.

Other issues affect organizations of various fields at the same time. For instance, societal debates about shareholder value versus stakeholder value question the societal function of stock corporations. Consequently, corporations of various industries were involved in these debates (Meyer & Höllerer, 2010). Together with industry associations and media outlets, they form an issue field that crosses various organizational fields and affects practices in quite different fields. For example, corporate social responsibility practices came into focus when corporations were asked to recognize interests of stakeholders other than their shareholders. Issue fields that cross various organizational fields can positively or negatively affect the adoption and adaptation of practices of organizations, which are not directly connected through exchange relationships or other relationships relying on interaction.

From a relational perspective, a shared issue creates a "relational space" (Wooten & Hoffman, 2008, p. 64) even for previously disconnected organizations. In public debates, some organizations become exemplary for typical positions in these debates and other organizations are compared with these typical organizations. In such a comparison, a relationship is constructed that is independent of interaction or exchange. For instance, when shareholder value practices are debated, organizations are asked to explain their position toward this issue in comparison to organizations with typical positions. The compared organization might react to the comparison relationship by referencing the other organization that functions as an example. Such references to other actors make the issue field visible even from a relational point of view (Wooten & Hoffman, 2008).

It is important to note that the nature of such references in issue fields is different from the relationships resting on interactions in an organizational field. Nevertheless, both types of relationships can interact over time: organizations with exchange relationships in an issue field can reference their partners publicly, and public references can function as a starting point to establish new communication and interaction relationships.

Translated into social network characteristics, an issue field consists of comparison and reference relationships, which either lay above an existing organizational field or connect organizations of various fields. While mutual recognition is essential in established organizational fields, in issue fields organizations are connected via comparison or single-sided references where mutualism is not necessary. Consequently, internal cohesion in issue fields is often lower than in organizational fields while connectivity of an issue field with other fields is typically higher.

### *Discursive Perspective on Issue Fields*

While membership in an organizational field is constructed through interaction and mutual recognition, membership in an issue field might stem from two sources: first, organizations join a debate by taking a discursive position on the discussed issue. If their contributions are recognized by other participants in the debate, then they become members of the issue field. Second, organizations can be added to an issue field even if they do not involve themselves actively or if they try to ignore invitations to contribute. For example, if civil society organizations start a debate on sustainability issues of the chemical industry, then media and policy organizations might join the debate actively while chemical companies and their industry associations might try to avoid these issues. Nevertheless, they will be referenced by civil society organizations, media, and parties again and again and at some point might start to react and join the issue field they tried to avoid (Hoffman, 1999).

While the identities of organizations in an organizational field are influenced by the field's purpose and the organizations' positions in the field structure, the identities of organizations in an issue field are in many cases untouched by the issue. For instance, one chemical company might join debates on sustainability without changing its identity while another company might adapt its self-representation extensively by reflecting sustainability topics. Especially in highly contested issue fields, the extent of adaptation can be interpreted as an expression of the position regarding the debated issue and should not be confused with membership in the issue field.

### *Field Configuration of the Sharing Economy*

Table 1 summarizes the two perspectives on organizational fields and issue fields.

To assess the current configuration of the sharing economy in light of these relational and discursive characteristics of organizational fields and issue fields, we ask the following empirical questions:

- *Relational perspective*: How densely are organizations involved in sharing economy debates connected with each other? And – even further – do we observe mutualism?
- *Discursive perspective*: Do densely connected organizations reflect an emerging field of the sharing economy in their organizational identities? And – more specifically – how central are field-specific sharing associations?

If we observed a center-periphery structure with a center populated by organizations with identities connected to the purpose of sharing, then we can conclude that the sharing economy has formed an organizational field. If we observed different clusters of higher density among organizations participating in debates about the sharing economy as an issue, then we can conclude that the sharing economy is an issue field that affects different fields. These two exemplary potential outcomes are not mutually exclusive: the center of a sharing economy issue field could be formed by a sharing economy organizational field.

***Table 1.*** Field Characteristics from Two Perspectives.

| | Organizational Field | Issue Field |
|---|---|---|
| Relational Perspective | High internal cohesion<br>Mutual awareness and recognition<br>Stratified positions<br>Low external connectivity | Single-sided references<br>Mutualism not necessary<br>Low internal cohesion<br>High external connectivity |
| Discursive Perspective | Organizational identity reflects<br>– shared purpose of the field<br>– role and position in field | Organizational identity does not need to reflect issues<br>Members participate in debates by taking positions on issue<br>Members can be taken into account on issue by others |

## DATA AND METHODS

We argue that the Internet provides a suitable empirical context to study field configurations from relational and discursive perspectives simultaneously. Two communicative characteristics of the Internet are thereby important in this study. First, the Internet provides the possibility to publicly display relations to other organizations (Powell, Horvath, & Brandtner, 2016). Organizations create weblinks to other organizations, which they recognize, endorse, and deem to be relevant (Powell et al., 2017). They link, for instance, suppliers and important customers, associations, cooperation partners, research institutes and media reports. Through such weblinks, organizations direct website visitors to their immediate network. Weblinks thus represent the willingness of organizations to share their audiences' attention with other websites. As such, weblinks reflect the embeddedness and position of organizations in their relational networks (Oberg, Schöllhorn, & Woywode, 2006). Consequently, the network of weblinks between actors in a field can be interpreted as a public representation of the network of social relations in a field (Powell et al., 2016). As such, we can use weblinks to reconstruct the network of social relations in the sharing economy.

Second, organizational websites have become central interfaces that organizations use to present themselves toward their audiences and to participate in debates (Powell & Oberg, 2017). The information organizations make publicly available on their websites – in particular on their "About Us," Our History," or "Who We Are" pages – represent claims about the organizations' identities (Bartel, Baldi, & Dukerich, 2016; Goffman, 1959). With these identity claims, organizations show how they are different from other organizations. Simultaneously, organizations reflect their membership in organizational fields and categories to be recognized and legitimized (Glynn & Navis, 2013). In addition, organizational self-representations through websites are also part of existing debates and thus contribute to the social construction of meaning on an issue (Berger & Luckmann, 1991; Green, 2004; Phillips, Lawrence, & Hardy, 2004). As a result, we can capture whether organizational identity claims reflect their belonging to the field of the sharing economy and the positions of organizations in debates on the sharing economy through analyzing organizational self-representations on the web.

To collect data on relational characteristics of the sharing economy, we reconstructed the sharing economy network on the World Wide Web by following the paths of weblinks between organizations that are involved in debates on the sharing economy. To capture discursive characteristics, we draw a theory-driven subsample of the identified organizations and analyze their online self-representations.

### *Data Collection*

We collected data in four steps: first, inspired by the idea that a field is formed around those organizations that create products and services, we developed a list of sharing organizations that often appear as prototypical examples in German media (e.g., Airbnb, Car2Go, or Betahaus). Following the theoretical expectations that meta-organizations are crucial, we added associations or informal initiatives that actively promote or discuss sharing economy models (e.g., Ouishare or Shareable). The result is a list of 37 organizations heavily involved in debates on the sharing economy either on the production side or as meta-organizations.

Second, we identified the URLs of the organizations on the starting list and used a web crawler (Oberg, Huppertz, & Woywode, 2006; Powell et al., 2017) to capture all of the outgoing links from these websites to other websites. The result of the second step was a list of more than 10,000 websites, which we sorted by the number of incoming links (indegree) in descending order. Interpreting the number of incoming links as a proxy for an organization's reputation from the perspective of the initial set (Scott, 2012; Wasserman & Faust, 1994), the first websites are most likely relevant for the sharing economy.

In the third step of data collection, we manually coded the set of websites with more than one incoming link to determine whether these organizations participate in debates on the sharing economy. For those organizations that are involved in debates on the sharing economy, we ran the web crawler again to collect all links among the full list of websites.

In a last step of data collection, we manually coded the years of founding and the type of organization (sharing organization, sharing-specific meta-organization, sharing-specific media, specialized media, venture capitalists, etc.) to obtain a first idea about the organizational demography. We observed sharing organizations, sharing-specific meta-organizations and other forms of organizations (nonsharing-specific media, think tanks, media organizations, associations, technology providers, Web 2.0 platforms, and investors).

### *Data Analysis*

We interpreted the resulting list of organizations involved in sharing economy debates and connected via public references as that part of the international issue field of the sharing economy that is recognized by German sharing organizations. The identified organizations and the weblinks among them can be analyzed as a network in which organizations represent nodes and the weblinks represent ties between these nodes. To make core structural features of the network visible, we limited the analysis in this chapter to the core of the network. The core consisted of 216 URLs – or, rather, organizations or initiatives behind these URLs – among which 3,386 directed references exist. We applied standard network analytical procedures to visualize and analyze relational data.

To obtain a first impression of the core of the issue field of the sharing economy, we created visualizations of the network using Gephi, an open-source network analysis and visualization software package (Bastian, Heymann, & Jacomy, 2009). We applied the Fruchterman–Reingold algorithm to define positions of nodes in the network (Fruchterman & Reingold, 1991). The algorithm introduces attraction forces between linked nodes and repulsion forces between unlinked nodes and by this means aims to find the optimal node position for a given network with respect to clusters of higher density relations. The size of nodes in these network visualizations reflects the indegree, which is the number of incoming weblinks to a focal organization's website from other organizations in the analyzed network.

To test whether relational characteristics of organizational fields can be identified in the reconstructed issue field, we applied the modularity algorithm provided in the Gephi software package to identify and analyze clusters of higher density and mutual connectivity in the network (Blondel, Guillaume, Lambiotte, & Lefebvre, 2008).

To interpret each cluster, we generated visualizations in which we highlight the respective cluster in the network. The size of nodes in these visualizations reflects the indegree within the cluster, meaning that only incoming links from other organizations within the same cluster are considered. This helped us to make comparisons between local and global positions of organizations. Following these indicators, we selected cases for each cluster for a qualitative in-depth analysis: cases for most important websites for each cluster and for specific network positions (e.g., brokers or hubs) were identified through visual analysis of the clusters. For each of these cases, we read the texts describing the organizations' missions and goals (e.g., "About Us," "Our History," or "Who We Are" pages) to assess whether they link their identities to the purpose of sharing or whether they contribute to sharing debates without adopting a sharing vocabulary in their self-representations. We also searched websites for information indicative of their roles and positions in the debates on the sharing economy. After bringing together the observations for cases of each cluster, we labeled the clusters "communities" if they shared a common subtopic in the sharing economy debate.

To compare field characteristics of these clusters, we calculated the following indicators: the average number of undirected linkages per cluster member to other members serves as an indicator for internal cohesion within a cluster. The average number of undirected linkages per cluster member to members of other clusters indicates the connectivity to other clusters. For a deeper understanding of connections within and between clusters, we further calculated the percentages of directed linkages between pairs of clusters in relation to all directed linkages in the whole network.

## FINDINGS

Being interested in the question of the extent to which we find characteristics of organizational fields in the reconstructed core of the sharing economy issue field, we started with an analysis of the whole structure of the core. Then we turned to clusters of higher density in the network and the discursive expressions of organizations in these clustered communities.

### *General Structure and Composition*

The network visualization in Fig. 1 shows the core of the sharing economy issue field. The node size reflects the number of incoming references from other members of the core.

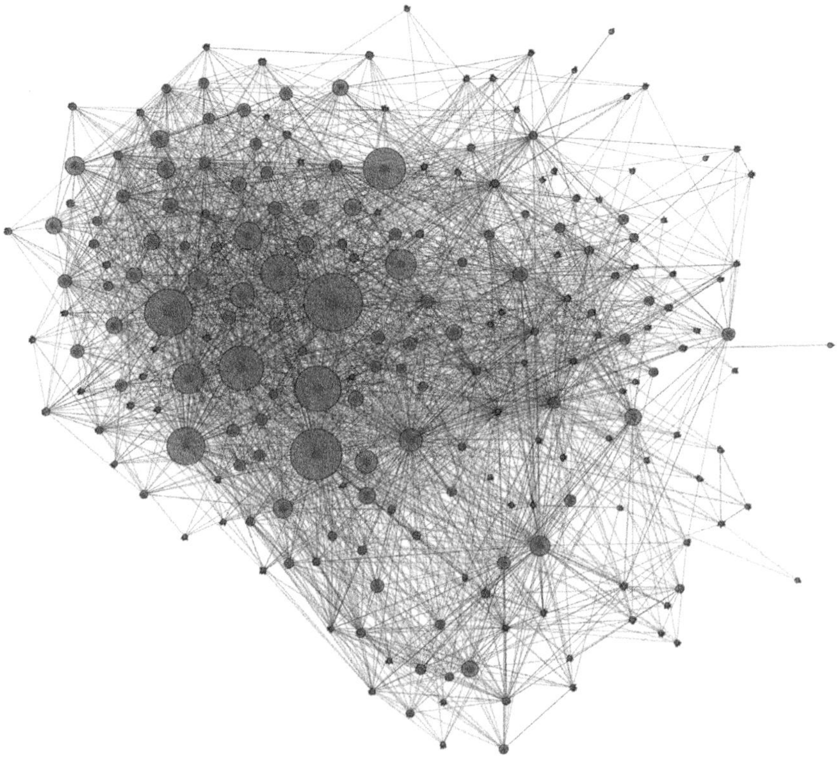

*Fig. 1.* General Structure.
Nodes: URLs of organizations.
Linkages: References on the Internet.
Positioning algorithm: Fruchterman–Rheingold.
Size of nodes: Indegree in the overall network.

We observe a skewed center-periphery structure with a densely connected area in the upper left part of the network with several organizations that are highly endorsed by many other members of the issue field. Astonishingly, the upper left part has no clear periphery above it or on its left side, but we observed an extended periphery on the right and bottom right. In this peripheral area, organizations are weakly connected and often only recognized by other peripheral organizations.

Because various forms of organizations can participate in the debate on the sharing economy, the position of sharing organizations is crucial for the question of whether the sharing economy starts to develop an organizational field. Fig. 2 highlights sharing organizations in black and sharing-specific meta-organizations in grey. Other forms of organizations (nonsharing-specific media, think tanks, media organizations, associations, technology providers, Web 2.0 platforms, and investors) remain white.

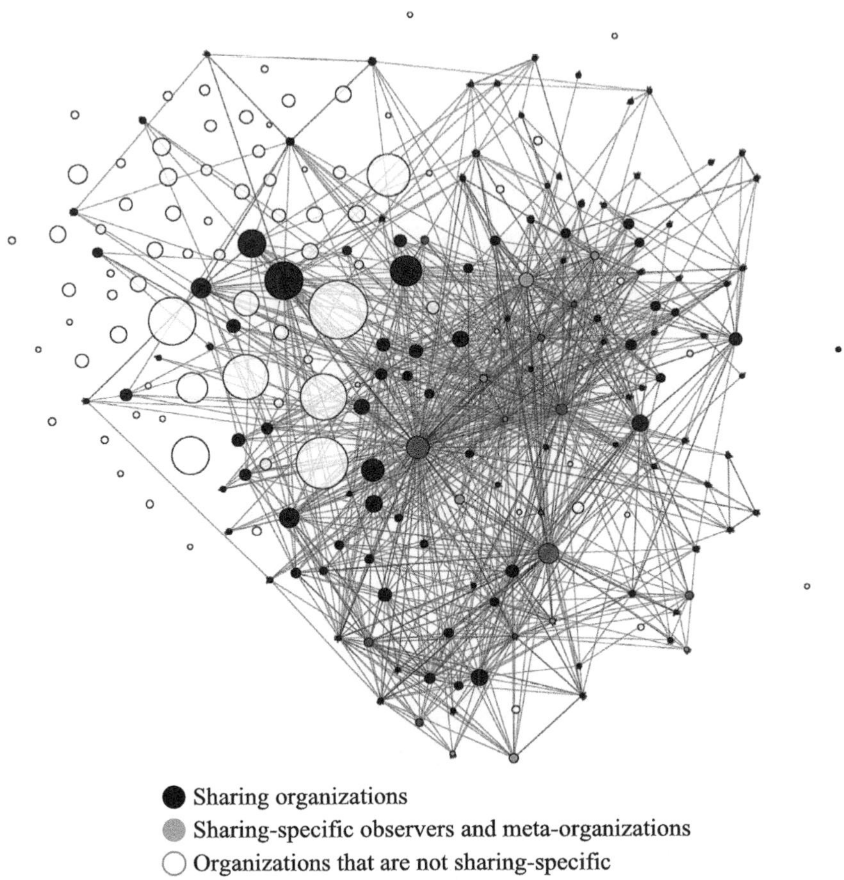


*Fig. 2.* Network with Sharing-specific Organizations Highlighted in Black and Grey.

Nodes: URLs of organizations.
Linkages shown: References on the Internet, where sharing-specific organizations are sender or receiver.
Positioning algorithm: Fruchterman–Rheingold.
Size of nodes: Indegree in the overall network.

Fig. 2 reflects the organizational demographic of the core of the sharing economy issue field: more than half of the organizations (around 53%) are sharing organizations. An additional 10% of organizations are sharing-specific meta-organizations that try to voice the interests of sharing initiatives or that report specifically about the sharing economy. The remaining 40% of organizations participate in the sharing debate without having a sharing-specific organizational form.

Interestingly, most sharing organizations are positioned in the periphery of the sharing economy issue field on the right and bottom right of Fig. 2. Although being actively involved in sharing, they do not dominate the issue field. Instead, highly endorsed organizations in the skewed center on the upper left have no sharing-specific organizational form. Contributions to discussions about the sharing economy come from organizations that are disconnected from sharing-specific forms but nevertheless highly linked and referenced by sharing organizations.

A second characteristic of an emerging organizational field is the public visibility of mutual support of field-specific actors. In Fig. 3, we selected bidirectional references between sharing-specific organizations. The size of nodes reflects the number of such ties.

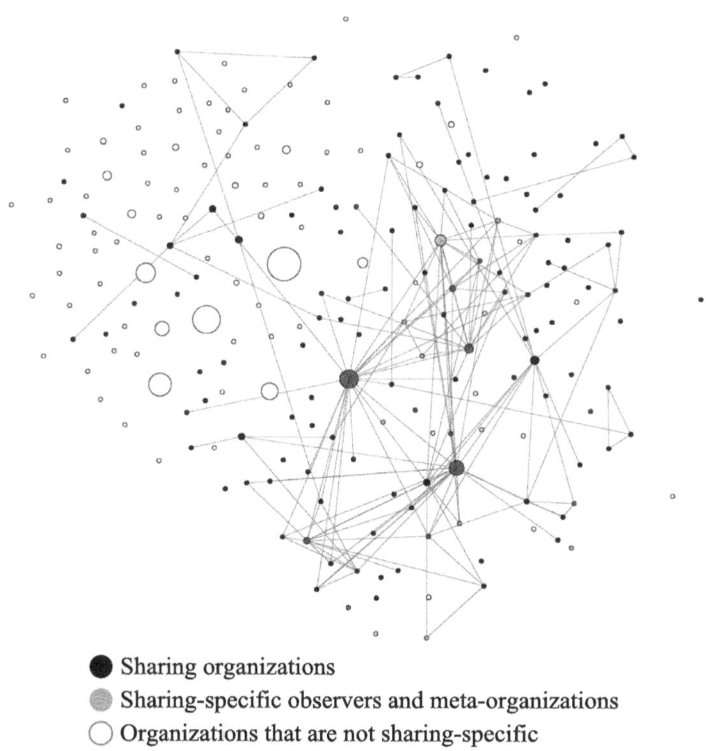


*Fig. 3.* Bidirectional Linkages among Sharing-specific Organizations.
Nodes: URLs of organizations,
Linkages shown: Bidirectional references on the Internet among sharing-specific organizations
Positioning algorithm: Fruchterman–Rheingold.
Size of nodes: Number of bidirectional ties.

We observed little mutualism between sharing organizations, but some mutual support between sharing organizations and sharing-specific meta-organizations. The emergence and mutual recognition of sharing-specific meta-organizations shows that there are attempts to organize sharing organizations within the sharing issue field and to voice their interests. Nevertheless, the sharing-specific organizations are in the periphery of the debate's field and their public mutual support did not create a density that affects the whole structure of the issue field.

In sum, the core of the issue field shows some mixed results regarding organizational field characteristics: there is a densely connected center of highly referenced organizations, but it is not populated by sharing-specific organizations; sharing-specific organizations show low levels of mutualism and mutual recognition of their own meta-organizations, but this happens in the periphery of the issue field.

### *Communities in the Network*

To deepen our understanding of the skewed center-periphery structure, we now turn to the analysis of clusters of higher density in the issue field. The Gephi modularity algorithm marked four clusters of higher internal density (see Fig. 4).

The peripheral area on the right and bottom right side splits up into three clusters (C1, C2, C3). The fourth cluster (C4) covers the center. In the next paragraphs, we analyze each clusters' community of organizations with their identity claims and positions in debates on the sharing economy. We summarize indicators for internal cohesion, connectivity, and directed linkages between pairs of clusters in relation to all directed linkages in Tables 2a and 2b and refer to the respective values in the following descriptions (in brackets).

#### *German Community*

We start with the cluster in the upper right corner of the periphery (see C1 in Fig. 5). It has the lowest internal cohesion of all clusters (3.64 undirected intracluster linkages per node, see Table 2a). This cluster covers the lowest fraction of all linkages in the network (2.69% of all linkages, see Table 2b). Surprisingly, the connectivity to other clusters is stronger than the internal cohesion (7.16 intercluster linkages per node compared to 3.64 intracluster links, see Table 2a). In addition, the cluster receives little attention from other clusters, while it links organizations from the central cluster more strongly than organizations within its own cluster (3.04% of all linkages compared to 2.69%, see Table 2b). Together, we observe strong structural indicators that this cluster does not form an organizational field itself.

When we turn to the composition of the cluster (see Fig. 5), we observe two highly recognized organizations: gruenderszene.de and deutsche-startups.de are two popular online news portals dedicated to the start-up scene in Germany.

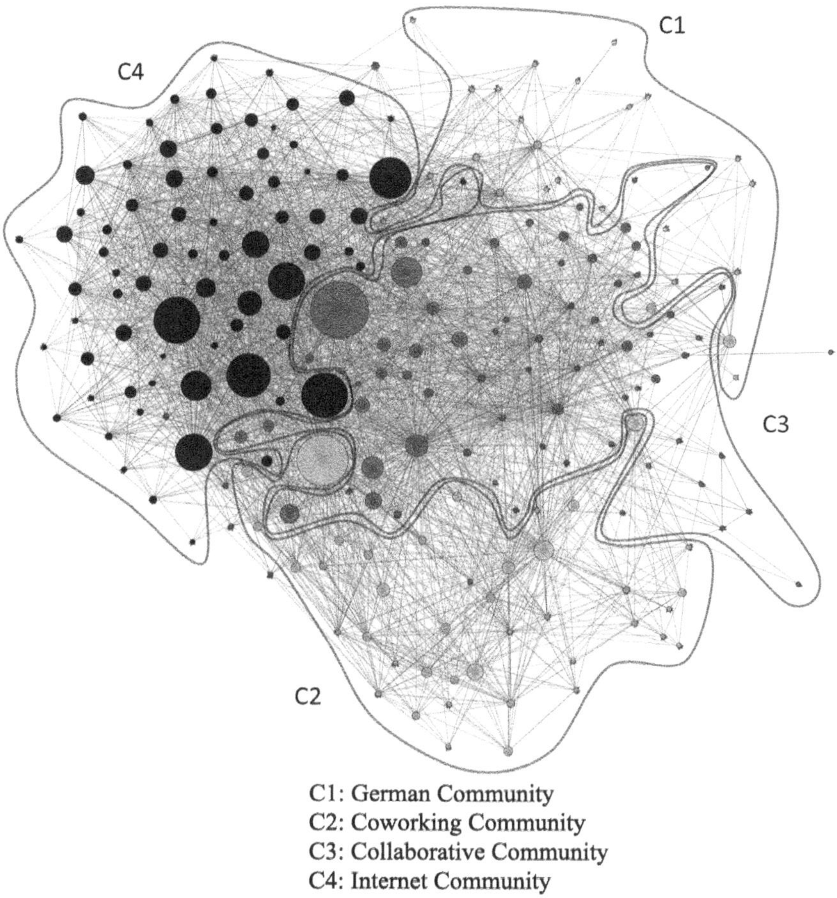


*Fig. 4.* Network with Four Communities.
Nodes: URLs of organizations.
Linkages shown: References on the Internet.
Positioning algorithm: Fruchterman–Rheingold.
Size of nodes: Indegree in the overall network.

***Table 2a.*** Comparative Indicators of Internal Cohesion and External Connectivity.

| | Average Number of Undirected Linkages Per Node | |
|---|---|---|
| | Intra-cluster | Inter-cluster |
| German Cluster | 3.64 | 7.16 |
| Coworking Cluster | 8.60 | 6.85 |
| Collaborative Cluster | 7.90 | 7.22 |
| Internet Cluster | 13.08 | 4.95 |

***Table 2b.*** Directed Connections Between Clusters.

| | Percentage of Linkages Between Pairs of Communities | | | |
|---|---|---|---|---|
| | German Cluster (%) | Coworking Cluster (%) | Collaborative Cluster (%) | Internet Cluster(%) |
| German Cluster | 2.69 | 0.80 | 1.45 | 3.04 |
| Coworking Cluster | 0.71 | 10.16 | 2.81 | 4.58 |
| Collaborative Cluster | 1.42 | 3.75 | 17.96 | 11.25 |
| Internet Cluster | 0.38 | 2.45 | 7.97 | 28.59 |

Tables 2a-2b. Network indicators of clusters.

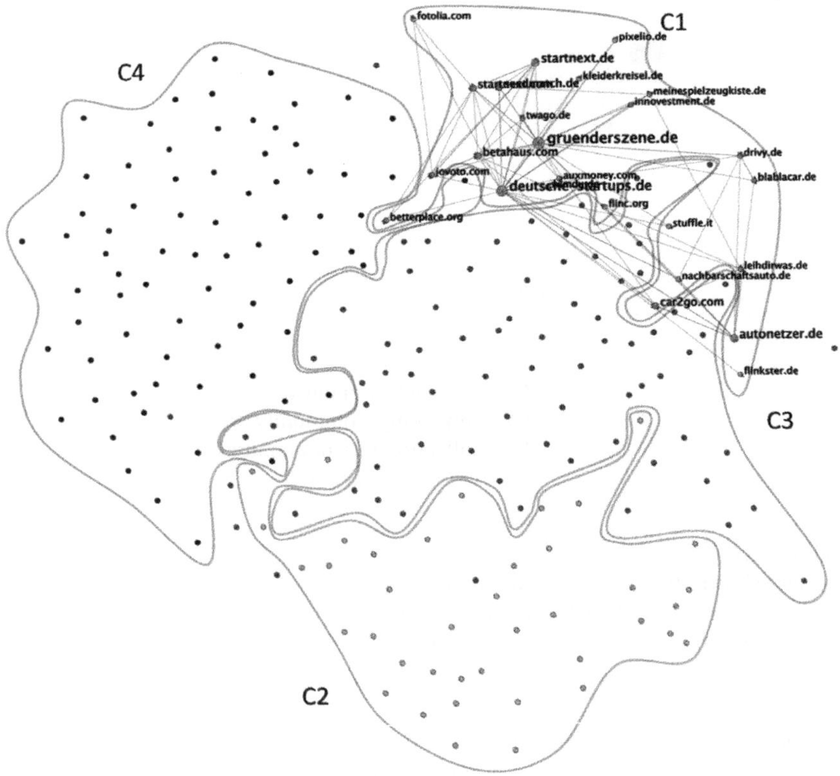


*Fig. 5.* German Community.

Nodes: URLs of organizations.

Linkages shown: References on the Internet between organizations that are part of the German Community.

Positioning algorithm: Fruchterman–Rheingold

Size of nodes of the German Community: Indegree in the community.

Size of other nodes: No meaning.

They are positioned at the upper part of the cluster, and deutsche-startups.de is at the border of two other clusters (C4 and C3). Both news portals have taken up the sharing topic during recent years and report on new foundings and developments. For instance, we found 424 articles and 10 job offerings since 2009 on Gruenderszene.de using the search term "sharing economy" and more than 50 articles on Deutsche-Startups.de since May 2012. As such, they represent relevant media contributing to debates on issues around the sharing economy in Germany.

Among the larger nodes is also startnext.de, the largest crowdfunding organization in Germany. We find this node at the top of the cluster, thus at a distance to other clusters and the network center. Startnext presents itself as dedicated to contributing to societal transformation toward more sustainability through supporting social enterprises and social innovation (Startnext, 2019). To do so, the organization builds on the idea of the "power of the crowd," where many people together provide financial resources for projects and founders. "Only together can we do great things!" (Startnext, 2019, translations by authors).

This community further consists of other sharing organizations (80% of organizations in this community) active in various sectors such as mobility or consumer goods. Some of these organizations present themselves as initiating or supporting change in the respective areas in which they are active. For instance, car2go.com, a car-sharing provider initiated by Daimler, describes itself as "at the heart of the sharing economy." It is further stated that "Car2go helped create the sharing economy we know today by disrupting the status quo … At car2go, we're shaping the future of mobility" (Car2go, 2019). We found the node car2go.com at the periphery of the cluster, bordering cluster 3 (C3).

What characterizes this cluster is that most organizations (almost 90%) were founded and are located in Germany. We thus called this community the German Community. That this community shows up in the sample of the sharing economy issue field is not surprising because we started our reconstruction of the issue field with sharing organizations active in Germany. Nevertheless, that there is a set of German organizations in the core of the issue field is not a methodological artifact because the organizations of the staring list could have ended up even more peripheral outside of the core of the issue field.

*Coworking Community*

The second cluster is located in the bottom right part of the network (see C2 in Fig. 6). The internal cohesion is twice as high as in the German community (8.60 undirected intracluster linkages per node, see Table 2a), and we observe almost three times as many linkages within this cluster (10.16% of all linkages, see Table 2b). The connectivity to organizations in other clusters (6.85 undirected intercluster linkages per node, see Table 2a) is only slightly weaker than the internal cohesion.

Turning to the internal network composition of the cluster (see Fig. 6), we observe that meetup.com is one of the most referenced organizations within this

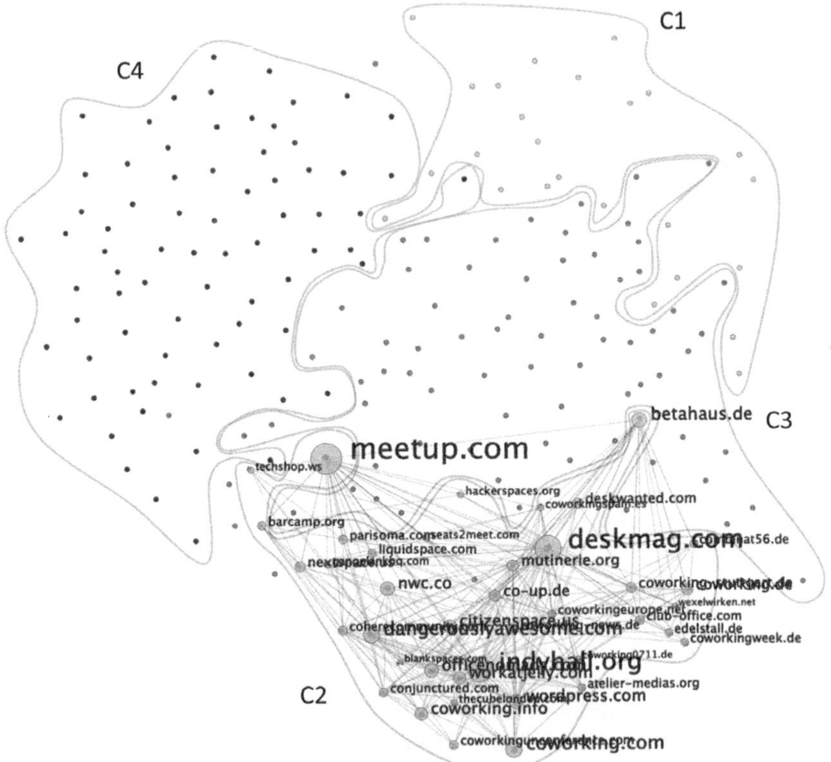


*Fig. 6:* Coworking Community.
Nodes: URLs of organizations.
Linkages shown: References on the Internet between organizations that are part of the Coworking Community.
Positioning algorithm: Fruchterman–Rheingold.
Size of nodes of the Coworking Community: Indegree in the community.
Size of other nodes: No meaning.

cluster. It is located at the cluster's edge, next to the center of the whole network, because it is highly regarded by organizations of the adjacent cluster in the center (70% of its linkages are intercluster linkages and 64% of these linkages are incoming endorsements). Meetup provides an online platform and membership software for groups for a variety of interests including hobbies and work. People can create local groups on the online platform and use the provided tools to organize physical meetings and events, which are called "meetups." With these offerings, the organization aims at strengthening the development of local communities through real-life encounters: "The real world is calling: Join a local group to meet people, try something new, or do more of what you love" (Meetup, 2018). We observe that proponents of the sharing economy use Meetup to organize events. In July 2019, 21 groups with almost 9,000 members existed in Germany for the search term "sharing economy." Worldwide, there were 234 meetups on that topic with more than 62,000 members. Facilitating the creation of sharing-specific groups, Meetup contributes to both debate on this issue and to creating relations between sharing economy actors.

Another strongly referenced organization in this cluster is deskmag.com, which is positioned at the center of the clusters' structure. *Deskmag* is important for providing visibility and legitimacy through referencing other organizations inside and outside of this cluster because it has twice as many outgoing references as incoming endorsements. Deskmag is an online magazine focusing on the issue of coworking, as one part of the sharing economy (Deskmag, 2018). The organization also conducts a yearly survey among providers of coworking spaces and publishes the results online. In addition, we found 104 articles when entering the keyword "sharing economy" (e.g., Kwiatowski, 2013; Rustrum, 2014). As such, Deskmag is actively participating in debates on coworking as a specific part of the sharing economy and on the sharing economy as a whole.

Among the most recognized coworking spaces in this community is indyhall.org, a coworking space founded in 2006 in Philadelphia, USA, and thus in the very early years of the emergence and spread of coworking spaces. Indy Hall is particularly recognized by organizations from the focal cluster, with 77% of its incoming linkages stemming from the focal cluster. As a result, the node indyhall.org can be found in the lower part of the cluster and thus at a large distance from other clusters. The slogan "Working Alone Sucks" (Indy Hall, 2019) that we find on Indy Hall's (2019) website nicely summarizes the organization's mission. "That's what you'll find at the heart of Indy Hall: great people building authentic and meaningful connections while doing their best work together.". In addition, Indy Hall subscribes itself to the core values of the global coworking movement, which are community, collaboration, sustainability, accessibility, and openness, thus presenting itself as an active member of that movement.

Overall, the cluster consists largely of sharing organizations (60%). Most of them are coworking spaces, where entrepreneurs, freelancers, and others are brought together in physical spaces provided by the sharing organizations. In addition to the examples, we find sharing-specific observers and collective actors (27.5%) engaged in the topic of coworking. Their theorizing of the concept of coworking implies that the concept is based on an ambiguous understanding of being self-employed. On the one hand, they point out advantages of working independently and autonomously. On the other hand, they emphasize social and economic disadvantages that stem from working alone, for which coworking provides a potential solution. Members of this community thereby present themselves as active members of the coworking movement. Based on these characteristics, we called this community the Coworking Community.

The high percentage of sharing organizations, the relevance of specific meta-organizations, and a shared topic are clear signs for the beginning formation of an organizational field on coworking. However, the low-to-medium internal cohesion suggests that the emerging organizational field structure is still not independent of other communities.

*Collaborative Community*

The third cluster is located in between the previous clusters on the right side of the periphery (see C3 in Fig. 7). This cluster has a similar internal cohesion as the Coworking Community (7.90 undirected intracluster linkages per node, see Table 2a), but covers a larger fraction of the relationships in the issue field than the previous two clusters together (17.96% of linkages, see Table 2b). The connectivity to other clusters (7.22 undirected intercluster linkages per node, see Table 2a) is equally strong as the internal cohesion. We observe a particularly strong connectivity to the cluster in the center. With 11.25% of linkages from this cluster to the cluster in the center and 7.97% of linkages from the central cluster to this one, it is the strongest connectivity between two clusters that we find in the network (see Table 2b).

The most important organization in this cluster is the online news portal techcrunch.com (see Fig. 7). We find this node at the edge of the cluster structure

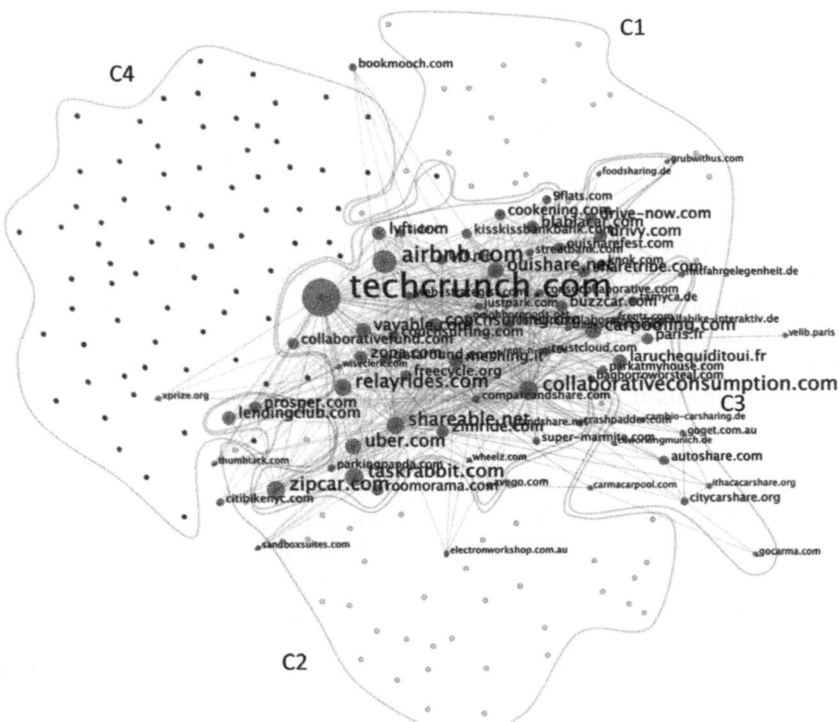


*Fig. 7.* Collaborative Community.

Nodes: URLs of organizations.

Linkages shown: References on the Internet between organizations that are part of the Collaborative Community.

Positioning algorithm: Fruchterman–Rheingold.

Size of nodes of the Collaborative Community: Indegree in the community.

Size of other nodes: No meaning.

next to the center of the issue field on the left. Techcrunch serves equally strong as sender and receiver of references. On its "About Us" pages, Techcrunch provides little explicit description of its mission or values. Instead, the organization presents a list of employees and shortly states "Meet the faces delivering top-notch reporting on the business of the tech industry" (Techcrunch, 2019). Instead of being focused on the sharing economy, Techcrunch covers topics around new technologies, the Internet, and the start-up scene, and it covers the sharing economy among these topics. In 2011, Techcrunch initiated Disrupt, a conference and networking event for founders, investors, hackers, and tech leaders taking place in various cities. The organization emphasizes its pioneering role: "Before there were tech conferences, there was Disrupt" (Techcrunch, 2019).

Among the larger nodes, we also find meta-organizations focusing on the sharing and collaborative economy such as ouishare.org and shareable.com. Both organizations function as hubs, which share the attention they receive with other organizations by referencing many organizations in the cluster and the overall network. Ouishare presents itself as a network of people dedicated to enhancing the development of the sharing economy and collaborative lifestyle. "It all started with the vision of transforming the world through sharing, using technology to organize as networks of peers and do business in a more open, collaborative and horizontal way" (Ouishare, 2018).

Members of the network serve as "connectors" in various geographical areas, mainly in Europe, where they aim to bring together and strengthen collaboration between local sharing organizations, activists, researchers, and other relevant actors. As a network, Ouishare convenes workshops, trainings for founders of sharing organizations, and large networking events such as the Ouishare Fest. Shareable plays a similar role, with a stronger focus on the United States. It presents itself as strongly rooted in the grassroots movement aiming to "solve today's biggest challenges, which old, top-down institutions are failing to address" (Shareable, 2018).

With their activities, these organizations contribute to mechanisms of early phases of institutionalization: they engage in proselytizing activities by spreading ideas and information to wide audiences; they serve as conveners by enabling exchanges and the creation of relations between organizations; and they invest in strengthening activities through providing resources and guidance (Powell et al., 2017). In sum, their activities can be interpreted as efforts toward further developing the field of the sharing or collaborative economy.

For the accommodation platform airbnb.com, we observe the highest number of endorsements for a sharing organization in this cluster. It is positioned at the edge of the cluster next to the center of the overall network. Airbnb receives many references both from inside and outside its cluster, but it is not very active in referencing other organizations in the network, with only 2% of its linkages being outgoing linkages. On its "About Us" page, Airbnb (2019b) presents itself as reshaping traveling and tourism: "Airbnb exists to create a world where anyone can belong anywhere, providing healthy travel that is local, authentic, diverse, inclusive and sustainable". In its press reports, it presents itself as part of the sharing economy, thereby emphasizing its pioneering role. "Since Airbnb's founding in 2008, our community has pioneered the development of the global sharing economy" (Airbnb, 2019a).

Other examples of highly referenced sharing organizations in this community are Uber, Zipcar, Taskrabbit, and Couchsurfing. All of them are among the early foundings in the sharing economy and have received much media attention, oftentimes being described as pioneers in their respective industries (Forbes, 2019). Zipcar (2019) describes itself as a car-sharing company and Couchsurfing's (2019) motto "share your life" suggests a belonging to the sharing economy. However, we did not find similar references on the websites of Uber (2019) and Taskrabbit (2019). Some of these fast-growing, economically successful start-ups – in particular Airbnb and Uber – are also among the most controversially debated sharing organizations, in addition to receiving regulatory and legal attention (Flew, 2018; Interian, 2016; Reader, 2016; Schwalbe & Peitz, 2016).

What most members of this cluster have in common is a focus on the sharing or collaborative economy, either because they are sharing organizations (71% of the cluster members) or because they actively promote a sharing and collaborative economy and lifestyle (14% are sharing-specific meta-organizations). We therefore called this cluster the Collaborative Community. The composition of organizations in this community – with large and highly visible sharing organizations, meta-organizations, and active supporters of the sharing discourse – shows important characteristics of an organizational field. However, the strong dependence on endorsements from other clusters in the issue field is a signal that this community has not formed an independent organizational field structure yet.

*Internet Community*

In the center on the left part of the core of the issue field, we observed the cluster with the highest internal cohesion (13.08 undirected intracluster linkages per node, see Table 2a) and the largest fraction of linkages (28.59% of linkages, see Table 2b). The connectivity to other clusters is much weaker than the internal cohesion (4.95 undirected intercluster linkages per node, see Table 2a), which is a clear sign that this cluster developed an internal structure independent of the other clusters. At the same time, this cluster receives larger fractions of cross-cluster references from other clusters in the field (see Table 2b).

A first group of highly recognized organizations in this cluster are media organizations such as fastcompany.com and wired.com (see Fig. 8). While Wired is at the cluster's center, Fast Company is positioned at the edge of this cluster, close to the Collaborative and the Coworking Communities. Fast Company positions itself as focusing on "world changing ideas," aiming to inspire "readers to think expansively … embrace change, and shape the future of business" (Fastcompany, 2019). "The breakthroughs and innovations" these media firms report on supposedly "lead to new ways of thinking, new connections, and new industries" (Wired, 2019). Within the last years, these media outlets have published articles from popular proponents and protagonists in the sharing economy debate – among others, Rachel Botsman (2013), Danielle Sacks (2011), Boyd Cohen (2018), Arun Sundararajan (2012), and Jeremiah Owyang (2013).

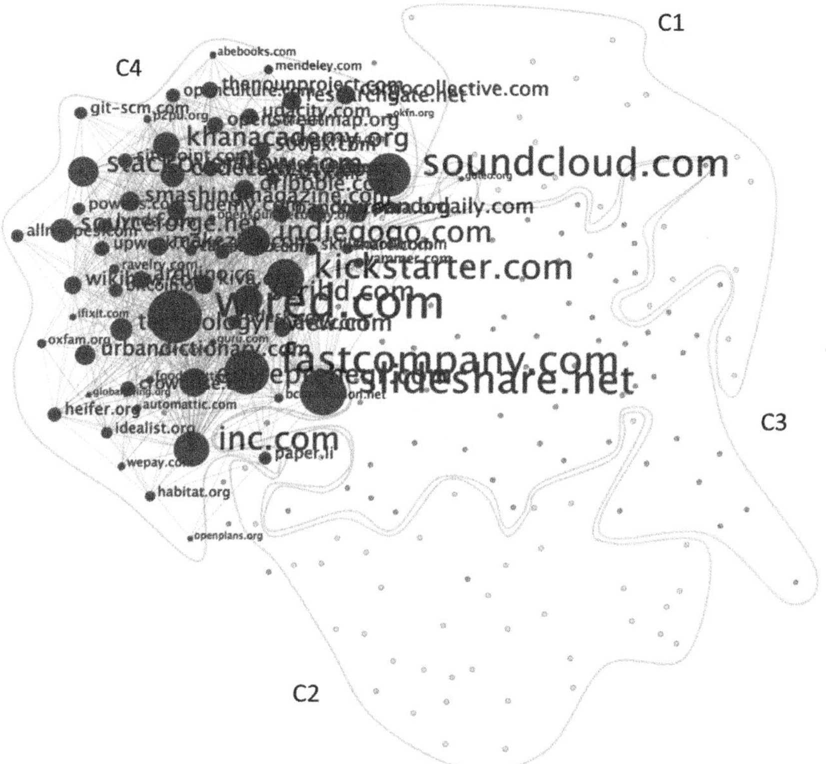


*Fig. 8.* Internet Community.
Nodes: URLs of organizations.
Linkages shown: References on the Internet between organizations that are part of the Internet Community.
Positioning algorithm: Fruchterman–Rheingold.
Size of nodes of the Internet Community: Indegree in the community.
Size of other nodes: No meaning.

These and many other articles describe business models of successful or new sharing organizations and discuss opportunities – and to some extant challenges – within the sharing economy. These media organizations serve as important proselytizers of the sharing idea and as strengtheners of sharing organizations (Powell et al., 2017). However, the sharing economy has not affected their identity.

A second group of important organizations in this cluster consists of interactive Web 2.0 platforms. Slideshare.com is the largest node from this group and can be found at the lower part of this cluster, at the border of the Collaborative Community. It presents its motivation as driven by the idea of sharing knowledge: "Founded in 2006 with the goal of making knowledge sharing easy" (Slideshare, 2019). We further observe that actors aiming to contribute to debates on the sharing economy upload presentations and sets of slides on the platform. Other platforms in this community have a stronger focus on programmers, designers, and entrepreneurs in the information technology sector for which they provide online courses and community functions (e.g., skillshare.com, slackoverflow.com, and lynda.com). They describe their missions as creating (expert) communities that typically coproduce content on the platform. They can thus serve as important sources of knowledge or learning and for community building for entrepreneurs in the context of the sharing economy.

A third set of organizations consists of venture capitalists (e.g., Kleiner Perkins and kpcb.com) and crowdfunding platforms (e.g., kickstarter.com). Kleiner Perkins (kpcb.com) is one of the leading venture capitalists investing in technology start-ups. It positions itself as the partner of "intrepid founders to build iconic companies that made history" (Kleiner Perkins, 2018). In recent years, Kleiner Perkins has invested in a number of sharing organizations including Uber and Airbnb. In addition, partners and employees at Kleiner Perkins engage in the debate on the sharing economy through public appearances or trend reports, thereby pointing to the opportunities offered in this area (e.g., Meeker, 2012; Wienetwork, 2016). For instance, Juliet de Baubigny, senior partner at Kleiner Perkins, described the sharing economy as follows: "Sharing is about slack capacity and it is to me about optimizing efficiency, and as an investor … it is about creating opportunities within that, particularly for entrepreneurs, a lot of them for women" (Wienetwork, 2016). She further emphasized the relevance of changes that sharing organizations initiate: "I think that Uber and Airbnb are among the most exciting companies out there right now. I don't think that they even have become started in terms of their potential." Uber "is not just about car services it is about the evolution of mass transportation, and city planning and transit. And it will have a profound effect". Crowdfunding platforms such as kickstarter.com or indiegogo.com represent a specific type of sharing organization. They provide financing possibilities for startups, thereby facilitating the "realization of creative projects" (Kickstarter, 2019) and the development of "groundbreaking products" and "the next big thing" (Indiegogo, 2019).

Among the technology providers, in the fourth group, we find several organizations that focus on enhancing and facilitating the use and development of open source solutions by providing software tools, hardware platforms, and possibilities for programmers to contribute and exchange (e.g., sourceforge.net, openstreetmap.org, and arduino.cc). These organizations tend to position themselves as nurturing new and innovative ideas and developments, partly with a normative mandate. For instance, Arduino (2019) positions itself as a "catalyst in the creation of the Maker Movement"; Automattic (2019) more broadly states that it is "passionate about making the web a better place." Other technology providers in this community develop payment technologies and systems that are particularly designed for digital platforms, for instance in the sharing economy (e.g., wepay.com and bitcoin.org).

Two additional observations are surprising: first, the most recognized nodes in the issue field of the sharing economy are not sharing organizations (only 20%) or sharing-specific meta-organizations (we find none in this cluster) but tech-media sites, knowledge-sharing platforms, venture capitalists, and technology providers. Second, the average organization participating in the issue field was founded in 2008, whereas the average organization in this cluster was founded in 2000. The center of the issue field on sharing is formed by organizations created during the Internet hype and the dot-com bubble. The importance of Internet technologies represents one major commonality in this cluster. Because of the composition of forms and their organizations' founding year, we labeled this central cluster the Internet Community.

The composition of the Internet Community suggests the existence of stratified roles based on a division of labor (DiMaggio & Powell, 1983). Central media outlets have the role of creators of attention and excitement for new issues and technologies in a way that encourages entrepreneurial activities. The role of interactive Web 2.0 platforms is to establish virtual spaces in the form of structures and tools to enhance knowledge sharing and community building among (potential) entrepreneurs. Technology firms, venture capitalists, and crowdfunding platforms serve as strengtheners and provide material support in the form of technologies or financing, through which it becomes possible to grasp new business opportunities. In addition, with a high level of cohesion and a low level of connectivity, the Internet Community shows an internal structure independent of the other communities.

Our findings further suggest a shared purpose and reflection of roles and positions in organizational self-representations. Inspiring and supporting founders with technology-driven ideas that have the potential to initiate change in existing fields or even to create new ones is part of how organizations in this community present themselves. High internal cohesion within a community suggests that these organizations recognize each other as relevant actors in such an endeavor. They have the shared purpose of nurturing different waves of tech entrepreneurs: during the dot-com years, they supported Internet start-ups; then, they made Web 2.0 platforms popular; and now, they have legitimized and strengthened sharing economy start-ups. The Internet Community is an organizational field in the issue field of sharing, which is highly relevant for emerging organizational fields such as the Collaborative Community and the Coworking Community. We can thus conclude that this cluster, with its relational and discursive characteristics, forms an organizational field.

## DISCUSSION

The sharing economy has evolved around issues such as "access instead of ownership" (Stokes, Clarence, Anderson, & Rinne, 2014), "collaborative consumption and production" (Botsman & Rogers, 2010), and "collaborative commons" (Rifkin, 2014). Our study's insights provide empirical support for this idea by showing that such issues have brought together various actors in debates on the sharing economy. The observation that it is not sharing organizations or sharing-specific meta-organizations that dominate this issue field and the identification of several communities allows us to speculate about the further development of the sharing economy.

One potential development is that the Collaborative Community develops further into an organizational field, and existing debates suggest a potential pathway for such a development. Within the last few years, meta-organizations in this community have increasingly turned to a specific subtopic. They report on platform cooperatives and promote the social movement that has evolved around them (Dönnebrink, 2019; Gorenflo, 2019; Marin, 2019; Pick, 2016). If meta-organizations succeed in increasing internal cohesion and consensus on the shared purpose among sharing organizations and other members of this movement, these efforts could lead to an organizational field of the collaborative economy or, more specifically, platform cooperatives.

A potential parallel pathway is that sharing organizations become members of established organizational fields in which they are active, such as mobility, tourism, and housing (Owyang, 2016). Sharing organizations initiate change and debates in existing fields because they introduce new technologies, practices, and organizational forms and because existing laws and regulations are not fully applicable to sharing organizations, thus initiating debates and potential changes in institutional arrangements (Codagnone & Martens, 2016; Heinrichs, 2013; Mair & Reischauer, 2017).

Our finding that the core of an issue field can be an organizational field whose collective identity is not influenced by the issue field suggests that we have identified an understudied field configuration. This field configuration shows relational characteristics typical of an organizational field, such as high internal cohesion, low connectivity, and stratified roles based on a division of labor. Other characteristics are high recognition within the issue field and being an important contributor to debates in the field. What further characterizes this field configuration is that it is more outwardly oriented than other field configurations. An important element of the collective identity in this field configuration is promoting activities that result in disruptions of existing industries and fields. We therefore call this field configuration the "disruptive field."

As issues related to disruption – for instance, digital, urban, or sustainability issues – are becoming increasingly prominent, with foundations, media and meta-organizations evolving around these issues, we would not expect the disruptive field we observe to be a single occurrence of that field configuration. For instance, we could imagine the fields evolving around the issues of climate change (Howard-Grenville, Hoffman, & Bhattacharya, 2007; Wittneben, Okereke, Banerjee, & Levy, 2012) or philanthropy (Horvath & Powell, 2016), becoming disruptive fields that support the spread of concepts, practices, and organizational models by which established fields are disrupted.

The combination of reconstructing the network of organizations involved in debates on the World Wide Web and analyzing the self-representations of these organizations allowed us to study different field configurations from a relational and discursive perspective simultaneously. Although recent work has contributed to theorizing on fields by combining ideas from both field concepts (Meyer & Höllerer, 2010; Powell et al., 2017; Zietsma, Groenewegen, Logue, & Hinings, 2017), frameworks and empirical studies disentangling but combining the relational and discursive perspective are – to the best of our knowledge – rare (see Furnari, 2018, for one model representing an exception). We argue that such a combination is fruitful for several reasons.

*Determining field configurations*. The distinction between organizational and issue fields is not binary. In the network core, we observed communities that showed some characteristics of organizational fields, while others were missing. The developed approach thus allows for a fine-grained analysis of field configurations and statuses. This also allows for deriving expectations on how fields might develop.

*Identifying overlaps between fields*. In observing an issue field with an organizational field at its core, our study provides an example of how to study and analyze the overlap and embeddedness of organizational and issue fields. Future research could start with an alternative sampling approach that uses established organizational fields populated by sharing organizations within the last years as a starting point – such as the fields of mobility or accommodation – and analyze how these fields overlap with the issue field of the sharing economy.

*Comparing field configurations*. The developed approach can also serve as a means to compare field configurations. Characterizing fields on both relational and discursive levels allows for teasing out similarities and differences between fields. With this study, we thus respond to recent calls to develop frameworks that enable taking a comparative lens in research on fields (Furnari, 2018; Greenwood et al., 2011; Scott, 2013).

Based on our snapshot of the network, our study lacks a longitudinal perspective. We observed that organizations in the network core already existed during the dot-com bubble, whereas many other organizations we identified were founded after 2008, but we do not have data on the development of the observed network over time. Arguing that an important part of the disruptive field's collective identity is promoting ever-new technologies and issues suggests that the observed network is fluid and will change over time. It would be interesting to repeat the analysis in some years to see whether the disrupting field has already distanced itself from debates on the sharing economy and has turned toward new issues – such as artificial intelligence – and to see whether the emerging fields of the Collaborative Community and the Coworking Community will have become fully developed organizational fields.

## REFERENCES

Arduino. (2019). *About Us*. Retrieved from https://www.arduino.cc/en/Main/AboutUs. Accessed on June 14, 2019.

Airbnb. (2019a). About us. Retrieved from https://press.airbnb.com/about-us/. Accessed on June 14, 2019.

Automattic. (2019). *Home*. Retrieved from https://automattic.com/. Accessed on June 16, 2019.

Airbnb. (2019b). Women hosts have earned over $10 billion on Airbnb. Retrieved from https://press.airbnb.com/women-hosts-have-earned-over-10-billion-on-airbnb/. Accessed on June 14, 2019.

Bartel, C., Baldi, C., & Dukerich, J. M. (2016). Fostering stakeholder identification through expressed organizational identities. In M. G. Pratt, M. Schultz, B. E. Ashforth, & D. Ravasi (Eds.), *The Oxford handbook of organizational identity* (pp. 474–493). Oxford: Oxford University Press.

Bastian, M., Heymann, S., & Jacomy, M. (2009). Gephi: An open source software for exploring and manipulating networks. *ICWSM*, *8*, 361–362.

Baum, J. A. C., & Oliver, C. (1991). Institutional linkages and organizational mortality. *Administrative Science Quarterly*, *36*(2), 187–218. https://doi.org/10.2307/2393353

Belk, R. (2014). Sharing versus pseudo-sharing in Web 2.0. *Anthropologist*, *18*(1), 7–23. https://doi.org/10.1080/09720073.2014.11891518

Berger, P. L., & Luckmann, T. (1991). *The social construction of reality: A treatise in the sociology of knowledge*. London: Penguin UK.

Blondel, V. D., Guillaume, J.-L., Lambiotte, R., & Lefebvre, E. (2008). Fast unfolding of communities in large networks. *Journal of Statistical Mechanics: Theory and Experiment*, *2008*(10), P10008. https://doi.org/10.1088/1742-5468/2008/10/P10008

Botsman, R. (2013). The sharing economy lacks a shared definition. Fast Company, November 22. Retrieved from https://www.fastcompany.com/3022028/the-sharing-economy-lacks-a-shared-definition

Botsman, R., & Rogers, R. (2010). *What's mine is yours: The rise of collaborative consumption*. New York, NY: HarperBusiness.

Car2go. (2019). Who we are. Retrieved from https://www.car2go.com/NA/en/hr/. Accessed on July 25, 2019.

Codagnone, C., & Martens, B. (2016, January). Scoping the sharing economy: Origins, definitions, impact and regulatory issues. Working Paper No. JRC100369, Institute for Prospective Technological Studies Digital Economy.

Cohen, B. (2018). Making sense of the many business models in the sharing economy. Fast Company, April 6. Retrieved from https://www.fastcompany.com/3058203/making-sense-of-the-many-business-models-in-the-sharing-economy

Cohen, M., & Sundararajan, A. (2015). Self-regulation and innovation in the peer-to-peer sharing economy. *University of Chicago Law Review Online*, *82*(1), 116.

Couchsurfing. (2019). About us. Retrieved from https://www.couchsurfing.com/about/about-us/. Accessed on June 14, 2019.

Deskmag. (2018). Retrieved from http://www.deskmag.com/de

DiMaggio, P. (1991). Constructing an organizational field as a professional project: The case of US art museums. Retrieved from https://nyuscholars.nyu.edu/en/publications/constructing-an-organizational-field-as-a-professional-project-th

DiMaggio, P. J., & Powell, W. W. (1983). The iron cage revisited: Institutional isomorphism and collective rationality in organizational fields. *American Sociological Review*, *48*(2), 147–160. https://doi.org/10.2307/2095101

Dönnebrink, T. (2019, April 26). Platform cooperativism: A global movement on the rise. Retrieved from https://www.shareable.net/platform-cooperativism-a-global-movement-on-the-rise/. Accessed on July 20, 2019.

Drori, G. S., Delmestri, G., & Oberg, A. (2013). Branding the university: Relational strategy of identity construction in a competitive field. In L. Engwall, & P. Scott (Eds.), *Trust in higher education institutions* (pp. 134–147). London: Portland Press.

Espeland, W. N., & Sauder, M. (2007). Rankings and reactivity: How public measures recreate social worlds. *American Journal of Sociology*, *113*(1), 1–40.

European Commission. (2016, June 2). A European agenda for the collaborative economy. Retrieved from http://ec.europa.eu/growth/single-market/services/collaborative-economy_en. Accessed on September 8, 2018.

Fastcompany. (2019). About us. Retrieved from https://www.fastcompany.com/about-us. Accessed on July 10, 2019.

Flew, T. (2018). Platforms on trial. *InterMEDIA*, *46*(2), 24–29.

Forbes. (2019). Airbnb, Snapgoods and 12 more pioneers of the "share economy." Retrieved from https://www.forbes.com/pictures/eeji45emgkh/airbnb-snapgoods-and-12-more-pioneers-of-the-share-economy/#7e2899e52cf6. Accessed on June 14, 2019.

Fruchterman, T. M. J., & Reingold, E. M. (1991). Graph drawing by force-directed placement. *Software: Practice and Experience*, *21*(11), 1129–1164. https://doi.org/10.1002/spe.4380211102

Furnari, S. (2018). When does an issue trigger change in a field? A comparative approach to issue frames, field structures and types of field change. *Human Relations*, *71*(3), 321–348.

Glynn, M. A., & Abzug, R. (2002). Institutionalizing identity: Symbolic isomorphism and organizational names. *Academy of Management Journal*, *45*(1), 267–280.

Glynn, M. A., & Navis, C. (2013). Categories, identities, and cultural classification: Moving beyond a model of categorical constraint. *Journal of Management Studies*, *50*(6), 1124–1137.

Goffman, E. (1959). *The presentation of self in everyday life*. New York, NY: Anchor Books.

Gorenflo, N. (2019, November 4). How platform coops can beat death stars like Uber to create a real sharing economy. Retrieved from https://www.shareable.net/how-platform-coops-can-beat-death-stars-like-uber-to-create-a-real-sharing-economy/. Accessed on July 20, 2019.

Greenwood, R., Raynard, M., Kodeih, F., Micelotta, E. R., & Lounsbury, M. (2011). Institutional complexity and organizational responses. *Academy of Management Annals*, *5*(1), 317–371. https://doi.org/10.1080/19416520.2011.590299

Grodal, S. (2007). The emergence of a new organizational field: Labels, meaning and emotions in nanotechnology. Doctoral Dissertation, Stanfort University. Retrieved from http://people.bu.edu/grodal/nanotechnology.pdf

Heinrichs, H. (2013). Sharing economy: A potential new pathway to sustainability. *GAIA-Ecological Perspectives for Science and Society*, *22*(4), 228–231.

Hinings, C., Logue, D., & Zietsma, C. (2017). Fields, institutional infrastructure and governance. In R. Greenwood, C. Oliver, T. B. Lawrence, & R. E. Meyer (Eds.), *The Sage handbook of organizational institutionalism* (pp. 163–189). London: Sage.

Hoffman, A. J. (1999). Institutional evolution and change: Environmentalism and the U.S. chemical industry. *Academy of Management Journal*, *42*(4), 351–371. https://doi.org/10.2307/257008

Horvath, A., & Powell, W. W. (2016). Contributory or disruptive: Do new forms of philanthropy erode democracy? In R. Reich, C. Cordelli, L. Bernholz, (Eds.), *Philanthropy in democratic societies: History, institutions, values* (pp, 87–112). Chicago and London: University of Chicago Press.

Howard-Grenville, J., Hoffman, A. J., & Bhattacharya, C. (2007). Who can act on sustainability issues? Corporate capital and the configuration of organizational fields. In *Organizations and the sustainability mosaic: Crafting long-term ecological and societal solutions* (pp. 193–215). Cheltenham: Edward Elgar Publishing.

Indiegogo. (2019). About us. Retrieved from https://www.indiegogo.com/about/our-story. Accessed on June 20, 2019.

Indy Hall. (2019). Retrieved from https://www.indyhall.org/. Accessed on July 15, 2019.

Interian, J. (2016). Up in the air: Harmonizing the sharing economy through Airbnb regulations. *Boston College International and Comparative Law Review*, *39*(1), 129.

Katz, V. (2015). Regulating the sharing economy. *Berkeley Tech Law Journal*, *30*(4), 1067. https://doi.org/10.15779/Z38HG45

Kickstarter. (2019). Retrieved from https://www.kickstarter.com/about?ref=global-footer. Accessed on June 20, 2019.

Kleiner Perkins. (2018). History in the making. Retrieved from https://www.kleinerperkins.com/partnerships/consumer. Accessed on October 2, 2018.

Kwiatowski, A. (2013, August 9). 5 tools for freelancers to delegate work easily. Retrieved from http://www.deskmag.com/en/5-tools-for-freelancers-to-delegate-work-easily-870

Maguire, S., Hardy, C., & Lawrence, T. B. (2004). Institutional entrepreneurship in emerging fields: HIV/AIDS treatment advocacy in Canada. *Academy of Management Journal*, *47*(5), 657–679. https://doi.org/10.2307/20159610

Mair, J., & Reischauer, G. (2017). Capturing the dynamics of the sharing economy: Institutional research on the plural forms and practices of sharing economy organizations. *Technological Forecasting and Social Change*, *125*, 11–20. https://doi.org/10.1016/j.techfore.2017.05.023

Malhotra, A., & Van Alstyne, M. (2014). The dark side of the sharing economy… and how to lighten it. *Communications of the Association for Computing Machinery*, *57*(11), 24–27. https://doi.org/10.1145/2668893

Marin, F. (2019, October 19). Post-capitalist entrepreneurship: reality or fiction? Retrieved from https://www.ouishare.net/article/post-capitalist-entrepreneurship-reality-or-fiction. Accessed on July 20, 2019.

Martin, C. J. (2016). The sharing economy: A pathway to sustainability or a nightmarish form of neoliberal capitalism? *Ecological Economics*, *121*, 149–159. https://doi.org/10.1016/j.ecolecon.2015.11.027

Meeker, M. (2012, December). *Internet Trends*. Talk presented at the Stanford, CA. Retrieved from https://www.slideshare.net/kleinerperkins/2012-kpcb-internet-trends-yearend-update/78-Consumer_Internet_White_SpaceTo_Be

Meetup. (2018). About us. Retrieved from https://www.meetup.com/about/. Accessed on October 7, 2018.

Meyer, R. E., & Höllerer, M. A. (2010). Meaning structures in a contested issue field: A topographic map of shareholder value in Austria. *Academy of Management Journal*, *53*(6), 1241–1262. https://doi.org/10.5465/amj.2010.57317829

Navis, C., & Glynn, M. A. (2010). How new market categories emerge: Temporal dynamics of legitimacy, identity, and entrepreneurship in satellite radio, 1990–2005. *Administrative Science Quarterly*, *55*(3), 439–471. https://doi.org/10.2189/asqu.2010.55.3.439

Negro, G., Koçak, Ö., & Hsu, G. (2010). Research on categories in the sociology of organizations. In G. Hsu, G. Negro, & Koçak, (Eds.), *Categories in markets: Origins and evolution* (pp. 3–35). Bingley: Emerald Publishing Limited.

Oberg, A., Huppertz, S., & Woywode, M. (2006). Do self-representations reveal invisible competition? Co-citation analysis in the World Wide Web. Presented at the Annuals Colloquium of the European Group of Organization Studies, Bergen, Norway.

Oberg, A., Schöllhorn, T., & Woywode, M. (2009). Isomorphism in organizational self-representation in the World Wide Web? Institutionalization processes regarding Internet self-representations of organizations. *Academy of Management Best Paper Proceedings* (Vol. 2009, No. 1, pp. 1–6). Briarcliff Manor, NY: Academy of Management.

O'Sullivan, N., & O'Dwyer, B. (2015). The structuration of issue-based fields: Social accountability, social movements and the Equator Principles' issue-based field. *Accounting, Organizations and Society*, *43*, 33–55. https://doi.org/10.1016/j.aos.2015.03.008

Ouishare. (2018). Our DNA. Retrieved from https://www.ouishare.net/our-dna. Accessed on October 5, 2018.

Owyang, J. (2013). The next big thing you missed: The sharing economy goes corporate. *Wired*, October 12. Retrieved from https://www.wired.com/2013/12/sharing-economy-goes-corporate/

Owyang, J. (2016). Honeycomb 3.0: The collaborative economy market expansion. Retrieved from http://www.web-strategist.com/blog/2016/03/10/honeycomb-3-0-the-collaborative-economy-market-expansion-sxsw/. Accessed on November 13, 2018.

Pick, F. (2016, October 24). Take back the music—With platform coops! Retrieved from https://www.ouishare.net/article/take-back-the-music-with-platform-coops. Accessed on July 20, 2019.

Powell, W. W., Horvath, A., & Brandtner, C. (2016). Click and mortar: Organizations on the web. *Research in Organizational Behavior*, *36*, 101–120. https://doi.org/10.1016/j.riob.2016.07.001

Powell, W. W., & Oberg, A. (2017). Networks and institutions. In R. Greenwood, C. Oliver, T. B. Lawrence, & R. E. Meyer (Eds.), *Sage handbook on organizational institutionalism* (pp. 446–476). Thousand Oaks, CA: Sage Publications.

Powell, W. W., Oberg, A., Korff, V. P., Oelberger, C., & Kloos, K. (2017). Institutional analysis in a digital era: Mechanisms and methods to understand emerging fields. In G. Krücken, C. Mazza, R. E. Meyer, & P. Walgenbach (Eds.), *New themes in institutional analysis* (pp. 305–344). Cheltenham: Edward Elgar.

Reader, R. (2016). In European court, Uber has to prove it is just a digital service. *Fast Company*, November 29. Retrieved from https://www.fastcompany.com/4025958/in-european-court-uber-has-to-prove-it-is-just-a-digital-service

Rifkin, J. (2014). *The zero marginal cost society: The Internet of things, the collaborative commons, and the eclipse of capitalism*. New York, NY: St. Martin's Press.

Rustrum, C. (2014). Escape Winter to Destination Cowork on Beach. *Deskmag*, October 14. Retrieved from http://www.deskmag.com/en/70-entrepreneurs-escape-winter-to-destination-cowork-on-beach-907

Sacks, D. (2011). The sharing economy. *Fast Company*, April 18. Retrieved from https://www.fastcompany.com/1747551/sharing-economy

Scholz, T. (2016). Platform cooperativism—Challenging the corporate sharing economy. Retrieved from http://www.academia.edu/download/44556273/scholz_platformcooperativism21.pdf

Schor, J. (2016). Debating the sharing economy. *Journal of Self-Governance & Management Economics*, *4*(3), 7. https://doi.org/10.22381/JSME4320161

Schütz, A. (1967). *The phenomenology of the social world*. Evanston, IL: Northwestern University Press.

Schwalbe, U., & Peitz, M. (2016). Kollaboratives Wirtschaften oder Turbokapitalismus? [Collaborative management or turbo-capitalism?]. *Perspektiven Der Wirtschaftspolitik*, *17*(3), 232–252. https://doi.org/10.1515/pwp-2016-0018

Scott, J. (2012). *Social network analysis*. London: Sage.

Scott, W. R. (2013). *Institutions and organizations: Ideas, interests, and identities*. London: Sage.

Shareable. (2018). About. Retrieved from https://www.shareable.net/about. Accessed on October 5, 2018.

Slideshare. (2019). About. Retrieved from https://de.slideshare.net/about. Accessed on June 14, 2019.

Startnext. (2019). Über startnext. Retrieved from https://www.startnext.com/info/startnext.html. Accessed on July 16, 2019.

Stokes, K., Clarence, E., Anderson, L., & Rinne, A. (2014). *Making sense of the UK collaborative economy*. London: Nesta.

Strang, D., & Meyer, J. W. (1993). Institutional conditions for diffusion. *Theory and Society*, *22*(4), 487–511.

Sundararajan, A. (2012). Why the government doesn't need to regulate the sharing economy. *Wired*, October 22. Retrieved from https://www.wired.com/2012/10/from-airbnb-to-coursera-why-the-government-shouldnt-regulate-the-sharing-economy/

Taskrabbit. (2019). Retrieved from https://www.taskrabbit.com/about. Accessed on June 14, 2019.

Techcrunch. (2019). Events. Retrieved from https://techcrunch.com/events/. Accessed on June 14, 2019.

Uber. (2019). About. Retrieved from https://www.uber.com/de/de/about/. Accessed on June 14, 2019.

Vith, S., Oberg, A., Höllerer, M. A., & Meyer, R. E. (2019). Envisioning the 'sharing city': Governance strategies for the sharing economy. *Journal of Business Ethics*, *159*(4), 1023–1046. https://doi.org/10.1007/s10551-019-04242-4

Walker, E. T., McCarthy, J. D., & Baumgartner, F. (2011). Replacing members with managers? Mutualism among membership and nonmembership advocacy organizations in the United States. *American Journal of Sociology*, *116*(4), 1284–1337. https://doi.org/10.1086/655753

Wasserman, S., & Faust, K. (1994). *Social network analysis: Methods and applications*. New York, NY: Cambridge University Press.

White, D. R., Owen-Smith, J., Moody, J., & Powell, W. W. (2004). Networks, fields and organizations: Micro-dynamics, scale and cohesive embeddings. *Computational & Mathematical Organization Theory*, *10*(1), 95–117. https://doi.org/10.1023/B:CMOT.0000032581.34436.7b

Wienetwork. (2016). The Sharing Economy—Juliet de Baubigny and Ken Parks. Retrieved from https://www.wienetwork.org/single-post/2016/10/19/The-Sharing-Economy—Juliet-de-Baubigny-and-Ken-Parks

Wired. (2019). About us. Retrieved from https://www.wired.com/about/press/. Accessed on July 10, 2019.

Wittneben, B. B. F., Okereke, C., Banerjee, S. B., & Levy, D. L. (2012). Climate change and the emergence of new organizational landscapes. *Organization Studies*, *33*(11), 1431–1450. https://doi.org/10.1177/0170840612464612

Wooten, M., & Hoffman, A. J. (2008). Organizational fields: Past, present and future. In R. Greenwood, C. Oliver, T. B. Lawrence, & R. E. Meyer (Eds.), *The SAGE Handbook of organizational institutionalism* (pp. 131–147). London: Sage.

Wruk, D., Oberg, A., Klutt, J., & Maurer, I. (2019). The presentation of self as good and right: How value propositions and business model features are linked in the sharing economy. *Journal of Business Ethics*, *159*(3), 997–1021. https://doi.org/10.1007/s10551-019-04209-5

Zietsma, C., Groenewegen, P., Logue, D. M., & Hinings, C. (2017). Field or fields? Building the scaffolding for cumulation of research on institutional fields. *Academy of Management Annals*, *11*(1), 391–450.

Zietsma, C., & Lawrence, T. B. (2010). Institutional work in the transformation of an organizational field: The interplay of boundary work and practice work. *Administrative Science Quarterly*, *55*(2), 189–221.

Zipcar. (2019). About us. Retrieved from https://www.zipcar.com/about. Accessed on June 14, 2019.

# CATEGORY KINGS AND COMMONERS: WITHIN AND CROSS-CATEGORY SPILL-OVERS IN THE SHARING ECONOMY

Pinar Ozcan, Kerem Gurses and Mareike Möhlmann


## ABSTRACT

*This chapter focuses on the largely unexplored within- and cross-category spill-overs between category kings and commoners within the field of the sharing economy. Going beyond the reputational spill-overs that are the main focus of extant literature, the authors also consider spill-overs in awareness, regulation, and customer usage between category kings and commoners, providing a holistic view of what it means to be a commoner in the same or adjacent category as a king. On the basis of a mixed-method study based on semi-structured interviews with UK sharing platforms and a consumer survey, the authors show that category commoners are affected by kings differently depending whether they are in the exact same sub-category or in an adjacent one within the same larger category. This chapter expands extant work on within and cross-category dynamics by taking the less popular perspective of the less visible category members. Studying these dynamics in the setting of the sharing economy also contributes to the authors' knowledge of what enables/hinders the growth of a new field as a whole. Finally, the findings have important policy implications.*


**Keywords**: Categories; category kings; spill-overs; corporate reputation; sharing economy; category commoners

**Theorizing the Sharing Economy: Variety and Trajectories of New Forms of Organizing**
**Research in the Sociology of Organizations, Volume 66, 163–185**

**ISSN: 0733-558X/doi:10.1108/S0733-558X20200000066008**

## INTRODUCTION

This chapter focuses on the largely unexplored spill-overs between category kings and commoners within and across the different sectors in the sharing economy. In addition to being highly visible members of many industries, category kings have attracted attention from researchers in various streams. Prior work has articulated "anchor tenants" in emergent geographic clusters (Powell, Packalen, & Whittington, 2012), market-dominant "kingpins" within industry value chains (Jacobides & Tae, 2015), and "cognitive referent" firms in novel product markets (Santos & Eisenhardt, 2009). However, most studies have overlooked what goes on with the majority of the members in the same category, that is, category commoners (McDonald & Eisenhardt, 2017), particularly how they might benefit/hurt from the existence and activities of category kings.

Our chapter addresses these questions by examining spill-overs within the context of sharing economy categories. Sharing economy is an umbrella term, associated with a plethora of similar concepts referred to as the platform economy, collaborative consumption, the gig economy, crowd-based capitalism, and access-based consumption (Bardhi & Eckhardt, 2012; Botsman & Rogers, 2010; Möhlmann, 2015; Sundararajan, 2016). In this chapter, we refer to the sharing economy as digitally enabled, peer-to-peer exchange platforms for goods and services that may or may not be for-profit, and that connect spare capacity with demand or offer access-over-ownership by enabling renting, lending, reselling, or swapping (Möhlmann, 2015). Within the sharing economy context, we refer to category kings as pioneering technology startups like *Airbnb* and *Uber* (Pontikes & Barnett, 2015), that have achieved a celebrity-like status and recognition from the public and dominate their respective categories. Unlike category kings, category commoners may stimulate less public attention (low visibility and limited coverage) and fading support (few resources and endorsements and limited market traction) (Mcdonald & Eisenhardt, 2017). In the UK, examples of category commoners may be the upscale accommodation sharing service *UnderTheDoormat*, a skill-sharing service based on a time-banking principle *Echo*, or the meal sharing service *Eatwith*.

Through a mixed-method study based on semi-structured interviews with UK sharing platforms and a consumer survey, this chapter expands extant work on categories by taking the less popular perspective of the commoner or "underdog" and by identifying the within and cross-category spill-overs that these category members receive from category kings. Going beyond the reputational spill-overs that are the main focus of extant literature, we also consider spill-overs in awareness, regulation, and customer usage between category kings and commoners, providing a holistic view of what it means to be a commoner. We find that category commoners are affected by kings differently depending whether they are in the exact same sub-category or in an adjacent one within the same larger category. While being in the same larger category (sharing platform), but a different sub-category as the category king is largely advantageous for commoners due to the increased awareness, trust, traffic, and regulatory conditions that the king creates for the category, being in the same sub-category as a category king is a double-edged sword. On the one hand, they can benefit from the same increased public awareness and better regulatory conditions described above. On the other hand, being lumped together with category kings carries the danger of being lost in the crowd, remaining undifferentiated from the category kings. In addition, the network effects make it difficult for a second, third etc. platform in the same category to attract both providers and users. Finally, the undesirable providers and users that the category king bans from its platform spill-over to these other platforms, which is difficult to detect and manage with limited resources.

Our study expands extant research on categories in several ways. First, we contribute to the burgeoning research on categories (Durand & Paolella, 2013) by distinguishing between category kings and commoners and how category kings' actions affect category commoners through several spill-over mechanisms, of which some are expected and some are paradoxical. Our study also extends previous literature by theorizing different effects of "category kingdom" based on whether or not the commoners are in the same sub-category. Studying these dynamics in the setting of the sharing economy contributes to our knowledge of how the sharing economy as a whole and firms in its sub-categories co-evolve. Most sharing economy research focuses only on a particular sector/category, for example, transportation (Chan & Shaheen, 2012; Greenwood & Wattal, 2017), or housing (Ert, Fleischer, & Magen, 2016), not paying attention to cross-category dynamics and how these dynamics affect the growth of the category as a whole.

Our findings also have important policy implications. We find that although category kings may be beneficial for increasing awareness for a new category as a whole, they may suppress their smaller competitors and achieve a monopolistic position. Checks and balances need to be put in place by regulators to prevent such outcomes. In addition, governments can set up and subsidize online trust building and compliance schemes, for example, a trust seal for the new category such that the rules and requirements of these schemes are not at deterring levels for the resource-poor category commoners in an emerging category.

The rest of the chapter first lays out the relevant literature on categories and category kings and commoners. We then describe our methodology and findings. Finally, we discuss our contributions to extant work on categories and the burgeoning sharing economy research. We conclude the chapter with policy implications and final words.

## THEORETICAL BACKGROUND

Previous studies advocate that constraints on new industries arise from a lack of knowledge, rendering organizations in emerging fields difficult to classify and comprehend (Meyer & Rowan, 1977; Zucker, 1977). Lack of familiarity with a new organizational population reduces survival and founding prospects (Hannan & Carroll, 1995; Hannan & Freeman, 1984; Singh, Tucker, & House, 1986). This lack of information means that potential entrepreneurs, employees, and exchange partners may find it difficult to understand how production and distribution are organized in the new industry (Aldrich & Fiol, 1994), inhibiting learning (Aldrich & Baker, 2001). The problem also extends to consumers of the new industry's products who may not understand the attributes of products (Rindova & Fombrun, 2001) or even know how to consume those products (Mezias & Boyle, 2002).

In such new industries, thus, early entry occurs in a context of great uncertainty with regard to the meaning, boundaries, and even the very existence of the industry (Aldrich & Fiol, 1994; Lounsbury, Ventresca, & Hirsch, 2003; Santos & Eisenhardt, 2009). Earlier work has shown the significance of socio-cognitive factors at the early stages of industry evolution (Clark, 1985; Kaplan & Tripsas, 2008; Lounsbury et al., 2003), and suggest a stronger focus on categorical dynamics since categories and their associated labels establish the focal points through which producers and consumers understand an evolving industry (Moreau, Markman, & Lehmann, 2001; Rosa, Porac, Runser-Spanjol, & Saxon, 1999).

### *Category Dynamics in Nascent Market Spaces*

Market categories are abstract schemes that classify merchandise and services into groups in line with their attributes and core features in a given market (e.g., Hannan, Polos, & Carroll, 2007), and categorical evolution in nascent market spaces can be divided into two major phases. In a preliminary phase of divergence, increasingly more categories are introduced and used; in the ensuing phase of convergence, a few categories start to win favor among market stakeholders, while many others are gradually abandoned (Suarez, Grodal, & Gotsopoulos, 2015). As experience and familiarization with the new product class increase, stakeholders end up with a better capacity to assess which of the product's features and uses are relevant and important. Categories that best capture and communicate such relevant dimensions are preferred and eventually start winning over other alternatives (Kennedy, Lo, & Lounsbury, 2010). This convergence of understandings and categories in an emerging industry constrain both the ability of producers and other stakeholders to introduce new categories, and their need for doing so. Shared understandings about the meaning of categories and about product characteristics that are deemed relevant and valuable do not allow for the introduction of novel categories. In addition, firms may find it more attractive to position their products in a well-established category because this allows them to reach a large pool of customers (Zuckerman, Kim, Ukanwa, & Von Rittmann, 2003). Producers that initially positioned their products in some of the categories that did not gain traction feel the pressure to reposition them, and producers that stick to categories that are wavering run the risk of being marginalized with lower chances of survival. Consequently, the rate at which new categories are introduced to the industry goes down, and the total number of categories also decreases due to abandonment of some of the categories. Over time, convergence toward a specific perception of the industry leads both producers and other stakeholders to move toward the category that best captures this perception. The preferred category thus progressively gains dominance and becomes the referent for the emerging industry and its products (Suarez et al., 2015).

As such, a dominant category may be defined as the conceptual schema that most stakeholders follow when they refer to products addressing similar needs and competing for the same market space (Suarez et al., 2015). As a dominant category becomes prominent, this dominance has implications for both the competition and other actors in the industry.

### *Intra-category Dynamics*

As categorical boundaries have clearer definitions, and categories gradually assume meanings of their own; that is, rather than being defined by the products that claim membership in them, they increasingly dictate the must-have product characteristics in order to be perceived as a legitimate member. Successive products are judged against these categorical requirements or "categorical test codes" (Hannan et al., 2007, p. 79), products that fit to the requirements of the category to which they claim membership are seen as legitimate members, while products that do not fit see their categorical claims questioned (Hannan et al., 2007). Stakeholders may even classify or reclassify a product regardless of the producer's categorical claims if they discover that it fits another category better (Bowker & Star, 2000). Industry boundaries and the notion of substitutability, thus, are not fully objective but, rather, socially constructed. In fact, categories emphasize the homogeneity of their members while also setting rules that differentiate members from non-members (Zerubavel, 1997). Simply having the same label and being part of the same category emphasizes the similarities between objects (Hannan et al., 2007) and stakeholders may perceive them as closer substitutes than they actually are. However, within the same category, we argue that some firms may have a higher standing than others, and at times, these differences may not be solely attributed to performance differences.

### *Category Kings and Commoners*

Prior work has articulated related characterizations of organizations that seem to be more prominent than others in a new category: a well-connected "anchor tenant" in an emergent geographic cluster (Powell et al., 2012), a market-dominant "kingpin" within an industry value chain (Jacobides & Tae, 2015), and a top-of-mind "cognitive referent" in a novel product market (Santos & Eisenhardt, 2009). Anecdotal accounts describe category kings – pioneering technology startups like Airbnb and Twitter that create and dominate new categories (Pontikes & Barnett, 2015). These companies have achieved a lopsided prominence and market share relative to their competitors and have essentially "closed the door behind them" in the category (Thiel, 2014). However, most prior work overlooked the also-rans in the industry that are called *category commoners* (McDonald & Eisenhardt, 2017). Compared to category kings, category commoners stimulate limited attention (low visibility and limited coverage) and fading support (few resources and endorsements and limited market traction) and recent research has even shed light on how firms end up becoming category kings or commoners through different strategies (Mcdonald & Eisenhardt, 2017). The distinction between category kings and commoners may be related to pure economic performance (i.e., category king/commoner may seem interchangeable with most/least successful firm) but this may not be fully objective, since category commoners may simply be lagging the king according to the perception of their audience. The reason category commoners may not fare as well in the eyes of their stakeholders as category kings is that, at times, category kings are perceived as "celebrities," and may get excessive attention from stakeholders and media, not leaving any room for category commoners to showcase themselves effectively to the stakeholders. Organizational celebrity is an important social approval asset that is given to an organization by audiences' high levels of attention and positive emotional responses (Pfarrer, Pollock, & Rindova, 2010; Pollock, Mishina, & Seo, 2015; Rindova, Pollock, & Hayward, 2006). Although category commoners may not be able to present themselves directly in such a positive light to their audience as much as the category kings, the actions of category kings may have consequences for the category commoners, through a reputational spill-over effect. Next, we define reputational spill-overs more generally and then review this phenomenon within the specific context of categories.

### *Reputational Spill-overs*

Reputational spill-over occurs when an event caused by the actions of one firm affects the reputation of others that are not involved with that event (Barnett & Hoffman, 2008; King, Lenox, & Barnett, 2002; Mohammad & Crane, 2015). It renders the traditional view of reputation as an expectation of future behavior based on the result of prior behavior incomplete since firms are attributed with similar behavioral expectations as others similar to them independent of their own actions. Consequently, audiences evaluate firms' reputations based on a mental classification of a greater representation of firms (Yu & Lester, 2008) and we observe that, in this case, the actions of one firm would influence the judgment made of another, leading to a common reputation among those firms (Barnett & King, 2008; King et al., 2002).

Extant research has found evidence for reputational spill-overs empirically. Goins and Gruca (2008) found that redundancy announcements U.S oil and gas industry firms negatively influence other firms within the industry that did not make such announcements. Spill-over effects on market valuations of firms, referred to as "information transfers," have been recognized with respect to managerial actions such as earnings announcements (Foster, 1981), bankruptcy (Lang & Stulz, 1992), drug withdrawals (Ahmed, Gardella, & Nanda, 2002) and new product introductions (Zantout & Chaganti, 1996) in the accounting and finance literature. Some firms may even experience more damage from spill-over effects from their competitors' actions than from their own actions, as studies of automobile recalls demonstrate (Jarrell & Peltzman, 1985).

Previous studies mostly attempt to provide a theoretical basis for how reputational spill-over occurs, therefore portray it in a relatively simplistic manner in that (1) the effects of a spill-over are considered constant between the firms that experience it, and (2) the scope of affected firms is limited to a single industry context (e.g., Barnett & Hoffman, 2008; King & Lenox, 2000; Yu, Sengul, & Lester, 2008). Such a narrow conceptualization constrains our understanding by failing to take into account facets of spill-over that make it complex and variable in nature – namely, the severity of its effect across different firms, and the full scope of firms that are subject to spill-over, including firms in different industries (Mohammad & Crane, 2015). Firms across industries should be considered in the scope of spill-overs since a firm's reputation can become entangled with firms outside of its industry through cross industry associations (Barnett & Hoffman, 2008), and may be affected by neighboring industries that the firm spans (Vergne, 2012). Thus, we can shed more light on reputational spill-overs through not only uncovering how spill-overs occur, but also by understanding how they vary in nature.

Our study addresses these questions and takes a wider view of spill-overs not only confined to reputational spill-overs reviewed above, within the context of sharing economy categories. Category spill-overs are positive or negative externalities arising from associating with a particular category. When two or more stakeholder-specific categories nourish each other over time, there are positive spill-overs, and when two or more stakeholder-specific reputations undermine each other over time, there are negative spill-overs. Studying the impact of category spill-overs can provide an enhanced understanding of how companies manage category associations and how different types of category associations generate spill-overs, which can have critical performance implications for member firms. This chapter sets out to shed light on such tensions by examining various types of spill-over effects occurring between various category actors, particularly the category kings and commoners in sharing economy. Next, we describe the methodology we followed for our study.

## METHODOLOGY

### *Research Setting*

Our research setting is the sharing economy organizations/platforms in the UK. Sharing platforms are becoming substantially more prevalent in day to day life and business activities. A *Time* magazine poll published in January 2016 estimated that 42 percent of Americans had already used a sharing economy service, and that 22 percent had provided one. Similarly, a cross-sector survey in the UK has shown that in 2017, 42 percent of the UK population used sharing platforms other than ecommerce platforms like ebay and gumtree, and close to half of these respondents use them more than once a month, constituting a 60 percent increase since 2016 (Ozcan, Mohlmann, & Krishnamoorthy, 2018). With such pervasiveness in the society, sharing economy firms are expected to generate trust, aid with community revival (Schor, 2016), and even reduce waste and increase the efficient use of resources (Hamari, Sjöklint, & Ukkonen, 2016), and thus, help solve societal problems (Uzunca, Rigtering, & Ozcan, 2018).

However, due to the sharing economy phenomenon still being quite recent, extant research lacks the indigenous theoretical groundwork to categorize and fully address sharing economy's impacts, dilemmas, and theoretical hurdles (Murillo, Buckland, & Val, 2017). In this case, grounding research on sharing economy in an already existing theoretical tradition is very beneficial to build a field of research, and at the same time, strengthen the field of practice (Mair & Reischauer, 2017). Since sharing economy has several sub categories, and since we observe that the sharing economy as a whole and its sub-categories co-evolve together, we posit that the categories research tradition would be an appropriate lens to study this co-evolution. The interaction between the more prominent firms, category kings – as we name them – and category commoners, both within, and cross-categories, is paramount to this co-evolution. Since category kings, albeit with different names/labels, have already been studied in the literature (Jacobides & Tae, 2015; Santos & Eisenhardt, 2009) this chapter takes the perspective of category commoner type sharing economy organizations in the UK and unveils their benefits and challenges of co-existing with category kings.

In order to unveil these benefits and challenges, we conducted an inductive study (Eisenhardt, 1989) with 30 semi-structured interviews with the UK sharing economy organizations/platforms, as well as industry experts, and members of the Sharing Economy UK (SEUK from here on), which is the major sharing economy trade association in the UK. SEUK aims (1) to champion and strengthen the sharing economy sector, (2) to ensure best practices among its members, and (3) to act as a single voice of its member organizations in the UK (SEUK, 2018). SEUK was launched in 2015, following the publication of a government-sponsored independent review written by the founder of LoveHomeSwap. Two years later, SEUK was incorporated into the Confederation of British Industry who is now managing the operations of the trade organization body. By the autumn of 2018, when we wrote this article, the SEUK board members were representatives of easyCar, Gumtree, Airbnb, Patchwork, and the legal practice Osborne Clark (SEUK, 2018). A plethora of different organizations/platforms that can be associated with different sub-industry categories have been granted SEUK membership by summer 2018, covering services such as the sharing of pre-owned goods (e.g., eBay and Gumtree), rental cars (e.g., easyCar and Zipcar), places to stay (e.g., Airbnb and Beds on Board), funding (e.g., Justgiving and Crowdcube), rides (e.g., Liftshare), parking (e.g., JustPark and Your Parking Space), professional services (e.g., Parcelly and TaskRabbit), and meals (e.g., MealSharing and Eatwith). These sharing platforms included both for-profit and not-for-profit organizations.

While different countries all around the world are experiencing a rise of the emerging sharing economy and face challenges on how to define its boundaries and how to regulate it, the UK context provides a valuable setting for our research. Large sharing economy brands such as Uber and Airbnb that are disrupting the economic landscape in many countries are active in the UK market. In addition, most sharing economy organizations/platforms tend to be located either in, or close to, the major metropolitan region of London. Due to this geographical proximity, even smaller and less well-known organizations/platforms tend to be involved in SEUK activities, providing us with valuable information about how the relationship between category commoners and category kings evolved in the UK context.

### *Data Sources*

Given the limited empirical work on our research question, we followed an inductive approach, where we analyzed the relationships between category commoners and category kings, as well as their interactions with their ecosystem. We used various sources for our data collection, capturing three different levels of analysis, including (1) the perspective of the SEUK trade association (and its management team), (2) the SEUK members comprising category commoners and category kings sharing economy organizations, and (3) sharing economy consumers. We draw on both qualitative and quantitative data.

The main source was in-depth semi-structured interviews with UK sharing economy organizations, as well as industry experts, and members of the SEUK management team. Access to data was facilitated in part through SEUK. One of the researchers approached SEUK in 2015, built a relationship and interviewed the member organizations. A total of 30 semi-structured interviews were conducted between 2015 and 2018, with an average duration of 60 minutes each. The interview questions were structured around the interviewees and their role, the business concepts and growth of respective sharing economy organizations/platforms they represent, as well as respective organizations' interactions with the trade association, other SEUK members, regulators, and consumers. In addition, two of the researchers regularly participated in SEUK member meetings. These provided a valuable source about the emergent role of SEUK and its role in the economic landscape of the UK, and allowed the researchers to observe members' and management team discussions in a non-artificial environment.

In order to classify the informants' organizations as category king or commoner, as well as to look at usage spill-overs between these platforms, we relied on a survey we conducted among sharing economy consumers in July 2017.[1] The survey was developed by two of the authors in close consultation with SEUK members. It was distributed by a commissioned research company based in the UK and gathered 1,200 valid and complete survey responses from a representative sample of the UK population (based on gender, income, education level, and place of residence). In the survey, respondents were asked several blocks of questions that unveiled their current sharing and non-sharing behavior and future motivations for sharing goods and services across different categories including rides, accommodation, and professional services.

### *Data Analysis*

The interviews and recordings of the meetings were transcribed. An individual case history was then constructed for each sharing organization following the data collection process. The case histories included interview, observational, and archival data (Eisenhardt, 1989; Yin, 1994) on each of the sharing platforms that we identified as either category king or commoner based on usage statistics in our quantitative survey (Ozcan et al., 2018) and supporting archival material. We triangulated these data, emphasizing themes that were supported by different data collection methods and confirmed by several informants (Jick, 1979).

We then began the cross-case analysis, looking for similar constructs and themes in the cases (Eisenhardt & Graebner, 2007). More specifically, we started analyzing our findings in order to spot the common positive and negative effects that category commoners documented as part of their experience. We used tables and other cell designs to compare several possible constructs at once (Miles & Huberman, 1994). As the theoretical frame clarified, we added comparison with the extant literature to highlight similarities and differences, strengthen the internal validity of findings, sharpen construct definitions and measures, and raise the generalizability of the findings.

For the complementing quantitative survey, we conducted a descriptive analysis of our survey data, which we made available to the academic and practitioner communities. We used the descriptive findings of the survey to inform our qualitative findings. Iteratively reflecting on our theoretical foundations and the empirical analyses based on qualitative and quantitative findings, we finally developed a theoretical model that captures our findings, described below.

## FINDINGS

Our interviews with sharing economy organizations as well as our consumer survey confirmed the existence of both category kings and commoners in the UK sharing economy setting. Table 1 presents a comparison of kings and commoners in different aspects in the UK context.

Among category kings and commoners we identified, we encountered both positive and negative spill-over effects of various kinds. Below, we discuss these within- and cross-category spill-overs following the same structure that is given in the visual illustration of these effects in Fig. 1.

### *Spill-overs in Regulatory Acceptance*

First, our interviews and observations revealed how commoner platforms in various categories benefited from kings' efforts in the political space for regulatory acceptance and favorable conditions. One of the main mechanisms through which commoners benefited from kings within and across the same category was through the activities of SEUK, as a founding member explains below:

> One of the big objectives of the sharing economy UK is to raise the profile of the sharing economy within the UK's political scene. If we didn't do it then we'd have regulations thrust upon us without the ability to consult and that was a big driver.

***Table 1.*** Comparison of Category Kings versus Commoners in Public Awareness and Usage.

| Sharing Platform | Sharing Sub-category | Public Awareness As Compared to the Second Largest Competitor in the Same Sub-category | Usage As Compared to the Second Largest Competitor in the Same Sub-category |
|---|---|---|---|
| Airbnb | Accommodation | 10-fold | 6-fold |
| Uber | Ride sharing | 20-fold | 12-fold |
| Easycar | Car sharing | 3-fold | 2-fold |
| Taskrabbit | Skill sharing | 2-fold | 2-fold |

*Source*: Warwick Business School Sharing Economy Consumer Survey (Ozcan et al., 2018).

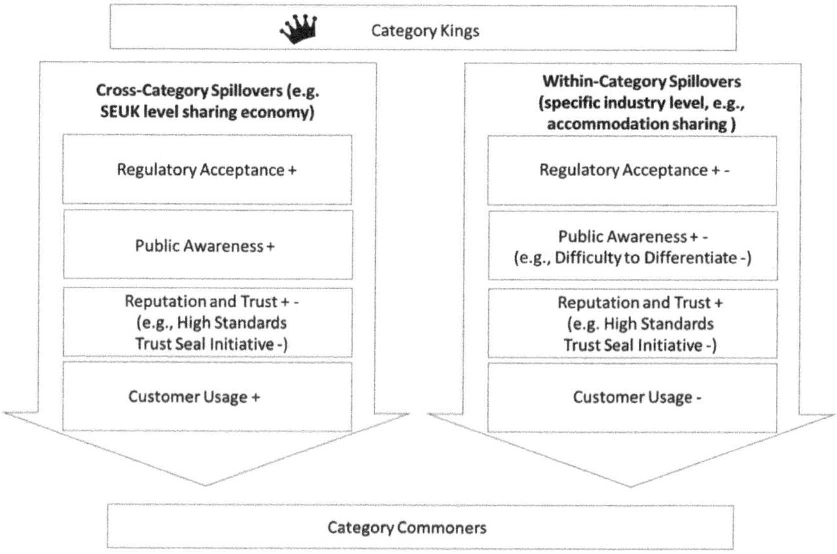


*Fig. 1.* Theoretical Model for Spill-overs from Category Kings to Commoners.

The media and communications manager of SEUK similarly described how their participation in political debates regarding the sharing economy is crucial for their members in order to navigate their regulatory uncertainty:

> Sharing economy may be popular with consumers, but it is still a new thing, especially for regulators. There are still many issues, like employment, taxes, that are not well defined for the space. So, it's crucial for us to help our members navigate this regulatory uncertainty and resolve it in their favour.

Funding the association in terms of annual fees represents a crucial means in order to push the regulatory agenda forward. Many category king organizations were founding members of this association and paid higher annual fees compared to commoners, as explained by another member below:

> I think what works for SEUK is having Airbnb involved, having that kind of cast to have our voices to be heard. Airbnb, Bla Bla Car, Taskrabbit, they pay more. But there are lots of people there who pay 1000 pounds a year for which I think they get incredibly rewarded.

Thus, category kings' financial support was crucial to support the wider range of activities that SEUK implemented for the members. However, not only did the category king organizations shoulder most of the financial burden, but also they tended to show more intensive engagement in SEUK, for instance by representing SEUK in meetings, being at the forefront of pushing regulatory acceptance forward. One SEUK executive described the involvement of the category kings as follows:

> The more established members don't just drive this effort financially, they also cooperate with us. They are often at the table with us as representatives of their sector, like Airbnb will often come with us to conversations with the government on accommodation sharing.

The second type of regulatory spill-over from category kings to commoners was through the direct political activities, or lack thereof, of the category kings. Our interviews showed that politically active category kings benefited from representing category commoners in the political space, as described by an executive from one of the large organizations that founded SEUK:

> It is important for us to fit into our environment and support our environment. This includes supporting smaller sharing platforms that could provide complementary services to us. Of course, while doing that, we also support smaller competitors, but this needs to happen .... It matters because when you lobby, it's very different to represent the entire UK sharing platforms versus when you do it just for yourself.

Interestingly, the positive spill-over of category kings' political efforts were not just to the smaller platforms within their sub-category (e.g., accommodation and ride sharing) but also cross-category, as described by a small organization executive in skill sharing:

> It's good for us because when someone like Airbnb talks to those guys <government>, their rhetoric is very much along the lines of "we're here as part of a larger sharing movement." They do it so that they don't look self-serving, and it's great for me!

We also discovered that not all category kings were politically active. A good example is Uber. A smaller ride-sharing platform founder explained how Uber's lack of engagement with institutional actors has made their life difficult.

> Up until recently, Uber has just not been engaging with any of the stakeholders. Their approach was, let our number of drivers and users speak for itself. But clearly, that didn't work out and in the meantime, it was extremely difficult for us to get a seat at the table with transportation authorities when Uber wasn't there.

### *Spill-overs in Public Awareness*

In our interviews, it was revealed that executives of category commoner organizations perceived both positive and negative within category spill-over effects. First, they experienced a positive effect, as category kings had greater resources for publicity. As described above, the efforts of SEUK to raise public awareness were beneficial for all organizations in the sharing economy. An SEUK member described:

> There was a full page on Sunday Times today on the rise of the sharing economy. SEUK has that kind of reach ...

Larger sharing economy organizations had different means to implement marketing activities. One founder of a commoner organization in the accommodation sector described this positive effect of category kings' PR efforts as follows:

> The likes of AirBnB got such big press and reach now. I don't know how many people but certainly many would have heard of Airbnb today and that helps in raising general awareness for the rest. I mean, there's still a long way to go but I think they've really moved this whole thing along.

Another member explained how category kings had become the way that people define the sharing economy category as a whole, as follows:

> Very few people would define the sharing economy because it is very difficult to define. More often people would give examples of companies that fit in the sharing economy to prove that they understand. So the examples they would give would be Airbnb and Uber typically.

We also observed an unexpected consequence of the awareness created by the category kings on commoners, which largely depended on whether they were located in the same category as the kings. For platforms that were in the same category as the category kings, there was a negative effect in terms of ability to differentiate their business model from these platforms. A great example is one accommodation platform that provides end-to-end service for hosts in the London area. In our interviews, the founder explained how they founded the platform for the purpose of serving the upscale market where hosts, who are typically executives working in the City, travel a lot, and do not have the time to prepare their apartment for sharing while they are gone. She explained:

> I think one of the big misnomers is that often people bundle them all together and just say, look, these are all platforms. But, when people talk about this stuff they actually see it all as one thing you know, my business, <others> for example, we actually all operate, so we manage the homes you know, we take care of everything from the cleaning, the linen that I was mentioning about, insurance, everything end-to-end so the homeowner basically puts everything into our care.

Similarly, the founder of another accommodation sharing platform explained:

> What they also don't really understand is they just think this is all Airbnb. There are many other formats out there that do different and sometimes better things.

But also category commoners in other categories, such as in transportation experienced similar difficulties. The founder of a smaller car-sharing platform explained how they had difficulty differentiating from ride-sharing companies, and in particular from the category king Uber:

> Car sharing is very different from ride sharing. But we see more and more that that's not clear to people. Whether they like it or not, what they tend to think of is Uber. That's one of our biggest challenges, I would say.

On the flipside, the category commoners in other categories experienced a positive effect of the heightened awareness for category kings in terms of raising awareness for their own business model because they could use the category king as a reference point: One car-sharing platform described this as follows:

> Coming out of London, when you speak to people and you explain to them, we're like Airbnb but for cars, they're like, ok!

Another organization used this effect to market their boat-sharing service by advertising on their platform:

> Airbnb for your boat .... Earn money when you're not on it!

Overall, we observed that the resources and efforts of category kings to raise awareness for the wider category of sharing economy and for their own sub-category had mixed effects for the category commoners. One the one hand, everyone else, whether they were in the same sub-category of sharing or a different one, experienced a positive effect from higher awareness created by the kings. But at the same time, as the entire category became associated with the business model of the category kings, those who were trying to differentiate from that model had trouble doing so.

### *Spill-overs in Reputation and Trust*

We differentiate awareness from reputation, which, based on extant literature, we define as the assessment, or the nature of the evaluation or judgement about a particular organization (Barnett, Jermier, & Lafferty, 2006). We observed that some of the heightened awareness around category kings created negative press coverage, which category commoners perceived as a negative effect on their own reputation, as apparent in the quotes below:

> All they see is in the press when there's an Airbnb disaster, people don't realise how much good activity happens in this space.

> There's a load of stuff where there's negative press and I don't feel like we do anything near what we should be doing in terms of proactive PR, you know, where we've got real data that can say look, here's the benefits that we're bringing, here's the opportunities that are created as a result of this. If we don't actually get out and proactively do more, I think we're then at the mercy of the negative press about these big players.

The interviews revealed that negative reputation is as likely to spill over as positive reputation. This applies to cross category and within-spill-overs alike.

> Do they see just the negative sides or also the positive sides? Once you see an imbalance there it also shows you that there should be more marketing towards marketing the benefits and then there's also like a public image problem, but this is something that needs to be worked on, right?

Reputation is an important factor in order to establish trust and increase consumer usage in digital platforms (e.g., Bolton, Greiner, & Ockenfels, 2013). Previous research has used the notion of "trust transfer," to refer to cross-level relationships, or "spill-overs," that occur across different hierarchy levels, potentially spanning from the organizational level to the interpersonal level (Rousseau, 1994; Stewart, 2003). Indeed, seminal work by Pavlou and Gefen (2004) and Gefen and Pavlou (2012) has shown that trust in organizations/institutions may influence interpersonal trust, such as trust in a community of individuals. In the presence of no or negative reputation, trust-building efforts become even more critical.

Through our interviews and observations, we observed how SEUK was engaged in broader trust-building efforts through a certification program called the "TrustSeal." The TrustSeal is a kitemark that certifies good practices of sharing economy companies, signaling that these act with high integrity and maintain high professional standards. It is awarded by a subcommittee of the SEUK board (mostly consisting of category kings). Among others, the subcommittee reviews criteria such as the implementation of identity and credential verification on respective sharing organizations, the provision of a credible insurance cover, the transparency of the pricing structure, and the implementation of security and data protections.

While the initiative has largely been pushed forward by the category kings in SEUK, however, one of the initial motivations for establishing the "TrustSeal" was to help small and less well-known SEUK members, since it would signal trustworthiness to potential users. A SEUK executive explained this as follows:

> Having this certification is potentially very important, particularly for our newer members to help establish themselves as a player that's legit.

However, it turned out that the costs involved in the application of the "TrustSeal," as well as the proper implementation of all criteria involved, were not affordable for many of the category commoners. Furthermore, some of the criteria set out in the "TrustSeal" requirements, such as the provision of insurance for its users, were difficult to implement by some of the category commoners because no third parties, for example, insurers, would collaborate with such small players. Those who were initially thought to profit most by this initiative could not afford getting onboard or live up to its requirements. By the summer of 2018, eight sharing economy companies had been awarded with the TrustSeal. These mostly consisted of larger platforms across different categories. The founder of a small organization commented:

> So, the TrustSeal is something that is good for us in theory. But the financial and the time dedication that it requires has really been off putting so far, and that's a pity, right? Because that becomes yet another factor that separates us from the big platforms that get all the business.

### *Spill-overs in Customer Usage*

In addition to observing the spill-overs between category commoners and kings in these different categories, we also looked at whether sharing organizations experienced customer usage spill-overs within the same category as well as across categories. Regarding usage spill-overs for platforms within the same category, we found, first of all, that due to network effects (Eisenmann, Parker, & Van Alstyne, 2006), which leverage a faster growth of the large organizations, there is very little positive spill-over effect between the usage of category kings to category commoners. One informant described:

> If you want to survive in a world where you have Airbnb, you need to offer something different, something that people can't get on Airbnb. Otherwise, why would they come to you?

As described above, differentiating from the large, well-known, and highly reputable organizations in terms of business model was another difficulty that category commoners faced, impacting the number of their subscribers. Customer usage spill-overs between category kings to category commoners seem to only kick in once users wanted to trick the system:

> In London, obviously there's the 90 day rule and you've got a lot of rogue landlords that are just doing Airbnb year-round, obviously Airbnb's been active in trying to crack down on that and limit people on their own platform to 90 days, but of course what then straight away happens is bad guys actually just go to another platform, because they are actively breaking the law.

When interviewed further, the founder explained how "not having by far as much in terms of resources" as Airbnb was a great problem in identifying and preventing the law-breakers on their platform.

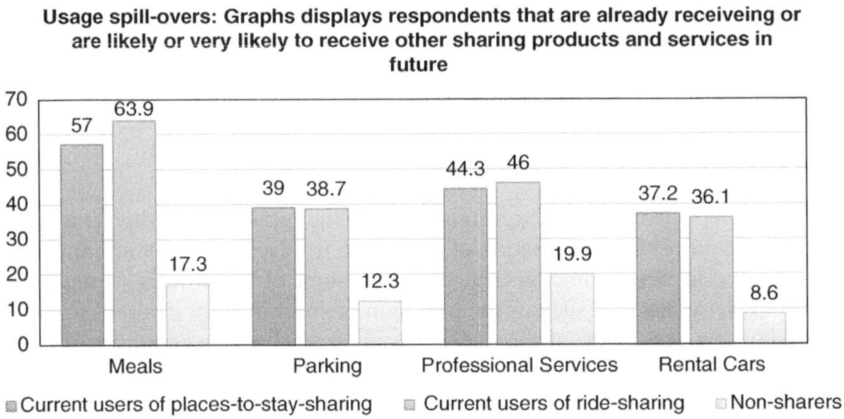


*Fig. 2.* Spill-overs in Usage. *Source*: Warwick Business School Sharing Economy Consumer Survey (Ozcan et al., 2018).

When we looked at spill-overs in usage across categories, our data revealed very different findings. Our consumer survey reveals that current users of the sharing economy are more likely to already receive other sharing products and services, or to do so in future compared to non-sharers (Fig. 2). In particular, our data reveals that more than 50 percent of current users of places-to-stay sharing (57 percent) and ride sharing (63.9 percent) already engage in meal sharing, or plan to do so in future, while this applies only to 17.3 percent of current non-sharers. Likewise, more than 40 percent of current users of places-to-stay sharing (44.3 percent) and ride sharing (46 percent) already participate on sharing economy platforms for professional services, or plan to do so in future, while this applies only to 19.9 percent of current non-sharers.

In addition to the increase in the general level of comfort using sharing platforms, our interviews show that there is complementarity in usage between platforms across certain sub-categories, as explained by a skill-sharing platform executive below:

> But look, let's also be clear, the explosion in growth of this particular industry really helps us. People that are renting out a room, they get people from us all the time because they are available, they are flexible, they can do multiple things, and they can fix things in the home quickly, they can also go and let people in. It really helps our business.

In this final section, we summarize our findings, discuss our contributions to extant literature and discuss avenues for future research.

## DISCUSSION

This chapter addresses the spill-over dynamics between category kings and commoners within the context of sharing economy categories, taking a wider view of spill-overs that is not only confined to reputation as discussed in previous literature. In doing so, we make several contributions to literature on the concepts of category kings and commoners, as well as on intra- and inter-category spill-overs between these actors, as detailed below. In this section, we summarize our findings and provide their immediate implications for research on categories. We then take a step back and discuss our contributions to the study of the sharing economy and the practical implications of our findings.

### *Category Kings and Commoners*

Our exploratory empirical study expands the extant research on categories in several ways. First, we contribute to the burgeoning research on categories (Durand & Paolella, 2013; Vergne & Wry, 2014) by distinguishing between category kings and commoners and how category kings' actions affect category commoners through several spill-over mechanisms as discussed above. Previous research focused either solely on category kings (Jacobides & Tae, 2015; Santos & Eisenhardt, 2009) or studied actors' strategies separately without considering the spill-over effects (Mcdonald & Eisenhardt, 2017).

Mirroring previous literature, we identified several category kings in the SEUK context and revealed that these organizations tend to take leadership roles in developing the wider market in which they operate. For instance, in the context of SEUK, they paid more for their membership than others and were more actively involved in lobbying activities of SEUK. In accordance with previous research that showed how reputable organizations such as celebrity firms receive substantial public attention and interest (Rindova et al., 2006), we find that category kings seem to have access to a lot of resources and thus the means to increase public awareness and to implement marketing and community outreach strategies in order to increase their entire category's, and therefore also their own image. We also find that they advocate initiatives that seek to increase consumer trust in this new category, as seen in the "TrustSeal" example described before.

In contrast to category kings, we used the term category commoners to refer to smaller, and less well-known sharing economy organizations. While there is an emergent body of research addressing category kings or celebrity firms (e.g., Zavyalova, Pfarrer, & Reger, 2017), research on category commoners is still in its infancy. Within the sharing economy literature, as well, most research studies focused on the assessment and discussion of well-known brands such as Airbnb and Uber (Baron 2018; Constantiou, Marton, & Tuunainen, 2017; Greenwood & Wattal, 2017) while scholars have not paid sufficient attention to the perspective of category commoners, or "underdogs" to address the challenges faced by these organizations.

We extend the existing literature by identifying a paradox that characterizes the relationship between category commoners and category kings. Based on our empirical analysis, we find that category commoners experience positive across category and within-category spill-overs. They can free-ride on the resources and efforts of category kings in increasing public awareness, as well as reputation for the entire category. Some of these advantages occur as spill-overs as category kings do marketing and community outreach to raise awareness and build trust for themselves. Others, particularly in the political sphere, occur as category kings consciously lead government relationships as representatives of their category because it is politically more advantageous for them to do so.

Paradoxically, we find that being associated with category kings may also result in substantial disadvantages for category commoners, in particular for those organizations associated within the same category. Indeed, customers and the public may face challenges in differentiating them from category kings, by focusing on similarities between respective companies, or broadly clustering their characteristics and features. Thus, category commoners may remain unrecognizable, making it hard to compete, or raise consumer awareness and trust for their distinct brand. Controversial press coverage about category kings may spill-over negatively to category commoners, as the public is unable to differentiate between distinct companies within the same category. While previous research has addressed how "infamy" (referring to extreme negative public attention of a well-known company), may result in substantial reputational consequences for an organization (Pollock et al., 2015), our findings indicate that negative public attention and reputation may trigger spill-overs and have an undesirable impact on other companies being associated with the same category.

Our study also extends previous literature by theorizing different effects of category kingdom based on whether or not the commoners are in the same sub-category. In the context of our study, we show that category kings can emerge at the highest level of hierarchy, that is, across categories. One example would be Airbnb – a very well-known organization with a large user-base, a category king dominating the sharing economy category as a whole. We see that all organizations classified within the broader sharing economy category experience positive or negative spill-overs from Airbnb's existence, depending whether or not they are in the same sub-category.

Associations with cross-category kings may result in distinct consequences and challenges for category commoners. Our data reveal that across categories, category kings increase customer usage as they raise awareness and trust for the category as a whole. However, being within the same lower hierarchy or sub-category may be challenging for category commoners due to increased difficulty in differentiating their reputation and services. These forces are described in Fig. 1. We further theorize that the downsides of categorization are further fueled by network effects (Katz & Shapiro, 1985). Sharing economy platforms with a larger user-base are of greater value to respective users, resulting in a faster growth of these platforms relative to their (smaller) counterparts, potentially increasing the gap between category kings and category commoners.

While our research has focused on the uni-directional spill-over effects from category kings to commoners, we also discovered that category kings benefit from the existence of commoners, particularly with regards to regulatory acceptance. We find that representing the entire sub-category (e.g., accommodation sharing) was a typical tactic of politically active category kings as this wider representation helped with their image in the regulatory space. Future research can explore other ways in which category commoners may help or hinder the growth of category kings.

### *Contributions to the Study of the Sharing Economy*

Following a call by Mair and Reischauer (2017) for further research in inter-field studies in the sharing economy, our study helps us uncover how the sharing economy as a whole and firms in its sub-categories co-evolve. Most sharing economy research focuses only on a particular sector/category, for example, transportation (Chan & Shaheen, 2012; Greenwood & Wattal, 2017), or housing (Ert et al., 2016), not paying attention to cross-category dynamics and how these dynamics affect the growth of the category as a whole. Conducting more inter-field level studies will shed light on the processes of change and as well as consequences not only for the studied fields but also for the society more generally (Mair & Reischauer, 2017).

The growth of the sharing economy is a significant phenomenon to study as sharing platforms can offer solutions to societal problems (Uzunca et al., 2018), with consequences for the welfare of society at large, such as generating trust and aiding community revival (Schor, 2016), or reducing waste and increasing the efficient use of resources (Hamari et al., 2016). However, sharing economy is also a complex phenomenon spanning across different sectors with different issues (e.g., safety and hygiene) that affect adoption in each one (Ozcan et al., 2018). By improving our understanding of the positive and negative spill-overs between sharing organizations across different sectors, our study contributes to our knowledge of what enables/hinders the growth of the category as a whole. For instance, trust is known to be one of the cornerstones of the sharing economy with significant implications for its growth (Botsman & Rogers, 2010; Möhlmann, 2015; Sundararajan, 2016). Previous research has found that many top sharing companies use online reputation-building mechanisms as an alternative to formal regulation in order to build trust in their companies (Murillo et al., 2017). In our study, we discover that trust spill-overs from category kings to category commoners within and across categories may also have an effect in overall trust to the category, subsequently impacting its growth and adoption. Here, we draw connections to the "trust transfer" literature (Gefen & Pavlou, 2012; Pavlou & Gefen, 2004; Rousseau, 1994; Stewart, 2003) and call for more cross-pollination between trust transfer research as applied to online marketplaces and reputation/trust research in more mainstream organization theory.

### *Policy Implications*

In addition to the contributions discussed above, we believe that our study puts forth important policy implications for the sharing economy. Previous studies already postulated that public policy actors need to refine their approach to regulation of the sharing economy (Murillo et al., 2017; Munoz & Cohen, 2017; Uzunca et al., 2018). By taking into account the dark side of spill-overs, we present novel policy implications for regulators. For instance, although category kings' visibility may help grow the awareness regarding the sharing economy category as a whole, they may eventually suppress the smaller players, commoners in their respective sub-categories, and achieve a monopolistic position based on the negative spill-over effects we identified in this chapter. Therefore, we posit that regulators should keep an eye on category kings and set up the necessary checks and balances to prevent monopolization of a given sharing economy category. Otherwise, we risk the sharing economy moving from being a grassroots movement for a "participatory, fair, and sustainable" society (Botsman & Rogers, 2010; Cohen & Kietzmann, 2014; Mazzela, Sundararajan, Déspous, & Möhlmann, 2016; Schor, 2016; Slee, 2015) to creating new centers of colossal economic power, replacing the previous incumbents to serve their own vested interests (Murillo et al., 2017).

Another important policy implication of our study is regarding the government's role in helping smaller sharing platforms establish trust among consumers. As our findings regarding the TrustSeal show, the efforts of industry associations in helping smaller organizations grow may not always be very effective especially if these associations are managed by larger organizations. A great responsibility falls on the government to set up schemes such as the TrustSeal that will allow small online organizations to build trust among potential users without incurring costs that are at deterring levels for these resource-poor organizations. Such policies will not only help smaller and innovative sharing platforms to prosper, but will help small organizations in other industries (e.g., fintech and healthtech) inject competition into their respective industries that are dominated by large and stale organizations.

## NOTE

1. Refer to https://www.wbs.ac.uk/wbs2012/assets/PDF/downloads/press/ResultsofUKSharingEconomyConsumerSurvery2017.pdf for more details on the survey.

## REFERENCES

Ahmed, P., Gardella, J., & Nanda, S. (2002). Wealth effect of drug withdrawals on firms and their competitors. *Financial Management*, *3*(31), 21–41.

Aldrich, H. E., & Baker, T. (2001). Learning and legitimacy: Entrepreneurial responses to constraints on the emergence of new populations and organizations. In C. B. Schoonhoven & E. Romanelli (Eds.), *The entrepreneurship dynamic: Origins of entrepreneurship and the evolution of industries* (pp. 207–235). Redwood, CA: Stanford University Press.

Aldrich, H. E., & Fiol, C. M. (1994). Fools rush in? The institutional context of industry creation. *Academy of Management Review*, *19*(4), 645–670.

Bardhi, F., & Eckhardt, G. M. (2012). Access-based consumption: The case of car sharing. *Journal of Consumer Research*, *39*(4), 881–898.

Barnett, M. L., & Hoffman, A. J. (2008). Beyond corporate reputation: Managing reputational interdependence. *Corporate Reputation Review*, *11*(1), 1–9.

Barnett, M. L., Jermier, J. M., & Lafferty, B. A. (2006). Corporate reputation: The definitional landscape. *Corporate Reputation Review*, *9*(1), 26–38.

Barnett, M. L., & King, A. A. (2008). Good fences make good neighbors: A longitudinal analysis of an industry self-regulatory institution. *Academy of Management Journal*, *51*(6), 1150–1170.

Baron, D. P. (2018). Disruptive entrepreneurship and dual purpose strategies: The case of Uber. *Strategy Science*, *3*(2), 439–462.

Bolton, G., Greiner, B., & Ockenfels, A. (2013). Engineering trust: Reciprocity in the production of reputation information. *Management Science*, *59*(2), 265–285.

Botsman R., & Rogers, R. (2010). *What's mine is yours: The rise of collaborative consumption*. New York, NY: Harper Collins.

Bowker, G. C., & Star, S. L. (2000). *Sorting things out: Classification and its consequences*. Cambridge, MA: MIT Press.

Chan, N. D., & Shaheen, S. A. (2012). Ridesharing in North America: Past, present, and future. *Transport Reviews*, *32*(1), 93–112.

Clark, K. B. (1985). The interaction of design hierarchies and market concepts in technological evolution. *Research Policy*, *14*(5), 235–251.

Cohen, B., & Kietzmann, J. (2014). Ride on! Mobility business models for the sharing economy. *Organization & Environment*, *27*(3), 279–296.

Constantiou, I., Marton, A., & Tuunainen, V. K. (2017). Four models of sharing economy platforms. *MIS Quarterly Executive*, *16*(4), 231–251.

Durand, R., & Paolella, L. (2013). Category stretching: Reorienting research on categories in strategy, entrepreneurship, and organization theory. *Journal of Management Studies*, *50*(6), 1100–1123.

Eisenhardt, K. M. (1989). Building theories from case study research. *Academy of Management Review*, *14*(4), 532–550.

Eisenhardt, K. M., & Graebner, M. E. (2007). Theory building from cases: Opportunities and challenges. *Academy of Management Journal*, *50*(1), 25–32.

Eisenmann, T., Parker, G., & Van Alstyne, M. W. (2006). Strategies for two-sided markets. *Harvard Business Review*, *84*(10), 92.

Ert, E., Fleischer, A., & Magen, N. (2016). Trust and reputation in the sharing economy: The role of personal photos in Airbnb. *Tourism Management*, *55*, 62–73.

Foster, G. (1981). Intra-industry information transfers associated with earnings releases. *Journal of Accounting and Economics*, *3*(3), 201–232.

Gefen, D., & Pavlou, P. A. (2012, September). The boundaries of trust and risk: The quadratic moderating role of institutional structures. *Information Systems Research*, *23*(3), 940–959.

Goins, S., & Gruca, T. S. (2008). Understanding competitive and contagion effects of layoff announcements. *Corporate Reputation Review*, *11*(1), 12–34.

Greenwood, B., & Wattal, S. (2017). Show me the way to go home: An empirical investigation of ride sharing and alcohol related motor vehicle fatalities. *MIS Quarterly*, *41*(1), 163–188.

Hamari, J., Sjöklint, M., & Ukkonen, A. (2016). The sharing economy: Why people participate in collaborative consumption. *Journal of the Association for Information Science and Technology*, *67*(9), 2047–2059.

Hannan, M. T., & Carroll, G. R. (1995). Theory building and cheap talk about legitimation: Reply to Baum and Powell. *American Sociological Review*, *60*(4), 539–544.

Hannan, M. T., & Freeman, J. (1984). Structural inertia and organizational change. *American Sociological Review*, *49*(2), 149–164.

Hannan, M. T., Polos, L., & Carroll, G. R. (2007). *Logics of organization theory, audiences, codes ecologies*. Princeton, NJ: Princeton University Press.

Jacobides, M. G., & Tae, C. J. (2015). Kingpins, bottlenecks, and value dynamics along a sector. *Organization Science*, *26*(3), 889–907.

Jarrell, G., & Peltzman, S. (1985). The impact of product recalls on the wealth of sellers. *Journal of Political Economy*, *93*(3), 512–536.

Jick, T. D. (1979). Mixing qualitative and quantitative methods: Triangulation in action. *Administrative Science Quarterly*, *24*(4), 602–611.

Kaplan, S., & Tripsas, M. (2008). Thinking about technology: Applying a cognitive lens to technical change. *Research Policy*, *37*(5), 790–805.

Katz, M. L., & Shapiro, C. (1985, June). Network externalities, competition, and compatibility. *American Economic Review*, *75*(3), 424–440.

Kennedy, M. T., Lo, J., & Lounsbury, M. (2010). Category currency: The changing value of conformity as a function of ongoing meaning construction. In G. Hsu & O. Kocak (Eds.), *Categories in markets: Origins and evolution* (pp. 369–397). Bingley: Emerald Publishing Limited.

King, A., Lenox, M., & Barnett, M. (2002). Strategic responses to the reputation commons problem. In A. Hoffman & M. Ventresca (Eds.), *Organizations, policy, and the natural environment: Institutional and strategic perspectives* (pp. 393–406). Stanford, CA: Stanford University Press.

King, A. A., & Lenox, M. J. (2000). Industry self-regulation without sanctions: The chemical industry's responsible care program. *Academy of Management Journal*, *43*(4), 698–716.

Lang, L. H., & Stulz, R. (1992). Contagion and competitive intra-industry effects of bankruptcy announcements: An empirical analysis. *Journal of Financial Economics*, *32*(1), 45–60.

Lounsbury, M., Ventresca, M., & Hirsch, P. M. (2003). Social movements, field frames and industry emergence: A cultural–political perspective on US recycling. *Socio-Economic Review*, *1*(1), 71–104.

Mair, J., & Reischauer, G. (2017). Capturing the dynamics of the sharing economy: Institutional research on the plural forms and practices of sharing economy organizations. *Technological Forecasting and Social Change*, *125*, 11–20.

Mazzela, F., Sundararajan, A., Déspous, V. B., & Möhlmann, M. (2016). How digital trust powers the sharing economy. *IESE Business Review*, *26*(5), 24–31.

McDonald, R., & Eisenhardt, K. (2017). Category kings and commoners: How market-creation efforts can undermine startups' standing in a new market. HBS Working Paper 16-095. Harvard Business School, Harvard University.

Mezias, S., & Boyle, E. (2002). *The organizational dynamics of creative destruction: Entrepreneurship and the creation of new industries*. New York, NY: Springer.

Möhlmann, M. (2015). Collaborative consumption: Determinants of satisfaction and the likelihood of using a sharing economy option again. *Journal of Consumer Behaviour*, *14*(3), 193–207.

Meyer, J. W., & Rowan, B. (1977). Institutionalized organizations: Formal structure as myth and ceremony. *American Journal of Sociology*, *83*(2), 340–363.

Miles, M. B., & Huberman, A. M. (1994). *Qualitative data analysis: An expanded sourcebook*. Thousand Oaks, CA: Sage.

Moreau, C. P., Markman, A. B., & Lehmann, D. R. (2001). "What is it?" Categorization flexibility and consumers' responses to really new products. *Journal of Consumer Research*, *27*(4), 489–498.

Mohammad, S., & Crane, A. (2015). *Theorizing reputational spillovers*. SSRN Working Paper.

Munoz, P., & Cohen, B. (2017). Mapping out the sharing economy: A configurational approach to sharing business modeling. *Technological Forecasting and Social Change*, *125*, 21–37.

Murillo, D., Buckland, H., & Val, E. (2017). When the sharing economy becomes neoliberalism on steroids: Unravelling the controversies. *Technological Forecasting and Social Change*, *125*, 66–76.

Ozcan, P., Mohlmann, M., & Krishnamoorthy, C. (2018). Who shares and who doesn't? Results of the UK sharing economy consumer survey 2017. Retrieved from https://www.wbs.ac.uk/wbs2012/assets/PDF/downloads/press/ResultsofUKSharingEconomyConsumerSurvery2017.pdf

Pavlou, P. A., & Gefen, D. (2004). Building effective online marketplaces with institution-based trust. *Information Systems Research*, *15*(1), 37–59.

Pfarrer, M. D., Pollock, T. G., & Rindova, V. P. (2010). A tale of two assets: The effects of firm reputation and celebrity on earnings surprises and investors' reactions. *Academy of Management Journal*, *53*(5), 1131–1152.

Pollock T. G., Mishina, Y., & Seo, Y. (2015). Falling stars: Celebrity, wrongdoing, and the fall from (and return to) grace. *Academy of Management Annual Meeting Proceedings*, *2015*(1), 15406–15406.

Pontikes, E. G., & Barnett, W. P. (2015). The persistence of lenient market categories. *Organization Science*, *26*(5), 1415–1431.

Powell, W. W., Packalen, K., & Whittington, K. (2012). Organizational and institutional genesis. In John F. Padgett & Walter W. Powell (Eds.), *The Emergence of Organizations and Markets* (p. 434). Princeton, NJ: Princeton University Press.

Rindova, V. P., & Fombrun, C. J. (2001). Entrepreneurial action in the creation of the specialty coffee niche. In C. B. Schoonhoven & E. Romanelli (Eds.), *The entrepreneurship dynamic* (pp. 236–261). Redwood, CA: Stanford University Press.

Rindova, V. P., Pollock, T. G., & Hayward, M. L. A. (2006). Celebrity firms: The social construction of market popularity. *Academy of Management Review*, *31*(1), 50–71.

Rosa, J. A., Porac, J. F., Runser-Spanjol, J., & Saxon, M. S. (1999). Sociocognitive dynamics in a product market. *The Journal of Marketing*, *63*, 64–77.

Rousseau. D. M. (1994). Now let's make multi-level research on trust doable. In F. J. Yammarino & F. Dansereau (Eds.), *Multi-level issues in organizational behaviour and processes* (pp. 159–166). Oxford: Elsevier.

Santos, F. M., & Eisenhardt, K. M. (2009). Constructing markets and shaping boundaries: Entrepreneurial power in nascent fields. *Academy of Management Journal*, *52*(4), 643–671.

Schor, J. (2016). Debating the sharing economy. *Journal of Self-Governance & Management Economics*, *4*(3), 7–22.

Singh, J. V., Tucker, D. J., & House, R. J. (1986). Organizational legitimacy and the liability of newness. *Administrative Science Quarterly*, *31*(2), 171–193.

Slee, T. (2015). *What's yours is mine: Against the sharing economy*. New York, NY: OR Books.

Stewart, K. J. (2003). Trust transfer on the world wide web. *Organization Science*, *14*(1), 5–17.

SEUK. (2018). Sharing economy United Kingdom. Retrieved from http://www.sharingeconomyuk.com/about-us. Accessed on August 20, 2018.

Suarez, F. F., Grodal, S., & Gotsopoulos, A. (2015). Perfect timing? Dominant category, dominant design, and the window of opportunity for firm entry. *Strategic Management Journal*, *36*(3), 437–448.

Sundararajan, A. (2016). *The sharing economy: The end of employment and the rise of crowd-based capitalism*. Cambridge, MA: MIT Press.

Thiel, P. (2014). *Zero to one: Notes on startups, or how to build the future*. New York, NY: Crown Publishing Group.

Uzunca, B., Rigtering, J. C., & Ozcan, P. (2018). Sharing and shaping: A cross-country comparison of how sharing economy firms shape their institutional environment to gain legitimacy. *Academy of Management Discoveries*, *4*(3), 248–272.

Vergne, J. P., & Wry, T. (2014). Categorizing categorization research: Review, integration, and future directions. *Journal of Management Studies*, *51*, 56–94

Vergne, J. P. (2012). Stigmatized categories and public disapproval of organizations: A mixed-methods study of the global arms industry, 1996–2007. *Academy of Management Journal*, *55*(5), 1027–1052.

Yu, T., & Lester, R. H. (2008). Moving beyond firm boundaries: A social network perspective on reputation spillover. *Corporate Reputation Review*, *11*(1), 94–108.

Yu, T., Sengul, M., & Lester, R. H. (2008). Misery loves company: The spread of negative impacts resulting from an organizational crisis. *Academy of Management Review*, *33*(2), 452–472.

Zantout, Z., & Chaganti, R. (1996). New product introductions, shareholders' wealth, and first-mover advantages. *Journal of Financial and Strategic Decisions*, *9*(3), 49–61.

Zavyalova, A., Pfarrer, M. D., & Reger, R. K. (2017). Celebrity and infamy? The consequences of media narratives about organizational identity. *Academy of Management Review*, *42*(3), 461–480.

Zerubavel, E. (1997). *Social mindscapes: An introduction to cognitive sociology*. Cambridge, MA: Harvard University Press.

Zucker, L. G. (1977). The role of institutionalization in cultural persistence. *American Sociological Review*, *42*(5), 726–743.

Zuckerman, E. W., Kim, T. Y., Ukanwa, K., & Von Rittmann, J. (2003). Robust identities or nonentities? Typecasting in the feature-film labor market. *American Journal of Sociology*, *108*(5), 1018–1074.

# "TURNING THE SHARING ECONOMY INTO A FAIR ECONOMY": STRATEGIC ISSUE WORK IN THE VIENNA CITY ADMINISTRATION

Sebastian Vith and Markus A. Höllerer

## ABSTRACT

*Over the last years, and under the umbrella of the "sharing economy," various new social practices and novel business models have been established worldwide. Such practices and models are perceived both as opportunity and challenge for existing (urban) public governance regimes. It is in this sense that the sharing economy has become a contested issue and regularly provokes bold governance responses. However, local governing authorities first need to interpret, negotiate, and establish what exactly is "at issue" in order to (re-)act adequately. While such "politics of signification" are well-studied, for instance, in social movements and public media discourse, research on the concerted framing activities of public administrations as well as on the strategic work that sets the stage for public policy-making is relatively sparse – and entirely lacking for the context of the sharing economy. In this chapter, the authors look behind the scenes of the policy-making in the City of Vienna, Austria. The empirical findings unearth six distinct mechanisms –"delimiting," "negotiating," "detailing," "linking," "justifying," and "situating" – that are strategically applied to shape the "Viennese way" of governing the sharing economy. This research develops an in-depth understanding of what the authors conceptually dub "strategic issue*

**Theorizing the Sharing Economy: Variety and Trajectories of New Forms of Organizing**
**Research in the Sociology of Organizations, Volume 66, 187–213**

**ISSN: 0733-558X/doi:10.1108/S0733-558X20200000066009**

*work": the manifold efforts that lead to, and underlie, in this case, the policy-making of a local government when it tries to come to terms with the governance challenges of the sharing economy.*

**Keywords**: Sharing economy; public governance; urban governance; policy-making; issue work; framing

## INTRODUCTION

New social practices that are centrally built around the idea of "sharing instead of owning" (Belk, 2007) – such as car sharing, apartment sharing, co-working, or community gardening – have been recently subsumed under the umbrella label of the "sharing economy." The underlying novel business models commonly rely on access-based collaborative consumption (Bardhi & Eckhardt, 2012; Botsman & Rogers, 2010) and affect traditional economic sectors as well as create entrepreneurial niches (Martin, 2016). The sharing economy therefore has been subject to controversial debate and is perceived as both an opportunity and a challenge: It is, as a recent comparative study for a number of leading global cities indicates, either embraced for its potential for "ecological transition" and "societal enhancement," more ambivalently evaluated as "market disruption," or negatively associated with "societal endangerment" (Vith, Oberg, Höllerer, & Meyer, 2019). Such varied assessment is, at least in part, due to the fact that many practices of the sharing economy are at odds with existing public governance regimes; for instance, they raise issues related to tax, employment, competition, or consumer law (e.g., Erickson & Sørensen, 2016; Frenken, Meelen, Arets, & van de Glid, 2015). As these and related governance questions manifest on the local level, cities and metropolitan areas have become the central arena in which these struggles and vested interest concerning the sharing economy are debated, negotiated, and addressed (Davidson & Infranca, 2016, 2017; Katz, 2015). Various stakeholders and interest groups – business associations, non-governmental organizations (NGOs), unions, consumer advocates, and incumbent companies, among many others – seek to influence this highly politicized debate and the policy-making process that leads to (regulatory) governance responses.

Local governing authorities are often confronted with the ambiguity and complexity of the sharing economy. As a consequence, they need to first interpret, negotiate, and establish what exactly is "at issue" and who has a say in the debate, and, above all, assign specific meaning to the sharing economy in order to be able to (re-)act adequately (Vith et al., 2019). In short, they need to engage in various activities around shaping and framing the focal issue. Framing theory and its core notion of "politics of signification" (Meyer, 2004; Snow & Benford, 1988) have been fruitfully applied and explored in broader policy research. While well-studied, for instance, for social movements (e.g., Benford & Snow, 2000), interest groups (e.g., De Bruycker, 2017; Lefsrud & Meyer, 2012), and in public media discourse (e.g., Gamson & Modigliani, 1989), research on the concerted framing practices of politicians, public officials, and selected key stakeholders as well as on their strategic efforts that set the stage for public policy-making has been relatively sparse in the domain of organization studies – and, to our best knowledge, is entirely lacking for the context of the sharing economy.

We address this shortcoming empirically by examining the manifold efforts that lead to, and underlie, the Vienna City Administration's policy-making when it tries to come to terms with the governance challenges of the sharing economy. While globally coined by emphasizing entrepreneurship and innovation (e.g., European Commission, 2016; European Parliament, 2016; OECD, 2016; World Economic Forum, 2013), Vienna took a rather bold position in explicitly postulating the goal of "turning the sharing economy into a fair economy" (Stadt Wien, 2016). Our intention is to unearth the strategic work and underlying social mechanisms that resulted in this very policy approach. It is in this sense that we are interested not only in how a governing authority positions itself toward a novel issue, but also equally in how this governing authority trims the issue to fit the pre-existing governance regime and the broader institutional arrangements in order to both enable and delineate future policy-making in the respective policy field.

Opting for a comprehensive case study approach (e.g., Langley & Royer, 2006; Yin, 2009), we analyze the Vienna City Administration's strategic actions regarding the sharing economy between 2014 and 2018 that subsequently led to the current policy outcome. As our goal here is theory elaboration (e.g., Lee, Mitchell, & Sablynski, 1999) rather than theory testing or conceptional reasoning, we examine empirical data in an iterative research process of consolidation, clustering, and reconciliation with existing theories, following the methodological procedure outlined by Gioia, Corley, and Hamilton (2013). We conducted interviews with all key actors and stakeholders involved in the policy-making process, and collected additional discursive material on the issue of sharing in advance (e.g., press releases by the Vienna City Administration and media articles). The case of Vienna provides an insightful research setting, also due to its remarkably stable political-administrative environment and a fairly bounded policy-making process for the sharing economy.

Our empirical findings unearth six distinct mechanisms – "delimiting," "negotiating," "detailing," "linking," "justifying," and "situating" – that are strategically applied in order to shape and legitimize the "Viennese way" of governing the sharing economy. These mechanisms (and their sequencing) are reflective of the focal institutional setting (e.g., Meyer & Scott, 1983; Scott, 1995) as well as of the political opportunity structure in place (e.g., Goodwin & Jasper, 2004; McAdam, 1996; Meyer & Höllerer, 2010). However, they also contain key elements of the deliberate and strategic work of a highly active agent. Our insights highlight actors, practices, and social mechanisms behind the politics of signification and allow for an in-depth understanding of what we here dub "strategic issue work."

The remainder of this chapter is organized as follows. In the next section, we expand on the phenomenon and conceptual orientation of our study. Subsequently, we briefly introduce the empirical design prior to presenting our findings in much detail in the central section of the chapter. We conclude with a discussion of main insights and core contributions.

## PHENOMENON AND CONCEPTUAL ORIENTATION

### *Sharing Economy: A Novel Phenomenon Leading to Policy Disruption*

Following Belk (2007, p. 127), sharing can be described as an "alternative to private ownership," including forms of lending, pooling, and otherwise joint allocation of resources. While the notion originally implied voluntary and ideology-driven practices as well as non-monetary transactions (Kornberger, Leixnering, Meyer, & Höllerer, 2018), it is now also used for contractual renting and leasing in return for payment – often with reference to organizations such as Airbnb and Uber, and/or to the sharing of goods and services more broadly (see, Belk [2014] for a detailed discussion on sharing and pseudo-sharing). The sharing economy is often juxtaposed to the "traditional" or "old economy," and researchers apply various approaches in order to make such distinction, including the comparison of underlying business models (e.g., Laamanen, Pfeffer, Rong, & Van de Ven, 2018; Wruk, Oberg, Klutt, & Maurer, 2019).

There has been wide acknowledgement of the phenomenon by a number of established institutions, such as the European Union (European Commission, 2016; European Parliament, 2016), the OECD (2016), and the World Economic Forum (2013). Their statements and position papers highlight the relevance of the topic and encourage national and local governments to proactively engage with the issue. Yet, from a public governance perspective, the phenomenon continues to pose a set of unanswered questions and considerable challenges. Governing authorities struggle to fully capture and address issues around sharing economy organizations with the policy solutions in place, and the existing regulatory toolbox seems of limited usefulness. Most notably, the de-territorial nature of many of these novel organizations, the rate by which some of them alter their respective business models, the fact that the majority of them is based on massive numbers of small-scale activities facilitated by online platforms (e.g., Zale, 2016), the core ideas of co-creation and co-consumption (and thus the blurred boundaries between members and customers of these organizations; see also Reischauer & Mair, 2018), and/or the startling lack of knowledge regarding the impact of this new socio-economic trend make it difficult for governing authorities to respond adequately with the governance regimes in place (Vith et al., 2019).

In consequence, policy disruption may result from the exploitation of ambiguous laws, from legal loopholes, as well as from business innovations for which existing regulations do not cater (Biber, Light, Ruhl, & Salzman, 2017). In the context of the sharing economy, legal gray areas can be found primarily in insurance and tax (e.g., Beretta, 2017), work and employment (e.g., Das Acevedo, 2016; Drahokoupil & Piasna, 2017), liability (e.g., Berke, 2016; McPeak, 2016), non-discrimination (e.g., Edelman, Luca, & Svirsky, 2017; Lutz & Newlands, 2018), and in the distinction between public and private activity (e.g., Katz, 2015). Regulatory shortcomings, according to Dyal-Chand (2015), are putting at risk (consumer) safety, market competition, workers' rights, and financial conduct.

Even though the sharing economy is a global phenomenon, it regularly plays out on the local level. Most importantly, the sharing economy is creating "distinctly local regulatory tensions" (Davidson & Infranca, 2017) and predominately manifests as an urban governance challenge (e.g., Davidson & Infranca, 2016). Cities have thus become a central arena in which issues concerning the sharing economy ought to be addressed, and local governments are confronted with challenges that are only partially covered by national regulation (e.g., Mazzucotelli Salice & Pais, 2017). In addition to these issues often being "diffuse, localized, and specialized" (Katz, 2015, p. 1080), a significant lack of knowledge and experience on the side of governing authorities has to be attested (e.g., Cohen, 2016; Gori, Parcu, & Stasi, 2015). So far, it seems that regulators have struggled to update and fine-tune existing regulations to also include the sharing economy, and reacted with bans, legalization, or enforcement (e.g., Katz, 2015). However, policy-makers do not just attribute challenges to the sharing economy; they also identify and embrace an array of opportunities. Indeed, a recent comparative study for a number of leading global cities indicates that a colorful mix of public, market, and environmental opportunities and challenges is currently associated with a wide range of public governance strategies (Vith et al., 2019).

### *Policy-making for the Sharing Economy*

With no clear precedents or "best practice"-templates for governing the sharing economy, each city and local government has to determine who will "take the lead on meeting with stakeholders, drafting ordinances and implementing new policies" (Hirshon et al., 2015, p. 6). A variety of approaches has been applied in order to address local concerns as well as to balance regulation and innovation. Rauch and Schleicher (2015) assume that governments adopt a combination of the following strategies: "subsidizing sharing firms" to encourage services that create public value; "harnessing sharing firms" to ensure fair competition and tax collection; and "contracting with sharing firms" to outsource public services. In a similar vein, Vith et al. (2019) highlight the application of eight specific public governance responses: "promotion," "regulation," "information," "partnering," "alignment," "expert knowledge," "technology," and "provision."

According to Davidson and Infranca (2017), the local regulatory response is shaped by a variety of factors linked to political power, "including the existing local political economy, the relative power of local incumbents, the particular local externalities sharing firms are generating, and the structure of local authority." A view that regards public policy merely as the course of action in order to solve a social problem neglects that every policy is "the product of political influence" (Hill, 1993, p. 47). Policy-making therefore involves negotiation, bargaining, and the accommodation of divergent vested interests. Following Osman (2002, p. 37), we regard public policy-making as the "complex interactive process influenced by the diverse nature of socio-political and other environmental forces." Easton (1965) highlights that policy-makers are confronted with demand and support from the environment, (such as from pressure groups, the media, consumer groups, and various other interest groups) that differ for each local setting. Moreover, scholars trace the variety in policy-making back to the different "administrative traditions" in place (e.g., Painter & Peters, 2010; Pollitt & Bouckaert, 2011), each having a dissimilar emphasis on control, coordination, and regulation based on different understandings of the state, law, government, and national or local culture more broadly. As a consequence, the roles assigned for policy-making equally differ (e.g., Rugge, 2012). Over the last decades, organizational reforms in the public sector have led to completely new forms of coordination (Ongaro, 2009), increased decentralization, and distributed decision-making in organizational networks (Powell, 1990) – and, subsequently, to novel modes of (network) governance (e.g., Osborne, 2010; Provan & Kenis, 2007).

Research on policy-making for the sharing economy is therefore well-advised to consider the socio-political environment as well as the different institutional arrangements and multi-stakeholder-relationships in place. However, while the strategies of governing authorities in response to opportunities and challenges need to be aligned with these prevailing cultural and socio-political structures (e.g., Biber et al., 2017), the social actor spearheading the policy-making process regularly has to come up with a coherent narrative for the issue at hand – as well as for the focal governance response. Our chapter will shed light on the underlying social mechanisms of how this is achieved.

### *Setting the Scene for Governing the Sharing Economy: The Crucial Role of Strategic Issue Work*

With a diversity of manifestations, unclear boundaries, and yet unknown implications, policy-making for the sharing economy is arguably more complex than for other issues or policy fields. The interpretations of what is actually part of the sharing economy, of who has voice in this debate and who has not, of the very opportunities and challenges that come with the sharing model, and of the consequences for a wide array of stakeholders (and of how to act upon them) resemble the central building blocks for how local governments approach the phenomenon and develop governance strategies.

Contested issues, such as the sharing economy (Vith et al., 2019), regularly undergo multiple processes of framing activity in order to assign meaning and define "what is at issue" (Gamson & Modigliani, 1989, p. 3) in the first place. As "schemata of interpretation" (Goffman, 1986), the resulting framings "locate, perceive, identify and label occurrences within [...] life space and the world at large" (Snow, Rochford, Worden, & Benford, 1986, p. 464; for a more recent overview of the framing literature, see Cornelissen & Werner, 2014). In conducting research on social movements, Snow and Benford (1988, p. 199) identify that the framing of an issue can conceptually be divided into three core framing "tasks": (a) "a diagnosis of some event or aspect of social life as problematic and in need of alteration"; (b) "a proposed solution to the diagnosed problem that specifies what needs to be done"; and (c) "a call to arms or rationale for engaging in ameliorative or corrective action." Framing activities therefore not only diagnose what is a (potential) problem; they also reveal specific moral or ethical positions, and on this basis suggest possible solutions (Benford & Snow, 2000). In a similar vein, March (1994) describes four generic mechanisms that are performed in order to cope with a focal issue: (a) the selective perception of an issue by defining boundaries that not only delimit the issue but also the potential actions toward it;

(b) the discursive splitting of the issue into separate phenomena that are easier to handle; (c) the identification of appropriate problem-solution behavior through generalizations; and (d) the locating of the specific phenomenon in the light of broader meaning structures.

Commonly, issues come with a relatively pre-defined "menu" of globally established interpretations, and actors will at least partially make use of the "repertoire of alternative interpretations that is available [...] to frame an issue" (Meyer & Höllerer, 2010, p. 1241). These global interpretations of an issue are routinely "translated" (e.g., Czarniawska & Sevón, 1996; Sahlin-Andersson, 1996) into a local setting and adapted to the prevailing circumstances (e.g., Höllerer, Walgenbach, & Drori, 2017; Wedlin & Sahlin, 2017). Even though social actors may – and often do – create novel framings for an issue, this is done vis-à-vis what Gamson (1992, p. 67) describes as the pre-existing "issue culture" of a field, creating an interplay between actors "who operate actively in the construction of meaning and socio-cultural processes that offer meanings." Activities of framing have been conceptualized as "identity work" (e.g., Brown & Toyoki, 2013) on the individual and social level, as "legitimacy work" regarding the perception or public image of a focal organization or social entity (Lefsrud, Graves, & Phillips, 2017; Treviño, den Nieuwenboer, Kreiner, & Bishop, 2014), or as "institutional work" maintaining, disrupting, or creating institutional arrangements (e.g., Lawrence, Leca, & Zilber, 2013; Lawrence & Suddaby, 2006). Indeed, with regard to the sharing economy, Mair and Reischauer (2017) explicitly propose to analyze the setting of boundaries and the prescription of practices for sharing from an institutional work perspective.

Framings guide action insofar as they assign specific meaning to events and occurrences (Benford & Snow, 2000). They can be purposefully crafted as ambiguous or vague in order to "neutralize" conflicting expectations (Meyer & Höllerer, 2016). Zald (1996), for instance, emphasizes that framings, as all cultural constructs, might be produced strategically, and that framing therefore is a strategic activity; however, he continues, we know relatively little in terms of constituent elements of and general processes around what he denotes as "strategic framing."

We here put an emphasis on the broader strategic efforts behind and prior to the framing of a contested issue – also stressing the overt or hidden agenda of the actor(s) driving it – as well as on the broader institutional embedding that is both relevant and impacted at the same time. For this purpose, we introduce the notion of "strategic issue work." It allows us to conceptualize a complex social entity such as a city administration as a more or less coherent political actor in the discourse and when facing a specific governance challenge. As such, it decides to a considerable degree – and often behind closed doors – on the cast of other actors involved, and thereby also determines who will have a say in future policy-making on the issue at hand. Most importantly, it may also directly trim the very issue itself in the first place in order to fit the existing governance regime and the broader institutional arrangements, and with this both enables and delineates a corridor for policy-making. Subsequent framing of the issue, from such a perspective, is then only able to a limited extent and against the rather restrictive political opportunity structure partly created through strategic issue work.

## EMPIRICAL DESIGN

### *The Case of the Vienna City Administration*

Since the late 1970s, Vienna, the capital city of Austria, has been consistently named as a prominent example for successful and well-balanced urban policy. The "Mercer Quality of Living Ranking" rated Vienna as the most livable city in the world for the tenth time in a row (Mercer, 2019); Vienna also replaced Melbourne on top of the Economist's recent "Global Liveability Ranking" (Economist Intelligence Unit, 2018). In addition, it is one of the fastest growing cities in Europe (Stadt Wien, 2018). Numerous awards and studies attest Vienna excellent premises for a dynamic development and a comfortable position in the global competition (Smart City Wien, 2019). Due to its status and sustained growth it is the prime arena for many new socio-economic developments in Austria – such as the sharing economy movement.

Many of Vienna's urban strategies are driven by a welfare state approach in public policy in order to keep urban development in balance and avoid segregation and social inequality. The broad acceptance of this rationale has also been due to a remarkably stable political-administrative environment: With the exception of Austro-fascism and Nazi-rule between 1934 and 1945, the social democrats have been in charge of political decision-making in Vienna for the last 100 years. From back in the 1920s, the city also carries its image as "Red Vienna" (e.g., Barnett & Woywode, 2004): during this period, a considerable number of initiatives in social, educational, and health services as well as in public and social housing were initiated that still exist today. To date, Vienna finds itself owning and providing shared resources such as, among others, public sport and recreational facilities, parks and gardens, libraries, a city bike system, educational and health care facilities, or housing cooperatives alongside a significant level of public and social housing (Stadt Wien, 2016, 2019).

Local governments in Austria act as largely independent administrative bodies, responsible for local spatial planning, social and health services, security issues, tourism, and traffic management, among a variety of other policy fields. Vienna also holds the secondary status of a federal state, which means that the City Council is at the same time the Federal State Parliament. Based on Austria's strong emphasis on the federal system, subnational decentralization, and the principle of subsidiarity (Kuhlmann & Wollmann, 2014), the Vienna City Administration has considerable means to formulate and implement policies. As Austria more broadly, Vienna displays a strong legalistic orientation and rule-of-law culture (Meyer, Egger-Peitler, Höllerer, & Hammerschmid, 2014; Painter & Peters, 2010).

Austria's national government has so far not embraced the sharing economy in an overly proactive manner. A "creative industries strategy," issued by the Federal Ministry of Science, Research, and Economy (BMWFW, 2016), named the sharing economy as one potential source for "creative entrepreneurship" but did not propose a specific course of action to promote it. So far, hardly any specific regulations or policies toward the sharing economy have been adopted on the national level. This is partially explained by the fact that the key economic sectors heavily affected by the sharing economy – that is, accommodation and mobility/transportation – are largely in the sphere of influence of local governments.

The case of Vienna provides a particularly insightful research setting: Vienna's position as an outstanding example of urban governance comes in combination with being a fruitful ground for various practices and models of sharing; a clear mandate within the city administration facilitates the re-narration of the policy-formulation process; and the stable political-administrative environment makes it relatively easy to demarcate the institutional embedding. Within the Vienna City Administration, the Department for Economic Affairs, Labor and Statistics coordinates the city's stance toward the sharing economy. In 2014, a process has been initiated that involves a range of key actors and stakeholders from inside and outside the Vienna City Administration in form of a strategic steering committee, resulting in an explicit position paper (Stadt Wien, 2016) and subsequent governance actions from 2016 onwards. This chapter aims at looking behind the scenes of the emergence of this policy approach.

### *Data and Method*

Applying a comprehensive and in-depth single case study approach (e.g., Langley & Royer, 2006; Yin, 2009), we explore the Vienna City Administration's attempts to come to terms with the governance challenges of the sharing economy between 2014 and 2018. Our data collection started with examining media releases and newspaper records dealing with the sharing economy in Vienna in order to sensitize the research team for the specificities of the empirical setting – and to reconstruct the sequence of events, activities, and decisions. This provided the backdrop for a set of nine in-depth semi-structured interviews with key decision-makers centrally involved in the policy-making process, including the initiator of the policy-formulation process, the leaders of various working groups, the members of the different municipal departments partaking in the city administration's strategic steering committee, and stakeholder representatives from outside the city administration that were invited to the table as well. Our goal was to get insights into the backstage of policy-making beyond formal processes – in particular, the informal practices as well as the perceived inferences and accounts used by individuals collectively crafting the overall narrative for governing the sharing economy in Vienna. All interviews were recorded and transcribed or, for a few cases where this was not possible, detailed protocols were written immediately after the interview. In order to ensure anonymity, we substituted interviewees' names with fictional first names. We sampled the interviews by first talking to all actors directly involved in the strategic steering committee and then asked for recommendations for additional interview partners. We followed such "snowballing-strategy" until no novel issues were mentioned in the interviews and no further informants were proposed. In addition to these interviews, we purposefully collected discursive material on the sharing economy, such as, for instance, official press releases by the City of Vienna as well as blog posts and documents on the websites of the Vienna City Administration that included formal statements of leading politicians and public officials. In addition, the city's position paper in 2016 on the sharing economy represents another central piece in our data collection in order to reconstruct and analyze the case. Finally, we extended our knowledge through participation at various events around the issue in Vienna (and beyond) and were able to conduct informal conversations with additional stakeholders that were affected but not formally included in the policy-formulation process (such as urban planners, NGOs, sharing economy organizations, and lobbyists).

It is important to note that we examine the case partly *ex post* and do not have time-authentic data for the entire observation period. For the qualitative coding and the identification of first order codes, we applied procedures suggested in qualitative content analysis (Mayring, 2014). In this first step, we adhered to the empirical data as much as possible and assigned coding units (i.e., quotes from the interviews, or passages from the texts) to inductively developed categories. Over time, we started comparing for similarities and differences among the many categories we identified, and eventually were able to reduce our categories to a more manageable number by consolidating and clustering them under new labels. We followed the procedure outlined by Gioia et al. (2013) to develop second order themes and, eventually, aggregate dimensions. As we were working with coding units from different sources, we also had to check for internal consistency of informants' accounts as well as analyzing converging or diverging patterns across data sources. We applied aspects of Langley's (1999) narrative strategy in order to reconstruct an overall narrative from the qualitative data; we extracted theoretically rich themes and continued to aggregate categories until distinct patterns became evident that conceptually addressed our central research interest (e.g., Gioia & Chittipeddi, 1991).

## FINDINGS

The following section presents two different perspectives on our data and analysis: A first part is a more descriptive re-narration of our case in order to present the "flow of activities and events" (Gehman et al., 2018) in a self-contained manner (Langley, 1999); this is important as it also explains the central policy outcome and therefore addresses the empirical dimension of our research question. A second part echoes the overarching themes (e.g., Alvesson & Kärreman, 2007; Gioia et al., 2013) that allow us to reorganize the empirical case in relation to our conceptual research question.

### *Sharing Economy and Policy-making in Vienna*

The sharing economy made its way into the Vienna City Administration rather through the back door and alongside a wider set of policies, such as an explicit open government (data) strategy (Kornberger, Meyer, Brandtner, & Höllerer, 2017). As early as 2011, the city launched the "Smart City Initiative" with the declared goal to assure "the best quality of life for all inhabitants of Vienna, while minimizing the consumption of resources [...] through comprehensive innovation" (Stadt Wien, 2014). Public officials first came in touch with the trend toward sharing when working on the annual tourism statistics in 2014 and being confronted with a significant number of unreported overnight stays via newly established peer-to-peer platforms such as Airbnb. Following an internal workshop, the Vienna City Administration commissioned a scientific study in order to address the topic from a more holistic perspective. With a focus on the transportation and accommodation sector, the study revealed potential negative consequences of the sharing economy and argued for public intervention (Europaforum Wien, 2015). As a result, the city administration – under the auspices of the Executive City Councilor for Finance, Business, Digital Innovation and International Affairs – initiated a strategic steering committee and several working groups that involved a number of municipal departments as well as invited representatives from interest groups such as the Vienna Economic Chamber, the Vienna Business Agency, the Chamber of Labor, the Vienna Tourist Board, the Federal Finance Ministry, housing and transport associations, and the labor union. In November 2015, the Vienna City Administration organized a themed conference where first insights were presented and discussed (MA23, 2015; Stadt Wien, 2015).

Based on the results of the individual working groups, the City of Vienna published, in February 2016, and in both German and English, a position paper titled "Turning the sharing economy into a fair economy in Vienna" (Stadt Wien, 2016). In this document, the administration establishes their view that sharing per se is not a novel phenomenon at all – rather, that the new governance challenge comes with commercial sharing via digital platforms. They postulate the following central policy goals: (a) to ensure protection of citizens and consumers; (b) to safeguard fair competition; (c) to prevent salary dumping and lower of social standards; and (d) to fight against social benefit fraud. The paper explicitly holds that the city "does not aim at regulating the sharing economy to death," yet it commits itself to "fair competition and the principle of 'good jobs'" (Stadt Wien, 2016, p. 2) as well as to applying the same set of rules to all kinds of business organizations. Special attention is given to the sectors of tourist accommodation and mobility/transportation. More implicitly, the position paper favors and supports a sharing economy that is firmly engaged in the non-profit sector and helps solving social and ecological problems in an urban setting. The proposed course of action includes the support of pilot projects, a comprehensive information campaign, exchange on legislation with federal government, European Union, and other European and global cities, as well as continued work of the strategic steering committee (Stadt Wien, 2016).

A large-scale information campaign started with the launch of a new website (www.sharing.wien.at) that featured, for instance, explanatory videos on issues that emerge from practices of sharing, guidelines for sharing of accommodation and private renting, a local tax calculator, as well as a number of further useful links. The content focuses on the legal framework in the core sharing economy sectors to provide a clear guidance about what is allowed in Vienna and what is not. Complementary ads consisting of bold slogans (e.g., "Whether at home or in the city – every community needs rules. Let's make the sharing a fair economy!") and cartoon illustrations were placed in local print media and on billboards. In addition, some more specific actions were taken: For instance, letters were sent to

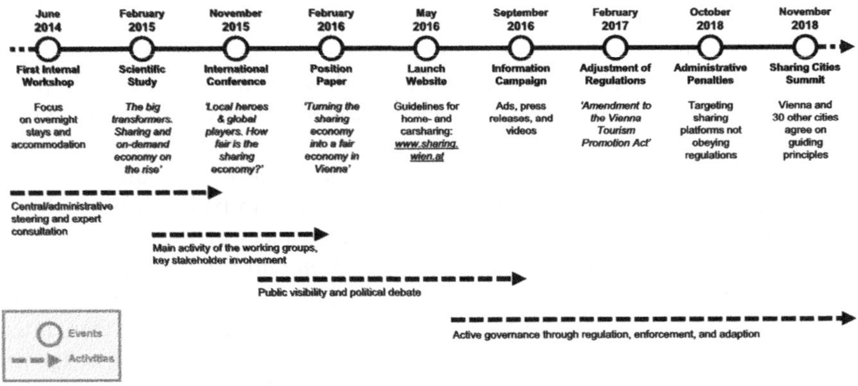


*Fig. 1.* Timeline of Events and Activities (Non-scaled).

tenants of social housing in order to inform them of the legal situation and the ban to rent out their homes to tourists, or city officials participated in townhall meetings in order to elaborate on the chosen governance approach.

In February 2017, the city administration adjusted first legal regulations: An amendment to the Vienna Tourism Promotion Act was passed, introducing reporting obligations for platform operators and fines for non-compliance. The law also opened up for individual platform providers to negotiate special agreements with the City of Vienna. However, these initiatives have hardly been successful, and several major platform providers refused to provide data at all. Discussions with Airbnb were terminated without an outcome in October 2018 after more than one year of negotiations, resulting in sustained administrative penalties on the company. Another working group on the revision of regulations for taxis and rental cars has not made public any of its results so far. In November 2018, Vienna participated at the Sharing Cities Summit in Barcelona where 31 cities from around the world agreed on guiding principles for the sharing economy. Fig. 1 exhibits and summarizes the timeline of events and activities.

### *Mechanisms of Strategic Issue Work in the Vienna City Administration*

> We can be observers and get run over by the development, or we proactively address the issue and shape it. – Paul (public official)[1]

Our case does not only provide insights into the central events and activities along Vienna's policy-making for the sharing economy. Analytically, we are also able unearth six distinct mechanisms of strategic issue work that are deployed in order to contextualize the issue, construct a consistent narrative for policy-making, and provide a rationale for intervention in terms of governance responses: (a) *delimiting* the issue from a (local) policy perspective; (b) *negotiating* the cast of actors; (c) *detailing* governance response strategies; (d) *linking* policy goals and governance responses with vested stakeholder interests; (e) *justifying* the modified governance regime; and (f) *situating* narrative and governance regime in the bigger picture.

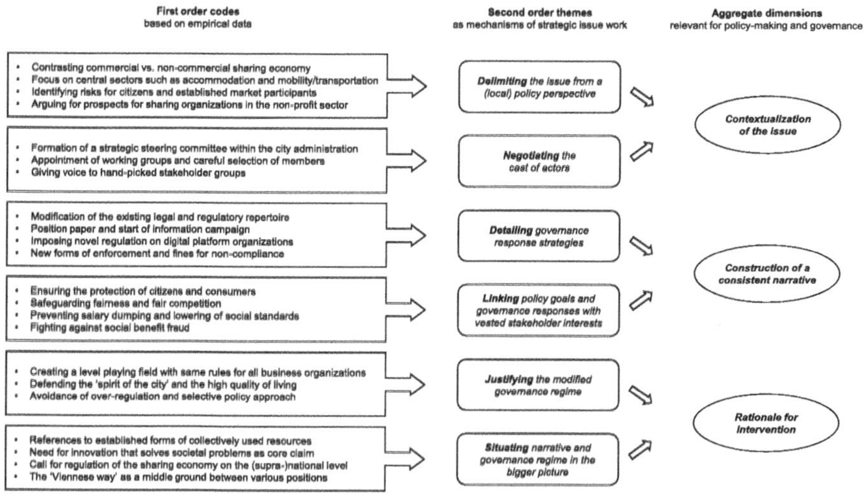


*Fig. 2.* Data and Coding Structure.

Fig. 2 exhibits the data and coding structure as well as the consolidation of empirical data (first order codes) to identified mechanisms of strategic issue work (second order themes) and core conceptual constructs (aggregate dimensions). In the following, each mechanism is described in detail.

## *Delimiting the Issue from a (Local) Policy Perspective*

> There are plenty of variations of the sharing economy. And that is the main problem, I guess. I cannot say that not-for-profit is always good and has no negative external effects. You need to assess this case by case. Profit-oriented organizations tend to have bigger effects, but they do not need to be bad per se. – Beatrice (public official)

> These platform organizations change the entire economic relations. They seem to be, at first sight, nice little alternative pop-up initiatives, but behind them are powerful billion-dollar companies. – Rita (politician)

> For us, sharing economy means something different. Big international and commercial providers unjustifiably benefitted so far. From now on, they are treated equally and also need to pay their dues. – Tina (politician)

The debate on the sharing economy brings to the fore the different interests, opinions, and interpretations within and across the plurality of stakeholders in the public, private, and civic sectors of society. Socio-political actors who are granted voice in policy-making try to influence the agenda by delimiting the issue with the vested interests of their clientele and a local policy perspective in mind (e.g., Vith et al., 2019). For instance, by contrasting the local non-profit sharing organizations and the often globally oriented for-profit sharing platforms, the sharing economy is split into two domains that are subject to rather different evaluation and policy approaches. The subsequent regulatory focus on global platform organizations and their distinct business model (Wruk et al., 2019) creates a bogeyman that is positioned outside the local sphere and relatively easy to criticize with the pooled forces of local stakeholders. Delimiting, however, goes beyond influencing the agenda of how to deal with an issue; it regularly involves trimming the issue, and with this, defining "what is at issue" (Gamson & Modigliani, 1989) in the first place. For instance, during meetings of the working groups, a focus is set on the policy fields of accommodation and mobility/transportation which further narrows down the scope of the issue; other aspects of the sharing economy worldwide, such as co-working, civic crowdfunding, or time-banking are of less prominence, if any at all, in the Viennese discourse. While never explicitly mentioned, it is rather obvious that the local debate and governance response strategies are set up and designed to target two international sharing economy organizations in particular: Airbnb and Uber. The discussions were accompanied, on the one hand, by an emphasis on potential risks for citizens and established market participants due to these large platform organizations – creating a duality between the (functioning) established order and external disturbances. On the other hand, multiple prospects for grass-root sharing in the non-profit sector were attested, thus further reinforcing the stark contrast between commercial and non-commercial aspects of sharing.

### *Negotiating the Cast of Actors*

> We had the mandate from the political level to address the topic proactively and find a clear position. However, we had to balance interests. – Elisabeth (public official)

> We invited associations and bodies that represented legitimate public interests. It was ok if others joined the debate, but we did not want actors that only represented themselves. This is why we did not invite any civil society actors. Because then I am facing only very particular interests. – Paul (public official)

> The interests of public and private, of employees and business organizations, of traditional and new economy collide. – Sarah (interest group representative)

The strategic steering committee operates from a relatively powerful position, as it has been set up by the Vienna City Administration and therefore is able to refer to a clear political-administrative mandate. The committee acts as the central gatekeeper in the ongoing debate and process of policy-making, claiming its own role and actively engaging in negotiations on who has a legitimate say with regard to the issue – and who has not. Much in line with the Austrian corporatist tradition (Höllerer, 2013), the "social partners" (for instance, labor unions and employer associations, among others) are granted a relatively prominent voice in the process early on, while direct citizen participation, for instance, is not relevant at all – not to our surprise, as governance topics are often framed as "expert discourse" in the local setting at hand (e.g., Jancsary, Meyer, Höllerer, & Barberio, 2017). Despite some initial contestation in the media, broad public agreement that a political intervention is preferred in order to face the rapidly emerging sharing economy that has developed over time. Specific interest groups, such as the taxi association and the hotel industry association, engage in concerted lobbying activities, while other stakeholders that originally were not considered increasingly push for inclusion in the conversation (for instance, the association of homeowners or individual sharing economy organizations). As a consequence, deciding whom to invite to which meeting increasingly becomes a crucial task for the Vienna City Administration and the strategic steering committee. Most interestingly, sharing economy organizations – as the main subject of governance responses – remain largely excluded from the debate and are not formally granted any voice to explain or defend their positions or business models. While one reason for this might have been the unwillingness of "incumbents" to invite the "intruders" to the table (see, for instance, the conflict between the taxi industry and Uber), a more significant one is the lack of any local representation of globally oriented sharing economy organizations, let alone a local mooring in the socio-economic landscape (see also Walgenbach, Drori, & Höllerer, 2017). This, however, in turn also accounts for an arguably low level of acceptance of the modified governance regime for the sharing economy sector in Vienna (see also, for instance, the [partial] withdrawal of companies such as oBike, ZipCar, or Uber from the Viennese market).

### *Detailing Governance Response Strategies*

> It was obvious to us that we need a strategy paper but even better a position paper that we can publish. So that it becomes clear to everyone that this is the official position of the City of Vienna on the topic. – Elisabeth (public official)

> We need to decide on the set of rules – and also need to be able to enforce them. – Karl (public official)

> Calls for tightening of the law must be carefully examined. In many cases, there is more of an enforcement problem, for instance missing data, than a lack of rules. – Daniel (public official)

While the formal decision-making authority for all regulatory action is eventually with the City Council, the steering committee plays a crucial role in the policy-making process and in preparing the details of the Vienna City Administration's governance response. It is important to hold that this has been an ongoing process that manifests in various regulatory instances and the strategic use of other governance tools, with the position paper serving as a guiding framework. While many aspects of policy-making occur on a merely discursive level, the actual operationalization of policy also includes the formulation of hands-on procedures and activities that target specific phenomena. Through the work accomplished by the detailing of governance response strategies, typical problems and typified solutions are linked, translated into the empirical setting, and narratives of cause and effect skillfully crafted often using vivid examples (e.g., Höllerer et al., 2017). These governance response strategies also act as both carriers and artifacts of issue interpretation; they entail proposed and favored solutions. The detailing of strategies involves reference to substantive measures, such as the modification of law and regulations, and the various forms of enforcement. In the case of Vienna, the working groups, however, display a preference on grasping the sharing economy with the legal and regulatory repertoire currently in place. They agree on updates and adaptions of existing legislation that, on the one hand, do not harm incumbent stakeholders but, on the other, make it possible to impose regulation on new digital platform organizations, in particular. For instance, the reporting obligation for sharing platforms represents an attempt to shift power positions and gain a firmer grip on this form of the sharing economy. In addition, novel ways of enforcement are discussed and fines for non-compliance significantly raised. The steering committee requested support from the city's legal department; first legislative changes are passed by the city government and enacted within a few months. In order to enhance attention for the outcomes of the working groups, the strategic steering committee also decides for a purposeful communication strategy that not only led to the publishing of the position paper but at the same time marked the start of a large-scale information campaign across the city.

### *Linking Policy Goals and Governance Responses with Vested Stakeholder Interests*

> The City of Vienna has pursued a constructive approach in the negotiations with Airbnb [...] that keeps tourism aligned with the interests of the citizens of Vienna and the local businesses. – Nathan (interest group representative)

> Some sharing economy business models are perfectly in line with the goals of the city [...]; [others] require regulation to avoid negative effects for the polity. – Martha (politician)

> We do not need a policy that promotes companies like Uber and Airbnb, but an appropriate set of rules that supports new business ideas while ensuring fair competition and protecting consumers. – Max (interest group representative)

Discursively, the policy goals and envisaged governance responses are purposefully linked to the interests of central and highly legitimate stakeholder groups in order to craft a convincing and consistent narrative that skillfully stiches together typical problems and typified solutions. First and foremost, the working groups emphasize goals that are crucial to the general public, the city's overall strategy, and the governance regime in place insofar as they resonate exceptionally well with the citizenry and, not unimportantly, the electorate. For instance, the account of citizen and consumer protection is centrally used to align the sharing economy and its future regulation to an understanding of a well-balanced society with a high level of quality of living for everyone as an undisputable socio-political objective. The emphasis on safeguarding fairness and fair competition, on the other hand, is an indirect concession to specific economic interest groups vital to urban life, such as the taxi and hotel industry associations who see their traditional business model at risk; both interest groups obviously play an important role in a city such as Vienna and therefore have strong bargaining power. In addition, explicit prevention of lowering social standards addresses the interests represented by labor unions and employee associations; the proclaimed fight against social benefit fraud and tax avoidance – in the context of undeclared work – aims at calming down tensions increasingly surfacing via the media. Interestingly, however, and much in line with above, no significant attempts of aligning governance responses with sharing economy organizations' interests have been recorded.

### *Justifying the Modified Governance Regime*

> One should call it *shadow* economy instead of *sharing* economy. – Melissa (interest group representative)

> We do not want to track down [users and service providers] with a burning sword. Rather, we believe that often ignorance prevails. – Rita (politician)

> Ultimately, it is about [...] preserving our high quality of life. – Karl (public official)

In order to promote their proclaimed narrative of "turning the sharing economy into a fair economy," the Vienna City Administration embarks actively on several endeavors in order to justify and legitimize a modified governance regime. It thereby relies on highly emotional slogans, often involving metaphorical elements, as well as bold visualizations. For instance, when the sharing economy is portrayed and demonized as a shadow economy doing harm to society, vigorous action to ensure that the same set of rules applies to everyone is hard to dispute. Reference to a level playing field and more abstract values such as fairness and equality have a strongly moralizing undertone and are used to justify the tightening of legislation. Invoking the high quality of life in Vienna, the world's leading lifestyle city, connects the championed governance approach to the broadly accepted image of the city as a livable environment for its citizens and visitors. On the other hand, by stating that they wish to avoid over-regulation, the Vienna City Administration justifies its selective policy approach that only targets specific players in the industry (i.e., the more globally oriented for-profit sharing economy organizations), and thereby absorbs concerns that additional laws and enforcements would also affect local businesses or the not-for-profit sector and grass-root initiatives. Together, these endeavors of justifying and legitimizing provide the solid basis of the Vienna City Administration's rationale for intervention and governance action.

### *Situating Narrative and Governance Regime in the Bigger Picture*

> Vienna thus chooses a middle ground: While some cities like Berlin rely on prohibitions and others like Amsterdam declare themselves as a sharing city, the Viennese way relies on both tradition and modernity. – Paul (public official)

> The same right must apply to all. Everyone has to obey the rules, whether in real or digital life. There must not be unfair competition! – Rita (politician)

> We think of the sharing economy not just as Airbnb, but rather as a broader structural shift. – Karl (public official)

Both narrative and modified governance regimes are explicitly contextualized. For instance, the position paper clearly makes historic references: By highlighting similarities with established forms of collectively used resources in Vienna, the city reinforces its mandate to govern the sharing economy and relates it to the long-lasting tradition of public intervention in the socio-economic sphere. In addition, however, the working groups issue a call for national-wide regulation of the sharing economy to address the more general problems. While the city prefers to alter state law in their favor in order to retain the capacity to act in the face of novel and emerging opportunities and challenges, calling for central regulation here is also a way to shuffle off responsibility for the side effects of globalization and digitization. In addition, the working groups emphasize the need for social innovation that tackles societal grand challenges – and with this somewhat pass the ball to organizations in the non-profit sector. Finally, the steering committee actively compares its own approach with those of other global cities. For instance, a supplementary "background report" that was commissioned in 2017 (Bartik & Lutter, 2017) as an unofficial follow-up to the 2015 expert study (Europaforum Wien, 2015) analyzes the legal framework, regulatory measures, and forms of cooperation in other European cities. Insights have been used to rhetorically portray the "Viennese way" as a middle ground between more extreme positions. It is in such a way that both the narrative and the modified governance regime in Vienna are used to situate the sharing economy (and the Viennese take on it, in particular) in the context of a greater development that is expected to change economic exchange and socio-economic behavior more fundamentally. This, eventually, made it easier for the city not only to regulate selected parts of the industry and embark on a large-scale information campaign, but also to engage in the very provision of municipal sharing services and pursue a welfare approach that supports or partners with local not-for-profit sharing initiatives that are not in conflict with the city's policy goals.

## DISCUSSION

We commenced this research endeavor based on the preliminary insight that we know relatively little about the "politics of signification," the concerted framing activities, and other forms of strategic and purposeful work performed by politicians and public officials when setting the stage for public policy-making in the context of the sharing economy. Our empirical findings unearth six distinct mechanisms of what we, in this chapter, dub "strategic issue work": "delimiting," "negotiating," "detailing," "linking," "justifying," and "situating." These mechanisms cluster in three different dimensions relevant to the policy-making process that partially build on each other (see also Fig. 2 above).

First, when the globally available idea of the "sharing economy" diffuses across cultural and geographical settings, one prerequisite for its local manifestation is the *contextualization of the global issue*. In a similar vein, Meyer and Höllerer (2010, p. 1241) argue that ideas

> must pass through powerful filters of local cultural and structural opportunities and constraints in order to mobilize legitimacy. Struggles over their meaning are intensified if they challenge the prevailing order.

Literature in organizational institutionalism refers to this process as "translation" (e.g., Czarniawska & Sevón, 1996; Sahlin-Andersson, 1996) or "re-contextualization" (Meyer, 2014). Translation occurs through acts of "editing" by local "experts" and (potential) adopters who reformulate meaning and ascriptions to activities and experiences "in the light of the present circumstances and visions" (Wedlin & Sahlin, 2017, p. 109). Höllerer et al. (2017) refer to such "glocalization" of organizational ideas, forms, and practices as an active process shaped by "knowledge entrepreneurs of various sorts." On a micro-level, this crucially implies the "manufacturing of consent" and the "avoidance of dissent," reflecting "the interests and goals of the actors involved as well as the local stocks of knowledge, local mobilizing structures and power constellations" (Meyer, 2014, p. 82) in the light of the issue at hand. Local policy-making for global issues, consequently, needs to be understood as an active process that centrally involves (re-)framing and adaption. As our case study shows, two mechanisms of strategic issue work correspond with such (re-)contextualization. Delimiting an issue is the purposeful framing in the light of the local socio-political context as well as the specific agenda-setting (e.g., Kingdon, 1984) with the interests of a focal clientele and policy perspective in mind. However, delimiting goes beyond influencing an agenda and regularly involves trimming and whipping the issue into shape in the first place – and with this, defining what is actually at issue (Gamson & Modigliani, 1989). Negotiating the cast of actors, then, produces an arrangement among local actors about the prerogative of interpretation of the issue. It defines who is inside the arena and has voice in the debate, and who has to stay out. We understand defining the cast of actors partly as an enactment of local "opportunity structures" (McAdam, 2010) rather than an entirely deliberate act. In tandem, delimiting and negotiating the cast of actors are the active equivalents of what others (e.g., Hunt, Benford, & Snow, 1994) label "boundary framing" and produce a diagnosis of the issue in the local context (Snow & Benford, 1988). In a similar vein, Denis, Langley, and Rouleau (2007, p. 185) refer to "problematization" in pluralist organizational settings as the "attempt to define an issue and offer an 'obligatory passage point' drawing an initial set of actors together to solve it."

A second dimension revealed in our work is the *construction of a consistent narrative*, broadly corresponding with the notion of framing as a "socially situated process of meaning construction" (Cornelissen & Werner, 2014, p. 183). Through the accomplishment of a third mechanism of strategic issue work (i.e., detailing governance response strategies), typical problems and typified solutions are linked and narratives of cause and effect skillfully crafted. Brandtner, Höllerer, Meyer, and Kornberger (2017, p. 1089) highlight, in this respect, the role of strategic governance responses as a way for governing authorities to engage with the complexity of an issue; they formulate detailed strategies "to stage consensus under conditions of diverging interests." This is supplemented by a fourth mechanism (i.e., linking policy goals and governance responses with vested stakeholder interests). Any perceived alignment of interest of key actors increases their willingness for further engagement in the endeavor (e.g., Denis et al., 2007). In fact, in our case the detailing of governance responses and the linking with stakeholder interests form the backbone for a consistent narrative around the policy-making. Such narratives serve the social function of "maintaining or reproducing stability and/or promoting or resisting change" (Vaara, Sonenshein, & Boje, 2016, p. 496). In a "polyphonic" organizational setting (Kornberger, Clegg, & Carter, 2006), where "many voices" articulate diverging interpretations of an issue, this communicative aspect of strategic issue work is crucial for striking the fine balance between stability and change that is needed to incrementally modify an established framework.

A third dimension is the provision of a clear *rationale for intervention* and governance action. In order to encompass a plurality of stakeholders with vested interests around a focal issue, such rationale for intervention strives for mobilizing pragmatic and moral legitimacy (Suchman, 1995) for the proposed way forward. Often building on emotionalization, the underlying narrative regularly uses metaphorical or visual language. The fifth mechanism of strategic issue work (i.e., justifying the modified governance regime) – reflects such an attempt to base the policy narrative on some sort of moral necessity. Yet another mechanism (i.e., situating narrative and governance regime in the bigger picture) helps to further anchor the narrative and governance response in the broader cultural and historical setting. Leixnering and Höllerer (2019), for instance, argue that a city's dynamic administrative arrangements and governance formations are firmly embedded in pre-existing narratives and have to be understood as specific instantiations of an unobservable "substance" (Friedland, 2009) – something that the authors refer to as the "spirit of a city." Our empirical study also demonstrates that local governments actively monitor their relative position vis-à-vis other entities they regard as peers. In tandem, justifying and situating broadly correspond with the motivational aspect of issue framing (Snow & Benford, 1988).

Overall, our work – drawing on the insights from a case study of the Vienna City Administration coming to terms with the governance challenges of the sharing economy – contributes to an in-depth understanding of the strategic engagement and issue work that underlies policy-formulation and policy-making. We highlight that the variety of new forms of organizing in the sharing economy (Maurer, Mair, & Oberg, this volume) is not uncontested, and that these novel forms are – as many organizational ideas and concepts – objects of intense debate, active (re-)framing, and adaptation. Thus, trajectories and consequences of the sharing economy are regularly co-constructed by dominant actors, such as governing authorities, politicians, and public officials. As a direct consequence, the question of good governance in and of the sharing economy (e.g., Cohen, 2016; Gori et al., 2015) depends much on the initial definition of what actually is at issue and who has a legitimate say in the debate. We empirically show that central actors deploy several mechanisms of strategic issue work in order to integrate and imbibe new social practices and novel economic models into an existing governance regime by (re-)contextualizing the issue, constructing a consistent narrative, and providing a clear rationale for intervention.

However, our case also indicates that the sequences of events and the specific manifestation of the rather abstract mechanisms of strategic issue work at least partly depend on the specific empirical setting. For instance, we assume that the power and experience of the actors involved, the novelty and contestedness of the issue, as well as the availability and potency of governance tools crucially influence the interplay of the mechanisms. Thus, the analysis of the case of Vienna – while an impressive example of how a society responds to new socio-economic phenomena – implies that this is not the only possible way, but that there might exist others. The "Viennese way" of governing the sharing economy is, for instance, strongly influenced by the notion of public welfare. Yet, the sharing economy is approached differently in other cities and governing authorities may apply alternative governance responses (e.g., Vith et al., 2019). Therefore, the contextual factors (i.e., the institutional setting and/or the cast of relevant actors) might explain why cities such as Amsterdam, London, or Paris vary significantly in their governance approach toward the sharing economy.

Conceptually, our research takes embedded agency seriously in the context of policy-making. The proclaimed turn toward practices (e.g., Lounsbury & Crumley, 2007) and work (e.g., Phillips & Lawrence, 2012) in organizational institutionalism has revived the "long running debate on how actors relate to institutions" (Abdelnour, Hasselbladh, & Kallinikos, 2017, p. 1775), and has induced "scholarly engagement with new forms of work that involve individuals and organizations" (Phillips & Lawrence, 2012, p. 223). We here have suggested the concept of issue work to describe and explore the strategic and entrepreneurial engagement of actors in designing, altering, or otherwise influencing a focal policy. Issue field (i.e., the cast of relevant actors), issue culture (i.e., the available menu of established interpretations and framing elements), and issue work (i.e., the strategic and entrepreneurial activities of shaping and framing) thus become three complementary components in the course of wrestling with a contested issue.

We acknowledge that strategic issue work exhibits a few striking similarities to institutional work. However, our proposed notion differs from institutional work (e.g., Lawrence & Suddaby, 2006) insofar as the focus of such work is not so much on creating, maintaining, or disrupting a specific institution (Lawrence, Suddaby, & Leca, 2011) but rather on directly targeting a malleable, often contested issue that requires local interpretation, trimming, modification, and charging with novel meaning. It equally differs from framing as it goes beyond the "core framing tasks" (e.g., Snow & Benford, 1988) and encompasses a wide range of strategic and purposeful activities that set the scene for framing to occur in the first place which also include more material manifestations and consequences beyond the discursive realm, such as, in our example, in ordinances, regulations, or funding.

Importantly, our study also indicates that governing authorities not only react to global developments in unique ways, but in fact claim "co-authorship" in bringing local instantiations to life. It is in this way that novel socio-economic models, such as the sharing economy, regardless of how globally taken-for-granted they appear, are not cast in stone. As researchers, we need to investigate how they are skillfully integrated in existing governance structures in local settings and purposefully employed by actors who use them to promote vested interests that are regarded as legitimate or relevant. Each and every translation and adaptation of a global template is therefore a creative process; and in the long run, local manifestations may even alter the global template through "bottom-up theorization." Höllerer et al. (2017, p. 232) refer to this as "rebound effects" within the process of glocalization and postulate that "established local-level practices influence the way global templates look." For instance, several cities around the globe have recently imposed stricter regulations, or even bans, on companies such as Airbnb and Uber (e.g., Rhodes, 2017; Tun, 2018). While not so long ago these were the uncontested figureheads of the new sharing movement, we ended up with a much more emancipated and nuanced understanding of sharing beyond Airbnb and Uber. Local governance responses seem to crucially impact the way in which the sharing economy unfolds, is perceived, and globally conceptualized (e.g., Geissinger, Laurell, & Sandström, 2018; Kornberger et al., 2018). It is in this sense that the "Viennese way" – with Vienna as a model city in terms of livability – might have wider implications by offering a narrative that is inspiring for policy-makers who engage in strategic issue work in other places – wherever that may be, and whatever the specific outcome may look like.

## ACKNOWLEDGMENTS

We wish to thank the Vienna City Administration and, in particular, its Department for Economic Affairs, Labor and Statistics for supporting our research. We appreciate comments from our colleagues Renate Meyer and Dennis Jancsary on a previous version of the manuscript, as well as constructive feedback from the reviewers and guest editors of *Research in the Sociology of Organizations*.

## NOTE

1. All quotes are translated by the authors.

## REFERENCES

Abdelnour, S., Hasselbladh, H., & Kallinikos, J. (2017). Agency and institutions in organization studies. *Organization Studies*, *38*(12), 1775–1792.

Alvesson, M., & Kärreman, D. (2007). Constructing mystery: Empirical matters in theory development. *Academy of Management Review*, *32*(4), 1265–1281.

Barnett, W. P., & Woywode, M. (2004). From Red Vienna to the Anschluss: Ideological competition among Viennese newspapers during the rise of national socialism. *American Journal of Sociology*, *109*(6), 1452–1499.

Bardhi, F., & Eckhardt, G. M. (2012). Access-based consumption: The case of car sharing. *Journal of Consumer Research*, *23*, 881–898.

Bartik, H., & Lutter, J. (2017). *Überblick über rechtliche Regulierungen für touristische Vermietung von Wohnraum in europäischen Städten*. Vienna: TINA Vienna.

Belk, R. (2007). Why not share rather than own? *Annals of the Academy of Political and Social Science*, *611*(1), 126–140.

Belk, R. (2014). Sharing versus pseudo-sharing in web 2.0. *Anthropologist*, *18*(1), 7–23.

Benford, R. D., & Snow, D. A. (2000). Framing processes and social movements: An overview and assessment. *Annual Review of Sociology*, *26*, 611–639.

Beretta, G. (2017). Taxation of individuals in the sharing economy. *Intertax*, *45*(1), 2–11.

Berke, D. (2016). Products liability in the sharing economy. *Yale Journal on Regulation*, *33*(2), 603–653.

Biber, E., Light, S. E., Ruhl, J. B., & Salzman, J. (2017). Regulating business innovation as policy disruption: From the Model T to Airbnb. *Vanderbilt Law Review*, *70*(5), 1561–1626.

BMWFW. (2016). Creative industries strategy for Austria. The creative industries – A key economic factor and driving force for Austria as a place of innovation. Retrieved from https://www.en.bmdw.gv.at/Innovation/Innovationandtechnologypolicies/Documents/Creative%20for%20Industries%20Strategy%20Austria.pdf

Botsman, R., & Rogers, R. (2010). *What's mine is yours. The rise of collaborative consumption*. New York, NY: Harper Business.

Brandtner, C., Höllerer, M. A., Meyer, R. E., & Kornberger, M. (2017). Enacting governance through strategy: A comparative study of governance configurations in Sydney and Vienna. *Urban Studies*, *54*(5), 1075–1091.

Brown, A. D., & Toyoki, S. (2013). Identity work and legitimacy. *Organization Studies*, *34*(7), 875–896.

Cohen, S. (2016). Urban sustainability and the sharing economy. Earth Institute, Columbia University. Retrieved from http://blogs.ei.columbia.edu/2016/10/10/urban-sustainability-and-the-sharing-economy

Cornelissen, J. P., & Werner, M. D. (2014) Putting framing in perspective: A review of framing and frame analysis across the management and organizational literature. *The Academy of Management Annals*, *8*(1), 181–235.

Czarniawska, B., & Sevón, G. (Eds.). (1996). *Translating organizational change*. Berlin & New York, NY: Walter de Gruyter.

Das Acevedo, D. (2016). Regulating employment relationships in the sharing economy. *Employee Rights & Employment Policy Journal*, *20*(1), 1–35.

Davidson, N. M., & Infranca, J. J. (2016). The sharing economy as an urban phenomenon. *Yale Law & Policy Review*, *34*(2), 215–279.

Davidson, N. M., & Infranca, J. J. (2017). The sharing economy and the upside of disrupting local governance. *Harvard Law Review Blog*. Retrieved from https://blog.harvardlawreview.org/the-sharing-economy-and-the-upside-of-disrupting-local-governance

De Bruycker, I. (2017). Framing and advocacy: A research agenda for interest group studies. *Journal of European Public Policy*, *24*(5), 775–787.

Denis, J.-L., Langley, A., & Rouleau, L. (2007). Strategizing in pluralistic contexts: Rethinking theoretical frames. *Human Relations*, *60*(1), 179–215.

Drahokoupil, J., & Piasna, A. (2017). Work in the platform economy: Beyond lower transaction costs. *Intereconomics*, *52*(6), 335–340.

Dyal-Chand, R. (2015). Regulating sharing: The sharing economy as an alternative capitalist system. *Tulane Law Review*, *90*(2), 241–309.

Easton, D. (1965). *A framework for political analysis*. Englewood Cliffs, NJ: Prentice Hall.

Economist Intelligence Unit. (2018). Global liveability index 2018. Retrieved from https://www.eiu.com/public/topical_report.aspx?campaignid=Liveability2018

Edelman, B. G., Luca, M., & Svirsky, D. (2017). Racial discrimination in the sharing economy: Evidence from a field experiment. *American Economic Journal: Applied Economics*, *9*(2), 1–22.

Erickson, K., & Sørensen, I. (2016). Regulating the sharing economy. *Internet Policy Review*, *5*(2), 1–13.

Europaforum Wien. (2015). The Big Transformers: Sharing- und On-Demand-Economy auf dem Vormarsch. Retrieved from https://www.wien.gv.at/statistik/pdf/big-transformers.pdf

European Commission. (2016). Collaborative economy. Retrieved from https://ec.europa.eu/growth/single-market/services/collaborative-economy_en

European Parliament. (2016). *The cost of non-Europe in the sharing economy. Economic, social and legal challenges and opportunities*. Brussels: European Parliamentary Research Service.

Frenken, K., Meelen, T., Arets, M., & van de Glid, P. (2015). Smarter regulation for the sharing economy. *The Guardian*, May 20. Retrieved from https://www.theguardian.com/science/political-science/2015/may/20/smarter-regulation-for-the-sharing-economy

Friedland, R. (2009). The endless fields of Pierre Bourdieu. *Organization, 16*(6), 887–917.

Gamson, W. A. (1992). The social psychology of collective action. In A. D. Morris & C. Mueller (Eds.), *Frontiers in social movement theory* (pp. 53–76). New Haven, CT: Yale University Press.

Gamson, W. A., & Modigliani, A. (1989). Media discourse and public opinion on nuclear power: A constructionist approach. *American Journal of Sociology*, *95*(1), 1–37.

Gehman, J., Glaser, V. L., Eisenhardt, K. M., Gioia, D., Langley, A., & Corley, K. G. (2018). Finding theory-method fit: A comparison of three qualitative approaches to theory building. *Journal of Management Inquiry*, *27*(3), 284–300.

Geissinger, A., Laurell, C., & Sandström, C. (2018). Digital disruption beyond Uber and Airbnb – Tracking the long tail of the sharing economy. *Technological Forecasting & Social Change*. published online before print June 23, 2018. doi:10.1016/j.techfore.2018.06.012

Gioia, D. A., & Chittipeddi, K. (1991). Sensemaking and sensegiving in strategic change initiation. *Strategic Management Journal*, *12*(6), 433–448.

Gioia, D. A., Corley, K. G., & Hamilton, A. L. (2013). Seeking qualitative rigor in inductive research: Notes on the Gioia methodology. *Organizational Research Methods*, *16*(1), 15–31.

Goffman, E. (1986). *Frame analysis: An essay on the organization of experience*. Boston, MA: Northeastern University Press.

Goodwin, J., & Jasper, J. (Eds.). (2004). *Rethinking social movements*. Lanham: Rowman and Littlefield.

Gori, P., Parcu, P. L., & Stasi, M. L. (2015). Smart cities and sharing Economy. EUI Working Paper RSCAS 2015/96. Retrieved from http://cadmus.eui.eu/bitstream/handle/1814/38264/RSCAS_2015_96.pdf

Hill, M. (Ed.). (1993). *The policy process: A reader*. London: Harvester Wheatsheaf.

Hirshon, L., Jones, M., Levin, D., McCarthy, K., Morano, B., Simon, S., & Rainwater, B. (2015). Cities, the sharing economy, and what's next. Retrieved from http://www.nlc.org/Documents/Find City Solutions/City-Solutions-and-Applied-Research/Report - Cities the Sharing Economy and Whats Next final.pdf

Höllerer, M. A. (2013). From taken-for-granted to explicit commitment: The rise of CSR in a corporatist country. *Journal of Management Studies*, *50*(4), 573–606.

Höllerer, M. A., Walgenbach, P., & Drori, G. S. (2017). The consequences of globalization for institutions and organizations. In R. Greenwood, C. Oliver, T. B. Lawrence, & R. E. Meyer (Eds.), *The SAGE handbook of organizational institutionalism* (2nd ed., pp. 214–242). Los Angeles, CA: SAGE.

Hunt, S. A., Benford, R. D., & Snow, D. A. (1994). Identity fields: Framing processes and the social construction of movement identities. In E. Laraña, H. Johnston, & J. Gusfield (Eds.), *New social movements: From ideology to identity* (pp. 185–208). Philadelphia, PA: Temple University Press.

Jancsary, D., Meyer, R. E., Höllerer, M. A., & Barberio, V. (2017). Towards a structural model of organizational-level institutional pluralism and logic interconnectedness. *Organization Science*, *28*(6), 1150–1167.

Katz, V. (2015). Regulating the sharing economy. *Berkeley Technology Law Journal*, *30*(4), 1067–1126.

Kingdon, J. W. (1984). *Agendas, alternatives, and public policies*. Boston, MA: Little, Brown & Co.

Kornberger, M., Clegg, S. R., & Carter, C. (2006). Rethinking the polyphonic organization: Managing as discursive practice. *Scandinavian Journal of Management*, *22*(1), 3–30.

Kornberger, M., Leixnering, S., Meyer, R. E., & Höllerer, M. A. (2018). Rethinking the sharing economy: The nature and organization of sharing in the 2015 refugee crisis. *Academy of Management Discoveries*, *4*(3), 314–335.

Kornberger, M., Meyer, R. E., Brandtner, C., & Höllerer, M. A. (2017). When bureaucracy meets the crowd: Studying "open government" in the Vienna City Administration. *Organization Studies*, *38*(2), 179–200.

Kuhlmann, S., & Wollmann, H. (2014). *Introduction to comparative public administration: Administrative systems and reforms in Europe*. Cheltenham & Northampton, MA: Edward Elgar.

Laamanen, T., Pfeffer, J., Rong, K., & Van de Ven, A. (2018). Editors' introduction: Business models, ecosystems, and society in the sharing economy. *Academy of Management Discoveries*, *4*(3), 213–219.

Langley, A. (1999). Strategies for theorizing from process data. *Academy of Management Review*, *24*, 691–710.

Langley, A., & Royer, I. (2006). Perspectives on doing case study research in organizations. *m@n@gement*, *9*(3), 81–94.

Lawrence, T. B., Leca, B., & Zilber, T. B. (2013). Institutional work: Current research, new directions and overlooked issues. *Organization Studies*, *34*(8), 1023–1033.

Lawrence, T. B., & Suddaby, R. (2006). Institutions and institutional work. In S. R. Clegg, C. Hardy, T. B. Lawrence, & W. R. Nord (Eds.), *The SAGE handbook of organization studies* (2nd ed., pp. 215–254). London: SAGE.

Lawrence, T., Suddaby, R., & Leca, B. (2011). Institutional work: Refocusing institutional studies of organization. *Journal of Management Inquiry*, *20*(1), 52–58.

Lee, T. W., Mitchell, T. R., & Sablynski, C. J. (1999). Qualitative research in organizational and vocational psychology, 1979–1999. *Journal of Vocational Behavior*, *55*(2), 161–187.

Lefsrud, L., Graves, H., & Phillips, N. (2018). Dirty oil or ethical oil? Visual rhetoric in legitimation struggles. In M. A. Höllerer, T. Daudigeos, & D. Jancsary (Eds.), *Multimodality, meaning, and institutions* (Research in the Sociology of Organizations, Vol. 54B, pp. 101–142). Bingley: Emerald Publishing Limited.

Lefsrud, L. M., & Meyer, R. E. (2012). Science or science fiction? Professionals' discursive construction of climate change. *Organization Studies*, *33*(11), 477–1506.

Leixnering, S., & Höllerer, M. A. (2019). *Keeping the spirit of a city alive: Resilience as a meta governance principle*. Vienna: WU Vienna working paper.

Lounsbury, M., & Crumley, E. T. (2007). New practice creation: An institutional perspective on innovation. *Organization Studies*, *28*(7), 993–1012.

Lutz, C., & Newlands, G. (2018). Choice and discrimination in the sharing economy. Working Paper. Weizenbaum Symposium, Berlin, May 15. Retrieved from https://papers.ssrn.com/sol3/papers.cfm?abstract_id=3241682

MA23. (2015). Die Wiener Vizebürgermeisterin Renate Brauner lädt zur internationalen Konferenz: Local Heroes & Global Players. Wie fair ist die Sharing Economy? Retrieved from https://www.sharing-economy.at/kos/WNetz?art=File.download&id=94&name=Local±Heroes%2BGlobal±Players_Programmfolder±DE.pdf

Mair, J., & Reischauer, G. (2017). Capturing the dynamics of the sharing economy: Institutional research on the plural forms and practices of sharing economy organizations. *Technological Forecasting & Social Change*, *125*, 11–20.

March, J. G. (1994). *A primer on decision making. How decisions happen.* New York, NY: The Free Press.

Martin, C. (2016). The sharing economy: A pathway to sustainability or a nightmarish form of neoliberal capitalism? *Ecological Economics*, *121*, 149–159.

Maurer, I., Mair, J., & Oberg, A. (2020). Variety and trajectories of new forms of organizing in the sharing economy: A research agenda. In I. Maurer, J. Mair, & A. Oberg (Eds.), *Theorizing the sharing economy: Variety, trajectories, and consequences of new forms of organizing*. (Research in the Sociology of Organizations, Vol. 66, pp. 1–23). Bingley: Emerald Publishing Limited.

Mayring, P. (2014). *Qualitative content analysis. Theoretical foundation, basic procedures and software solution*. Klagenfurt, Austria: SSOAR. Retrieved from http://nbn-resolving.de/urn:nbn:de:0168-ssoar-395173

Mazzucotelli Salice, S. & Pais, I. (2017). Sharing economy as an urban phenomenon: Examining policies for sharing cities. In P. Meil & V. Kirov (Eds.), *Policy implications of virtual work. Dynamics of virtual work* (pp. 199–228). Cham, Switzerland: Palgrave Macmillan.

McAdam, D. (1996). Conceptual origins, current problems, future directions. In D. McAdam, J. D. McCarthy, & M. N. Zald (Eds.), *Comparative perspectives on social movements: Political opportunities, mobilizing structures, and cultural framings* (pp. 23–40). Cambridge: Cambridge University Press.

McAdam, D. (2010). *Political process and the development of black insurgency, 1930–1970*. Chicago, IL: University of Chicago Press.

McPeak, A. A. (2016). Sharing tort liability in the new sharing economy. *Connecticut Law Review*, *49*(1), 171–225.

Mercer. (2019). Quality of living ranking. Retrieved from https://mobilityexchange.mercer.com/insights/quality-of-living-rankings

Meyer, J. W., & Scott, W. R. (1983). *Organizational environments*. Beverly Hills, CA: SAGE.

Meyer, R. E. (2004). *Globale Managementkonzepte und lokaler Kontext. Organisationale Wertorientierung im österreichischen öffentlichen Diskurs*. Wien, Austria: WUV.

Meyer, R. E. (2014). 'Re-localization' as micro-mobilization of consent and legitimacy. In G. S. Drori, M. A. Höllerer, & P. Walgenbach (Eds.), *Global themes and local variations in organization and management: Perspectives on glocalization* (pp. 79–89). New York, NY: Routledge.

Meyer, R. E., Egger-Peitler, I., Höllerer, M. A., & Hammerschmid, G. (2014). Of bureaucrats and passionate public managers: Institutional logics, executive identities, and public service motivation. *Public Administration*, *92*(4), 861–885.

Meyer, R. E., & Höllerer, M. A. (2010). Meaning structures in a contested issue field: A topographic map of shareholder value in Austria. *Academy of Management Journal*, *53*(6), 1241–1262.

Meyer, R. E., & Höllerer, M. A. (2016). Laying a smoke screen: Ambiguity and neutralization as strategic responses to intra-institutional complexity. *Strategic Organization*, *14*(4), 373–406.

OECD. (2016). *OECD tourism trends and policies 2016*. Paris, France: OECD Publishing.

Ongaro, E. (2009). *Public management reform and modernization. Trajectories of administrative change in Italy, France, Greece, Portugal and Spain*. Cheltenham: Edward Elgar Publishing.

Osborne, S. (2010). *The new public governance? Emerging perspectives on the theory and practice of public governance*. New York, NY: Routledge.

Osman, F. A. (2002). Public policy making: Theories and their implications in developing countries. *Asian Affairs (Dacca)*, *24*(3), 37–52.

Painter, M., & Peters, B. G. (Eds.). (2010). *Tradition and public administration*. Basingstoke: Palgrave Macmillan.

Phillips, N., & Lawrence, T. B. (2012): The turn to work in organization and management theory: Some implications for strategic organization. *Strategic Organization*, *10*(3), 223–230.

Pollitt, C., & Bouckaert, G. (2011). *Public sector reform. A comparative analysis: New public management, governance, and the neo-Weberian state* (3rd ed.). Oxford: Oxford University Press.

Powell, W. W. (1990). Neither market nor hierarchy: Network forms of organization. *Research in Organizational Behavior*, *12*(1), 295–336.

Provan, K. G., & Kenis, P. (2007). Modes of network governance: Structure, management, and effectiveness. *Journal of Public Administration Research and Theory*, *18*(2), 229–252.

Rauch, D. E., & Schleicher, D. (2015). Like Uber, but for local government law: The future of local regulation of the sharing economy. *Ohio State Law Journal*, *76*(4), 901–963.

Reischauer, G., & Mair, J. (2018). Platform organizing in the new digital economy: Revisiting online communities and strategic Responses. In L. Ringel, P. Hiller, & C. Zietsma (Eds.), *Toward permeable boundaries of organizations?* (Research in the Sociology of Organizations, Vol. 57, pp. 113–135). Bingley: Emerald Publishing Limited.

Rhodes, T. (2017). Uber: Which countries have banned the controversial taxi app. *The Independent*, September 22. Retrieved from https://www.independent.co.uk/travel/news-and-advice/uber-ban-countries-where-world-taxi-app-europe-taxi-us-states-china-asia-legal-a7707436.html

Rugge, F. (2012). Administrative legacies in Western Europe. In B. G. Peters & J. Pierre (Eds.), *The SAGE handbook of public administration* (pp. 228–240). London: SAGE.

Sahlin-Andersson, K. (1996). Imitating by editing success: The construction of organizational fields. In B. Czarniawska & G. Sevón (Eds.), *Translating organizational change* (pp. 69–92). New York, NY: Walter de Gruyter.

Scott, W. R. (1995). *Institutions and organizations*. Thousand Oaks, CA: SAGE.

Smart City Wien. (2019). Awards, studies and rankings. Retrieved from https://smartcity.wien.gv.at/site/en/the-initiative/awards-studies-and-rankings

Snow, D. A., & Benford, R. D., (1988). Ideology, frame resonance and participant mobilization. *International Social Movement Research*, *1*, 197–217.

Snow, D. A., Rochford, E. B., Worden, S. K., & Benford, R. D. (1986). Frame alignment processes, micromobilization, and movement participation. *American Sociological Review*, *51*(4), 464–481.

Stadt Wien. (2014). Smart city Wien framework strategy. Retrieved from https://smartcity.wien.gv.at/site/files/2019/07/Smart-City-Wien-Framework-Strategy_2014-resolution.pdf

Stadt Wien. (2015). Konferenz "local heroes & global players". Retrieved from https://www.wien.gv.at/wirtschaft/standort/peer-economy-konferenz.html

Stadt Wien. (2016). Turning the sharing economy into a fair economy in Vienna. Retrieved from https://www.wien.gv.at/wirtschaft/standort/pdf/share-economy-in-vienna.pdf

Stadt Wien. (2018). Wien in Zahlen 2018. Retrieved from https://www.wien.gv.at/statistik/pdf/wieninzahlen-2018.pdf

Stadt Wien. (2019). History of Vienna – The making of a capital. Retrieved from https://www.wien.gv.at/english/history/overview

Suchman, M. (1995). Managing legitimacy: Strategic and institutional approaches. *The Academy of Management Review*, *20*(3), 571–610.

Treviño, L. K., den Nieuwenboer, N. A., Kreiner, G. E., & Bishop, D. G. (2014). Legitimating the legitimate: A grounded theory study of legitimacy work among ethics and compliance officers. *Organizational Behavior and Human Decision Processes*, *123*(2), 186–205.

Tun, Z. T. (2018). Top cities where Airbnb is legal or illegal. *Investopedia*. Retrieved from https://www.investopedia.com/articles/investing/083115/top-cities-where-airbnb-legal-or-illegal.asp

Vaara, E., Sonenshein, S., & Boje, D. (2016). Narratives as sources of stability and change in organizations: Approaches and directions for future research. *Academy of Management Annals*, *10*(1), 495–560.

Vith, S., Oberg, A., Höllerer, M. A., & Meyer, R. E. (2019). Envisioning the 'sharing city': Governance strategies for the sharing economy. *Journal of Business Ethics*, *159*(4), 1023–1046.

Walgenbach, P., Drori, G., & Höllerer, M. A. (2017). Between local mooring and global orientation: A neo-institutional theory perspective on the contemporary multinational corporation. *Research in the Sociology of Organizations*, *49*, 99–125.

Wedlin, L., & Sahlin, K. (2017). The imitation and translation of management ideas. In R. Greenwood, C. Oliver, T. B. Lawrence, & R. E. Meyer (Eds.), *The SAGE handbook of organizational institutionalism* (2nd ed., pp. 102–127). Los Angeles, CA: SAGE.

World Economic Forum. (2013). Young global leaders sharing economy dialogue position paper. Retrieved from http://www3.weforum.org/docs/WEF_YGL_CircularEconomyInnovation_PositionPaper_2013.pdf

Wruk, D., Oberg, A., Klutt, J., & Maurer, I. (2019). The presentation of self as good and right: How value propositions and business model features are linked in the sharing economy. *Journal of Business Ethics*, *159*(4), 997–1021.

Yin, R. K. (2009). *Case study research: Design and methods* (4th ed.). Thousand Oaks, CA: Sage.

Zald, M. N. (1996). Culture, ideology, and strategic framing. In D. McAdam, J. McCarthy, & M. Zald (Eds.), *Comparative perspectives on social movements: Political opportunities, mobilizing structures, and cultural framings* (pp. 261–274). Cambridge: Cambridge University Press.

Zale, K. (2016). When everything is small: The regulatory challenge of scale in the sharing economy. *San Diego Law Review*, *53*(4), 949–1016.

# REGULATING THE SHARING ECONOMY: A FIELD PERSPECTIVE

Stefan Kirchner and Elke Schüßler*

## ABSTRACT

*Critics increasingly highlight the dark sides of the sharing economy resulting from the insufficient regulation of competition, labor, or taxes in its for-profit sector. In this chapter, the authors argue that regulatory solutions for the sharing economy hinge on the understanding of the ways in which the sharing economy is organized. Here, digitalization undermines established regulation through underlying organizational shifts pertaining to places, labor inputs and output responsibilities. Mapping out the field of actors that are or could be involved in regulating the sharing economy, the authors highlight a particular role played not only by digital platforms as market organizers, but also of a variety of other public and private actors such as standard setting organizations, social movements, trade unions, organized buyers and sellers, incumbents, or policy makers. The authors suggest that an understanding of sharing economy markets as fields can not only capture the highly organized nature of the sharing economy, but also serve to untangle the contestations and power dynamics unfolding among various actors engaged in different regulatory issues associated with the sharing economy. Seeing "Uberization" as a next development stage away from the modern corporation after global supply chains, the authors highlight regulatory challenges associated with the even more individualized and dispersed way in which sharing*

*The authors are grateful for comments and suggestions made by Hans Pongratz, by the editors of this volume and by the anonymous reviewers. The work was partially funded by the German Federal Ministry of Labour and Social Affairs (project number: FIS.00.0014.18).

**Theorizing the Sharing Economy: Variety and Trajectories of New Forms of Organizing**
**Research in the Sociology of Organizations, Volume 66, 215–236**

**ISSN: 0733-558X/doi:10.1108/S0733-558X20200000066010**

*economy markets are organized and also discuss new opportunities for regulation provided by digital technology.*

**Keywords**: Sharing economy; market organization; organizational fields; regulation; sociology of markets; new forms of organizing; global supply chains

## 1. INTRODUCTION

Not that long ago, the rise of the sharing economy created a vision for a more sustainable and democratic way of producing and consuming goods and services, essentially laying the digitally mediated foundation for a fairer society (Botsman & Rogers, 2010; Rifkin, 2011; Schor & Fitzmaurice, 2015). However, the rise and worldwide success of profit-driven companies like Uber, Lyft, or Airbnb that operate under the guise of "sharing" has turned attention to the variety of exchange models found under the same label (e.g., Belk, 2014, 2017) and has spurred a debate about whether the sharing economy rather presents an unleashed form of neoliberal capitalism (for an overview, see Fitzmaurice et al., 2018; Murillo, Buckland, & Val, 2017).

Recent definitions highlight that the sharing economy includes both commercial and non-commercial forms of sharing and a variety of business models that may or may not be digitally mediated (Hartl & Hofmann, 2019). Our focus in this chapter lies on digital platforms that facilitate commercial sharing activities among peers such as Airbnb, Uber, or Lyft. These platforms are often linked to a broader phenomenon described as the platform economy (Kenney & Zysman, 2016) or platform capitalism (Langley & Leyshon, 2017) and criticized for issues such as distorted competition, precarious working conditions, tax evasion, and increased social inequality (e.g., Fernández-Macías, 2018; Malhotra & Alstyne, 2014; Peticca-Harris, deGama, & Ravishankar, 2018; Schor, 2017; Schor & Attwood-Charles, 2017). Just as regulators around the world are trying to catch up with the sharing economy, and the platform economy more broadly, organizational scholars (e.g., Kornberger, Leixnering, Meyer, & Höllerer, 2018; Mair & Reischauer, 2017; Schor & Vallas, 2020, forthcoming; Uzunca, Rigtering, & Ozcan, 2018) as well as legal scholars (e.g., De Stefano, 2016; Prassl & Risak, 2016) are searching for ways of theorizing this new phenomenon.

In one of these efforts, Jerry Davis (2016a, 2016b) argued that sharing economy companies, with their digital platforms as the dominant organizational model, present only the most recent stage in a long-term and profound transformation. In this transformation, organizational models are shifting away from the vertically integrated modern corporation toward a price and market-oriented economic structure in which companies like Uber employ relatively few regular employees (mostly programmers), but provide a digital infrastructure for a vast number of independent and often individualized service providers (sellers) and consumers (buyers). Davis portraits this stage of *Uberization* as a further escalation of what he calls *Nikefication*. The latter denotes a first major shift away from the vertically integrated cooperation toward global supply chains driven forward by outsourcing dynamics. Whereas in *Nikefication* corporations still played an important role as lead firms or suppliers, *Uberization*, according to Davis, seems to abandon the organizational structures of the modern corporation and its principles altogether. Although its actual scope and newness is still debated, the novel way of organizing value creation in the sharing economy caught many established regulatory mechanisms and institutions off guard and often rendered them practically ineffective (e.g., Howcroft & Bergvall-Kåreborn, 2018; Martin, Upham, & Klapper, 2017), making the emergence of the sharing economy seem an uncoordinated and unregulated endeavor.

In this chapter, we argue that both regulatory challenges and their solutions hinge on our understanding of the ways in which the sharing economy is organized. Specifically, we argue that by simply stating a decline of organizations in favor of market-based mechanisms of coordination, as broadly argued by Davis, the importance of organizational structures and mechanisms that underlie the rise and success of the sharing economy is dramatically underestimated. Drawing on economic sociology and understanding markets as fields (Fligstein, 2001a, 2001b), we posit that the rise of platforms in the sharing economy is, in fact, a highly organized process undertaken by market organizers that establish and operate digital marketplaces. Digitization lends itself to particular ways of loosened couplings of organizational structures (Kirchner & Beyer, 2016; Weick, 1976). These forms of loosened couplings create a need for coordination that, in our view, is best captured by the notion of organized digital marketplaces (Ahrne, Aspers, & Brunsson, 2014). Key to understanding the regulatory challenges of the sharing economy is, thus, not to view this process as an erosion of organizations, but as a substantial shift of organizational structures. We therefore also posit that attempts at regulating the potential dark sides of the sharing economy do, could, and should involve various organizational actors. Our chapter thus deals with the following questions: What are the underlying reasons for why established regulatory efforts fail to get a hold with Our chapter thus deals with the following questions the sharing economy? What role do different organizations play in the process of regulating the sharing economy?

## 2. THE ORGANIZATIONAL SHIFTS OF "UBERIZATION" THAT UNDERMINE REGULATION

As broadly argued by Davis (2016a, 2016b), the emergence of sharing economy companies lies on a historical trajectory that erodes established organizational structures, particularly that of the modern corporation. By installing information and communication technologies (ICTs), especially mobile devices, Uberization seems to render the modern corporation as an efficient way of organizing the production inputs and outputs redundant. The success of Uber and other sharing economy companies hereby questions fundamental theoretical assumptions about the role of organizations in the economy. Coase (1937) and many others (e.g., Marsden, 1999; Simon, 1951; Williamson, 1991) argued that, under certain conditions such as uncertainty of transactions and asset-specific investments, firms that steadily employ a designated workforce realize an advantage over market mechanisms. The rise and success of digital platforms undermines these organizational principles and the associated taken for granted assumptions, since the possibilities of digital technology facilitate the on-demand matching of tasks with a specialized labor force on an unprecedented scale.

To better understand the organizational shifts resulting from digitization, the concept of, coupling which distinguishes between states of tight and loose coupling of organizations and their elements (Orton & Weick, 1990; Weick, 1976), provides useful insights. Broadly speaking, tight coupling constitutes a state where organizational elements are highly interrelated and tied together by a strong bond. Loose coupling, in contrast, describes a state where organizational elements still relate to each other, yet allow for a high degree of flexibility and adaptability of single elements. The modern corporation, best exemplified by the Fordist production company (Boyer & Freyssenet, 2003), represents a tightly coupled organizational system. Here the industrial organization is tightly coupled to one specific place, a designated labor force, and a particular product. The idea is that employees work in a factory to manufacture a product – a car in a case of Ford – that would eventually roll out of the factory and be sold to consumers. This stylized model often implicitly serves as key reference point in the current debate about the sharing economy.

The process of digitalization, understood as the pervasive diffusion and use of ICT, gradually enabled more loosely coupled organizational structures. ICT allowed organizations to loosen its couplings to one specific place, to a designated labor force, and to the responsibilities for a specific product. To develop our argument, we posit that three basic mechanisms advanced by digitalization allowed for fundamental shifts in industrial organization: delocalization, delegation, and intermediation (see also Kirchner & Beyer, 2016).[1]

### *2.1. Delocalization – Loosening Coupling with One Specific Place (Location)*

Digitalization loosens the couplings between organizations and one specific place through the mechanism of delocalization. Delocalization thrives on the specific properties of digital technology, especially mobile ICT or cloud computing, that translate physical objects and communications into a digital format: the physical CD evolved into an MP3 that can easily be stored and copied; the paper file transformed into a digital document that can be transferred, copied, and edited with considerably less effort; retail stores evolved into online stores and warehouses with digital logistics. To some extent, digitalization rids persons, communications, and objects of organizations from their physical properties, removing traditional physical boundaries and enabling much quicker exchanges and reduced communication and search costs (e.g., Langlois & Garzarelli, 2008).

Delocalization driven by digital technology can be seen as an extension of a larger transformation that is often described in broad terms such as globalization or transnationalization (see Flecker & Schönauer, 2016). It is important to note here that persons, communications, and objects still require locations and still occupy places: just think of a personal computer, a home office with internet access, a laptop on a train or the hard drives of a cloud server. The important difference is that digitalization greatly reduces the dependence of organizations on a specific place, for example, a factory or an office building (e.g., Evans & Schmalensee, 2016). Knoblauch and Löw (2017) argue that digitalization fosters a "re-figuration of space," allowing for novel relations between space and social entities, including organizations.

### *2.2. Delegation – Loosening Coupling with a Designated Labor Force (Input)*

Digitalization loosens the couplings between organizations and a designated labor force through the mechanism of delegation. Delegation evolved in a longer process in various forms of atypical and contingent employment (e.g., Kalleberg, 2001; Marchington, Grimshaw, Rubery, & Wilmott, 2005), intensified by a general move to outsource non-core processes to external contractors including various forms such as offshore production and fragmented value chains (e.g., Flecker, 2009; Haidinger, Schönauer, Flecker, & Holtgrewe, 2014; Helfen, 2015). In these organizational shifts, ICT often serves as a facilitator for outsourcing or fragmentation of production inputs (Kakabadse & Kakabadse, 2000). Delegation also flourishes on the parallel mechanism of delocalization, because a loosened tie to a specific place allows organizational processes to span across various locations and subcontracted organizations.

Current developments in internet technology accelerate outsourcing activities and create new forms of delegation. This development is most prominent in the proliferation of prosumers, crowdsourcing, and "gig work" (Bauer & Gegenhuber, 2015; Kleemann, Voß, & Rieder, 2008), which includes people who are not formal employees in essential value creation processes. In general, delegation denotes a shift in which organizations distance themselves from important inputs, especially labor, but also assets or resources (ranging from actual manufacturing equipment to data storage in cloud computing). Pertaining to the labor force, delegation enables organizations to operate novel and often highly disintegrated labor and fragmented production processes. This shift from inter-organizational networks and global supply chains toward platform-mediated markets and crowds concerns basic tasks as much as highly innovative ones.

### *2.3. Intermediation – Loosening Coupling with Responsibility for a Concrete Product (Output)*

The final mechanism, intermediation, loosens the coupling between organizations and the responsibilities for a concrete output, the product sold, or the service performed. Digitalization enables intermediary positions for specialized actors that connect external sellers and buyers on a digital marketplace. Sharing economy companies like Uber, Lyft, and Airbnb hereby organize so-called two-sided or multi-sided markets (Evans, 2011; Hagiu & Wright, 2015; Rochet & Tirole, 2003), extracting a fee for connecting a large number of buyers and sellers (Langley & Leyshon, 2017). From an organization-of-markets perspective (Ahrne et al., 2014), sharing economy companies organize digital marketplaces as "profiteers," because they operate a market infrastructure for their own economic interest. Profiteers enable the digital marketplace, for example, by offering participatory architectures and evaluative infrastructures (Kornberger, 2017), yet cede most of the responsibilities to the sellers and buyers treating their relation as ordinary market transaction.

In the case of the sharing economy, intermediation is combined with delocalization and delegation: platforms intermediate sharing activities between buyers and sellers that are highly dispersed, often using mobile devices and app interfaces (delocalization) to integrate them into a digital marketplace. Sharing economy companies require actors (sellers) who are not formally employed with the company yet are willing to provide their labor power on the marketplace (delegation). Similarly, platforms also heavily rely on unpaid consumers (buyers) who reliably and continuously rate seller's performance that facilitate the transactions on their marketplace (see below). The loosened couplings with the location, the inputs, and the outputs of production enables novel organizational structures and business models of the sharing economy and allow market organizers to reap a major share of the value created (e.g., see Powell, 2016).

Overall, digitalization allows for highly loosened organizational structures, severing ties to one specific place, a designated workforce and the responsibilities for a particular product.[2] This enables the intermediary position of the market organizer operating a digital platform as a digital marketplace.

### *2.4. Three Development Stages, Loosened Couplings, and the Ineffectiveness of Regulation*

The new mode of capitalist market economies currently embodied by platforms such as Uber, Lyft, or Airbnb substantially challenges the traditional way of regulating economic activities. However, this challenge has been long underway even before the sharing economy rose to its current success. The trajectory of modern capitalist market economies can well be illustrated and historically contextualized by connecting the three mechanisms of digitalization with Davis' (2016a, 2016b) three broad stages of the transformation (see Table 1). This processual view will

***Table 1.*** Mode of Organization, Development Stages and Levels of Loosened Couplings.

| Mode of Organization | Industrial Organization | Post-industrial Organization | Market Organizer |
|---|---|---|---|
| Mechanism of loosened couplings | | | |
| Delocalization (place) | Low | Medium | High |
| Delegation (input) | Low | Medium | High |
| Intermediation (output) | Low | Low | High |
| Stages, governance, and labor | | | |
| Stages | Modern Corporation | Nikefikation | Uberization |
| Central governance mechanism | Hierarchy | Network | Market |
| Dominant labor pattern | Careers | Jobs | Tasks |

*Source*: own depiction based on Davis (2016a, 2016b).

help us in identifying avenues for regulating the sharing economy. Importantly, technological developments have not spurred these developments alone, but are deeply entangled with neoliberal politics of the last four decades that come with an ideology of state-regulated marketization, privatization, and individualization (Beck, 2000; Djelic & Quack, 2018).

As already argued above, levels of delocalization, delegation, and intermediation are low in an ideal-typical Fordist factory. This changed in the intermediate stage of Nikefication, because transnationalization and outsourcing processes transformed organizational structures into spatially dispersed production networks already relying less on a specific place and a designated labor force. Yet, labor is typically still employed for jobs, for example, in the form of multi-employer networks (Marchington, Rubery, & Grimshaw, 2011), and production processes are still organized around particular products, albeit intermediated by lead firms that sometimes add not much more than their brand to the final physical product.[3] In the shift toward Uberization, market organizers started to operate digital platforms that facilitate the provision of services for a vast number of consumers without a formal employee status or enduring sub-contracting relations. Thus, while Nikefication has eroded careers in the modern corporation into jobs in a post-industrial organization, Uberization seemingly dissolved jobs into tasks on a digital marketplace.

From a governance perspective, this succession of stages can be viewed as a steady progression of central governance mechanisms moving from organizational hierarchy over networks to markets (Powell, 1990; Williamson, 1991). Most established regulation (e.g., labor, health and safety, and taxation) coevolved in the development stage of the modern corporation. Targeting the very organizational structures of the modern corporation (e.g., a Fordist company) and its dominant labor and production patterns, sharing platforms operate in regulatory loopholes, treating the lack or lag of effective regulation and regulatory gray zones as a strategic opportunity. Uber, for instance, is said to have a strategy of trying something out and asking for forgiveness later (Kenney & Zysman, 2016; Thelen, 2018). Uber also engaged in framing activities to avoid regulation, such as defining itself as separate from the existing, highly regulated taxi industry (Collier, Dubal, & Carter, 2018). Many traditional regulating efforts require a mode of tight coupling of place, labor, and product to take effect: they work best when there is a specific location (e.g., factory and nation-state), a designated workforce identified by a clear and enduring employment relationship (e.g., full-time employees), and well-defined production output sold and answered for by a company (e.g., a branded car or shoe). The loosened couplings between the organization, a specific place, a designated workforce, and a particular product realized by the sharing economy bypass the established regulation.

Already firms in the Nikefication stage escaped traditional regulation, because outsourcing dynamics blurred established boundaries with a designated workforce, scattering labor input across many different forms of employment and subcontracted factories in fragmented value chains. Here, regulating issues such as labor standards remains a challenge, especially as nation-states increasingly cede regulation to private actors such as managers (Scherer & Palazzo, 2011), non-governmental organizations, unions, or consumers (Donaghey, Reinecke, Niforou, & Lawson, 2014), resulting in a complex – yet often state-facilitated – ecology of actors operating in national and transnational arenas (Djelic & Quack, 2018).

However, although market organizers tend to frame relations as simple transactions between the two market sides, they take up an important intermediary position with the power to define who participates in the marketplace or to set rules and sanctions (Kirchner & Schüßler, 2019; also Kornberger, 2017). Thus, sharing economy markets include hierarchical and network modes of governance, too. Just as supply chains still include hierarchical organizations as lead firms and suppliers and can be governed using market, network, or hierarchical modes of governance (Helfen, Schüßler, & Sydow, 2018), sharing economy platforms are typically hosted by a classic, hierarchical organization (Uber Technologies, Inc., for instance) and rely on various modes of governing market transactions. At the same time, the sharing economy typically involves even more dispersed and atomistic actors than those found in global supply chains, thus calling for different regulatory approaches.

In the following sections, we suggest that applying a field perspective allows us to not only capture which organizations are shaping the sharing economy and in which ways (Mair & Reischauer, 2017), but more specifically also to outline avenues in which regulators can move beyond viewing the sharing economy as markets toward viewing them as highly organized markets, involving a field of multiple organizational actors and multiple modes of governance.

## 3. THE FIELD OF ACTORS INVOLVED IN REGULATING THE SHARING ECONOMY

With a number of regulatory issues such as competition and anti-trust, labor, social policy, inequality and discrimination, taxation, the circumvention of local regulations or consumer safety accompanying the rise of the sharing economy, various organizational actors such as incumbents, consumer organizations, NGOs, unions, citizens' initiatives, as well as public officials have become involved in its regulation (Biber, Light, Ruhl, & Salzman, 2017; Collier et al., 2018; Thelen, 2018). Moving beyond a narrow focus on single organizations, a field perspective introduces a relational view on organizations that perceive each other as relevant, even though they may not necessarily directly interact as market actors (Fligstein, 2001a, 2001b; Fligstein & McAdam, 2012). Since incumbent organizations often face challengers, fields exhibit particular dynamics reflecting the established power relations in a field and attempts to change them by challenger organizations or social movements (Fligstein, 1996; 2001a, 2001b). To some extent, the rise of the sharing economy can be viewed as the establishment of a new field forcing itself into a broader societal ecosystem where it challenges established relations and regulations and interacts with other fields (Mair & Reischauer, 2017).

We start out by mapping the actors participating in regulating the sharing economy before discussing the broader implications of this field perspective. The central organizational actors comprise the market organizers themselves, traditional regulatory actors, other private actors and civil society (see Uzunca et al., 2018 for an overview).

### *3.1. Regulating by Market Organizers*

The first group of organizational actors that heavily engages in regulating the sharing economy hides in plain sight: the organizers of the digital marketplaces. As we argued above, companies like Uber, Lyft, and Airbnb do not simply intermediate connections through matchmaking; they actively curate connectivity (van Dijck, 2013), strategically govern their online communities (Mair & Reischauer, 2017), implement governance structures to prevent undesirable user behavior (Hartl, Hofmann, & Kirchler, 2016), or foster trust through the setup of evaluative infrastructures (Kornberger, 2017).

Historically, intermediaries are a common feature in many markets (Ahrne et al., 2014) as they fulfill various functions (Bessy & Chauvin, 2013), including buying and reselling products, matching transaction partners, advising market participants, evaluating products, persons, and organizations, as well as guaranteeing and monitoring transactions. Usually intermediaries take on one role to perform a specialized function for a given market, that is, being a seller, a matchmaker, an evaluator, an advisor, a mediator, or a broker. Earlier, we argued that digitalization enables a specific kind of intermediary, the organizer of a digital marketplace. This digital intermediary extensively combines several functions of many other specialized intermediaries: sharing economy platforms serve simultaneously as matchmaker, evaluator, advisor, mediator, and broker to facilitate their digital marketplace.

Being extensive intermediaries sets sharing economy platforms apart from various regular intermediaries in other markets. In the sharing economy, market organizers install elaborate measures to facilitate transactions on their digital marketplaces, thereby addressing the basic coordination problems that hamper social order on markets (Beckert, 2009; Kirchner & Beyer, 2016). They provide comprehensive information to allow for a valuation of services, they construct a frame for competition at the marketplace, and they ensure the smooth cooperation of buyers and sellers, for example, by installing reputation systems and granting insurances. Market organizers decide on the technical infrastructures and extensive rules that they monitor and sanction. They also constantly reconfigure their app interfaces or the evaluation systems in a way that fosters transactions and attracts more sellers and buyers (Kirchner & Schüßler, 2019). The related literature discusses the underlying regulative structures under the terms algorithmic management, algorithmic governance, or algorithmic bureaucracy (Czarniawska, 2019; Kirchner & Schüßler, 2019; Lehdonvirta, 2016; Müller-Birn, Dobusch, & Herbsleb, 2013). These technically enabled systems tend to employ various forms of "soft power" (Rosenblat & Stark, 2016) to govern user activities in order to eventually capture value.

Overall, the market organizers of the sharing economy thus introduce and maintain very elaborate organizational and technical structures to establish a digital market order and actively regulate their marketplaces. Therefore, digital marketplaces of the sharing economy need to be highly organized in order to operate. A sufficiently stable market order involving extensive intermediation efforts constitutes a precondition to extract fees. By the same token, the sharing economy is far from being an unregulated societal arena. Market organizers engage in regulating their digital marketplaces with substantial efforts to allow their business model to grow and prosper. From this perspective, sharing economy companies like Uber, Lyft, and Airbnb engage in regulating their marketplaces by introducing and maintaining a system of private governance which constitutes the very core of their revenue model and the business success of their digital marketplaces.

### *3.2. Regulating By Traditional Regulators (Governments and Municipalities)*

The second group of organizations involved in regulating the sharing economy are official bodies such as governments or communal agencies (e.g., Interian, 2016). The rise of sharing economy companies like Uber, Lyft, and Airbnb exposes regulatory gaps and causes policy disruptions (Biber et al., 2017). Thus, official organizations like transport agencies or zoning committees find themselves entangled with sharing economy developments right away, as the developments force decisions on the legality of the new marketed services. When looking at efforts to regulate the cases of Uber, Lyft, and Airbnb, we identify three broad patterns of how official organizations actually faced or could face regulatory challenges:

(1) *Accommodate and hope*: An accommodate-and-hope approach to the sharing economy refrains from obstructing the emerging sharing economy markets and hope for effective self-regulating market mechanisms to emerge. The underlying idea is that competition on these multi-sided markets produces efficient outcomes for consumers and regulates itself in a way that maximizes the utility for all involved parties. The deregulation of taxi services in the USA (Thelen, 2018) provides a case in point here: official organizations changed the regulatory framework to accommodate the new business models of Uber and Lyft that allowed regular persons to provide individual transport services (e.g., UberPop service) that was previously restricted to taxi companies and registered taxi drivers.

(2) *Ban and restore*: A ban-and-restore approach, in contrast, bans activities right away. Regulators deem sharing economy marketplaces as illegal. Uber in Germany provides a case in point (Thelen, 2018): German regulators essentially disallowed the radical delegation of taxi services to regular persons with a private car (UberPop service) and thus stopped Uber from establishing its intermediary position on its marketplace. German authorities reinforced existing regulation that individual transport requires a taxi license for the driver. Hence, regulation inhibited the loosened couplings of the Uber

marketplaces and effectively restored the established taxi model – a model that is already loosely coupled, yet still requires registered taxi drivers the Uber model would have undermined. Regarding the case of labor, critical accounts suggest to redefine market organizers as employers, so that sellers on the marketplaces should be viewed as employees (Fernández-Macías, 2018; Malin & Chandler, 2017; Prassl & Risak, 2016). In the light of our argument, this approach could be understood as an attempted return to the stage of the modern corporation, because the employee status would restore an organizational structure of tight coupling. Not surprisingly, Uber itself acknowledges the employee status as one of its major risk factors for its business model (Uber Technologies, Inc., 2019).

(3) *Trim and adjust*: A trim-and-adjust approach sits in the middle between the two other options. Instead of little regulation or harsh regulation, regulators allow sharing economy marketplaces to operate, but trim unwanted branches and adjust market organizers' activities to defined boundaries. Here, Uber in Sweden provides a good example (Thelen, 2018) where authorities allowed Uber to operate parts of its marketplace, yet required it to comply with the general frameworks, especially enforcing drivers' tax payments. Like Germany, Sweden disallowed the radical delegation to regular persons with their private cars (UberPop service), yet allowed Uber to act as taxi operator enforcing requirements for drivers to officially register and to adhere to adapted tax policies. Here, official organizations limit the business model and slightly adjust the established regulatory framework.

Trim and adjust also seems to be the general approach to cope with Airbnb (Interian, 2016; Uzunca et al., 2018). The rise of Airbnb especially produced unintended consequences for cities across the world (e.g., Dobusch, 2019). Communal regulators increasingly noted that housing in desired inner-city regions was removed from the regular housing market and instead commodified as Airbnb offers for tourists. This not only increased housing prices and makes inner-city accommodation increasingly unaffordable, but it also changed the character of the city quarters as tourists would gradually replace residents. Current regulatory approaches trim the Airbnb model, requiring a host to register with the city and pay tax (Interian, 2016) and limiting the nights of subletting per year, thereby inhibiting the increasing number of professional and commercial sellers. Also, cities require Airbnb sellers to comply with certain standards (e.g., fire alarms and property insurance) (Hill, 2016).

Overall, actual regulation by official organizations contains a mix of these three options, often leaning toward a trim-and-contain approach, although the relationships between platforms and regulators vary across countries (Thelen, 2018; Uzunca et al., 2018).

### *3.3. Regulating by Private Actors and Civil Society*

The third group of organizational actors relevant for regulating the sharing economy comprises private and civil society actors such as incumbents, collective business and labor organizations, or alternative organizational forms and social movements. These may either support or challenge for-profit sharing economy platforms.

(1) *Collective business organizations (trade associations and standardization organizations)*: Trade associations, a common feature in many markets (Fligstein, 2001a), represent the interests of their members and try to influence and shape regulation and industry policy. Here, market organizers ally to tackle common issues or combat regulatory threats. This could range from knowledge exchange to lobbing and standard setting. An example from the adjacent crowdsourcing field is a code of conduct regarding fair crowdwork conditions developed and signed by several German crowdworking platforms.[4] The introduction and monitoring of industry standards as a regulating effort could also stem from specialized standardization organizations (Brunsson & Jacobsson, 2000) that already emerged in the stage of Nikefikation (e.g., Reinecke, Manning, & von Hagen, 2012). Standardization organizations could certify certain aspects of the products provided by the marketplaces. However, market organizers already regulate various aspects of standardization themselves (e.g., user evaluations, registration, and product categories) and could proactively shield themselves against external regulatory influence.

(2) *Labor organizations (trade unions)*: Because sharing economy companies require work efforts from many persons to operate their marketplaces, labor organizations could be potentially involved in regulating the emerging employment issues. However, the loosened couplings of organizations between a specific place, a designated labor force, and product responsibility complicate a traditional representation of labor interests. The majority of work in the sharing economy is performed by spatially dispersed sellers acting in a status of formal self-employment. The organizational shifts of Uberization, especially abandoning the employment relationship, erodes the modern corporation and at the same time also inhibits established practices of labor representation, for example, by trade unions (see Lehdonvirta, 2016; Wood, Graham, Lehdonvirta, & Hjorth, 2018). Because the modern corporation and trade unions coevolved, established forms of labor representation usually require the tightly coupled organizational structure of the modern corporation to take effect. Furthermore, shifting the legal frame from regulating labor in organizations to market regulation invokes very different regulatory patterns, such as cartel law, because sellers would then illegally agree on prices and conditions. This situation thwarts a straightforward union-driven approach to regulating the sharing economy. However, digital technology might provide communication means to rally and organize workers outside the main formal channels, for example, by using online forums or online groups (Berg, Furrer, Harmon, Rani, & Silberman, 2018). To date, the German service sector union Verdi, to draw on another example from crowdsourcing, has published position papers on crowdwork, is funding studies and workshops, and has opened a consultation service for crowdworkers as first steps toward a union response strategy.

(3) *Incumbents and competitors*: In their stock exchange reports, Uber and Lyft note that competition presents a substantial risk to their business model (Lyft, 2019; Uber Technologies, Inc., 2019). Beside the oligopolistic competition between different digital marketplaces or providers in the notorious "winner take all"-markets (Rochet & Tirole, 2003), startups or established firms from adjacent industries try to invade the sharing economy field. For example, German car manufactures increased their activities in the taxi and ridesharing market. Since 2014, the Daimler company fully controls the "Mytaxi" app-company (now called Free Now) that provides an independent marketplace for regular taxi rides in German cities, also offering shared rides and rides by rental car drivers. In 2019, the Volkswagen company launched "Moia" a ridesharing service in the city of Hamburg that operates with an exclusively produced electrical van and regularly employs drivers. In both cases, incumbent car companies introduce alternative models into the growing sharing economy field, thus impacting on sharing platforms' business models as well as, potentially, the regulatory environment.

(4) *Alternative organizational forms and social movements*: Other alternative organizations that follow a less conventional form often evolve from social movements (Zald, Morrill, & Rao, 2005). While in the for-profit sharing economy alternatives do not play a major role, the platform cooperativism movement (Scholz, 2016) provides a salient example in the current debate. Kornberger et al. (2018) see the "ideal-type" organizational model of the sharing economy organization as a mix of a platform organization and social movements, able to balance both the economic and the moral dimension of sharing. Ironically, the sharing economy started out as a social movement to provide non-profit alternatives, yet was swiftly colonized by for-profit market organizers that thrive on venture capital. As challengers, alternative organizations might be able to advance into market niches establishing a countermovement to the rise and success of the current sharing economy companies, like Uber, Lyft, and Airbnb. This includes the short-term lodging platform "fairbnb.coop," the New York City-based ridesharing company "Juno," or the Denver-based driver-owned taxi cooperative "Union Taxi." These examples show that alternative organizations emerge and could pressure established market organizers to adapt their marketplace models, thereby also effectively regulating activities in the sharing economy.

(5) *Buyers, sellers, and surrogate actors*: Both sellers of goods and services and buyers can shape the regulatory environment once they organize collectively. As argued by Collier et al. (2018; also Thelen, 2018) in the case of Uber, to date drivers depend largely on surrogate actors in lobbying for their interests. Drivers across the world drove court cases against the company arguing that they should not be viewed as "Uber partners," but as Uber employees. A ruling or revised regulation in their favor could effectively reinstate a traditional organizational model restoring an employment relationship, with all its rights, benefits, and responsibilities. This would block the mechanisms of delegation and intermediation forcing Uber to act as formal employer. Consumers of Uber share interests with both challengers (Uber) and

incumbents (existing taxi service providers), because the former provides both high supply and low cost of service and the latter fights for consumer protection and safety. Through this dual strategy, consumers' interests have been addressed in various legislative ventures, leading to both preserved regulations for existing providers and weak regulations for Uber. Drivers, in turn, have approached attorneys to represent their interests, but to date efforts to litigate against Uber have not been successful in bringing about regulatory change for more worker protection. From our perspective, sellers or buyers would have to collectively organize, for example, in a cooperative or a social movement, to effectively regulate the sharing economy if official regulators do not engage.

## 4. REGULATING THE SHARING ECONOMY: TOWARD A FIELD PERSPECTIVE

In this chapter, we argued that digitalization facilitates specific organizational structures that underlie the sharing economy. These organizational structures enable market organizers like Uber, Lyft, and Airbnb to create and operate their digital marketplaces. Our analysis shows that the sharing economy represents only the most recent stage of an ongoing transformation of organizational structures in which the modern corporation, marked by a hierarchical mode of governance, becomes not dissolved, but increasingly embedded in a complex web of individual and organizational actors whose activities are coordinated using plural modes of governance. While extensive outsourcing already substantially challenged established regulatory approaches, the sharing economy moves even further away from the world of the modern corporation. By the mechanisms of delocalization, delegation, and intermediation, activities on the digital marketplaces become detached from one specific place, a designated workforce and the responsibilities for a specific product. This process removes the organizational connectors for established regulation and renders many traditional approaches ineffective.

Yet, we showed that notions describing the sharing economy as markets fail to account for the activities of the market organizers as well as other organizational actors involved in shaping the sharing economy. We thus proposed to consider the sharing economy as a field that comprises various organizational actors and different modes of governance, all of which can provide avenues for regulation. While our chapter only provides a starting point, elaborating further on a fields perspective would allow us to unpack the different actors involved in configuring new market orders and to understand the complex dynamics of collaboration and contestation unfolding among these actors. Whether fields are perceived as markets (Fligstein, 2001a), as strategic action fields (Fligstein & McAdam, 2012), or as issue fields (Hoffman, 1999), such an endeavor also includes unpacking the power relations in markets which appear to be unilaterally organized by digital platforms as intermediaries (see Dolata, 2019).

While our argument provides a conceptual frame to tackle the pending question of regulating the sharing economy, the emerging organizational structures and field dynamics are still in flux and many aspects need to be studied more extensively. In the light of our argument, we would like to highlight and discuss several aspects.

First, regulation by market organizers like Uber, Lyft, and Airbnb cannot be underestimated. To run their business models, sharing economy companies implement a rule of private governance and thereby regulate activities of sellers and buyers. Sundararajan (2016) argued that "reputation replaces regulation" in the sharing economy. He stressed that the desire to make profits self-regulates the behavior of buyers and sellers more effectively than government regulation would. This view overlooks the fact that market organizers interfere heavily in shaping these reputational systems and install other technical infrastructures to operate their digital marketplaces (Ahrne et al., 2014; Kirchner & Beyer, 2016; Kornberger, 2017). Also, sharing economy companies do not routinely allow for sellers' and buyers' participation in platform-level decision making (Gegenhuber, Ellmer, & Scheba, 2018). Thus, although sharing economy companies often claim to realize alternative forms of the economy, a key interest – at least of the dominant platforms – is to satisfy investors by securing quasi-monopoly positions and extract fees (Langley & Leyshon, 2017).

Second, traditional regulators respond to these developments by using various approaches. The accommodate-and-hope approach considers sharing economy marketplaces mostly as intermediaries of matchmaking that greatly reduce the transaction costs for market participants. However, this view easily underestimates the underlying power structure of digital marketplaces (Dolata, 2019). Whereas competition between sellers is fierce on the marketplace itself, market organizers dwell in comparably comfortable positions with only few other competing marketplaces. The Uber case shows that once the cycle between supply and consumer demand had risen, it has proven very difficult to effectively counteract the diffusion of Uber (Thelen, 2018). Because of the prominent role played by network externalities, such constellations are prone to create path-dependent solutions that might produce socially undesirable outcomes (Sydow, Schreyögg, & Koch, 2009).

A ban-and-restore approach of official organizations targets the foundations which the sharing economy companies require to operate. This approach is especially salient in the employment status of sellers (drivers or hosts) on digital marketplaces. However, to ban sharing economy marketplaces and restore conditions of earlier organizational structures – such as a regular employment relationship – requires substantial effort. Regulators need to constantly oppose the strong forces of digitalization, especially rival startups and consumer demands. Also, banned companies stock the opportunity to implement their model on a later date, when conditions might turn out more favorable.

A current regulatory initiative in California (the so called "AB 5 bill"), adds another layer to the ongoing struggle between official regulators and sharing economy companies. The new regulation rules the self-employment status of Uber and Lyft drivers to be illegal, thus, departing from the accommodate-and-hope regulation pattern in the USA. Banning radical delegation and reattaching responsibilities to the market organizers constitutes a shift towards a ban-and-restore path. However, applying our field approach, we assume that sharing economy companies will try to evade and fight this unfavorable regulation as it threatens the core of their organizational structures. The settlement of this regulatory struggle, in the heartland of the platform economy, will most likely provide a critical juncture in the regulation of the sharing economy.

A trim-and-adjust approach by official organizations could prove best suited for the tensions inherent in the sharing economy. It would allow popularity among customers and job creation on the one hand, while threatening existing employment and undermining tax or employment regulation on the other (Dudley, Banister, & Schwanen, 2017). In practice, though, it appears quite difficult to implement regulation that effectively trims and adjusts. Often regulators have no or very limited access to marketplace data (Hill, 2016). Thus, enforcing regulation by fines or taxation proves costly. Additionally, rules on the marketplaces might shift to evade targeted regulation and reinforce the legal positions as mere intermediaries.

The systematic inability to enforce established regulation could trigger new regulatory paradigms that better connect with the intermediation structures of the marketplace. The shift from tightly to loosely coupled organizational structures could be paralleled by a shift to regulating intermediated loose couplings. Instead of focusing on dispersed buyers and sellers on the marketplace, regulators could reconnect responsibilities to the market organizers, for example, by directly taxing market transactions that in turn is redistributed among citizens. As extensive intermediaries, sharing economy companies store the data and command the digital infrastructure to effectively implement such regulation of loose couplings. In this sense, digital technology also provides new avenues for regulation that were not available in the stage of Nikefication.

Third, we also considered the regulating efforts of adjacent and alternative organizations. Trade associations might facilitate the exchange and cooperation of various sharing economy companies and lobby for favorable regulation or agree on common standards. Specialized standard organizations could provide general guidelines for sharing economy companies and monitor the compliance. Adjacent organizations that traditionally represented labor interest are unions. The mechanisms of digitalization especially undermine unionization efforts as workers are locally dispersed, not formally employed and the market organizers refrain from responsibilities, highlighting their mere intermediary status. While in the case of Uber drivers took strike and protest action to protest against Uber's policies, outbursts remain temporary and locally limited. As of yet, there is no general movement to unionize drivers.

However, the very same digital technology driving delocalization, delegation, and intermediation can also support alternative forms of worker representation. For the crowdsourcing field, Lehdonvirta (2016), for instance, describes examples where algorithms have contributed to uniting globally dispersed workers so that they can mutually support each other by sharing information in internet-based communities (see also Wood et al., 2018). Also, for crowdsourcing, The German union IG Metall, for instance, has established a Crowdsourcing Code of Conduct in 2015. Signatories to this code signal that they adhere to local wage standards. Similar activities could influence sharing economy companies to change their policies and to provide more democratic forms of participation (Ellmer, Gegenhuber & Schüßler, 2019).

Civil society might foster the emergence of social movements that evolve into alternative organizers of digital marketplaces. Building on the same mechanism as the sharing economy, social movements thus might produce social forms that counteract the "dark side" of digital marketplaces, and digital infrastructures might contribute to their global diffusion (Adler, 2015). The platform cooperativism movement (Scholz, 2016) might introduce new approaches to the sharing economy that better align with labor interests and other social outcomes. However, considering the organizational structure of cooperatives, this alternative might encounter practical difficulties such as slower decision-making processes due to a high consensus-orientation or little capital. Also, such cooperative alternatives would face substantial resistance from incumbents, who will fiercely seek to defend their established market positions. Incumbents in the sharing economy comfortably rest on funding by venture capital as well as on strong, technologically induced network effects enabling their quasi-monopoly positions (Langley & Leyshon, 2017). This uneven situation likely confines alternative organizational forms to niches that might successfully tap into local initiatives or patterns of moral consumption. Yet, even if alternative organizational forms of market organizers could introduce a viable market order, it seems quite likely that this would again attract profiteers and venture capital aiming to transform or absorb the viable alternative organizational forms in for-profit ventures. Finally, sharing economy companies actually employed social movement-like strategies to rally support for a favorable regulation successful in the USA which indicates that mobilization strategies are not exclusive to non-profit alternative organizations. It is noteworthy here that the literature hints at substantial international differences regarding the framing and legitimation strategies of sharing economy platforms, regulatory responses, and the interplay with civil society (e.g., Mair & Reischauer, 2017; Thelen, 2018; Uzunca et al., 2018).

Overall, this discussion indicates that effective regulating efforts need to take the central role of market organizers into account, regardless of whether official organizations try to ban activities, whether actors agree to certain standards, or whether unions or social movements target the sharing economy practices or promote alternative organizational models. A field perspective highlights the possible interplay between these various organizational actors to achieve a certain regulatory outcome. For example, official organizations or unions could support social movements and foster the emergence of non-profit market organizers of digital marketplaces that allow for more democratic participation by sellers (and buyers) and socialize platform ownership (Martin et al., 2017; Scholz, 2016). While digitization has created new regulatory challenges through mechanisms of delocalization, delegation, and intermediation, digital technology also provides new regulatory opportunities, for instance regarding the mobilization of even highly dispersed actors or regarding the availability of data for monitoring violations and compliance.

## NOTES

1. Note that each of the mechanisms entails a counter mechanism under the conditions of digitalization. Delocalization always requires a form of re-localization that enables social exchange between spatially dispersed entities. Delegation requires forms of control so that forwarded tasks are carried out according to specifications. Mediation requires a form of appropriation enabling intermediaries to secure their share in the value capture process (e.g., by raising fees).

2. It is important to note that we do not argue that these three mechanisms exclusively pertain to digitalization. Delocalization (e.g., transport companies) or delegation (sales businesses, historical putting-out or domestic systems) can be found in diverse societal areas. Also, intermediaries are common in many markets and it is easy to find non-digital examples, such as supermarkets, temporary agencies or stock exchanges. However, the combination of these three mechanisms enables the organizers of digital marketplaces in the sharing economy.

3. Davis' argument on the Uberization of the whole economy essentially posits broad claims. Whether Uber provides a template for the whole economy seems questionable and remains to be studied. However and most importantly, the claims allow us to situate current developments in the sharing economy in a historical perspective of consecutive and layered transformations. Here, it is important to point out that besides outsourcing other forms, like franchising (Biber et al., 2017), also introduced preceding organizational structures, also thriving on delocalization and delegation.

4. For details see http://www.crowdsourcing-code.de/.

## REFERENCES

Adler, P. S. (2015). Book review essay: The environmental crisis and its capitalist roots: Reading Naomi Klein with Karl Polanyi—Naomi Klein: This changes everything: Capitalism vs. the climate. *Administrative Science Quarterly*, *60*(2), NP13–NP25.

Ahrne, G., Aspers, P., & Brunsson, N. (2014). The organization of markets. *Organization Studies*, *36*(1), 7–27.

Bauer, R. M., & Gegenhuber, T. (2015). Crowdsourcing: Global search and the twisted roles of consumers and producers. *Organization (Lond)*, *22*(5), 661–681.

Beck, U. (2000). *What is globalization?* Cambridge: Polity Press.

Beckert, J. (2009). The social order of markets. *Theory and Society*, *38*(3), 245–269.

Belk, R. (2014). You are what you can access: Sharing and collaborative consumption online. *Journal of Business Research*, *67*(8), 1595–1600.

Belk, R. (2017). Sharing without caring. *Cambridge Journal of Regions, Economy and Society*, *10*(2), 249–261.

Berg, J., Furrer, M., Harmon, E., Rani, U., & Silberman, M. S. (2018). *Digital labour platforms and the future of work: Towards decent work in the online world.* Geneva, Switzerland: International Labour Office.

Bessy, C., & Chauvin, P.-M. (2013). The power of market intermediaries: From information to valuation processes. *Valuation Studies*, *1*(1), 83–117.

Biber, E., Light, S. E., Ruhl, J., & Salzman, J. (2017). Regulating business innovation as policy disruption: from the Model T to Airbnb. *Vanderbilt Law Review*, *70*(5), 1561–1626.

Botsman, R., & Rogers, R. (2010). *What's mine is yours. How collaborative consumption is changing the way we live*. London: Collins.

Boyer, R., & Freyssenet, M. (2003). *Produktionsmodelle: eine Typologie am Beispiel der Automobilindustrie*. Berlin, Germany: edition sigma.

Brunsson, N., & Jacobsson, B. (2000). *A world of standards*. Oxford: Oxford University Press.

Coase, R. H. (1937). The nature of the firm. *Economica*, *4*(16), 386–405.

Collier, R. B., Dubal, V. B., & Carter, C. L. (2018). Disrupting regulation, regulating disruption: The politics of Uber in the United States. *Perspectives on Politics*, *16*(4), 919–937.

Czarniawska, B. (2019). Overwhelmed by overflows? In B. Czarniawska & O. Löfgren (Eds.), *Virtual red tape, or digital v. paper bureaucracy* (pp. 170–190). Manchester: Lund University Press.

Davis, G. F. (2016a). Can an economy survive without corporations? Technology and robust organizational alternatives. *Academy of Management Perspectives*, *30*(2), 129–140.

Davis, G. F. (2016b). What might replace the modern corporation? Uberization and the web page enterprise. *Seattle University Law Review*, *39*, 501–515.

De Stefano, V. (2016). Non-standard work and limits on freedom of association: A human rights-based approach. *Industrial Law Journal*, *46*(2), 185–207.

Djelic, M.-L., & Quack, S. (2018). Globalization and business regulation. *Annual Review of Sociology*, *44*(1), 123–143.

Dobusch, L. (2019). Dynamics of the sharing economy between commons and commodification. *Momentum Quarterly, Zeitschrift für Sozialen Fortschritt*, *8*(2), 109–115.

Dolata, U. (2019). Privatization, curation, commodification. Commercial platforms on the Internet. *Österreich Zeitschrift für Soziologie*, *44*(Suppl 1), 181–197.

Donaghey, J., Reinecke, J., Niforou, C., & Lawson, B. (2014). From employment relations to consumption relations: Balancing labor governance in global supply chains. *Human Resource Management*, *53*(2), 229–252.

Dudley, G., Banister, D., & Schwanen, T. (2017). The rise of Uber and regulating the disruptive innovator. *The Political Quarterly*, *88*(3), 492–499.

Ellmer, M., Gegenhuber, T. K., & Schuessler, E. S. (2019). Exploring Crowdworker Participation on Digital Work Platforms. In Academy of Management Proceedings (Vol. 2019, No. 1, p. 14552). Briarcliff Manor, NY: Academy of Management.

Evans, D. S. (2011). *Platform economics: Essays on multi-sided businesses*. Chicago, IL: Competition Policy International.

Evans, D. S., & Schmalensee, R. (2016). *Matchmakers: The new economics of multisided platforms*. Boston, MA: Harvard Business Review Press.

Fernández-Macías, E. (2018). Automation, digitisation and platforms: Implications for work and employment. In Eurofound (Ed.), *Research report* (pp. 1–34). Luxembourg: Publications Office of the European Union.

Fitzmaurice, C. J., Ladegaard, I., Attwood-Charles, W., Cansoy, M., Carfagna, L. B., Schor, J., & Wengronowitz, R. (2018). Domesticating the market: Moral exchange and the sharing economy. *Socio-Economic Review*. https://doi.org/10.1093/ser/mwy003.

Flecker, J. (2009). Outsourcing, spatial relocation and the fragmentation of employment. *Competition & Change*, *13*(3), 251–266.

Flecker, J., & Schönauer, A. (2016). The production of 'Placelessness': Digital service work in global value chains. In J. Flecker (Ed.), *Space, place and global digital work* (pp. 11–30). London: Palgrave Macmillan.

Fligstein, N. (1996). Markets as politics: A political-cultural approach to market institutions. *American Sociological Review*, *61*(4), 656–673.

Fligstein, N. (2001a). *The architecture of markets. An economic sociology of twenty-first-century capitalist societies*. Princeton, NJ: Princeton University Press.

Fligstein, N. (2001b). Social skill and the theory of fields. *Sociological Theory*, *19*(2), 105–125.

Fligstein, N., & McAdam, D. (2012). *A theory of fields*. Oxford: Oxford University Press.

Gegenhuber, T., Ellmer, M., & Scheba, C. (2018). *Partizipation von CrowdworkerInnen auf Crowdsourcing-Plattformen: Bestandsaufnahme und Ausblick*. Düsseldorf, Germany: Hans Böckler Stiftung.

Hagiu, A., & Wright, J. (2015). Multi-sided platforms. *International Journal of Industrial Organization*, *43*, 162–174.

Haidinger, B., Schönauer, A., Flecker, J., & Holtgrewe, U. (2014). Value chains and networks in services: Crossing borders, crossing sectors, crossing regimes? In M. Vidal & M. Hauptmeier (Eds.), *The comparative political economy of work and employment relations* (pp. 98–118). Houndsmills: Palgrave Macmillan.

Hartl, B., & Hofmann, E. (2019). Sharing economy. In K. Gangl & E. Kirchler (Eds.), *A research agenda for economic psychology* (pp. 154–168). Cheltenham: Edward Elgar Publishing.

Hartl, B., Hofmann, E., & Kirchler, E. (2016). Do we need rules for "what's mine is yours"? Governance in collaborative consumption communities. *Journal of Business Research*, *69*(8), 2756–2763.

Helfen, M. (2015). Institutionalizing precariousness? The politics of boundary work in legalizing agency work in Germany, 1949–2004. *Organization Studies*, *36*(10), 1387–1422.

Helfen, M., Schüßler, E., & Sydow, J. (2018). How can employment relations in global value networks be managed towards social responsibility? *Human Relations*, *71*(12), 1640–1665.

Hill, S. (2016). *The California challenge. How (not) to regulate disruptive business models*. Berlin, Germany: Friedrich-Ebert-Stiftung, Division for International Dialogue.

Hoffman, A. J. (1999). Institutional evolution and change: Environmentalism and the U.S. Chemical Industry. *The Academy of Management Journal*, *42*(4), 351–371.

Howcroft, D., & Bergvall-Kåreborn, B. (2018). A typology of crowdwork platforms. *Work, Employment and Society*, *33*(1), 21–38. doi:0950017018760136.

Interian, J. (2016). Up in the air: Harmonizing the sharing economy through Airbnb regulations. *Boston College International & Comparative Law Review*, *129*(1), 129–161.

Kakabadse, N., & Kakabadse, A. (2000). Critical review – Outsourcing: A paradigm shift. *Journal of Management Development*, *19*(8), 670–728.

Kalleberg, A. L. (2001). Organizing flexibility: The flexible firm in a new century. *British Journal of Industrial Relations*, *39*(4), 479–504.

Kenney, M., & Zysman, J. (2016). The rise of the platform economy. *Issues in Science & Technology*, *XXXII*(3), 61.

Kirchner, S., & Beyer, J. (2016). Die Plattformlogik als digitale Marktordnung. Wie die Digitalisierung Kopplungen von Unternehmen löst und Märkte transformiert. *Zeitschrift für Soziologie*, *45*(5), 324–339.

Kirchner, S., & Schüßler, E. (2019). The organization of digital marketplaces. In G. Ahrne & N. Brunsson (Eds.), *Organization outside organization* (pp. 131–154). Cambridge: Cambridge University Press.

Kleemann, F., Voß, G. G., & Rieder, K. (2008). Un(der)paid Innovators: The commercial utilization of consumer work through crowdsourcing. *Science, Technology & Innovation Studies*, *4*(1), 5–26.

Knoblauch, H., & Löw, M. (2017). On the spatial re-figuration of the social world. *Sociologica* (2), 1–28.

Kornberger, M. (2017). The visible hand and the crowd: Analyzing organization design in distributed innovation systems. *Strategic Organization*, *15*(2), 174–193.

Kornberger, M., Leixnering, S., Meyer, R. E., & Höllerer, M. A. (2018). Rethinking the sharing economy: The nature and organization of sharing in the 2015 refugee crisis. *Academy of Management Discoveries*, *4*(3), 314–335.

Langley, P., & Leyshon, A. (2017). Platform capitalism: The intermediation and capitalisation of digital economic circulation. *Finance and Society*, *3*(1), 11–31.

Langlois, R. N., & Garzarelli, G. (2008). Of hackers and hairdressers: Modularity and the organizational economics of open-source collaboration. *Industry and Innovation*, *15*(2), 125–143.

Lehdonvirta, V. (2016). Algorithms that divide and unite: Delocalisation, identity and collective action in 'microwork'. In J. Flecker (Ed.), *Space, place and global digital work* (pp. 53–80). Basingstoke: Palgrave Macmillan.

Lyft, I. (2019, March 1). Form S-1 registration statement – As filed with the securities and exchange commission. Retrieved from https://www.sec.gov/Archives/edgar/data/1759509/000119312519059849/d633517ds1.htm. Accessed on July 12, 2019.

Mair, J., & Reischauer, G. (2017). Capturing the dynamics of the sharing economy: Institutional research on the plural forms and practices of sharing economy organizations. *Technological Forecasting and Social Change*, *125*, 11–20.

Malhotra, A., & Alstyne, M.V. (2014). The dark side of the sharing economy … and how to lighten it. *Communications of the ACM*, *57*(11), 24–27.

Malin, B.J., & Chandler, C. (2017). Free to work anxiously: Splintering precarity among drivers for Uber and Lyft. *Communication, Culture & Critique*, *10*(2), 382–400.

Marchington, M., Grimshaw, D., Rubery, J., & Wilmott, H. (2005). *Fragmenting Work: Blurring organizational boundaries and disordering hierarchies*. Oxford: Oxford University Press.

Marchington, M., Rubery, J., & Grimshaw, D. (2011). Alignment, integration, and consistency in HRM across multi-employer networks. *Human Resource Management*, *50*(3), 313–339.

Marsden, D. (1999). *A theory of employment systems: Micro-foundations of societal diversity: Micro-foundations of societal diversity*. Oxford: Oxford University Press.

Martin, C. J., Upham, P., & Klapper, R. (2017). Democratising platform governance in the sharing economy: An analytical framework and initial empirical insights. *Journal of Cleaner Production, 166*, 1395–1406.

Müller-Birn, C., Dobusch, L., & Herbsleb, J. D. (2013). Work-to-rule: the emergence of algorithmic governance in Wikipedia. Proceedings of the 6th *international conference on communities and technologies*. (C&T '13). ACM, New York, pp. 80–89. doi: 10.1145/2482991.2482999.

Murillo, D., Buckland, H., & Val, E. (2017). When the sharing economy becomes neoliberalism on steroids: Unravelling the controversies. *Technological Forecasting and Social Change, 125*, 66–76.

Orton, J. D., & Weick, K. E. (1990). Loosely coupled systems: A reconceptualization. *The Academy of Management Review, 15*(2), 203–223.

Peticca-Harris, A., deGama, N., & Ravishankar, M. N. (2018). Postcapitalist precarious work and those in the 'drivers' seat: Exploring the motivations and lived experiences of Uber drivers in Canada. *Organization*, doi:1350508418757332.

Powell, W. W. (2016). A sociologist looks at crowds: Innovation or invention? *Strategic Organization, 15*(2), 289–297.

Powell, W. W. (1990). Neither market nor hierarchy: Network forms of organization. *Research in Organizational Behavior, 12*, 295–336.

Prassl, J., & Risak, M. (2016). Uber, Taskrabbit, & Co: Platforms as employers? Rethinking the legal analysis of crowdwork. *Comparative Labor Law & Policy Journal*, Forthcoming (Oxford Legal Studies Research Paper No. 8/2016. Oxford: University of Oxford).

Reinecke, J., Manning, S., & von Hagen, O. (2012). The emergence of a standards market: Multiplicity of sustainability standards in the global coffee industry. *Organization Studies, 33*(5–6), 791–814.

Rifkin, J. (2011). *The third industrial revolution: how lateral power is transforming energy, the economy, and the world*. New York, NY: Palgrave Macmillan.

Rochet, J.-C., & Tirole, J. (2003). Platform competition in two-sided markets. *Journal of the European Economic Association, 1*(4), 990–1029.

Rosenblat, A., & Stark, L. (2016). Algorithmic labor and information asymmetries: A case study of Uber's drivers. *International Journal of Communication, 10*(27), 3758–3784.

Scherer, A. G., & Palazzo, G. (2011). The new political role of business in a globalized world: A review of a new perspective on CSR and its implications for the firm, governance, and democracy. *Journal of Management Studies, 48*(4), 899–931.

Scholz, T. (2016). *Platform cooperativism. Challenging the corporate sharing economy*. New York, NY: Rosa Luxemburg Foundation.

Schor, J. (2017). Does the sharing economy increase inequality within the eighty percent?: Findings from a qualitative study of platform providers. *Cambridge Journal of Regions, Economy and Society, 10*(2), 263–279.

Schor, J. B., & Attwood-Charles, W. (2017). The "sharing" economy: labor, inequality, and social connection on for-profit platforms. *Sociology Compass, 11*(8), e12493.

Schor, J., & Fitzmaurice, C. J. (2015). Collaborating and connecting: the emergence of the sharing economy. In L. A. Reisch & J. Thøgersen (Eds.), *Handbook of research on sustainable consumption* (pp. 410–425). Cheltenham: Edward Elgar.

Schor, J., & Vallas, S. (2020, forthcoming). Understanding the Gig Economy. Annual Review of Sociology.

Simon, H. A. (1951). A formal theory of the employment relationship. *Econometrica, 19*(3), 293–305.

Sundararajan, A. (2016). *The sharing economy: The end of employment and the rise of crowd-based capitalism*. Cambridge, MA: The MIT Press.

Sydow, J., Schreyögg, G., & Koch, J. (2009). Organizational path dependence: Opening the black box. *Academy of Management Review, 34*(4), 689–709.

Thelen, K. (2018). Regulating Uber: The politics of the platform economy in Europe and the United States. *Perspectives on Politics, 16*(4), 938–953.

Uber Technologies, Inc. (2019, April 11). Form S-1 registration statement – As filed with the Securities and Exchange Commission. Retrieved from https://www.sec.gov/Archives/edgar/data/1543151/000119312519103850/d647752ds1.htm. Accessed on July 12, 2019.

Uzunca, B., Rigtering, J. P. C., & Ozcan, P. (2018). Sharing and shaping: A cross-country comparison of how sharing economy firms shape their institutional environment to gain legitimacy. *Academy of Management Discoveries, 4*(3), 248–272.

van Dijck, J. (2013). *The culture of connectivity: A critical history of social media*. Oxford: Oxford University Press.

Weick, K. E. (1976). Educational organizations as loosely coupled systems. *Administrative Science Quarterly*, *21*(1), 1–19.

Williamson, O. E. (1991). Comparative economic organization: The analysis of discrete structural alternatives. *Administrative Science Quarterly*, *36*(2), 269–296.

Wood, A. J., Graham, M., Lehdonvirta, V., & Hjorth, I. (2018). Good gig, bad gig: Autonomy and algorithmic control in the global gig economy. *Work, Employment and Society*, *33*(1), 56–75. doi:0950017018785616.

Zald, M. N., Morrill, C., & Rao, H. (2005). The impact of social movements on organizations. In G. F. Davis, D. McAdam, W. R. Scott, & M. N. Zald (Eds.), *Social movements and organizations* (pp. 253–279). Cambridge: Cambridge University Press.

# INDEX

*Note*: Page numbers followed by "*n*" indicate notes.


Abductive approach, 32
Access economy, 114–118
Access-based consumption, 164
Accommodate-and-hope approach, 224, 229
Ad hoc regulations, 97
Airbnb, 10, 63, 69, 94, 120, 151–152, 164, 170, 177, 197, 216, 219–220, 225
Alternative organizational forms, 226–227
Amazon Mechanical Turk (AMT), 63
Analysis levels in sharing economy, 7–8
Anti-trust laws, 90
Apartment sharing, 188
Austria's national government, 194
Austro-fascism, 194

B2B model, 26
B2C model, 26
Ban-and-restore approach, 224, 229
Bazaar governance, 30
BlaBlaCar, 63
Bottom-up theorization, 207
Boundary framing, 205
Brokerage, 9–11
Business model, 26–29, 36
  characteristics, 36
  of organizations, 42
  in pure-market governance, 38
  in sharing-economy organization, 26
Buyers, 227

C-Form governance, 30
Capitalist market, 88
Car sharing, 175, 188
Category/categories, 9–10, 13, 164–165
  commoners, 10, 164, 167–168, 179–180
  dynamics in nascent market spaces, 166
  kings, 164–165, 167–168, 179–180
  spill-overs, 169
Central media outlets, 155
City Council, 194
Civil society, 230
  organizations, 136
  regulating by, 225–227
Clan governance, 30–32
Clan-hierarchy hybrid, 27, 45–47
Classic entrepreneurs, 112
Clusters, 140
Co-authorship, 207
Co-consumption, 190
Co-creation, 190
Co-working, 188
  community, 147–149
Coding, 70
Cognition, 8–9
Cognitive framing, 110
Cognitive legitimacy, 85
Collaborative community, 150–152
Collaborative consumption, 164
Collaborative economy field, 115–116
Collective business organizations, 226
Command-and-control frameworks, 90
Commons, 119–120
Community/communities, 26, 144
  co-working, 147–149
  collaborative, 150–152
  community-member incentives, 32
  coworking, 147–149
  gardening, 188
  German, 144–147

governance, 26, 28–29, 36
Internet, 152–155
logic, 99–100
in sharing economy, 27–28
Competition law, 93
Competitors, 226
Consumers, 56
Contracting with sharing firms, 191
Control practices, 30
Conventional content analysis, 70
Cooperativism movement, 227
Coordinated network led by strong leaders, 121–122
Corporate social responsibility practices, 135
Corporations, 92
logics, 88–90, 98–99
Correlations, 82
Correspondence analysis, 62, 66–69
Couchsurfing, 152
Coupling, 217–218
Creative entrepreneurship, 194
Creative industries strategy, 194
Cross-case analysis, 171
Crowd-based capitalism, 164
Crowd-funding platforms, 154–155
Culture, 120
Customer usage, spill-overs in, 177–178

Decentralized technology, 119
Delegation, 231*n*1
Delegation–loosening coupling with designated labor force, 218–219
"Delimiting" mechanism, 189, 198, 204
Delocalization, 231*n*1
Delocalization–loosening coupling with specific place, 218
Descriptive analysis of survey data, 172
Descriptive coding approach, 70
Descriptive statistics, 81
*Deskmag*, 149
Detailing governance response strategies, 201–202
"Detailing" mechanism, 189, 198, 204
Deutsche-startups.de (online news portals), 144
Digital marketplace, 91
Digital platforms, 84, 217
Digitalization, 218, 220
Digitization, 217
Discursive framing, 109, 110
Discursive perspective, 137
on issue fields, 136–137
on organizational fields, 134–135
Disincentive practices, 46
Disrupt, 151
Disruptive field, 133, 156
Diverse and paradox, 4–5
Do-ocracy, 122
Dominant category, 166

*Eatwith*, 164
*Echo*, 164
Ecological transition, 188
Emergent structuring of variety, 8
Emotional dissonance, 58
Emotional labor, 57–59
correlations, 82
descriptive statistics, 81
peer-to-peer social interaction, 56–57
practices, 57, 71
qualitative platform analysis, 69–73
quantitative surveys, 62–66
research design, 61–62
in sharing economy, 59–61
Empathy, 71
Entrepreneurs, 114, 132
Entrepreneurship in emerging and contested fields, 109–112
"Explaining", 5–6

"Fairbnb.coop" platform, 227
Family logic, 87
*Fast Company*, 152
Fields (*see also* Issue fields; Organizational fields), 13–14
configuration of sharing economy, 137
emergence, 109

field-internal hierarchy, 134
field-internal structuration processes, 134
field-specific meta-organizations, 135
Firms, 168–169
First-level codes, 18
Food Assembly, 121
Formal participant observations, 34
Framings, 192–193
theory, 188
Functional economy (*see* Access economy)

Gender, 64
Gephi software, 139–140
German community, 144–147
German sharing organizations, 139
Gift economy, 118–119
Gig economy platforms, 84–85, 164
difference between gig and sharing platforms, 95–96
historical configuration of corporation, market, and state logics, 88–90
institutional logics, 85–88
institutional misalignments in platform economy, 90–96
resolving institutional misalignments, 96–100
Glocalization, 204–205, 207
Governance
approach, 9, 12–13
practices, 9, 11–12
in sharing economy, 27–28
structure, 29–32
Governing variety, 8
Governments, 223–225
Great diversity, 4
Gruenderszene.de (online news portals), 144

Harnessing sharing firms, 191
Health insurance scheme, 98
Hierarchical stratification, 134
Hierarchy governance, 29–32
Hilfr (Danish domestic cleaning platform), 99
Horizontal structuration, 134–135

"Ideal-type" organizational model, 227
In-depth qualitative platform analysis, 62
Incentive systems, 38, 41
Incumbents, 226
organizations, 222
Indegree, 139–140
Indiegogo.com, 154
Industry boundaries, 167
Indy Hall, 149
Informal participant observations, 34
Information and communication technologies (ICTs), 217
Information transfers, 168
Innovation communities, 28
Institutional complexity, 88
Institutional entrepreneurship, 112–113
coordinated network led by strong leaders, 121–122
network of individuals, 123
in pluralistic field, 111–112
in SE field, 121
showcasing dynamics, contradictions, and controversies, 124–125
theorization of, 126
Institutional logics, 10, 85–88, 90
Institutional misalignments
band aid solutions, 97–98
community logic, 99–100
corporation logic, 98–99
market logic, 99
parallel corporation logics, 92–94
parallel market logics, 91–92
in platform economy, 90–91
platforms, 96–97
research agenda, 100–102
resolving, 96
Institutional pluralism, 88
Institutional scholars, 84
Institutional work, 14

Interactive Web 2.0 platforms, 155
Intermediaries, 223
Intermediation–loosening coupling with responsibility, 219–220
Internal cohesion in issue fields, 136
Internet, 138
  community, 152–155
Interpretive coding, 70
Intra-category dynamics, 167
Issue fields (*see also* Organizational fields)
  discursive perspective on, 136–137
  relational perspective on, 135–136

Joint mobilization of plural framings, 121
Juno (New York City-based ridesharing company), 227
Justifying mechanism, 189, 198, 204
Justifying modified governance regime, 203

Kickstarter.com, 154

*La Ruche Qui Dit Oui* project, 121
Label-sharing economy, 132
Labor laws, 90
Labor organizations, 226
Labor union, 84
Libertarianism, 120–121
"License-based only" model, 95
Linear regression, 62–64
"Linking" mechanism, 189, 198, 204
Linux, 119
Local governing authorities, 188
Local regulatory response, 191
Logics, 9–10
Loose coupling, 218, 230
Lyft, 216, 219–220

Market
  categories, 166
  disruption, 188
  governance, 29, 31–32
  logic, 87–90, 92, 99
  market-based mechanisms of coordination, 217
  market-hierarchy hybrid, 27, 42–45
  organizers, 222–223
MAXQDA 12 software, 35
Mediation, 231*n*1
Meetup, 148
Mercer Quality of Living Ranking, 194
Meta-organizations, 139, 151
Methodological approach in sharing economy, 5–7
Mixed methods research, 61
Monitoring procedures, 38
Multi-national home-sharing platforms, 69
Multi-sided markets, 219
Municipalities, 224–225
Mutualism, 144

Nazi-rule, 194
Negative press coverage, 176
"Negotiating" mechanism, 189, 198, 204
Network
  externalities, 92
  of individuals, 123
  visualization, 140–141
"New phenomenon", 4
Nikefication, 216, 220–221
Non-governmental organizations (NGOs), 188
Normative messaging, 60

Online communities, 28
  command-and-control activities in, 30
Online platforms, 92
Order
  coping with variety, 15
  from order to variety, 14–15
  from variety to, 13–14
Organizational fields (*see also* Issue fields), 85–86, 108, 111, 132–133
  discursive perspective on, 134–135
  relational perspective on, 133–134

Organizational/organizations, 56, 138, 141
celebrity, 168
institutionalism, 85, 204
reforms, 192
websites, 138
Organized digital marketplaces, 217
OuiShare, 108–109, 112, 121, 123–124, 151
OuiShare Fest Evolution, 117

Parallel corporation logics, 92–94
Parallel market logics, 91–92
Peer-to-peer (P2P)
car sharing platforms, 96
foundation platform, 119–120
model, 26
platforms, 28, 84, 92
sharing economy, 56
Platform economy, 90, 164
institutional misalignments in, 90–96
Platforms (*see also* Gig economy platforms; Qualitative platform analysis), 84, 96
capitalism, 108
co-ops, 99–100
crowd-funding, 154–155
digital, 84, 217
multi-national home-sharing, 69
online, 92
P2P, 28, 84, 92
platform-mediated service experiences, 56
ride-hailing, 92
ride-sharing/ride-hailing, 69
sharing, 60, 95–96, 169
skill-sharing, 178
Plurality in emerging and contested fields, 109–112
POC 21 project, 121
Policy disruption, novel phenomenon leading to, 190–191
Policy implications for sharing economy, 181–182
Policy-makers, 191
Policy-making for sharing economy, 191–192
Politics of signification, 188
Positive emotions, 58
Positive rating system assessment, 64–65
Practice, 8–9
Principal component analysis, 64
Principal-agent problems, 89
Private actors, regulating by, 225–228
Problematization, 205
Product market logic, 91
Product-service systems, 33
Professions, 86
Providers, 56
Public awareness, spill-overs in, 174–176
Public governance responses, 191
Public visibility of mutual support, 143
Pure clan, 27
Pure market, 27
governance, 37–39
Pure-clan governance, 39–42

Qualitative content analysis, 69
Qualitative platform analysis, 69, 72–73
data and sample, 69
method, 69–70
results, 70–71
Quality assessment, 91
Quality-control mechanisms, 94
Quantitative survey measures, 61
Quantitative surveys, 62
correspondence analysis, 66–69
linear regression, 62–64

Rating/review system, 64
Re-figuration of space, 218
Rebound effects, 207
Recruiting practices, 45
"Redistribution markets", 33
Regulation, 84
ineffectiveness of, 220–222
Regulatory acceptance, spill-overs in, 172–174

Relational perspective, 137
on issue fields, 135–136
on organizational fields, 133–134
Relational space, 136
Reputation
reputation-based feedback mechanisms, 60
spill-overs in, 168–169, 176–177
Respect, 71
Ride-hailing platforms, 92
Ride-sharing/ride-hailing platforms, 69

Second-level codes, 18
Self-employed individuals, 93, 98
Self-employed supplier, 93
Self-regulating by market organizers, 222–223
Sellers, 227
Semi-structured interviews, 112
Service experiences co-creation, 60
Service industries, 58
Shareable.com, 151
Shareholder value practices, 136
ShareNL, 108
Sharing economy (SE), 2, 17*n*1, 26, 84, 108–110, 132–133, 164–165, 175, 188, 216
access economy, 114–118
actors involved in regulating, 220–227
clan-hierarchy hybrid, 45–47
commons, 119–120
communities in network, 144–155
community and governance in, 27–28
concept of governance structure, 29–30, 32
contemporary research on organizations, 15–17
contributions to study of, 181
data analysis, 35–36, 139–140
data and methods, 138–140
data collection, 33–34, 138–139
delimiting issue from (local) policy perspective, 199–200
emotional labor in, 59–61
field configuration, 137
findings, 36, 140–155
framework for theorizing, 5–15
gift economy, 118–119
institutional entrepreneurship in, 111–112, 121–125
joint mobilization of plural framings, 121
libertarianism, 120–121
market, hierarchy, and clan governance, 31
market-hierarchy hybrid, 42–45
methodology, 112–113
novel phenomenon leading to policy disruption, 190–191
organizations, 26–27
peer-to-peer, 56
as phenomenon of variety and dynamics, 3–5
plural framings and entrepreneurial action, 110–111
policy-making for, 191–192
and policy-making in Vienna, 196–198
pure market governance, 37–39
pure-clan governance, 39–42
regulating, 227–231
research approach and sample, 32
results, 114
semantic network of depictions, 4
structure and composition, 140–144
theory, 133–137
timeline of events and activities, 198
types of governance, 36–37
variety of community governance, 28–29
Sharing Economy UK (SEUK), 170–171, 173, 179
"Sharing instead of owning", 1
Sharing organizations, 139, 142, 144
Sharing platforms, 60, 169
difference between gig platform and, 95–96

Sharing-specific meta-organizations, 139, 142–144
Silicon Valley, 121
Single governance, 30
Situating narrative and governance regime, 203–204
"Situating" mechanism, 189, 198, 204
Skewed center-periphery structure, 141
Skill-sharing platform, 178
Slideshare.com, 153
Smart City Initiative, 196
Snowballing-strategy, 195
Social
  actors, 193
  hospitality, 56
  interaction, 71
  media, 102*n*3
  movements, 86, 226–227
  partners, 200
  relationships, 118–119
Societal endangerment, 188
Societal enhancement, 188
Socio-cognitive factors, 166
Socio-economic phenomenon, 4–5
Socio-political actors, 199
Socio-political legitimacy, 85
Spill-overs, 164
  in customer usage, 177–178
  data analysis, 171–172
  data sources, 170–171
  findings, 172–178
  methodology, 169–172
  in public awareness, 174–176
  in regulatory acceptance, 172–174
  in reputation and trust, 176–177
  research setting, 169–170
  theoretical background, 165–169
  theoretical model for, 173
Stakeholders, 90, 167
Standardization organizations, 225–226
Standards, 14
Startnext, 147
State logics, 87, 88–90
State-owned company, 87
Stock corporations, 135
Strategic framing, 193
Strategic governance responses, 205
Strategic issue work, 192–193, 207
  mechanisms in Vienna City Administration, 198–199
Strategic steering committee, 200–201
Structural equivalence, 134
Structuration processes, 134
Subsidizing sharing firms, 191
Substitutability, 167
Surrogate actors, 227

Taskrabbit, 152
Taxi rides, 84
Techcrunch.com (online news portal), 150–151
Technology firms, 155
Tesla, 135
Theorization
  of institutional entrepreneurship, 126
  in pluralistic field, 111–112
Tight coupling, 218
Trade associations, 225–226
Trade unions, 226
Traditional regulators, regulating by, 223–225
Translation, 204–205
Transport agencies, 224
Trim-and-adjust approach, 224–225, 229
Trust, spill-overs in, 176–177
Trust transfer, 176, 181
TrustSeal, 176–177, 179, 182
Two-sided markets, 219

Uber, 10, 63, 66, 69, 95, 152, 154, 164, 170, 216, 219–220
  rating system, 59
Uberization, 216
  delegation–loosening coupling with designated labor force, 218–219
  delocalization–loosening coupling with specific place, 218

intermediation–loosening coupling with responsibility, 219–220
organizational shifts, 217–219
UberPop, 95
"Understanding", 5–6
trajectories of new forms of organizing, 13–15
variety of new forms of organizing, 8–13
*UnderTheDoormat*, 164
Uni-directional spill-over effects, 180
Union Taxi, 227
Urban governance, 191, 195
URLs of organizations, 139

Variety, 8
coping with, 15
to order, 13–14
from order to, 14–15
theoretical inquiry for understanding, 9–13
Venture capitalists, 154–155
Vertical structuration, 134–135
Vienna City Administration
data and coding structure, 199
data and method, 195–196
detailing governance response strategies, 201–202
empirical design, 194–196
findings, 196–204
justifying modified governance regime, 203
linking policy goals and governance responses, 202
negotiating cast of actors, 200–201
phenomenon and conceptual orientation, 190–193
policy-making, 189
situating narrative and governance regime, 203–204
strategic issue work mechanisms in, 198–199
Vienna Tourism Promotion Act, 198
Viennese way, 206, 208

Walk-through method, 69–70
Weakening state logics, 94
Weblinks, 138
*Wired Company*, 152

Zipcar, 152
Zoning committees, 224

Printed and bound by CPI Group (UK) Ltd, Croydon, CR0 4YY

13/09/2026

14961058-0002